Biographical Memoirs

NATIONAL ACADEMY OF SCIENCES

NATIONAL ACADEMY OF SCIENCES
OF THE UNITED STATES OF AMERICA

Biographical Memoirs

VOLUME XLVI

NATIONAL ACADEMY OF SCIENCES
WASHINGTON, D.C. 1975

INTERNATIONAL STANDARD BOOK NUMBER 0-309-02240-1

LIBRARY OF CONGRESS CATALOG CARD NUMBER 75-839

Available from

PRINTING AND PUBLISHING OFFICE, NATIONAL ACADEMY OF SCIENCES
2101 CONSTITUTION AVENUE, N.W., WASHINGTON, D.C. 20418

PRINTED IN THE UNITED STATES OF AMERICA

CONTENTS

PREFACE

The *Biographical Memoirs* is a series of volumes containing the biographies of deceased members of the National Academy of Sciences and bibliographies of their published scientific works. Each biographical essay has been written by a fellow member of the Academy familiar with the professional career of the deceased, with only occasional exceptions. These volumes, therefore, provide a record of the lives and work of some of the most distinguished leaders of American science as witnessed and interpreted by their colleagues and peers.

The National Academy of Sciences is a private, honorary organization of scientists and engineers elected on the basis of outstanding contributions to knowledge. Established by a Congressional Act of Incorporation on March 3, 1863, and supported by private and public funds, the Academy works to further science and its use for the general welfare by bringing together the most qualified individuals to deal with scientific and technological problems of broad significance.

Biographical Memoirs

VOLUME XLVI

Hans T. Clarke

HANS THACHER CLARKE

December 27, 1887–October 21, 1972

BY HUBERT BRADFORD VICKERY

D URING THE third and fourth decades of the present century, the discipline long known as physiological chemistry underwent extensive transformation into a discipline more properly referred to as biological chemistry—the chemistry of living tissue. This transformation came about, at least in part, as a result of the recognition by the university authorities concerned with appointments of department heads, of the fact that progress in the science was most likely to occur if persons trained fundamentally as pure chemists—either organic or physical—were to take over the direction of the departments. Outstanding among the many such appointments of the period was that of Hans Thacher Clarke, in 1928, as head of the Department of Biological Chemistry at the College of Physicians and Surgeons of Columbia University. With a background of some fourteen years of industrial research at Eastman Kodak Company on the large-scale production of developers, dyes, and, after the war, of a wide assortment of organic substances previously imported from Germany, he brought to Columbia a vast and detailed knowledge of the organic chemical literature and an unexcelled personal skill and resourcefulness in organic synthesis. Within a few years he had assembled one of the strongest faculties in this country, and his department promptly attracted students and visitors of the highest qualifications.

3

Today, his graduates are among the leaders of American bio-chemistry.

Hans Thacher Clarke was born of an American father and a German mother on December 27, 1887, in Harrow, England. His father, Joseph Thacher Clarke (1856–1920), son of a Boston, Massachusetts, physician who died when the son was twelve, was educated in Germany and became an archeologist who, with another young man, excavated Assos, an ancient city near the site of Troy, and subsequently prepared the lavishly illustrated final reports for the Archeological Institute of America.* His interest in photography led him to design and produce a magazine camera, the "Frena," which in turn brought him to the attention of George Eastman. They met in 1886, became close personal friends, and shortly afterwards Clarke was appointed to be the European representative of Eastman affairs, a position in which his knowledge of European languages, of art, and, incidentally, of music, for he was a competent cellist, eminently fitted him. This relationship led quite naturally to the appointment of Hans Clarke, his son, who had become a highly trained organic chemist, when, at the outbreak of the war in 1914, it became necessary for the Eastman Kodak Company to undertake the manufacture of the photographic chemicals that previously had been imported from Germany.

Hans Clarke's mother was Agnes von Helferich (1858–1935), the daughter of Hans von Helferich, Professor of Political Economy at the University of Munich. A cousin, B. Helferich, was Emil Fischer's private assistant during the period in 1912 and 1913 when Clarke worked in Fischer's Laboratory.

There seems to be little information in family records about Clarke's grandfather, Luther Whipple Clarke (1825–1868), save that he was born in Marietta, Ohio, and practiced medicine in

---

* Joseph T. Clarke, Francis H. Bacon, and Robert Koldewey, *Expedition of the Archaeological Institute of America: Investigations at Assos* (London: Barnard Quaritich, Henry Sotheran and Co., 1902).

Boston from about 1850. His wife was Mary Gray Thacher (1823–1875), the daughter of a well-known Boston merchant who could trace her ancestry back through a long line of New Englanders to John Howland and others who came over in the *Mayflower*. Her direct ancester was Antony Thacher, a clergyman. He and his wife were the only survivors of a ship that was wrecked in 1635 on what became known as Thacher Island near Gloucester. They were traveling from Newbury to Marblehead, Massachusetts, to take up Thacher's duties as minister of the church there.

Hans Clarke was the second child in a family of two boys and two girls. He has recorded that he "was exposed from early childhood to intellectual and musical stimuli. Independent reading in an extensive and catholic parental library was encouraged, and [I] took part in family string quartets from the age of eight." He attended the University College School in London from 1896 to 1905, where he "preferred subjects (such as algebra) which had a scientific flavor and, in the last two years definitely recognized chemistry as a major interest." He especially disliked Latin grammar, but enjoyed modern languages that were imaginatively taught. His home occupations, "apart from music and general reading, were mainly manual (carpentry and metal work). Practical chemistry and glassblowing were encouraged, and facilities for them were provided in the home."

In 1905 Clarke entered University College, London, where he concentrated on the study of chemistry under Sir William Ramsey, J. N. Collie, and Samuel Smiles. A minor field of study was physiology, under E. H. Starling. It was in this period that he was first exposed to physiological chemistry, for he took a course given by R. H. Aders Plimmer that involved the isolation of a few crystalline proteins, carbohydrates, and amino acids as well as lecithin and kephalin, and also some exercises in urine analysis. He has recorded that "these exercises did not greatly appeal to me; I found them intellectually far less rewarding than the rich fare offered by Collie and Smiles in their courses on organic chemistry."

This is an interesting comment from a man who later became one of the leaders of modern biochemistry in this country. It suggests the reason why he always insisted that his students acquire a fundamental training in organic chemistry before tackling biochemistry itself. It was also in this period that he was active in athletics, playing rugby football and tennis. He was twice heavyweight boxing champion of the school.

After graduation as B.Sc. in 1908, he continued in research with Smiles and A. W. Stewart, while holding a minor teaching position.

In 1911 he was awarded an 1851 Exhibition scholarship and spent three semesters in the laboratory of Emil Fischer in Berlin and one with A. W. Stewart at Queen's College, Belfast. He found that although Fischer visited him almost daily to discuss his work, discussion between the students of their problems was sharply discouraged. He has reported, "This was so contrary to British tradition that I was interested to find out the reason; it appeared that most of the chemists who were working on topics of their own were retained as consultants by one or another of the German manufacturing firms, which had priority on any patentable discoveries made by the individuals concerned. This system appeared to me, as it still does, as being at variance with the prime function of an academic laboratory." On his return from the studies in Germany and in Belfast, he was awarded the D.Sc. degree by the University of London.

Clarke had been occasionally consulted on organic chemical matters by his father's friend George Eastman, and early in the summer of 1914 he was asked by Eastman to come to Rochester to evaluate a newly invented process for the chemical modification of cellulose. Here he found that he was the only organic chemist employed by the company. However, with the outbreak of the war in August and the subsequent impossibility of obtaining chemicals from Germany, he soon became involved in devising methods for the large-scale synthesis of developers and sensitizing dyes. The research laboratory itself was enlarged and in 1918 began the preparation of many substances in short supply in this country. The organic chemicals division of Kodak was thus started. He was also active in contributing methods to *Organic Syntheses* and in checking many methods contributed by others to this publication.

In 1928, at the suggestion of his friend H. D. Dakin, Clarke was invited to become Professor of Biological Chemistry and head of the department in the College of Physicians and Surgeons of Columbia University. The medical school had recently moved to its then new location on West 168th Street, New York, and the department was ill-equipped. Under Clarke's vigorous direction and with the aid of grants from the Chemical Foundation, this situation was soon corrected; the library was greatly enlarged, and a large open laboratory was provided for the graduate students. Clarke always maintained that students who worked in close proximity learned more from each other than from their teachers.

The small but extremely able faculty was promptly enlarged, and the department soon became the home of a long and distinguished list of postgraduate students and visitors, many of whom were German refugees who remained for years, ultimately becoming members of the faculty. Of the ninety-four graduate students who were trained under Clarke's direction, forty-three later attained sufficient eminence to be elected members of one or another of the six societies that form the Federation of American Societies for Experimental Biology; and several are today heads of biochemistry departments or leaders of productive research groups in various institutions throughout the country.

Clarke's first publication, a paper with Smiles on diethoxythioxan, initiated an interest in organic compounds of sulfur that remained throughout his life. Of approximately thirty journal papers in which he described the synthesis of new compounds, no less than eighteen deal with such substances. The year and a half he spent in Fischer's laboratory was devoted to the synthesis of thiazans, which he prepared for the first time, and to the study of the reactivity of analogous compounds that contained nitrogen, oxygen, or sulfur in all of the possible pairs.

The fourteen years at the Kodak research laboratory resulted in few publications in the journal literature, but in this period there were twenty-six descriptions of the preparation of a wide variety of substances published in *Organic Syntheses*. He also acted as one of the checkers of no less than sixty-five preparations submitted by others. A number of other preparations were contributed after the removal to Columbia in 1928. He also served as the editor of two of the annual volumes of this series.

Clarke retained a connection with the Kodak research laboratory for the rest of his life. On leaving Rochester, he was invited to serve as a consultant who would spend two days a month with the organic research group. He resigned from this responsibility only in 1969 when the deterioration of his health made it necessary.

The years at Columbia were happy ones. Clarke has recorded that "my chief activities, listed in the order in which they absorbed my time were: 1) training of graduate students, 2) experimental research, 3) instruction of medical students, 4) administration . . . with the passage of the years, the amount of time available for research with my own hands (I could never work at ease with a technical assistant) continually decreased, finally dwindling to about ten percent." The parenthesis in this statement is especially interesting. Clarke was a master glassblower, and his bench and shelves were littered with devices for special uses that he had made himself—liquid-liquid extractors, distillation columns, filtering apparatus, and so forth. These items were fragile, and their use was sometimes by no means obvious. Aside from the difficulty of explaining to an assistant what he wanted done, was the danger that the use of this equipment in inexperienced hands might lead to the necessity of a repair job at the blast lamp: thus, his unease.

The problem of the graduate student who applied for admission to Clarke's laboratory was a serious one. The professor refused to pay much attention to college grades, but required a long personal interview in which the applicant's course work, his laboratory experience, and especially his capacity to coordinate such background as he had acquired in college were thoroughly discussed. If the impression made was favorable, the student was admitted, but then was frequently told to go back to college and broaden his acquaintance with organic and physical chemistry at both theoretical and practical levels. He was also directed to take courses in biology, if deficient in this discipline. To many, this was a devastating blow, but there was no alternative. A year later they were welcomed into the courses in biochemistry where they soon found that the additional training had been necessary. When the time arrived for the selection of a research problem, Clarke gave the student a wide choice, especially if he had developed some special interest. There was no attempt to direct him into some field allied to the professor's personal research. Thus, the list of titles of papers with graduate students in his bibliography ranges from studies of fatty acids, of amino acids, and of analytical methods, to a problem having to do with rickets in children and another concerning plasma volume. Nevertheless, a considerable number of students chose to work on amino acids and especially on cystine, the most puzzling amino acid of all. With deliberate pedagogic intent, Clarke took advantage of the large laboratory, where all of the graduate students worked, to ensure a wide degree of diversification in the themes of departmental research.

Clarke's personal research led to a number of important and useful advances. With the cooperation of a number of graduate students, he established the details of the reduction of cystine by sulfite, studied the form of labile sulfur in proteins, and found conditions under which the whole of the cystine sulfur could be converted into the so-called lead-blackening sulfur, previously a most confusing problem. Perhaps his best-known contribution was his development in 1935 of the structure of the sulfur-containing moiety of R. R. Williams' recently isolated specimen of pure vitamin B. Williams had found that the crystalline vitamin could be decomposed by treatment with sulfite into two substances, one of which he recognized to be a pyrimidine derivative. The other substance was a strong nitrogenous base containing sulfur. He submitted this material to Clarke, who promptly recognized that its stability to alkaline plumbite before treatment with nitric acid and its lability afterwards indicated that it contained a thiazole nucleus. This enabled Williams to write a tentative structure for the vitamin, the details of which were later corrected. Clarke and Gurin next synthesized a thiazole derivative that was identical to Williams' basic substance obtained from the vitamin. In this brilliant accomplishment Clarke made shrewd use of the results of his studies with other students of the properties of cystine.

A further example of his extraordinary resourcefulness in developing the formula of an organic substance containing sulfur was related to the writer by Professor duVigneaud, whose extended studies of biotin had led in 1942 to the accumulation of data that suggested a possible structure. One evening, he laid the data before Clarke and asked what he thought the structure might be. Clarke pondered for a short while and then wrote a formula that to his mind conformed with the evidence. DuVigneaud then took from his pocket a sheet of paper on which he had written the structure that he had derived. The two formulas were identical in every detail.

In addition to his duties at Columbia and Kodak, Clarke found time for other and extensive professional relationships. In Rochester, he had been chairman of the local section of the American Chemical Society (1921) and was a member of the Editorial Board of *Organic Syntheses* (1921–1932). In 1924–1925 he was chairman of the Division of Organic Chemistry of the American Chemical Society. He was an associate editor of the *Journal of the American Chemical Society* from 1928 to 1938 and on the Editorial Board of the *Journal of Biological Chemistry* from 1937 to 1951. In 1942 he was president of the Harvey Society and was chairman of the New York Section of the American Chemical Society in 1946. He was president of the American Society of Biological Chemists in 1947 and a member of the Biochemical and Nutrition Study Section of the United States Public Health Service from 1948 to 1957. He was also a member of the Committee on Research of the American Philosophical Society during the same period. An important honor was to be appointed Science Attaché at the American Embassy in London in 1951–1952.

A great responsibility was placed upon him in 1944 when he was asked to be Assistant to the Director of OSRD to coordinate the many reports of the then highly confidential research on penicillin. Later he served, together with Sir Robert Robinson and Professor J. R. Johnson as editor of the huge book in which these researches were published by the Princeton University Press in 1949.

Clarke retired from Columbia in 1956 at the mandatory age of 68 and accepted a long-standing invitation from a former student, Professor Joseph Fruton, to come to New Haven to the biochemical laboratory in the Graduate School as a guest of Yale. Here for nearly eight years, Clarke enjoyed the luxury of full-time research. He was an active participant in seminars, attended occasional lectures, gave a short course of lectures on antibiotics a few times, and was always available to students who were puzzled over some problem in organic chemistry. His glassblowing skill was frequently in demand for the repair or development of apparatus. In 1968 the University required the laboratory space he was occupying for newly appointed members of the department, and Clarke then accepted an invitation from Dr. Sidney Farber to continue his work at the Children's Cancer Research Foundation in Boston. Here he spent the years from 1963 to 1970, when increasing ill health compelled him to discontinue active research. He had been engaged since the Yale days in a study of the action of hypochlorite on sulfanilate with the object of preparing azobenzene-4,4'-disulfochloride, a reagent he had suggested to Professor F. M. Richards as possibly useful for interaction with proteins. This turned out to be by no means a simple problem, and he spent years in isolating and identifying the numerous unexpected by-products that were formed. The outcome was the publication in 1971 of his last paper, which contains registry numbers of more than twenty new compounds isolated or prepared in the course of the investigation.

Clarke was elected to the National Academy of Sciences in 1942 and received the King's Medal for service in 1948. The University of Rochester awarded him an honorary degree in 1953 and Columbia in 1957. He was a skilled editor, who invariably improved the many manuscripts that passed through his hands while serving on the boards of the *Journal of the American Chemical Society* and the *Journal of Biological Chemistry*. His own writing was characterized by clearness, brevity, and grace of statement, qualities that he passed on to many of his students, and by his vast scholarship. He was rarely at a loss, in discussing some organic reaction, to point out significant analogies and other examples.

An important phase of Clarke's life resulted from his pur-chase in 1929 of about fifty acres of property in Scotland, Con-necticut, mostly woodland, but with a charming old house and huge barn and several acres of open fields. Here he brought up his young family of two sons and two daughters to share in the frequently heavy labor involved in damming a brook to form a swimming pool, building a dormitory to accommodate the children when the frequent guests arrived, developing the lawn, mowing the fields, maintaining the buildings, and plant-ing and caring for several acres of conifers on what had been low-grade pasture land. Not only his children, but guests were also soon drawn into these activities, so that a weekend with the Clarkes could sometimes develop into an exhausting ex-perience. Clarke was a large and very strong man skilled with axe, saw, and scythe, and had little patience with the weak-nesses of his less well-endowed friends.

No account of Hans Clarke would be complete without mention of his interest in music. That he played in family groups from childhood has been mentioned. His favorite instru-ment was the clarinet, which he played at almost a professional level. He was competent on the viola and the double bass, and when occasionally called upon by the Rochester orchestra, could play the bass clarinet. He married Frieda Planck, daugh-ter of Professor Adelbert Planck and niece of Max Planck, as well as an accomplished violinist, in 1914. Together in Rochester, they played frequently with an amateur orchestra and in smaller groups. Later in New York they played with a small group of friends for twenty-five years, usually in private, but occasionally in concert.

In these groups Clarke was a demanding performer. Every marking of the music for tempo and phrasing was noted, and a mistake by some unlucky member would bring a shout of protest. His knowledge of chamber music was extensive. He had inherited his father's large library and had added to it. He could produce on demand the parts for almost any chamber music, including those of many of the more modern composers, all of which he played with taste and fine discrimination. An accident to his right hand with a scythe in 1960 brought an end to his clarinet playing, but did not interfere with the playing of string instruments.

There were four children, two boys and two girls, all of whom were brought up to use tools skillfully and to play an instrument in the frequently assembled chamber music groups. Their mother died in 1960, and in 1963 Clarke married Flora de Peyer, who survives him.

Clarke was widely recognized as one of the finest organic chemists of the period in this country. He had friends and colleagues both here and in Britain and Germany with whom he frequently corresponded on technical matters. His students were devoted to him, and a memorial meeting in New York shortly after his death brought together a large group in spite of inclement weather. At this meeting, a number of his musical friends played several of his favorite works, and brief addresses were made by former associates. He leaves a gap in American biochemistry that will be difficult, if not impossible, to fill.

IN PREPARING THIS MEMOIR, I have had the use of a document Clarke deposited with the Academy in the 1950s and supplemented in 1968. Also of his "Impressions of an Organic Chemist in Biochemistry," published by *Annual Reviews of Biochemistry* in 1958, of a bibliography and other documents kindly sent to me by Dr. J. Meienhofer of the Jimmy Fund in Boston, and of much genealogical and other information from his son, Dr. Eric Clarke, and from Mrs. Clarke. For all of this help, I am most grateful.

BIBLIOGRAPHY

KEY TO ABBREVIATIONS:

Arch. Intern. Med. = Archives of Internal Medicine
Ind. Eng. Chem. = Industrial and Engineering Chemistry
J. Am. Chem. Soc. = Journal of the American Chemical Society
J. Biol. Chem. = Journal of Biological Chemistry
J. Chem. Soc. = Journal of the Chemical Society (London)
J. Org. Chem. = Journal of Organic Chemistry

1909

With S. Smiles. Diethoxythioxan: a relation between the refractive power and chemical activity of some sulphur compounds J. Chem. Soc., 95:992.

1910

The relation between reactivity and constitution of certain halogen compounds. J. Chem. Soc., 97:416.

1911

Handbook of Organic Analysis. London, E. Arnold, Ltd., 4th ed., 1926.
With S. Smiles. Synthesis of derivatives of thioxanthone. III. 1,4-Dihydroxythioxanthone. J. Chem. Soc., 99:1535.
The relation between residual affinity and chemical constitution. II. Certain compounds of nitrogen. J. Chem. Soc., 99:1927.

1912

4-Alkyl-1,4-thiazans. J. Chem. Soc., 101:1583–90.
The relation between residual affinity and chemical constitution. III. Some heterocyclic compounds. J. Chem. Soc., 101:1788–1809.
Introduction to the Study of Organic Chemistry. London, Longmans Green & Co. Ltd.

1913

With A. K. Macbeth and A. W. Stewart. Colors produced by tetranitromethane with compounds containing elements capable of showing change of valency. Proceedings of the Chemical Society, 29:161.
The relation between residual affinity and chemical constitution. IV. Some open-chain compounds. J. Chem. Soc., 103:1689–1704.

With A. W. Stewart. Über die ultraviolette Absorption des reinen Azetone überhalb $\lambda 332\mu\mu$. Physikalische Zeitschrift, 14:1049.

1918

Examination of organic developing agents. Ind. Eng. Chem., 10: 891–95.

1919

With C. E. K. Mees. A new yellow dye and filters made from it. Ind. Eng. Chem., 11:454–55.

1920

Manometer for vacuum distillation. J. Am. Chem. Soc., 42:786.

1921

With I. N. Hultman and A. W. Davis. The automatic separator in esterifications and other preparations. J. Am. Chem. Soc., 43: 366–70.

1922

Rare organic chemicals. Ind. Eng. Chem., 14:836–37.

1923

With E. J. Rahrs. Laboratory fractionating column. Ind. Eng. Chem., 15:349.

With E. R. Taylor. Separation of xylenes. J. Am. Chem. Soc., 45:830–33.

With R. Phillips. The preparation of alkylguanidine. J. Am. Chem. Soc., 45:1755–57.

1924

With R. R. Read. A modification of Sandmeyer's synthesis of nitrites. J. Am. Chem. Soc., 46:1001–3.

With W. W. Hartman. The preparation of thioacetic acid. J. Am. Chem. Soc., 46:1731–33.

1926

With E. J. Rahrs. A "bubbler" laboratory fractionating column. Ind. Eng. Chem., 18:1092.

1927

With W. E. Bachmann. Mechanism of Wurtz-Fittig reaction. J. Am. Chem. Soc., 49:2089–98.

With E. R. Taylor. The lower fatty acids of coconut oil. J. Am. Chem. Soc., 49:2829–31.

1929

With C. J. Malm. The action of fatty acids on cellulose. J. Am. Chem. Soc., 51:274–78.

1930

With H. Zahnd. The estimation of sulfur in organic compounds. J. Am. Chem. Soc., 52:3275–79.

With L. D. Behr and J. W. Palmer. The estimation of bromides in biological material. J. Biol. Chem., 88:131–35.

With J. M. Inouye. Some observations on the action of alkali upon cystine and cysteine. J. Biol. Chem., 89:399–419.

1931

With J. M. Inouye. The alkaline deamination of derivatives of cysteine. J. Biol. Chem., 94:541–50.

With S. Graff. Determination of plasma. Vol. I. The dye method. Arch. Intern. Med., 48:809.

With S. Graff, D. A. D'Esopo, and A. J. B. Tillman. Determination of plasma. Vol. II. The rate of dye mixing. Arch. Intern. Med., 48:821.

1932

With L. D. Behr. l-p-Methoxyphenylalanine. J. Am. Chem. Soc., 54:1630–34.

With H. B. Gillespie. Benzenesulfonylguanidines. J. Am. Chem. Soc., 54:1964–68.

With H. B. Gillespie. The action of acetic acid upon certain carbohydrates. J. Am. Chem. Soc., 54:2083–88.

The action of sulfite upon cystine. J. Biol. Chem., 97:235–48.

With J. W. Palmer. The elimination of bromides from the blood stream. J. Biol. Chem., 99:435–44.

With G. S. Babcock, M. R. Brethen, A. W. Davis, E. E. Dregers, W. W. Hartman, W. R. Kirner, T. F. Murray, E. J. Rahrs, R. R.

Read, and E. R. Taylor. Contributions to *Organic Syntheses,* ed. by H. Gilman, collective volume I. New York, John Wiley & Sons, Inc. Contributions by Clarke and others include: Acid ammonium *o*-sulfobenzoate, Benzenesulfonyl chloride, Benzil, Benzoic anhydride, Bromo-*n*-caproic acid, *α*-Bromonapthalene, Catechol, *o*-Chlorobenzoyl chloride, Epichlorohydrin, Ethyl oxalate, Ethyl propane-1,1,2,3-tetra-carboxylate, *n*-Heptyl alcohol, Methyl red, *m*-Nitrotoluene, Oxalic acid (anhydrous), Phloroglucinol, Quinoline, *o*-Sulfobenzoic anhydride, *o*-Tolunitrite and *p*-Tolunitrite, Tricarballylic acid, 1,3,5-Trinitrobenzene, and 2,4,6-Trinitrobenzene.

1933

With H. Zahnd. Labile sulfur in proteins. J. Biol. Chem., 102: 171–86.
With H. B. Gillespie and S. Z. Weisshaus. The action of formaldehyde on amines and amino acids. J. Am. Chem. Soc., 55: 4571–87.

1934

With R. M. Herbst. Oxidation of amino acids by silver oxides. J. Biol. Chem., 104:769–88.
With J. S. Fruton. Chemical reactivity of cystine and its derivatives. J. Biol. Chem., 106:667–91.
With S. Gurin. Allocation of free amino groups in proteins and peptides. J. Biol. Chem., 107:395–419.
With G. L. Foster and H. B. Vickery. Über die "neue Methode zur Darstellung von Aminen aus Aminosäuren" von Wada. Biochemische Zeitschrift, 272:376–79.

1935

With S. Gurin. Studies of crystalline vitamin B_1. XII. The sulfur-containing moiety. J. Am. Chem. Soc., 57:1876–81.
With D. Blumenthal. Unrecognized forms of sulfur in proteins. J. Biol. Chem., 110:343–49.

1936

With E. Borek. Carboxymethoxylamine. J. Am. Chem. Soc., 58:2020–21.

1937

With S. Ratner. The action of formaldehyde upon cysteine. J. Am. Chem. Soc., 59:200–206.

1938

With M. Bovarnik. Racemization of tripeptides and hydantoins. J. Am. Chem. Soc., 60:2426–30.

With A. Mazur. The amino acids of certain marine algae. J. Biol. Chem., 123:729–40.

With K. Bloch. N-Methylcysteine and derivatives. J. Biol. Chem., 125:275–87.

With E. Borek. Compounds related to canaline and canavanine. J. Biol. Chem., 125:479–94.

Natural amino acids. In: *Organic Chemistry,* by H. Gilman, chap. 10, vol. II. New York, John Wiley & Sons, Inc.

1941

With A. Mazur. Lipids of diatoms. J. Biol. Chem., 141:283–89.

1942

Editor. *Dynamic State of Body Constituents,* by Rudolph Schoenheimer. Cambridge, Harvard University Press.

With A. Mazur. Chemical components of some autotrophic organisms. J. Biol. Chem., 143:39–42.

1943

With H. H. Mason and D. J. McCune. Intractable hypophosphatemic rickets with renal glycosuria and acidosis (the Fanconi syndrome). American Journal of Diseases of Children, 65:81.

With H. J. Bean, L. D. Behr, and E. R. Taylor. Contributions to *Organic Syntheses,* ed. by A. H. Blatt, collective volume II. New York, John Wiley & Sons, Inc. Contributions by Clarke and others include: β-Alanine, α-Aminobutyric acid, o-Chlorobenzoic acid, and o-Toluic acid.

1944

Preparation of o-aminobenzyl- and β-aminoethylthiazolium salts. J. Am. Chem. Soc., 66:652.

1945

With H. B. Vickery. The amino acid composition of proteins. Science, 102:454–56.

1949

Editor. With J. R. Johnson and Sir Robert Robinson. *The Chemistry of Penicillin.* Princeton, Princeton University Press.

1954

Editor. *Ion Transport Across Membranes.* New York, Academic Press Inc.

1955

Cysteic acid monohydrate. In: *Organic Syntheses,* ed. by E. C. Horning, collective volume III, p. 226. New York, John Wiley & Sons, Inc.,

With S. M. Nagy. Pentaacetyl *d*-glucononitrite. In: *Organic Syntheses,* ed. by E. C. Horning, collective volume III, p. 680. New York, John Wiley & Sons, Inc.

1956

With S. Korman. Carboxymethylamino acids and peptides. J. Biol. Chem., 221:113–31.

Carboxymethyl proteins. J. Biol. Chem., 221:133–41.

1959

Resolution of DL-β-hydroxybutyric acid. J. Org. Chem., 24:1610.

1968

The action of hypochlorite on sulfanilate. J. Org. Chem., 36:3816.

P. Debye

PETER JOSEPH WILHELM DEBYE

March 24, 1884–November 2, 1966

BY J. W. WILLIAMS

VITAE

Peter Joseph Wilhelm Debye was born on March 24, 1884, at Maastricht, the Netherlands. His education began in the elementary and secondary schools there; it continued at the Technische Hochschule in Aachen. His first degree, achieved in 1905, was in electrical engineering. During the Aachen period Debye came under the influence of two exceptionally able physicists, Professors Max Wien and Arnold Sommerfeld, and with their encouragement and guidance remained there for a short additional period with an appointment as Assistant in Technical Mechanics. When Sommerfeld was called to Munich in 1906 as Professor of Theoretical Physics he invited Debye to accompany him as his assistant. Debye there completed his doctoral program in July 1908 and was promoted to privatdozent in 1910. By this time it was abundantly evident that he was well on the way to an illustrious career in physics.

In 1911 Debye received an appointment at the University of Zurich as Professor of Theoretical Physics. He returned to the Netherlands in 1912 to accept a position as Professor of Theoretical Physics at the University of Utrecht. The next invitation, two years later, was from Göttingen to take charge of the theoretical section of the Physics Institute. Within a

23

short time he became director of the institute, and he lectured on experimental physics until after the end of World War I.

Debye returned to Zurich in 1920, this time to become Professor of Physics and director of the Physics Laboratory at the Eidgenössische Technische Hochschule. An equivalent position at the University of Leipzig opened in 1927, and he was invited to fill it. From 1934 to 1940 he served as director of the Max Planck Institute of the Kaiser Wilhelm Institute for Physics at Berlin-Dahlem and Professor of Physics at the University of Berlin.

The Berlin post turned out to be his last in Europe. Immediately following its termination (for political reasons) he became Professor of Chemistry and, later, also chairman of the Department of Chemistry at Cornell University at Ithaca, New York. The promotion to emeritus status came in 1950. It was during the Ithaca period that Debye became an American citizen.

The quality of his scientific work gained him many honors and distinctions. A number of them have been listed to form an endpaper for this Memoir. Election to the National Academy of Sciences (U.S.) came first as a Foreign Associate (1931) and then as a Member (1947).

A different type of recognition came in 1939. A shoulder-length bust, a gift of the natives of his birthplace, Maastricht, was there unveiled in his honor to adorn the town hall. It has been noted by others that this distinction probably pleased Debye above all others.

Professor Debye married Mathilda Alberer in 1913. There were two children, a son, Peter Paul Rupprecht (b. 1916), and a daughter, Mathilda-Maria (b. 1921). He died on November 2, 1966.

THE SCIENTIST

In the Nobel Prize citation to Debye (1936) one reads, "for his contributions to our knowledge of molecular structure through his investigations on dipole moments and on the diffraction of x-rays and electrons in gases." The structure of atoms and molecules was indeed a subject of major and continuing interest with Debye; it extended over the years from studies of the arrangements of the electrons in the simplest of the atoms to measurements of the average end-to-end distance in macromolecules of the "random-coil" type. One might have elected to consider in a single section those contributions that are related to the structure of matter, but here the attempt will be made to conform more closely to the outline Debye himself selected for his *Collected Papers* (1954), a volume that was presented to him by his students and friends and by the publisher on the occasion of his seventieth birthday, in 1954. In this way there is retained to some degree a chronological order, another plan that might have been adopted.

The articles presented in this compendium, fifty-one titles, constitute somewhat less than one quarter of the total number of his contributed papers. In even this portion one finds an impressive record of high-level achievement. The main subject areas are four in number: "X-Ray Scattering," "Dipole Moments," "Electrolytes," and "Light Scattering." A fifth unit is made up of "Miscellaneous Contributions." In the development and description of the researches, the reports are invariably replete with that same skill for which the author came to be known as a speaker and lecturer, namely, consummate proficiency in the description of a difficult and intricate subject in a lucid and well-organized fashion. A study of these and the other Debye contributions is indeed a rewarding experience.

X-RAY SCATTERING

The story has often been told of how, after learning about the progress of a study of the passage of light through crystals by Ewald and Sommerfeld at Munich in 1910–1912, Von Laue became interested in the passage of very short waves through such materials. He reasoned that if the wavelength of the radiation were of the same order as the distance between the structural units a diffraction effect should be obtained. For the experimental test he suggested that x rays be used; the result strongly supported the correctness of his anticipation of a diffraction of the x rays by the crystals. As a result of this experiment a whole new subject, x-ray analysis, had been created.

Though the analysis came to be recognized as being simple in principle, there were certain complications in detailed application. Debye, well informed about the research activities at Munich, was quick to perceive that refinements of several kinds were necessary if the analyses were to have quantitative character. His treatments of two of them, the temperature effect (1914) and the atomic scattering factor effect (1915), are representative of great pioneering achievement.

In the first of these efforts Debye made calculations of the influence of the thermal vibrations of solids on the x-ray diffraction pattern. His earlier experience with the famous theoretical evaluation of the heat capacities of crystalline solids (1912) served him well in this endeavor. Using the same general idea, that the thermally induced atomic displacements in the crystal may be described as being elastic waves that are propagated through the material, he developed a mathematical expression to describe the temperature dependence of the x-ray structure amplitude factor. Introduced was the quantity now known as the Debye, or Debye-Waller, temperature factor. (Waller, later on, had made some adjustments.) Incidentally, this factor is essential to an understanding of the Mössbauer effect.

A consideration of the atomic scattering factor, Debye's second of the two refinements discussed in x-ray analysis, is of vital importance in structure determination. For the analysis, observed intensities of the spectra are compared with those calculated for assumed electronic arrangements of the structural elements. The calculations require a knowledge of the atomic scattering factor, a quantity that describes the result of interference effects within the scattering atoms.

For atoms of different sizes and kinds the scattering power for the x rays varies. Further, the waves scattered from the different parts of the electron cloud that surrounds a nucleus will be diffracted with phase differences in the direction of observation. The total amplitude is thus a function of the scattering angle and the distribution of the electron density about the atom. The atomic scattering factor, the quantity calculated, is defined as the ratio of the actual amplitude to that which would be produced by a single Thomson electron under the same experimental conditions.

Debye was able to take these several factors into quantitative account (1915). He demonstrated that as the angle of scattering increases, these phase differences become larger, so that the effective number of scattering units becomes smaller. The scattering factor, f, is now a quantity smaller than the total number of electrons in the atom. The factor depends on the wavelength, λ, of the incident rays in such a way that it is a function of $\sin \theta / \lambda$, with θ being the Bragg angle of diffraction. For example, it was possible for Debye to construct the curve for the distribution of diffracted x-ray intensity to be expected from Bohr atoms with their electrons arranged in circular orbits about their nuclei.

It was at this time, 1915, that Debye first recorded his conclusions that in matter of any state one never finds a completely random arrangement of atoms and molecules, and that perfect crystallinity is not required for the diffraction of x rays. It was pointed out in this renowned article (1915) that even in gases the atoms are not completely random in their order. This observation was the beginning of a whole sequence of experimental researches by Debye concerned with the scattering of x rays by gases, liquids, and amorphous solids. In such systems the curve of diffraction intensity versus angle of diffraction should show broad maxima and minima. However, Debye's first experimental test, conducted with Scherrer (1916), produced an unanticipated result. The test substance was finely powdered lithium fluoride, but the x-ray diffraction pattern that was observed consisted of the sharp spots characteristic of diffraction by a crystal lattice. The formation of the sharp rings was properly explained as being due to the intersection on the photographic plate of a succession of conical beams from randomly oriented crystals. It was in this way that a new and useful method of x-ray analysis, the "powder method," was discovered.

Debye persisted in his researches in x-ray optics. In an article published somewhat later (1925), his thoughts were refined, extended, and summarized. He reaffirmed that it should be possible to observe diffraction effects that are interpretable in terms of the structure of the atoms and the molecules, irrespective of their physical state. More definitively, the thought was still to the effect that certain arrangements of any given atom with respect to its neighbors are more probable than others; thus it should be possible to obtain information about them by an x-ray analysis, regardless of the state of matter. For liquids on exposure to x rays a small number of broad and diffuse halos are produced in scattering. Two factors determine the outline of these halos; Debye early called them "inner" and "outer" interferences, with those of the first kind being between waves scattered by atoms belonging to the same molecule, while those of the second kind derive from intermolecular interferences. It is now known that this distinction cannot generally be made.

For the molecular structure determination it was reasoned that the "outer" interferences should vanish if the system were "diluted," as in a gas. In this way, the mathematical analysis and interpretation should be greately simplified. The intensity factor, I, scattered by the gas should be an average effect, one described by a well-known Debye formula

$$I = k \sum_{1}^{n} \sum_{1}^{n} f_i f_j \frac{\sin x_{ij}}{x_{ij}},$$

in which the magnitude x_{ij} is proportional to the distance l_{ij} from atom i to atom j and f_i and f_j are their atomic scattering factors. The sums include the cases where $i = j$. For the angle of scattering, 2θ, of rays of wavelength λ (of the primary radiation),

$$x_{ij} = 4\pi l_{ij} \frac{\sin\theta}{\lambda}.$$

The formula is written for a molecule that consists of n atoms.

The scattering curve is thus a composite of as many individual curves as there are atomic distances in the molecule. Each such distance produces an intensity that increases and decreases as the angle of scattering is increased; the importance of the several interatomic distances is measured by the product of the scattering factors.

The results of the first experiments with gases, those from Debye's laboratory, were reported from Leipzig (1929). The reasoning had been correct; interference rings were produced by the scattering of x rays even from the simplest of molecules. For instance, from the photometered records of the rings, the chlorine–chlorine interatomic distances in carbon tetrachloride could be established with precision. Since the model for this molecule is taken to be a tetrahedron, this single distance suffices to define the complete structure. A more definitive and expanded account of similar researches, extended to certain other molecules, appeared within another year (1930).

It was at this time that Mark and Wierl * presented a preliminary description of their investigations showing that the Debye formula descriptive of the scattering of x rays by a gas, a brief outline of which appears above, could also be applied to describe the scattering of electron rays by gases. Physically, there is one difference. The electron interferences provide information about the positions of the atomic nuclei themselves, while the x-ray interferences reveal the locations of the centers

* H. Mark and R. Wierl, "Electron Diffraction, by a Single Molecule," *Naturwissenschaften* 18 (1930) : 205.

of gravity of the electron clouds about them. What is really ascertained in either case is the position of the atom centers, the desired quantity.

For reasons that need not be here described, electron diffraction became at once the preferred experiment. Though it is true that the actual number of molecules to which these methods may be applied remains small, still with modern computational devices and vastly improved equipment, electron diffraction has become a method of great utility and high precision for the evaluation of molecular structure.

Concurrently with the study of gaseous structure Debye, with Menke (1930), conducted experimental researches to determine the inner structure of liquids by x-ray analysis. The scattering pattern now represents the superposition of the two interference phenomena, an intramolecular part and an intermolecular part. It was argued that if these two parts could be separated, it would become possible to draw conclusions about the structure of the liquid. Mercury, a monatomic liquid, was selected as being a suitable test substance. With this choice the separation of inner and outer effects becomes possible. The separation of the contributions to the scattering pattern was achieved, and, by using an analysis of the type that had been presented already, by Zernicke and Prins,* it was possible to compute a distribution function to describe the probability of finding the molecules in the liquid at particular separations. This probability distribution curve for mercury demonstrated that even in the liquid there is found to be a quasi-crystalline state. The term "clustering" has been applied to short-range order situations of this general type; one finds it used in several other Debye discussions, in particular in his description of the underlying principles of electrolytic solution behaviors and in his treatments of the critical state.

---

* F. Zernike and J. A. Prins, "The Bending of X-Rays in Liquids as an Effect of Molecular Arrangement," *Zeitschrift für Physik* 41 (1927) : 184.

In these ways it was proven that there is no absolutely sharp distinction between the amorphous and crystalline states. The general subject was again given definitive overall and more modern consideration in a critical review published rather recently (1960). The volume in which this article appears provides a good idea of the enormous amount of work that has been done in structural studies of various types of amorphous materials, an area in which Debye was the pioneer.

DIPOLE MOMENTS

It is as a consequence of their asymmetrical (electrical) structure that most molecules possess a permanent dipole moment; the magnitude of this characteristic entity is a quantitative measure of the polarity of the molecule. The practical unit of dipole moment is 1×10^{-18} e.s.u., now universally known as the debye, with symbol (D).

Sixty years after the appearance of the original Debye contributions on the subject (1912; 1913), the measurement and interpretation of molecular dipole moments continues unabated. Of the two articles, one was addressed to the problem of the behavior of a dielectric in a static electric field and the other to the case in which the electric field varies sinusoidally with time. The full significance of their teachings was not immediately recognized in chemical circles. The reports had appeared in journals for subjects in physics, and they were mathematical in character. This situation changed with the appearance of two more lengthy discourses by Debye: the renowned article in the Marx *Handbuch der Radiologie* (1925) and the record of a course of lectures presented at the University of Wisconsin in early 1927 and published later in book form (1929) with the title "Polar Molecules." In these publications the subject matter was superbly summarized, organized, and enriched, and it came quickly to the attention of the physicists, who in turn communicated their interest to friends in chemistry. In the United States Professors K. T. Compton and R. C. Tolman were of great influence in this way.

To provide an indication of continuing interest we may note that beginning in 1955 at least three monographs that summarize advances in the subject have made their appearance: C. P. Smyth, "Dielectric Behavior and Structure," United States; N. E. Hill, W. E. Vaughan, A. H. Price, and M. Davies, "Dielectric Properties and Molecular Behavior," Great Britain; and V. I. Minkin, O. A. Osipov, and Yu. A. Zhdanov, "Dipole Moments in Organic Chemistry," the Soviet Union. An earlier Methuen pocket-size monograph, *Dipole Moments,* by R. J. W. LeFevre is now in its third edition; we consider this source of information to be an excellent introduction to the subject.

Debye, in his treatment of the electrical case, made use of the Langevin statistical theory of orientation for the permanent magnetic moments of paramagnetic molecules. In doing so, he took cognizance of the fact that matter is built up of electrically charged units. Prior to 1912 it had been recognized that many molecules, ammonia and water for example, showed abnormally high electrical susceptibilities, ones for which there was no explanation. By analogy with the magnetic problem Debye reasoned that such asymmetric molecules must possess finite and permanent electrical moments and that their total electrical polarizations result from two contributions, a displacement of electrons and atoms in the molecule and an orientation in the electrical field of the molecule as a whole. For the actual application in any given case it was necessary to devise means for the quantitative evaluations of each of these polarizations. The result, another well-known Debye equation that can be applied to polar gases at low pressures or (less exactly) to dilute solutions of polar substances in a nonpolar solvent, provides the means to compute the dipole moment, μ. It is, in molar form,

$$P = \frac{4\pi}{3} N \ (\alpha + \mu^2/3kT).$$

The quantity P, which Debye called the molar polarization, is evaluated experimentally by means of the Clausius–Mossotti formula, which involves dielectric constant and density data. As the formula is written, the term a measures the sum effect of electronic and atomic polarizations of a molecule as the field is applied; it is a constant that is independent of temperature. The quantity $\mu^2/3kT$ represents the orientation polarization, again per molecule. The equation demonstrates that a plot of P versus $1/T$ (T = absolute temperature) should be linear. From the slope of the line the dipole moment of the molecule is calculable.

At the time of its inception the dipole moment was the principal source of information about molecular structure. Now such data for small molecules of the rigid type have become of lesser significance because of the incidence of the x-ray and electron diffraction techniques (of Debye) and of modern spectroscopic methods.

There are molecules for which the P versus $1/T$ plot is nonlinear, with downward concavity. This result indicates that the molecular dipole moment is not independent of temperature; it can be explained by an intramolecular rotation of polar groups. Such effects are observed all the way from relatively small molecules to "random-coil" polymers in which, for example, -C-C- linkages occur. The particular finite value of the dipole moment observed at any temperature for molecules with internal rotations about such linkages then becomes the root-mean square value averaged over all the rotational positions.

For the molecule 1, 2-dichloroethane, for example, a rotation of the two -CH$_2$Cl groups about the -C-C-bond could be established. In this instance the rotations are of the "hindered" rather than "free" type. The molecular configuration possesses a center of symmetry when the two Cl atoms are at their greatest distance apart, the *trans* form, and the dipole moment in this arrangement is zero. In any other configuration, the dipole moment is finite and increases with increasing angle of internal rotation; it reaches a maximum value in the *cis* form, with an azimuthal angle of 180°. A third rotational state, the gauche form, has an azimuthal angle of $\Phi = \pm 120°$. These three rotational states serve to represent and characterize the staggered forms of the molecule.* In this way it becomes possible to compute a fractional occupation of each state and its relative potential energy.†

With F. Bueche, Debye (1951) applied this relatively simple idea of internal rotations to an organic high-polymer system. It will be indicated later that one may gain information about the average size of coiled polymer molecules in solution from light scattering measurements. However, the average coil diameter found by this experiment is usually much larger than would be calculated for a "random-coil" molecule of the same molecular weight and with unhindered rotaion about the bonds that link the monomeric structural units. The difference was ascribed to a restriction of the rotations about these bonds, and a model was devised by which its effect could be quantitatively taken into account.

It may be mentioned that there have been established by dipole moment studies cases where free and unhindered rotations are encountered. An interesting example in polymer chemistry is that of the omega-hydroxydecanoic acid esters.‡ The result, the interpretation of which is actually a triumph of the Debye dipole theory, provided early and ample justification for the universal use by polymer chemists of the "random-coil" model for their macromolecules.

The concept of the orientation of dipolar molecules in an

---

* S. Mizushima, *Structure of Molecules* (New York: Academic Press, Inc., 1954), p. 7.

† Cf. for example, C. L. Braun, W. H. Stockmayer, and R. A. Orwoll, "Dipole Moments of 1,2-Disubstituted Ethanes and Their Homologs. An Experiment for Physical Chemistry," *Journal of Chemical Education* 47 (1970) : 287.

‡ W. B. Bridgman and J. W. Williams, "Polar Group Orientation in Linear Polymeric Molecules. The ω-Hydroxydecanoic Acids," *Journal of the American Chemical Society* 59 (1937) : 1579; J. Wyman, Jr., "A Dielectric-Constant Study of ω-Hydroxydecanoic Acid Polymers," *Journal of the American Chemical Society* 60 (1938) : 328.

electric field, this time an alternating one, was applied by Debye (1913) in the explanation of the behavior of the two dielectric constants, real and imaginary, that are to be observed. (Permittivity and loss factor are better terms when frequency dependence is involved.) The basic principle is that when the field is applied, or released, a finite time will be required for the molecules to come to their equilibrium orientation because there is a viscous resistance to these rotatory motions. The range of frequency over which the real dielectric constant is variable extends from the static field to one that oscillates so rapidly as not to provide for any rotational motion of the polar molecule at all; the theory thus describes a typical molecular relaxation process. The accompanying constant, called the time of relaxation, is made available from measurements of the frequency variation of either the real dielectric constant or the energy absorption for the system; in solutions this time constant may be related to molecular size and shape.

The arguments and equations presented in connection with the frequency dependence problem have perhaps been of greatest interest in electrical engineering. One difficulty with the Debye theory has been that, written in terms of molecular dimensions and the internal friction of the medium, it leads to equations of quite the same mathematical form as an alternative explanation of Wagner * that is founded upon inhomogeneity of substance without reference to any molecular mechanism. There is nothing vague about the Debye model, and one can readily appreciate its appeal to those who work to elucidate the molecular behavior of electrically insulating materials. The model's main fault may be that it is too definitive in character.

ELECTROLYTES

As physical chemistry was taught in the early 1920's one of its major subdivisions was a description of the electrochemical

* Cf. in H. Schering, *Isolierstoffe in der Elektrotechnik* (Berlin: Springer, 1924), p. 1.

behavior of electrolyte solutions. But in this particular area one encountered many perplexing situations; overall its consideration was not a satisfying experience for either teacher or student. Clearly, a new idea was needed, and while Debye may not have provided it he did achieve great success in transforming a new postulate into an effective and practical working tool.

In particular, there was a fundamental problem in that the simple laws of Arrhenius and van't Hoff, so successful in application for the study of the equilibrium and transport properties of weak electrolytes (organic acids and bases), failed utterly when applied to account for these same kinds of data for solutions of the strong electrolytes (salts, certain inorganic acids and bases). In the latter situations the starting point, a mass action law equilibrium, was clearly inconsistent with the results of extensive sets of experiments. The answer was found in the assumption that the strong electrolytes are completely dissociated when dissolved in water. This representation had been considered by others, notably by Bjerrum and Sutherland and, using it, Milner * had actually computed the osmotic coefficient (a quantity that is simply related to the activity coefficient) for the electrolytes. Certainly, it may be said that the Milner analysis is, in principle, a solution of the thermodynamic problem, but there remained substantial mathematical difficulties such that the result had to be expressed in graphical and impractical ways.

For the treatment of the equilibrium properties, another mathematical route was selected by Debye and Hückel (1923). The results were presented in quantitative expressions that could be adapted simply and directly to freezing-point depression and related data for dilute strong-electrolyte aqueous systems. In the classical theory the ions had been treated as independently active units. In the new analysis it was the

* S. R. Milner, "Virial of a Mixture of Ions," *The Philosophical Magazine* 23 (1912) : 551; "The Effect of Interionic Forces on the Osmotic Pressure of Electrolytes," *The Philosophical Magazine* 25 (1913) : 742.

electrostatic forces exerted between the ions that proved to be the basic causes of the observed nonideality of solution behavior—hence the term "interionic attraction theory." Actually, for sufficiently dilute electrolyte solutions, it became possible for Debye and Hückel to calculate in advance of any experiment what would be the observed osmotic pressure (or freezing point lowering, etc.) for salts of different valence types at a given ionic strength (a function of the electrolyte concentration) in an aqueous solution. The restriction to dilute solution behaviors made easier an otherwise very involved mathematical problem.

Still with reference to the first of the Debye–Hückel papers and the freezing point depression problem, we amplify these remarks. The argument is based on the application of well-known laws of electrostatics and together with the Maxwell–Boltzmann statistics. The ions were considered to be spheres of the same diameter, with their charges spread out in spherical symmetry. The solvent was a medium of uniform dielectric constant, a quantity unchanged by the addition of the solute ions.

The ions in solution might be expected to be in random thermal motion. However, because of the charges they carry, there will be, as a time average, more ions of opposite sign than those of the same sign in a neighboring small element of volume about any individual ion upon which attention is focused. As a result there is a structure in the system, one which is neither completely regular nor completely random in character. Each ion is thus subject to an average net electrostatic attraction by all of the other ions, and a clustering results. The magnitude of this attraction is a function of the product of the charges of the ions and the mean distance between them (concentration of the solution). The potential energy of any arbitrary central ion in the solution is lower as compared to what the energy would have been if the ion had possessed zero charge. The magnitudes of ionic attractions and repulsions were described by Coulomb's law, a fact that leads eventually to the square root of concentration behaviors for both equilibrium and transport behaviors observed by experiment in dilute solutions of strong electrolytes.

In the theory it was the most probable distribution of an ionic atmosphere about a central ion that was first determined. Then, the average electrical potential of a given ion due to the presence of all the other ions was calculated. The calculation involved the combination of the Poisson differential equation, in which potential is related to the average electrical charge density, with the Boltzmann distribution theorem. It was the approximations here introduced to effect a simplification of the mathematical problem that have become the cause of much later comment. Certainly, they restrict the application of the theory largely to dilute aqueous solutions.

With a knowledge of this potential, the excess free energy due to the electrostatic interactions was computed. It is related to the several measures of solution nonideality, for instance, the osmotic coefficient from freezing-point depression data, and even more simply, the activity coefficient.

In the common usage of today it is the activity coefficient which is sought. Debye (1924) was prompt in his appreciation of its advantage in use over the osmotic coefficient; he recognized that his earlier presentation with Hückel (1923) could be greatly simplified if written in terms of the activity coefficient. It is the equivalent of this second derivation of the limiting thermodynamic law that is almost universally reproduced in the modern physical chemistry texts. The title of this article is, in translation, "Osmotic Equation of State and Activity of Dilute Strong Electrolytes." In the introduction to this report one finds the German equivalent of the sentences, "Besides, I have in the meantime come across some laws on the activity of strong electrolytes which G. N. Lewis discovered in a purely experimental way. I am glad to have this opportunity to emphasize the special importance of these fine investigations, the more so since the laws of Lewis can be explained very easily by the proposed theory."

The appreciably more difficult transport problem of electrical conductance was the subject of the second of the basic Debye–Hückel theoretical treatments (1923). On the basis of the Arrhenius theory, the variation of the equivalent electrical conductance with electrolyte concentration was explained by the change in the relative number of the ions, the carriers of the current, as a function of concentration—a law of mass action effect. While this explanation remains correct to a good approximation for weak electrolytes, it could not account for the square root of concentration decrease in equivalent conductance with increasing concentration that had already been found experimentally by Kohlrausch and others for the strong electrolytes. Here, per equivalent of electrolyte, the number of carriers of electricity remains substantially constant (in dilute solution); it is the ion mobilities that decrease with increasing electrolyte concentration, again an effect of the interionic attractions. The discussion was now focused on two properties of the ionic atmosphere, a relaxation time effect and an electrophoretic effect. Although this time absolute values could not be computed, Debye and Hückel were able to demonstrate that for the limiting law the two progressive decreases in ion mobilities with increasing salt concentration are each proportional to the square root of the equivalent concentration. In their first treatment of the transport problem Debye and Hückel did not fully take into account the effect of the Brownian movement of the ions during the time of their displacement in the electrical field. The required modification was provided by Onsager, and the combined result is called today the Debye–Hückel–Onsager theory.

With the appearance of these papers there began a whole new era in the treatment of systems containing electrolytes. Debye himself continued to recognize new areas in the subject and to treat them with his customary aplomb. Immediately following the publication of the fundamental disclosures he indicated (1923) at length that his simple limiting law for the activity coefficient of a strong electrolyte can be directly applied in the explanation of the change in solubility of a difficultly soluble salt caused by the addition to the solution of a salt without a common ion. The quantity $\log s/s_0$ versus square root of the ionic strength is linear, and $\log s/s_0$ is a direct measure of -log $\gamma_\pm$, for the difficultly soluble salt. The quantities s and s_0 are the solubilities of the saturating salt in the presence and absence, respectively, of the added electrolyte, and $\gamma_\pm$ is its mean activity coefficient.

In two papers on the "salting-out effect," Debye (1925; 1927) showed that the separation of organic solutes from saturated aqueous systems on salt addition is largely a consequence of the inhomogeneous electrical field produced by the localized charges carried by the ions. Again, these accounts do not take into consideration the fact of the presence of other forces, especially in that one is no longer dealing with dilute solutions.

In further connection with the transport problem Debye and Falkenhagen (1928) reasoned that because of the finite time of relaxation of the ionic atmosphere there must be a frequency dependence of the electrical conductivity for a strong electrolyte in solution. Further it was indicated that the Wien observation of a deviation from Ohm's law when high field strengths are applied in the measurement could be interrelated with the frequency dependence problem. Although the experiments are difficult to perform, the detailed prediction of the dependence of conductance on the frequency of the applied field was later verified by direct experiment, an establishment of the sufficiency of the Debye model to explain not only the conductance behavior, but also to provide treatments of other transport problems, such as diffusion and viscosity, again for dilute strong electrolyte solutions.

The Debye papers descriptive of his interionic attraction

theory have influenced profoundly the course of research in several related areas. We mention but two of them:

1. The velocity of ionic reactions is modified as salt is added to the system. These effects are not generally due to any direct action of the salt; they are due rather to the electrostatic forces between the ions as they influence the velocity constants for the reaction. The bearing of modern electrolyte theory on the reaction kinetics has been treated in an authoritative fashion by Bell.*

2. There has been much confusion in the literature of the protein physical chemist as data for typical equilibrium and transport experiments have been interpreted. The system used is traditionally that of water, protein, and salt, a three-component system, one which requires detailed mathematical interpretation. By the simple expedient of the addition of excess salt, called "supporting electrolyte," and attention to certain experimental details, the influence of the charge on the macroion is largely suppressed, and the problem is reduced in complexity to that encountered in the analysis of a two-component, neutral molecule system. Casassa and Eisenberg † have discussed this problem as it relates to osmotic pressure, light scattering, and sedimentation equilibrium in such systems.

LIGHT SCATTERING

The final period of Debye's life began in 1940 when he arrived at Cornell University. Debye now applied his talents to macromolecular and colloid chemistry and began at once to provide new ideas and ways for their study. Now, the central theme was again the interaction of radiation and matter. He recognized that just as the wavelength of x rays is comparable to the size of atoms in the crystal, so is the corresponding length of light rays of the same order as the dimensions of the polymer molecules and colloidal particles. As the result one finds in the

* R. P. Bell, *Acid-Base Catalysis* (Oxford: Clarendon Press, 1941).
† E. F. Casassa and H. Eisenberg, "Thermodynamic Analysis of Multi-Component Solutions," *Advances in Protein Chemistry* 19 (1964): 287.

literature theoretical analyses by which light-scattering experiments may be interpreted in terms of macromolecular size, radius of gyration, and even of the end-to-end distance of the macromolecular unit when it has the random-coil configuration. There are also significant extensions of our knowledge of the structure of colloidal particles and porous solids.

Of the two kinds of mathematical analysis for light scattering from solutions, the vibrating dipole theory of Hertz * and the density fluctuation theory of von Smoluchowski † and of Einstein,‡ the latter is the more generally applicable.

A basic quantity is the turbidity, τ, described by an exponential law of common form:

$$I = I_0 e^{-\tau r}.$$

This statement has as a source the vibrating dipole theory. In it I and I_0 are the scattered and incident light intensities, respectively, and r is the distance between the scattering center and the point of observation. The turbidity is thus the extinction coefficient in cm^{-1}. In experimental quantities it can be written as:

$$\tau = \frac{32\pi^3}{3} \frac{v}{\lambda^4} \left[\frac{1}{n_0} \frac{dn}{dc} \right].$$

It will be noted that this formula contains the familiar Rayleigh scattering factor $(\lambda^4)^{-1}$. With v, the number of macromolecules per cubic centimeter, which is equal to cN/M, the molecular weight (M) is introduced and $\tau = HMc$. The concentration (c) is the weight of solute per cubic centimeter of solution, H is the familiar light-scattering constant in $(\lambda^4)^{-1}$, and dn/dc is the refractive index increment.

Fluctuation theory may be used with advantage in the calculation of the excess scattering by a dissolved substance. From an

---

* H. Hertz, "Die Kräfte electrischen schwingungen, behandelt nach der Maxwellschen theorie," *Annalen der Physik* 36 (1888) : 1.

† Smoluchowski, *Annalen der Physik* 25 (1908) : 205.

‡ A. Einstein, "Theory of the Opalescence of Homogeneous and of Mixed Liquids in the Neighborhood of the Critical Region," *Annalen der Physik* 33 (1910) : 1275.

Einstein relation between osmotic pressure and light scattering Debye obtained the general expression to describe the light-scattering behavior as a function of solute concentration (c) for a binary nonideal solution of neutral macromolecules whose size is small in comparison with the wavelength of the monochromatic light. It is:

$$\frac{Hc}{\tau} = \frac{1}{M} + 2Bc,$$

in which B is the osmotic pressure second virial coefficient.

With intramolecular interference of the light, such as is found in larger and flexible molecules, the situation becomes much more complicated because a particle-scattering factor now must be introduced into the essential working equations. Debye's classical and original work on the atomic scattering factor in x-ray analysis pointed the way for him to relate the angular dissymmetry of the light scattering now involved to particle shape. The particle-scattering factor contains a size parameter, angle of scattering, and wavelength dependence.

The application of the Einstein and Rayleigh equations for light scattering to the determination of the molecular size of macromolecules in solution did not originate with Debye. There were the earlier Putzeys and Brosteaux * and the Gehman and Field † contributions; proper and generous references to these papers were made in the Debye reports. But, as is typical, Debye did make the procedure a practical one, so much so that immediately following the appearance of his disclosures there began an explosive development of organic high-polymer chemistry—the subject matter of which had now been taken out of the realm of the descriptive and into exact science.

Further, the light-scattering techniques were applied to other types of systems, such as silicates and soap micelles. In an interesting series of papers, published during the period 1948–1951,

* P. Putzeys and J. Brosteaux, "The Scattering of Light in Protein Solutions," *Transactions of the Faraday Society* 31 (1935) : 1314.

† S. D. Gehman and J. E. Field, "Colloidal Structure of Rubber in Solution," *Industrial and Engineering Chemistry* 29 (1937) : 793.

Debye, with several collaborators, used the techniques to learn about micelle formation in solutions of paraffin-chain salts. Both the size and the shape of the micelles were considered. An objective was to determine the number of primary units of which they are composed and whether all the micelles are alike in size; another was to describe the mechanism of micelle formation.

Of the two theoretical accounts of the Debye theory of micelle formation appearing in the literature (1949), the New York Academy of Sciences article is the more definitive. It should be mentioned, however, that both Reich * and Ooshika † believe Debye to be seriously in error in his treatment of the problem. Both critics agree that the stable micellar size must be the one that results in a minimum of free energy for the system as a whole rather than for the individual micelle, as Debye had postulated. (Although an interval of two years between the appearance in the literature of the two criticisms is evident, the original manuscripts reached their respective editorial offices in August 1953, actually within one week of each other. The presumption is that they were conceived and published independently.)

In the final period of his scientific life, Debye became greatly interested in the phenomenon of critical opalescence and lectured widely and enthusiastically on the subject. Under certain circumstances small molecules may form aggregates of a size comparable to the wavelength of light, again a typical clustering phenomenon. A study of the scattering of light from such systems provides information about the distance of nearest approach of the molecules, which is taken to be a measure of the range of molecular interaction. But here, and apparently without full realization, the work of Debye had been largely, but

---

* I. Reich, "Factors Responsible for the Stability of Detergent Micelles," *Journal of Physical Chemistry* 60 (1956) : 257.

† Y. Ooshika, "Theory of Critical Micelle Concentration of Colloidal Electrolyte Solutions," *Journal of Colloidal Science* 9 (1954) : 254.

not completely, anticipated by Ornstein and Zernike *; their distribution function to ascertain this distance was the one used by Debye. Their study was concerned with density fluctuations in the critical region; the basic article bears the title "Accidental Deviations of Density and Opalescence at the Critical Point of a Single Substance." There exists in the literature a series of papers over a period of some eight years in which these authors continued the development and description of various phases of the problems related to the clustering tendency of molecules in the critical state and the resultant opalescence.

MISCELLANEOUS

Of the papers assigned to the miscellaneous category by Debye for his *Collected Works,* lack of space requires that but two of the items receive mention. Both are of such consequence that accounts of them appear in most of the better modern texts of physical chemistry.

The earlier one has to do with the theory of the heat capacity of solids (1912). According to an old empirical rule of Dulong and Petit, the heat capacity per gram-atom of an element in the solid state is 6.2 calories. In the attempt to account for this value theoreticians had believed it to result from an equipartition of energy, but as more accurate data for the temperature dependence of the heat capacity were made available it became evident that this could not be the complete explanation, especially at the lower temperatures. The experimental fact is that the heavy and soft elements possess this value for the heat capacity per gram-atom at room temperature, but for the light and hard elements much higher temperatures are required for its attainment. At the low temperatures all the solid elements show heat capacities lower than 6.2 calories per gram-atom.

* L. S. Ornstein and F. Zernicke, "Accidental Deviation of Density and Opalescence at the Critical Point of a Single Substance," *Proceedings of the Royal Academy of Sciences of Amsterdam* 17 (1914) : 793.

The model used by Debye was to treat the solid as a continuum filled with elastic waves rather than as a system of oscillators. In spite of very involved mathematical operations he succeeded in deriving a formula that gives an excellent representation of the heat capacity at constant volume, c_v, as a function of temperature. It contains his famous T^3 law for the quantity c_v at very low temperatures, while still accounting for the fact that c_v does not increase indefinitely as the temperature is increased.

The later miscellaneous Debye paper, "Some Remarks on Magnetization at Low Temperatures" (1926), is another thoroughly imaginative and impressive item. (The same procedure was described independently by the American physical chemist Giauque, and concurrently in time.) Herein is presented in detail the principle of adiabatic demagnetization as a method for the production of very low temperatures. In it, a paramagnetic salt is inserted between the poles of a powerful magnet contained in a bath of liquid helium. As the field is turned on, the magnetic dipoles are oriented, with the production of heat; in turn, this heat is absorbed in the bath. Following the strong magnetization, the salt is insulated from its surroundings. On decrease of the field strength the orientation of the dipoles moves toward randomization, increasing the potential energy at the expense of the kinetic energy of the molecules. Accordingly, the temperature of the salt is decreased. The difficult experiment came gradually into fruitful application, beginning with Giauque in 1933.

Debye did not write many monographs and review articles. In addition to the definitive article on dipole theory in the Marx *Handbuch der Radiologie* (1925; 1934), his "Polar Molecules" of 1929 has served as a great stimulus to chemists. Interest in this volume has continued, with paperback reprints having been made available in 1945 and again in 1960. The Chu and the Prock-McConkey books, records of two series of lectures by

Debye (Cornell and Harvard), provide valuable information about molecular interactions and the forces responsible for them.

The overall record, of which but a small part has been herein depicted, must demonstrate that in his lifetime Professor Debye made many brilliant contributions of great value to physics, to chemistry, and to certain of their borderline disciplines. In these writings he has left a precious legacy for physical scientists. In every sense and by universal acclaim he was indeed one of the leading scientists of our century.

THE MAN

As an individual Professor Debye was held in universal affection and esteem by those who knew him. One description, taken from a Harvard University citation, is particularly apt— "a large-hearted physicist who gladly lends to the chemist a helping hand." He was the kind of person Maurice Hindus had in mind when he wrote, "A student needs to come under the influence of only one exciting professor to feel the effects of it all his life, even to have the course of his life changed." He was readily approachable, a very friendly person to whom one could go for advice in research and come away fully rewarded. No one was beneath his personal encouragement; he was patient and understanding with all.

The many honors and distinctions that came with the passing of the years did not in any way change him. He was modest and realistic about them. He never forgot his old friends and associates, nor did his interest in science diminish with increased time or frame. To the end his generosity, friendliness, and concern for others were commensurate with his mental prowess.

Whether as classroom teacher or as special lecturer he was renowned for his facility of expression. This apparent ease of exposition must have required concerted effort at organization. Nowhere were his abilities to explain scientific principles better demonstrated than in his lectures for the large introductory physics courses presented during the Zurich and Leipzig periods. The concomitant lecture table displays were correspondingly pertinent and skillful; here again it was obvious that much thought and time had gone into their preparation.

In his years in the United States Debye became an inveterate traveler. He gave lectures and seminars outside of Ithaca almost weekly. At meetings his appearances invariably meant large audiences, for from his discussions at them the new and unexpected was the rule. He possessed the ability to explain scientific ideas and principles to a wide variety of audiences, and wherever he went he was received as a desirable and agreeable lecturer.

It has been noted elsewhere * that Debye was "an affectionate husband, father, and grandfather." His hobbies were few, such as gardening, fishing, and collecting cacti. There were periods when his lengthy activities in his rose garden might have brought concern to an observer, but more often than not they were followed by extraordinary bursts of scientific activity; a new idea had been elaborated during the out-of-doors time.

As a result of my own relationships with him I must note that Professor Debye did indeed have true kindness of heart, along with his rare vigor of intellect.

THE AUTHOR is indebted to colleagues both here at the University of Wisconsin and at the California Institute of Technology for their advice and help. Drs. E. W. Hughes, W. E. Vaughan, P. Bender, and J. D. Ferry have read portions of the manuscript, have given wise counsel, and have made useful suggestions.

Subject to certain revisions and modifications, the bibliography which is here included has been taken from the Debye Memoir written by Professor Mansel Davies for the 1970 volume, *Biographical Memoirs of the Fellows of the Royal Society* (London). Too, he has read the manuscript and raised certain questions in connection with it. For the permission of Dr. Davies to make use of both bibliography and suggestions, I am deeply grateful.

* F. A. Long, "Peter Debye—An Appreciation," *Science* 155 (1967) : 979.

A substantial portion of this memoir was written in the hospitable Millikan Library of the California Institute of Technology at Pasadena.

HONORS AND DISTINCTIONS

ACADEMIES

National Academy of Sciences, Washington, D.C.
New York Academy of Sciences, New York
American Academy of Arts and Sciences, Boston
American Philosophical Society, Philadelphia
Franklin Institute, Philadelphia
Royal Dutch Academy, Amsterdam, Holland
Royal Society, London, England
Royal Institution of Great Britain, London, England
Royal Danish Academy, Copenhagen, Denmark
Academies of Berlin, Göttingen, Munich, Germany
Academies of Brussels and Liège, Belgium
Royal Irish Academy, Dublin, Ireland
Papal Academy, Rome, Italy
Indian Academy, Bungalore, India
National Institute of Science, India
Real Sociedad Española de Fisica y Quimica, Madrid, Spain

MEDALS

Rumford Medal (Royal Society, London), 1930
Lorentz Medal (Royal Dutch Academy, Amsterdam), 1935
Nobel Prize in Chemistry, 1936
Franklin Medal (Franklin Institute), 1937
Willard Gibbs Medal (American Chemical Society, Chicago), 1949
Max Planck Medal (German Physical Society), 1950
Nichols Medal (American Chemical Society, New York), 1961

HONORARY DEGREES

Brussels and Liège (Belgium)
Oxford (England)
Prague (Czechoslovakia)
Sofia (Bulgaria)
Aachen and Mainz (West Germany)

Zürich, E. T. H. (Switzerland)

Harvard, St. Lawrence, Colgate, Notre Dame, Holy Cross, Brooklyn Polytechnic, Boston College, Providence College, and Clarkson Institute of Technology (United States)

LECTURESHIPS

Paris (France)

Liège (Belgium)

Oxford and Cambridge (England)

Harvard, Michigan, Columbia, California, Southern California, Massachusetts Institute of Technology, California Institute of Technology, and Wisconsin (United States)

BIBLIOGRAPHY

KEY TO ABBREVIATIONS

Angew. Chem. = Angewandte Chemie

Ann. Phys. = Annalen der Physik

Ber. Verh. Saech. Akad. Leipz. math.-naturwiss. Kl. = Berichte über die Verhandlungen der Saechsischen Akademie zu Leipzig, mathematisch-naturwissenschaftlich Klasse

Bull. sci. Acad. Roy. Belg. = Bulletin des sciences, Academie Royale de Belgique

C. R. Soc. Suisse Phys. = Comptes rendus de la Société Suisse de Physique

Ergeb. tech. Röntgenk. = Ergebnisse der technischen Röntgenkunde

J. Appl. Phys. = Journal of Applied Physics

J. Chem. Phys. = Journal of Chemical Physics

J. Colloid Sci. = Journal of Colloid Science

J. Phys. Chem. = Journal of Physical Chemistry

J. Phys. Colloid Chem. = Journal of Physical and Colloid Chemistry

J. Polym. Sci. = Journal of Polymer Science

Nachr. Akad. Wiss. Goett. math.-phys. Kl. IIa = Nachrichten der Akademie der Wissenschaften in Goettingen, mathematisch-physikalische Klasse, IIa

Natuur-en Geneeskd. Congr. = Natuur-en Geneeskundige Congress

Phys. Eindhoven = Physica, Eindhoven

Phys. Rev. = Physical Review

Phys. Z. = Physikalische Zeitschrift

Rev. univ. mines (Liège) = Revue universelle des mines (Liège)

Sitzungsber. Bayer. Akad. Wiss. math.-naturwiss. Kl. = Sitzungsberichte der Bayerischen Akademie der Wissenschaften, mathematisch-naturwissenschaftliche Klasse

Trans. Am. Electrochem. Soc. = Transactions of the American Electrochemical Society

Trans. Faraday Soc. = Transactions of the Faraday Society

Verh. Dtsch. Phys. Ges. = Verhandlungen der Deutschen Gesellschaft für Physik

Verh. Schweiz. Naturforsch. Ges. Freib. = Verhandlungen der Schweizerischen Naturforschenden Gesellschaft, Freiburg

Z. Elektrochem. = Zeitschrift für Elektrochemie und angewandte physikalische Chemie

Z. Phys. = Zeitschrift für Physik

Z. phys. Chem. = Zeitschrift für physikalische Chemie

Z. tech. Phys. = Zeitschrift für technische Physik

1907

Wirbelströme in Stäben von techteckigem Querschnitt. Zeitschrift für Mathematik und Physik, 54:418.

1908

Eine Bemerkung zu der Arbeit von F. A. Schulze. Einige neue

Methoden zur Bestimmung der Schwingungszahlen höchster hörbarer und unhörbarer Töne usw. Ann. Phys., 25:819.

Das elektromagnetische Feld um ein Zylinder und die Theorie des Regenbogens. Phys. Z., 9:775; also in Verh. Dtsch. Phys. Ges., 10(20):741.

1909

Näherungsformeln für die Zylinder funktionen für grosse Werte des Arguments und unbeschränkt veränderliche Werte des Index. Mathematische Annalen, 67:535.

Der Lichtdruck auf Kugeln von beliebigen Material. Ann. Phys., 30:57.

Das Verhalten von Lichtwellen in der Nahe eines Brennpunktes oder einer Brennlinie. Am. Phys., 30:755.

1910

Stationäre und quasistationäre Felder. In: *Encyklopädie der Mathematischen Wissenschaften*, vol. 5, *Physik*, Teil 2, p. 395. Leipzig, B. G. Teubner.

Zur theorie der Elektronen in Metallen. Ann. Phys., 33:441.

Semikonvergente Entwickelungen für die Zylinder-funktionen und ihre Ausdehnung ins Komplexe. Sitzungsber. Bayer. Akad. Wiss. math.-naturwiss. Kl., no. 5, p. 1.

With D. Hondros. Elektromagnetische Wellen an dielektrischen Drähten. Ann. Phys., 32:465.

Die Berechnung der Moleküldimensionen aus Radiometerbeobachtungen. Phys. Z., 11:115.

Der Wahrscheinlichkeitsbegriff in der Theorie der Strahlung. Ann. Phys., 33:1427.

1911

Die Frage nach der atomistischen Struktur der Energie. Vierteljahrsschrift der Naturforschenden Gesellschaft in Zurich, 56:156.

Über Abweichungen vom Curie-Langevin'schen Gesetz und ihren Zusammenhang mit der Quantenhypothese. Verh. Schweiz. Naturforsch. Ges. Freib., 94:220; also in C. R. Soc. Suisse Phys., 1er août, 1911.

1912

Zur Theorie der spezifischen Wärmen. Ann. Phys., 39:789.

Einige Resultate einer kinetischen Theorie der Isolatoren. Phys. Z., 13:97.

1913

Zur Theorie der anomalen Dispersion im Gebiete der langwelligen elektrischen Strahlung. Verh. Dtsch. Phys. Ges., 15:777.

With W. Dehlinger. Die kinetische Theorie der Materie in ihrer modernen Entwicklung (Ausgang aus der Utrechter Antrittsreder von Prof. P. Debye). Archiv Elektrotechnik, 2:167.

Zustandsgleichung und Quantenhypothese. Nachr. Akad. Wiss. Goett. math.-phys. Kl. IIa, 1913:140; also in Phys. Z., 14:317.

Über den Einfluss der Wärmebewegung auf der Interferenzerscheinungen bei Röntgenstrahlen. Verh. Dtsch. Phys. Ges., 15:678.

Über die Intensitätsverteilung in den mit Röntgenstrahlen erzeugten Interferenzbildern. Verh. Dtsch. Phys. Ges., 15:738.

Spektrale Zerlegung des Röntgenstrahlen mittels Reflexion und Wärmebewegung. Verh. Dtsch. Phys. Ges., 15:857.

With A. Sommerfeld. Theorie des lichtelektrischen Effektes vom Standpunkt des Wirkungsquantums. Ann. Phys., 41:873.

1914

With J. Kern. Über die Behandlung gekoppelter Systeme nach der Methode der Eigenschwingungen. Phys. Z., 15:490.

Zustandsgleichung und Quantenhypothese mit einem Anhang über Warmeleitung. In: *Vorträge über die kinetische Theorie der Materie und der Elektrizität. Math. Vorlesgn,* vol. VI. Leipzig, B. G. Teubner.

Interferenz von Röntgenstrahlen und Wärmebewegung. Ann. Phys., 43:49.

1915

Die Konstitution des Wasserstoff Moleküls. Sitzungsber. Bayer. Akad. Wiss. math.-naturwiss. Kl., 1915:1.

Zerstreuung von Röntgenstrahlen. Ann. Phys., 46:809; also in Nachr. Akad. Wiss. Goett. math.-phys. Kl. IIa., 1915:70.

1916

With P. Scherrer. Interferenzen an regellos orientierten Teilchen im Röntgenlicht. I. Phys. Z., 17:277; also in Nachr. Akad. Wiss. Goett. math.-phys. Kl. IIa., 1916:1.

With P. Scherrer. Interferenzen an regellos orientierten Teilchen im Röntgenlicht. II. Nachr. Akad. Wiss. Goett. math.-phys. Kl. IIa, 1916:16.

Die Feinstruktur wasserstoffähnlicher Spektren. Phys. Z., 17:512; also in Nachr. Akad. Wiss. Goett. math.-phys. Kl. IIa, 1916:161.

Quantenhypothese und Zeeman-Effekt. Phys. Z., 17:507; also in Nachr. Akad. Wiss. Goett. math.-phys. Kl. IIa, 1916:142.

1917

Konzentrationselement und Brownsche Bewegung. Phys. Z., 18:144.

Der erste Elektronenring der Atome. Phys. Z., 18:276; also in Nachr. Akad. Wiss. Goett. math.-phys. Kl. IIa, 1917:236.

With P. Scherrer. Über die Konstitution von Graphit und amorpher Kohle. Nachr. Akad. Wiss. Goett. math.-phys. Kl. IIa, 1917:180.

With P. Scherrer. Interferenzen an regellos orientierten Teilchen im Röntgenlicht. III. Die Kohlenstoffmodifikationen. Phys. Z., 18:291.

Optische Absorptionsgrenzen. Phys. Z., 18:428.

Die Atomanordnung von Wolfram. Phys. Z., 18:483.

1918

With P. Scherrer. Atombau. Phys. Z., 19:474; also in Nachr. Akad. Wiss. Goett. math.-phys. Kl. IIa, 1918:101.

1919

Das molekulare elektrische Feld in Gasen. Phys. Z., 20:160.

1920

Die neuen Forschungen über den Bau der Molekule und Atome. Verhandlungen der Gesellschaft deutscher Naturforscher und Ärzte, 86:239.

Die van der Waalsschen Kohäsionskräfte. Phys. Z., 21:178; also in Nachr. Akad. Wiss. Goett. math.-phys. Kl. IIa, 1920:55.

1921

Adsorptie van elekenische molekulen. Phys. Eindhoven, 1:362.

Molekularkräfte und ihre Elektrische Deutung. Phys. Z., 22:302.
Moleculaire krachten van electrischen Oorsprong. Handelingen v. het. XVIII Vdld. Natuur-en Geneeskd. Congr., Utrecht.

1922

Laue-interferenzen und Atombau. Naturwissenschaften, 10:384.

1923

Zerstreuung von Röntgenstrahlen und Quantentheorie. Phys. Z., 24:161.
With E. Hückel. Zur Theorie der Elektrolyte. I. Gefrierpunktserniedrigung und verwandte Erscheinungen. Phys. Z., 24:185.
With E. Hückel. Zur Theorie der Elektrolyte. II. Das Grenzgesetz für die elektrische Leitfähigkeit. Phys. Z., 24:305.
Kinetische Theorie der Gesetze des osmotischen Drucks bei starken Elektrolyten. Phys. Z., 24:334; also in Recueil des travaux chimiques des Pays Bas et de la Belgique, 42:597.
De moderne ontwikkeling van de elektrolyt-theorie. Handelingen v. het. XVIII Vdld. Natuur-en Geneeskd. Congr., Maastricht.
Over Ionen en Hun Activiteit. Chemisch Weekblad, 20:562.

1924

With E. Hückel. Bemerkungen zu einem Satze über die Kataphoretische Wanderungsgeschwindigkeit suspendierter Teilchen. Phys. Z., 25:49.
Osmotische Zustandsgleichung und Aktivität verdünnter starker Elektrolyte. Phys. Z., 25:97.

1925

Molekulare Kräfte und ihre Deutung. Verh. Schweiz. Naturforsch. Ges. Freib., 106:128.
Note on the scattering of x-rays. Journal of Mathematics and Physics, 4:133.
Theorie der elektrischen und magnetischen Molekulareigenschaften. In: *Handbuch der Radiologie. Die Theorien der Radiologie,* ed. by E. Marx, vol. VI, p. 597. Leipzig, Academische Verlagsgesellschaft.
With L. Pauling. Inter-ionic attraction theory of ionised solutes. IV. The influence of variation of dielectric constant on the limit-

ing law for small concentrations. Journal of the American Chemical Society, 47:2129.

With J. McAulay. Das elektrische Feld der Ionen und die Neutralsalzwirkung. Phys. Z., 26:22.

With A. Huber. Een proef over de instelling van paramagnetische molukulen. Phys. Eindhoven, 5:377.

1926

Die Grundgesetze der elektrischen und magnetischen Erregung vom Standpunkte der Quantentheorie. Phys. Z., 27:67.

Molekulare Kräfte und ihre Deutung. Umschau, 30:905; also in Verh. Schweiz. Naturforsch. Ges. Freib., 106:128.

Einige Bemerkungen zur Magnetisierung bei tiefer Temperatur. Ann. Phys., 81:1154.

Bemerkung zu einigen neuen Versuchen über einen magnetoelektrischen Richteffekt. Z. Phys., 36:300.

With W. Hardmeier. Anomale Zerstreung von a-Strahlen. Phys. Z., 27:196.

With W. Hardmeier. Dispersion anomale des rayons alpha. C. R. Soc. Suisse Phys., 8:131.

1927

Wellenmechanik und Korrespondenzprinzip. Phys. Z., 28:170.

With C. Manneback. The symmetrical top in wave mechanics. Nature, Lond., 119:83.

Report on conductivity of strong electrolytes in dilute solutions. Trans. Faraday Soc., 23:234.

Das elektrische Ionenfeld und das Aussalzen. Z. phys. Chem., 130:56.

Über die Zerstreuung von Röntgenstrahlen an amorphen Körpern. Phys. Z., 28:135.

Dielectric constants of electrolyte solutions. Trans. Am. Electrochem. Soc., 51:449.

1928

Die elektrischen Momente der Molekeln und die zwischenmolekularen Kräfte. Z. Elektrochem., 34:450.

Editor of Sommerfeld Festschrift. Die Zeitlichen Vorgänge in Elektrolytlösungen. In: *Probleme der Modernen Physik*, p. 52. Leipzig, S. Hirzel.

Über elektrische Momente. Atti del Congresso Internazionale dei Fisici, Como, 1927. Bologna, N. Zanichelli.

With H. Falkenhagen. Dispersion von Leitfähigkeit und Dielektrizitätskonstante bei starken Elektrolyten. Phys. Z., 29:121; also in Z. Elektrochem., 34:562.

With H. Falkenhagen. Dispersion der Leitfähigkeit und der Dielektrizitätskonstante starker Elektrolyte. Phys. Z., 29:401.

1929

With L. Bewilogua and F. Ehrhardt. Zerstreuung von Röntgenstrahlen an einzelnen Molekeln. Phys. Z., 30:84.

Interferometrische Messungen am Molekül. Phys. Z., 30:524; also in Berichte Züricher Vorträge, Juli 1–4.

Polar Molecules. Wisconsin lectures. New York, Chemical Catalog Co.

With L. Bewilogua and F. Erhardt. Interferometrische Messungen am Molekül. Ber. Verh. Saech. Akad. Leipz. math.-naturwiss. Kl., 81:29.

1930

Röntgeninterferenzen an isomeren Molekülen. Phys. Z., 31:142.

Röntgenzerstreuung an Flüssigheiten und Gasen. Phys. Z., 31:348.

Röntgeninterferenzen und Atomgrösse. Phys. Z., 31:419.

With H. Menke. Bestimmung der inneren Struktur von Flüssigkeiten mit Röntgenstrahlen. Phys. Z., 31:797.

Interferometrische Bestimmung der Struktur von Einzelmolekülen. Z. Elektrochem., 36:612.

Interference measurements with single molecules. Proceedings of the Physical Society of London, 42:340.

1931

A note on comparison of electrolytic resistance at low and radio frequencies. Indian Journal of Physics, 6:261.

With H. Menke. Untersuchung der molekularen Ordnung in Flüssigkeiten mit Röntgenstrahlung. Ergeb. tech. Röntgenk., 2:1.

1932

The dispersion of conductivity in different solvents, pp. 32–33; Interferometric measurement of atomic distances in molecules, pp.

204–209; Anomalous dispersion in solids, p. 207. In: *Chemistry at the Centenary* (1931). British Association for the Advancement of Science. Cambridge, Heffer & Sons, Ltd.

Polar molecules. Congrès International d'Electricité, Paris. Sect. 1. Rapport No. 1.

De polaritare molecularum. Pontificia Academia della Scienze, Nuovi Lyncei, Nuncius Radiophonicus, no. 14, p. 3.

With F. W. Sears. On the scattering of light by supersonic waves. Proceedings of the National Academy of Sciences, 18:409.

Schallwellen als optische Gitter. Ber. Verh. Saechs. Akad. Leipz. math.-naturwiss. Kl., 84:125.

Zerstreuung von Licht durch Schallwellen. Phys. Z., 33:849.

1933

Die elektrische Leitfähigkeit von Elektrolytlosüngen in starken Feldern und bei hohen Frequenzen. Z. Elektrochem., 39:478.

With H. Sack. Demonstration des Hochfrequenzeffektes bei Elektrolyten. Z. Elektrochem., 39:512.

15th Faraday lecture. Relations between stereochemistry and physics. Journal of the Chemical Society, London, 1933:1366.

A method for the determination of the mass of electrolytic ions. J. Chem. Phys., 1:13.

Streuung von Röntgen- und Kathodenstrahlen. Ergeb. tech. Röntgenk., 3:11.

1934

Röntgen und sein Entdeckung. Abhandlungen des Berliner Deutschen Museums, 6:83.

Die Physik der Atomkerne. Vortrag des Bund der Freunde der Technischen Hochschule München.

With H. Sack. Theorie der elektrischen Moleküleigenschaften. In: *Handbuch der Radiologie. Die Theorien der Radiologie,* ed. by E. Marx, vol. VI, pt. 2, p. 69. Leipzig, Akademische Verlagsgesellschaft.

Einfluss des molekularen Feldes auf den Verlauf adiabatischer Entmagnetisierungsprozesse bei tiefsten Temperaturen. Ber. Verh. Saech. Akad. Leipz. math.-naturwiss. Kl., 86:105.

Energy absorption in dielectrics with polar molecules. Trans. Faraday Soc., 30:679.

Hochfrequenzverluste und Molekülstruktur. Phys. Z., 35:101.

Die magnetische Methode zur Erzeugung tiefster Temperaturen.
Phys. Z., 35:923; also in Z. tech. Phys., 15:499.
With H. Sack and F. Coulon. Expériences sur la diffraction de la
lumière par des ultrasons. Comptes rendus de l'Academie des
Sciences, Paris, 198:922.

1935

Kernphysik. Angew. Chem., 48:381.
Les propriétés diélectriques du point de vue moléculaire. Rev.
univ. mines (Liège), 11:176.
Analyse des essaies de sédimentation. Rev. univ. mines (Liège), 11:
266.
La rotation des molécules dans les liquides. Bull. sci. Acad. Roy.
Belg., 21:166.
Relations entre la constitution chimique et les propriétés diélec-
triques. Bulletin de la Société Chimique de Belgique, 44:167.
Der Rotationszustand von Molekülen in Flüssigkeiten. Phys. Z.,
36:100; also in Bull. sci. Acad. Roy. Belg., 21:166.
Dielektrische Sättigung und Behinderung der freien Rotation in
Flüssigkeiten. Phys. Z., 36:193.

1936

Dielectric properties of pure liquids. Chemical Reviews, 19:171.
Der Weg zum absoluten Nullpunkt. Umschau, 40:41.
Die tiefsten heute erreichten Temperaturen. Forschungen und
Fortschrifte, 12:22; idem, English version. The lowest tempera-
tures yet established. Research Progress, 2:89.
Bemerkung zu dem Artikel von E. Gehrcke: "Wie die Energiever-
teilung der schwarzen Strahlung in Wirklichkeit gefunden
wurde." Phys. Z., 37:440.

1937

Das Kaiser-Wilhelm-Institut für Physik. Naturwissenschaften, 25:
257.
Johann Diderik van der Waals. Nederlands tijdschrift voor natuur-
kunde, 4:257.
With W. Ramm. Grundlagen der Strahlungsphysik. In: Die Welt
der Strahlen, ed. by H. Woltereck. Leipzig, Verlag Quelle &
Meyer.
With H. Sack. Constantes diélectriques, moments électriques.
Tables annuelles des constantes, Nr. 2. Paris, Hermann et Cie.

Structure in electrolytic solutions. Journal of the Franklin Institute, 224:135.
With W. Ramm. Hochfrequenzverluste und quasikrystalline Struktur von Flüssigkeiten. Ann. Phys., 28:28.
Die Untersuchung der freien Elektronen in Metallen mit Hilfe von Röntgenstrahlen. Phys. Z., 38:161.
Methoden zur Bestimmung der elektrischen und geometrischen Struktur von Molekülen. Nobelvortrage. Angew. Chem., 50:3. English version. Nobel Lectures—Chemistry 1922–1941. New York, N.Y., Elsevier Publ. Co. (1966).

1938

A contribution. In: *Physique Générale*. Paris, Hermann et Cie.
Wege der modernen Forschung in der Physik. Stahl Eisenhuettenwes, 58:1.
With M. H. Pirenne. Über die Fourieranalyse von interferometrischen Messungen an freien Molekülen. Ann. Phys., 33:617.
Die Geburt des Wirkungsquantums. Z. tech. Phys., 19:121.
Abkühlung durch adiabatische Entmagnetisierung. Ann. Phys., 32:85.
With W. Ramm. Dispersion und Absorption polarer Substanzen. Nuovo Cimento, 15:226.
Die paramagnetische Relaxation. Phys. Z., 39:616.

1939

Die quasikrystalline Struktur von Flüssigkeiten. Z. Elektrochem., 45:174.
Über den tiefsten heute erreichbaren Temperaturen. Schriften der Deutschen Akademie für Luftforschung, No. 3, p. 8.
Das Sektorverfahren bei der Aufnahme von Elektroneninterferenzen. Phys. Z., 40:507.
Untersuchung eines neuen Vorschlags zur Fourier-Analyse von Elektronenaufnahmen. Phys. Z., 40:573.
Zur Theorie des Clusiusschen Trennungsverfahrens. Ann. Phys., 36:284.

1941

The influence of intramolecular atomic motion on electron diffraction diagrams. J. Chem. Phys., 9:55.

1942

Reaction rates in ionic solutions. Trans. Am. Electrochem. Soc., 82:265.

1944

Magnetic approach to the absolute zero of temperature. American Scientist, 32:229.
Light scattering in solutions. J. Appl. Phys., 15:338.

1945

Angular dissymmetry of scattering and shape of particles. Technical Report no. 637. Washington, D.C., Rubber Reserve Company.

1946

The intrinsic viscosity of polymer solutions. J. Chem. Phys., 14:636.
With R. H. Ewart, C. P. Roe, and J. R. McCartney. The determination of polymeric molecular weights by light scattering in solvent-precipitant systems. J. Chem. Phys., 14:687.

1947

The structure of polymers in solution. Record of Chemical Progress, 8(1/2):1.
Molecular weight determination by light scattering. J. Phys. Colloid Chem., 51:18.

1948

The structure of polymers in solutions. Les Grosses molécules en solution. Homage national à Paul Langevin et Jean Perrin, p. 39. Collège de France, Paris.
Light scattering in soap solutions. J. Colloid Sci., 3:407.
With A. M. Bueche. Thermal diffusion of polymer solutions. In: High Polymer Physics, ed. by H. A. Robinson, p. 497. Brooklyn, Chemical Publishing Co., Inc.
With A. M. Bueche. Intrinsic viscosity, diffusion and sedimentation rate of polymers in solution. J. Chem. Phys., 16:573.

1949

Light scattering in soap solutions. Annals of the New York Academy of Sciences, 51:575.

Light scattering in soap solutions. J. Phys. Colloid Chem., 53:1.

With R. V. Nauman. The scattering of light by sodium silicate solutions. J. Chem. Phys., 17:664.

With A. M. Bueche. Scattering by an inhomogeneous solid. J. Appl. Phys., 20:518.

With A. M. Bueche. Light scattering by inhomogeneous solids. India Rubber World, 119:613.

With W. M. Cashin. Determination of molecular weights and sizes by absorption. Phys. Rev., 75:1307.

1950

With A. M. Bueche. Scattering by inhomogeneous materials. Colloid Chemistry, 7:33.

With A. M. Bueche. Light scattering by concentrated polymer solutions. J. Chem. Phys., 18:1423.

Estructura de altos polimeros estudiada por metodos opticos. Anales de la Real Sociedad Española de Fisica y Quimica (Madrid) Ser. B, 46:343.

1951

With R. V. Nauman. Light scattering investigations of carefully filtered sodium silicate solution. J. Phys. Colloid Chem., 55:1.

With F. Bueche. Dielectric constant of polystyrene solutions. J. Phys. Colloid Chem., 55:235.

With E. W. Anacker. Micelle shape from dissymmetry measurements. J. Phys. Colloid Chem., 55:644.

With C. W. Tait, R. J. Vetter, and J. M. Swanson. Physical characterization of cellulose xanthate in solution. J. Polym. Sci., 7:261.

With W. M. Cashin. Effect of small refractive-index differences between solution and solvent on light scattering. J. Chem. Phys., 19:510.

With F. Bueche. Electric moments of polar polymers in relation to their structure. J. Chem. Phys., 19:589.

With F. Bueche and W. M. Cashin. Expressions for turbidities. J. Chem. Phys., 19:803.

With F. Bueche. A study of crystallite sizes in polymers by a light scattering method. Phys. Rev., 81:303.

1952

With J. O. Edwards. Long-lifetime phosphorescence and the diffusion process. J. Chem. Phys., 20:236.

With F. Bueche. Distribution of segments in a coiling polymer molecule. J. Chem. Phys., 20:1337.

With F. Bueche and W. M. Cashin. The measurement of self-diffusion in solid polymers. J. Chem. Phys., 20:1956.

With J. O. Edwards. A note on the phosphorescence of proteins. Science, 116:143.

1954

Equilibrium and sedimentation of uncharged particles in inhomogeneous electric fields. In: *Ion Transport Across Membranes,* p. 273. New York, Academic Press, Inc.

With P. P. Debye, B. A. Eckstein, W. A. Barber, and G. J. Arquette. Experiments on polymer solutions in inhomogeneous electrical fields. J. Chem. Phys., 22:152.

With P. P. Debye and B. H. Eckstein. Dielectric high frequency method for molecular weight determinations. Phys. Rev., 94: 1412.

With W. A. Barber, P. P. Debye, and B. H. Eckstein. A field-induced-diffraction method for molecular-weight determinations. Phys. Rev., 94:1412.

The Collected Papers of Peter J. W. Debye. New York, Interscience Publishers Inc.

1955

With N. T. Notley. The extension of polystyrene chains; dependence on molecular weight and solvent. J. Polym. Sci., 17:99.

Structure of gel-catalysts by low angle x-ray scattering. American Chemical Society Directory of Petroleum Chemistry, General Papers, No. 33, p. 35.

1957

With H. R. Anderson, Jr., and H. Brumberger. Scattering by an inhomogeneous solid. II. The correlation function and its application. J. Appl. Phys., 28:679.

With N. T. Notley.   Dimensions of linear polystyrene molecules in solution: molecular weight dependence for low molecular weights.   J. Polym. Sci., 24:275.

With H. Brumberger.   Low-angle scattering of x-rays by glasses. J. Phys. Chem., 61:1623.

1958

With P. Dorefuss and N. T. Notley.   Polymerization of isopropenylstyrene.   J. Polym. Sci., 28:611.

With W. Prins.   Micellar dispersion of α-monoglycerides in benzene and chlorobenzene.   J. Colloid Sci., 13:86.

1959

Röntgenstreuung in Körpern mit regelloser Struktur.   Z. Phys., 156: 256.

With R. L. Cleland.   Flow of liquid hydrocarbons in porous Vycor. J. Appl. Phys., 30:843.

Angular dissymmetry of the critical opalescence in liquid mixtures. J. Chem. Phys., 31:680.

With L. K. H. van Beek.   Effect of adsorbed water on the optical transmission properties of isotropic powders.   J. Chem. Phys., 31:1595.

With J. Daen.   Stability considerations on non-viscous jets exhibiting surface or body tension.   Physics Fluids, 2:416.

Strukturbestimmung von Körpern mit regelloser Struktur mit Hilfe von Streustrahlung.   In: *Physikertagung Berlin 1959*.   Mosbach, Baden, Physik Verlag.

1960

Scattering of radiation by non-crystalline media.   In: *Noncrystalline Solids*, ed. by V. D. Fréchette, p. 1.   New York, John Wiley & Sons.

Paul Scherrer und die Streuung von Röntgenstrahlen.   Basel-Stuttgart, Birkhäuser Verlag, GmbH.

Die Winkelverteilung der kritischen Opalezenz und die Messung molekularer Wechselwirkung.   Makromolekulare Chemie, 35A: 1.

With A. Prock and G. McConkey. Inhomogeneous field method for the study of large polarizable particles. J. Chem. Phys., 32:234.

With H. Coll and D. Woermann. Critical opalescence of polystyrene solutions. J. Chem. Phys., 32:939.

With H. Coll and D. Woermann. Critical opalescence of polystyrene in cyclohexane. J. Chem. Phys., 33:1746.

Arnold Sommerfeld und die Überlichtgeschwindigkeit. Physikalische Blätter, 16:568.

With H. Coll. Non-ionic detergents in non-aqueous solvents. PB 146,513. Washington, D.C., U.S. Department of Commerce, Office of Technical Services.

With H. Coll. Non-ionic detergents in non-aqueous solvents. II. Critical opalescence of binary liquid mixtures: the system polystyrene–cyclohexane. PB 149,895. Washington, D.C., U.S. Department of Commerce, Office of Technical Services.

1961

With R. V. Nauman. The slow change in turbidity of sodium silicate solutions. J. Phys. Chem., 65:5.

With R. V. Nauman. The refractive indices of sodium silicate solutions. J. Phys. Chem., 65:8.

With R. V. Nauman. A light scattering study of the aggregation of acidified sodium silicate solutions. J. Phys. Chem., 65:10.

With B. Chu. Critical opalescence of polystyrene in cyclohexane: transmission measurements. AD 264,359. Washington, D.C., U.S. Department of Commerce, Office of Technical Services.

With B. Chu. Critical opalescence of polystyrene in cyclohexane: range of molecular forces and radius of gyration. AD 264,360. Washington, D.C., U.S. Department of Commerce, Office of Technical Services.

1962

Molecular forces. In: *International Symposium on Electrolytes,* ed. by B. Pesce, p. 1. Proceedings of a conference, Trieste, 1959. Oxford, Pergamon Press, Inc.

Interatomic and intermolecular forces in adhesion and cohesion. In: *Symposium on Adhesion and Cohesion,* ed. by Philip Weiss, p. 1. Proceedings of a conference, Warren, Michigan, 1961. New York and Amsterdam, Elsevier Pub. Co.

With D. Woermann and B. Chu. Critical opalescence of polystyrene in cyclohexane: transmission measurements. J. Chem. Phys., 36:851.

Critical opalescence and the range of molecular interaction. Pontificiae Academiae Scientiarum, Scripta Varia, 22:53.

With B. Chu and D. Woermann. Critical opalescence of polystyrene in cyclohexane: range of molecular forces and radius of gyration. J. Chem. Phys., 36:1803.

With B. Chu and H. Kaufmann. Critical opalescence of binary liquid mixtures: methanol–cyclohexane and aniline–cyclohexane. J. Chem. Phys., 36:3378.

With B. Chu. Spectrophotometry and light scattering on supported platinum. J. Phys. Chem., 66:1021.

With H. Coll. The association of α-monoglycerides in non-aqueous solvents. J. Colloid Sci., 17:220.

With H. Kaufmann, K. Kleboth, and B. Chu. Angular dissymmetry of critical mixtures: aniline–cyclohexane: aniline-l-hexene. Transactions of the Kansas Academy of Sciences, 66:260.

With B. Chu. Critical opalescence of polystyrene in ethylcyclohexane. AD 266,258. Washington, D.C., U.S. Department of Commerce, Office of Technical Services.

Topics in Chemical Physics, ed. by A. Prock and G. McConkey. Harvard lectures. New York, Elsevier Pub. Co.

1963

Structure determination by radiation scattering. Chemical Engineering News, 41:92.

With B. Chu and D. Woermann. Viscosity of critical mixtures. J. Polym. Sci. Ser. A, 1:249.

With D. Woermann and B. Chu. Critical opalescence of polystyrene in ethylcyclohexane. J. Polym. Sci. Ser. A, 1:255.

With B. Chu and H. Kaufmann. Molecular configuration of polystyrene in benzene. J. Polym. Sci. Ser. A, 1:2387.

Light scattering and molecular forces in electromagnetic scattering. In: *Interdisciplinary Conference on Electromagnetic Scattering,* ed. by Milton Kerker. Oxford, Pergamon Press, Inc.

1964

The early days of lattice dynamics. In: *Lattice Dynamics,* ed. by

R. F. Wallis. Proceedings of Copenhagen conference, August 1963. London, Pergamon Press, Inc.

Flüssigkeiten, Gase, Makromoleküle: kritische Streuung und die Reichweite der Molekularkräfte. Zeitschrift für Kristallographie, Kristallgeometrie, Kristallphysik, Kristallchemie, 120: 113.

Light scattering as a tool. Official Digest of the Federation Society of Paint Technology, 36:518.

With D. Caulfield and J. Bashaw. Critical opalescence of binary mixtures: perfluorotributylamine-isopentane. J. Chem. Phys., 41:3051.

With K. Kleboth. An electrical field effect on the critical opalescence. AD 604,494. Washington, D.C., U.S. Department of Commerce, Office of Technical Services.

1965

Hans Falkenhagen zum 70 Geburtstag am 13 mai 1965. Z. Phys. Chem., 1965:228, 289.

Spectral width of the critical opalescence due to concentration fluctuations. Physical Review Letters, 14:783.

With K. Kleboth. Electrical field effect on the critical opalescence. J. Chem. Phys., 42:3155.

Static homogeneous electrical field effect on critical opalescence. Ithaca, N.Y., Cornell University Report No. TR-9. NASA N65-11285.

Surface determination by x-ray scattering. In: *Coloquio sobre Quimica Fisica de Procesos en Superficies Solidas,* pp. 1–11. Madrid, Consejo Superior de Investigaciones Cientificas.

1966

Light-scattering as a tool. Pure and Applied Chemistry, 12:23.

With J. Bashaw, B. Chu, and D. M. Tancredi. Critical opalescence of the polystyrene–cyclohexane system: small-angle x-ray scattering. J. Chem. Phys., 44:4302.

With C. C. Gravatt. The behavior of non-ionic detergents in nonpolar solvents. AD-642604, N67-16150. Washington, D.C., U.S. Department of Commerce, Office of Technical Services.

With C. C. Gravatt and M. Ieda. Electric field effect on the critical opalescence. II. Relaxation times of concentration fluctuations.

Report AD-642606, N67-16129. Washington, D.C., U.S. Department of Commerce, Office of Technical Services.

With C. C. Gravatt. Behavior of non-ionic detergents in non-polar solvents. AD-642604. Washington, D.C., U.S. Department of Commerce, Office of Technical Services.

1967

With C. C. Gravatt and M. Ieda. Electric field effect on the critical opalescence. II. Relaxation times of concentration fluctuations. J. Chem. Phys., 46:2352.

With C. C. Gravatt. Measurement of relaxation times of concentration fluctuations by the electric field effect on critical opalescence. AD-657208, N67-38297. Washington, D.C., U.S. Department of Commerce, Office of Technical Services.

Molecular Forces. Baker Lectures, Cornell. (Book: B. Chu) New York, Elsevier Pub. Co.

1968

With R. T. Jacobsen. Direct visual observation of concentration fluctuations in a critical mixture. J. Chem. Phys., 48:203.

Clarence H. Graham

CLARENCE HENRY GRAHAM

January 6, 1906–July 25, 1971

BY LORRIN A. RIGGS

CLARENCE H. GRAHAM was an experimental psychologist whose principal contributions to science lie in the areas of vision and visual perception. Psychophysical and electrophysiological experiments on retinal interaction effects occupied his attention in the 1930's at Clark University. In the 1940's at Brown University he explored animal and human vision by a variety of behavioral techniques and made significant contributions to military problems of visual surveillance and selection of personnel during the Second World War. The remainder of his career, at Columbia University, was devoted mainly to studies of form, depth and motion perception, and the discrimination of color.

Before giving a more detailed account of Graham's life and accomplishments, let me attempt the difficult task of picturing him as an individual. It was in the early days at Clark and at Brown that I knew him best. I can see him now, hands locked behind his head, feet crossed aloft at the right-hand corner of his desk, analyzing the report just handed him by one of his students. "Absurd," he would murmur, but his eyes would be twinkling, and, as likely as not, "poor damned bastard," would be the next remark. Then he would take up a red pencil and cross out large sections of the manuscript, rewriting and re-

rewriting it until it assumed an almost totally new, but immeasurably better-organized form.

With an interest that was wide-ranging and keen, Clarence Graham delighted in observing humanity's foibles, but never without a hint of warm compassion. Each of the men and women, seventy in all, who wrote a doctoral dissertation under his direction can testify to his abhorrence of sloppy thinking and his intolerance of failure to live up to the intellectual capacity one was judged to possess. In Graham's own work, in fact, the standards he held out for himself were so high that he found it difficult to tolerate any error at all. Like all perfectionists, he suffered agonies of remorse over any slip, no matter how trivial, that found its way into his lectures or published articles. Perhaps it was a stern New England upbringing that imposed these strictures upon his behavior, yet allowed him to be among the most generous and considerate of masters in his relationships with a student.

From his birth in 1906 until his doctorate in 1930 Graham remained in Worcester, Massachusetts. His parents had emigrated from County Donegal in Ireland, and his father was a skilled metal worker in a Worcester factory. Clarence was the oldest of four children. He entered public school at the age of five and graduated from high school at seventeen. As a schoolboy he put in long hours, not only in study but also in part-time employment to supplement the family's income and prepare for his own higher education. In an autobiographical sketch he recalled that, during the summer following his graduation from high school, he worked a forty-eight-hour week at a steel wire mill, earning forty cents an hour. Thus was developed the pattern of hard work that lasted him the rest of his life, a pattern that left him no time for idleness and little even for the traditional forms of recreation.

Clark University in Worcester was primarily a graduate school, but in 1923 it accepted Graham as one of a small number of undergraduates to qualify for admission. So strong was his intellectual curiosity that he started immediately to explore many areas of the humanities and sciences. Finally, after nearly three years of college life, he selected psychology as his major subject. This choice he attributes mainly to the fact that a member of the faculty, John Paul Nafe, took a personal interest in the small band of students who were interested in the laboratory side of psychology at that time. Nafe, whose work was mainly in the cutaneous senses, had what Graham called a magical ability to communicate to others his fascination with the phenomena of perception. This, too, stayed with Graham the rest of his life.

Undergraduate and graduate education overlapped one another at Clark, and the entire faculty of psychology consisted of four men who shared in the teaching at all levels. Graham soon found himself drawn into the graduate program of research, and his formal enrollment in the graduate program followed immediately the attainment of his undergraduate degree. Walter Hunter was the strongest figure of the group, a benevolent dictator who was to be Graham's chief mentor, not only in these years at Clark but also, later on, at Brown. Hunter, at the height of his own research career, early saw in Graham the signs of intellectual talent that would one day take him far beyond the borders of Worcester, Massachusetts.

At the graduate level Graham again explored several possible lines of work before settling down to a final choice. Within the first year experiments on visual perception claimed his main interest and were summarized in his earliest publication (1929). In the subsequent two years of graduate work, Graham became dissatisfied with the subjectivity and essentially qualitative nature of most work in visual perception. In this he was no doubt influenced most strongly by Walter Hunter, who had recently written a paper entitled, "The Subject's Report."

The main thrust of that paper was to reject "introspection" as a method by which a subject analyzes his own sensory processes. Hunter turned the emphasis onto the recording, by the experimenter, of the language responses of his subject. Graham, indeed, went even further than Hunter in insisting on a behaviorist interpretation of what a subject reports about what he perceives. The whole process is seen as one of setting up the conditions under which the subject is to give a verbal response, preferably a response that is itself restricted to one of a limited number of alternatives. The task of the experimenter is then simply that of taking an objective record of the responses that the subject makes. Thus is the subjectivity of visual perception brought under the objective control of scientific research. This sort of thinking led Graham to use one of the standard psychophysical methods, in which the subject is forced to say "yes" or "no" with respect to his perception of very weak stimuli, in determining binocular summation in the fovea at threshold (1930). Furthermore, the nature of that problem was such that physiological explanations were required. Thus Graham was led to the realization that postdoctoral training in neurophysiology would greatly benefit his career in vision and visual perception.

The year 1930, at the beginning of the period of economic depression, was undoubtedly a most difficult one for finding a postdoctoral research or teaching position, and Graham was fortunate to obtain a one-year appointment in psychology at Temple University in Philadelphia. A five-course teaching load did not discourage him from exploring other opportunities in the Philadelphia area, and soon he made contact with the new laboratory of the Johnson Foundation for Medical Physics. This group, at the University of Pennsylvania, had been established by Detlev Bronk, and two future Nobel laureates were beginning their work there. Ragnar Granit was the one who immediately welcomed Graham as a collaborator in research, and Keffer Hartline later took Graham to Woods Hole for the summer. During that summer, indeed, they accomplished their historic dissection of the optic nerve of *Limulus* in order to make the earliest records of single-unit activity in the visual system (Hartline and Graham, 1932). Graham won a National Research Council fellowship for the continuation of this work with Hartline in 1931–1932 at the Johnson Foundation. During that year Graham also found time to take a course with Jacobs on the quantitative treatment of experimental data in general physiology. This completed the formal training of Clarence Graham for his lifework of teaching and research in vision, with emphasis on quantification and physiological interpretation of the data.

Three universities were to share in Graham's academic productivity: Clark, 1932–1936; Brown, 1936–1945; and Columbia, 1945–1971. At each in succession he established an experimental facility for vision research, gathered around him a group of graduate and postdoctoral students, and built up the curriculum in the areas of his special competence.

At Clark Graham began a series of psychophysical studies on the spatial interaction that takes place when two or more adjacent areas of the retina are stimulated by light. This program, together with related neurophysiological studies by E. D. Adrian, Granit, and others, he summarized ably in a chapter contributed to the new (1934) *Handbook of General Experimental Psychology,* edited by his colleague, Carl Murchison. Several of his earliest graduate students got their start in research by participating in various parametric experiments that still stand as definitive for human observers under various conditions of light and dark adaptation.

Likewise at Clark, he enlisted my aid in the pursuit of some electrophysiological experiments along the lines of those he had started with Granit and Hartline. An old string galvanometer, borrowed from Hudson Hoagland, was used in early studies of the electroretinogram (ERG) in the rat, pigeon, and frog. For these studies homemade direct-current amplifiers, wick electrodes, animal holders, and shielding equipment were assembled at minimum cost in a small toolshop used by all the graduate students.

A feature of the ERG experiments on the white rat was to strap the animal to a miniature table and place a cotton wick electrode in contact with the cornea of the eye. Graham was extremely anxious to get ERG records of high quality, and this made it necessary to immobilize the animal by tightening the restraining straps. Graham was caught squarely between his anxiety to get records of high quality and his sympathy for the animal. Throughout the experiment he would repeatedly tighten the straps around the rat's head, meanwhile chanting, "Poor damned animal; poor *damned* animal!"

One more enterprise begun at Clark was Graham's course in the quantitative treatment of experimental data. This seminar gave his graduate students an insight into such mathematical manipulations as numerical transforms, curve fitting, and the testing of hypotheses to account for the results of an experiment. Over the next forty years this kind of course was continued, not only by Graham but by his followers in many other universities. Courses having a similar aim were those of Jacobs in physiology, Daniels in chemistry, and Worthing in physics. But the Graham course for the first time brought experimental psychology into line with other sciences with respect to the processing of data for effective publication in journals and books.

When Hunter was called to the chairmanship at Brown in 1936, he took Graham with him to represent sensory and physiological psychology in a department that had already achieved a considerable status in experimental psychology under the preceding head, Leonard Carmichael. Together with Schlosberg, Hunt, and Kemp they taught large numbers of undergraduates and gradually expanded the graduate program of seminars and research. The old frame dwelling at 89 Waterman Street had to provide offices for all the department, so that the research in vision had to be conducted in small basement rooms that included a former furnace room and several adjoining coal bins. The judicious use of partitions and hallways made of this basement a suite of cubicles in which both animal and human research in vision could be set up.

The five years at Brown preceding the Second World War Graham has called "some of the happiest of my life." Those joining the staff included Donald Lindsley, Lorrin Riggs, and Carl Pfaffmann. Graduate students brought into the Graham orbit of research included Fred Mote, Robert Gagne, Neil Bartlett, Conrad Mueller, and William Verplanck. Other than teaching, there were few constraints on this group's avid pursuit of experiments. At odd hours, too, classroom space could be used for poker games, ping-pong, and musical outpourings.

World War II brought another phase of Graham's career, that of organizing large teams of research personnel for specific projects related to the war effort. A major portion of this work centered around the visual aspects of gunfire control, especially in the tracking of aircraft targets. Two other team efforts were for the selection of specialized military personnel, and the screening of recruits with problems of emotional instability. The supervision of these projects was at Brown, but they were conducted also at a dozen other locations throughout the country, and about one hundred and fifty persons participated in them. Among those from the Brown psychology group were Bartlett, Berry, Gagne, J. McV. Hunt, Mote, Mueller, Riggs, Solomon, Stellar, and Verplanck. In recognition of his key role in setting up these programs, Graham was awarded the Presidential Certificate of Merit in 1948.

At the conclusion of the war in 1945, Graham was called to his final academic appointment, that of successor to Robert S. Woodworth at Columbia. Thus, at the age of thirty-nine, he ascended to greatly enlarged facilities and opportunities by comparison with those he had left at Clark and then at Brown.

Now he found himself directing as many as eight or ten Ph.D. theses, while at the same time teaching the advanced course for graduate students in experimental psychology and sharing with Selig Hecht a graduate seminar in vision. In 1947 Hecht died, and Graham fell heir to much of his specialized equipment. In addition, Hecht's former collaborator, Yun Hsia, came to work with Graham on problems of color vision. Hsia had been a student in psychology with R. S. Woodworth. Together he and Graham conducted many extensive studies of normal color vision and a number of explorations of color-blind visual functions. Perhaps the most significant of the Graham and Hsia studies was that of a woman with normal color vision in one eye and dichromatic vision in the other. Of particular interest was the fact that this subject saw only two hues in her dichromatic eye; wavelengths shorter than 502 nm were seen as a blue that matched 470 nm as seen by the normal eye, while wavelengths longer than 502 nm were seen as yellow, matching a wavelength of 570 nm as seen by the normal eye. The 502-nm wavelength could therefore be regarded as a neutral point of the spectrum, appearing white to the subject and separating the two basic receptor systems that were present in her dichromatic eye.

A large number of graduate students owe the beginning of their research careers to Graham in his years at Columbia. Among them may be mentioned Munehira Akita, Howard Baker, Shakantala Balaraman, Aleeza Beare, Eda Berger, John L. Brown, John Coulson, Leonard Diamond, John Foley, Barbara Gillam, Elaine Hammer, David Henderson, Robert Herrick, Gerald Howett, Joyce Kerr, Herschel Leibowitz, Alfred Lit, V. V. Lloyd, George Long, Barbara Mates, Leonard Matin, Conrad Mueller, Celeste McCullough, Joel Pokorny, Joan Pollock, Philburn Ratoosh, Vivianne Smith, Harry Sperling, Florence Veniar, Gary Yonemura, and Richard Zegers. Graham's marriage to Dr. Hammer took place in 1949, and she devoted herself to his welfare until his death in 1971.

During the Columbia years Graham edited, and wrote a considerable part of a book, *Vision and Visual Perception* (1965), with co-authors J. L. Brown, N. R. Bartlett, Y. Hsia, C. G. Mueller, and L. A. Riggs. This volume summarized the field in a definitive fashion for students and research workers. Also during these years Graham spent an academic sabbatical leave as scientific liaison officer with the Office of Naval Research in London, 1952–1953. This was an important post in providing contacts between European laboratories and those of the United States in experimental psychology. During a visit to Japan in August and September of 1952, he conducted an intensive seminar for faculty members from several of the leading Japanese universities, to acquaint them with research going on in the United States in vision and visual perception. A direct result of this enterprise was the visits to the United States of a number of the participants and their students, some of whom completed their graduate or postdoctoral education in this country. Indeed, it is true that Graham introduced such topics as visual contrast and figural aftereffects into Japanese experimental psychology.

During the last four years of his life, Graham suffered several physical setbacks, including a heart attack, pneumonia, and a broken hip. With care and encouragement from his wife, he kept up his writing and maintained contact with his laboratory. Even under these trying conditions he continued to be generous of his time and interest in his graduate students. But the uphill fight was lost in the summer of 1971, and he died on July 25. A memorial service was held on August 6 at which many of his former students, friends, and associates paid tribute to his memory.

Among the honors accorded him during his lifetime are the following: Howard Crosby Warren Medal, Society of Experimental Psychologists, 1941; election to the National Academy of Sciences, 1946; Presidential Certificate of Merit, 1948; Honorary Sc.D. Degree from Brown University, 1958; Certificate of

Appreciation, Office of Naval Research, 1961; Tillyer Medal, Optical Society of America, 1963; Distinguished Scientific Contribution Award, American Psychological Association, 1966.

The book *Vision and Visual Perception* will unquestionably stand for a long time to come as a monument to its editor and principal author, Clarence Graham. Aside from its factual material, uniquely present in this one volume at the time of its publication, in 1965, the book exemplifies three of the main themes of Graham's own life.

First, and most important, is the theme of objectivity. Undoubtedly, the objective orientation of the book owes itself to the behaviorist tradition in American psychology, a tradition with which Graham was closely identified through his early association with Walter Hunter and his later contacts with B. F. Skinner. His introductory chapter, "Some Basic Terms and Methods," goes to great lengths (some would say too great lengths) in expounding the behaviorist views on such visual sensations as hue, brightness, and saturation. Of hue, for example, Graham says, "The term is to be understood as either a label for or as an inferred effect . . . in the following stimulus–response sequence: (a) instructions to a subject who has had a past history with the vocabulary represented in the instructions, (b) the presentation of radiant energy to the subject, and (c) the subject's responses." In a later chapter, Graham quotes Skinner, with respect to the names that are attached to hues, as follows: "If the person says 'green' to light of wavelength 530 mμ, such a response obtains social approval; it is the 'correct response.' " The point of all this is to approach the entire subject of color vision with the aim of avoiding the ambiguities that might creep in if anything so personal and subjective as color naming were to be used as a major source of information. Instead, Graham emphasized that truly scientific studies of color vision must fulfill the criteria of objectivity. That is, the stimulus situation must be carefully specified and controlled, and the responses of the subject must be carefully tabulated by the experimenter. Among the stimulus conditions are not only the primary ones, such as the wavelength, luminance, and other dimensions of the light, but also the instructions to the subject and the various environmental and physical conditions under which the experiment is carried out. The instructions should typically limit the subject to two possible responses, such as "match" or "mismatch" in the case of color judgments and "seen" or "not seen" in determining a threshold. Standard psychophysical procedures may then be used to estimate the critical value of the stimulus at which the judgment shifts from one category to the other; this value yields a quantitative definition of the subject's sensory discrimination. Certainly, it is true that objectivity was an important consideration in the selection of material to be included or excluded in the coverage of the Graham book, particularly with respect to certain fields of visual perception.

A second point of major emphasis in Graham's thinking was the physiological basis for vision and visual perception. In this regard he differed strongly with Skinner and other psychologists of behaviorist backgrounds. Perhaps it was his lifelong association with neurophysiologists, beginning with Granit and Hartline, that led him to the conviction that hypotheses about vision should be mainly physiological. In any event, he included in the coverage of the 1965 book specific chapters on the structure, electrophysiology, and photochemistry of vision. Furthermore, a majority of the specific topics in vision and visual perception are handled in such a way as to emphasize the probable physiological bases for the findings.

The third characteristic of Graham's approach to vision, also clearly exemplified in the book, is his attention to the quantitative analysis of data. There are many instances of his care in fitting curves to data, testing theoretical models against experimental results, and illustrating by graphical displays the essential features of research information.

Those of us who were privileged to write doctoral dissertations under Graham's direction remember his meticulous editing of manuscript, checking and rechecking of data, and laborious reworking of tables and graphs to maximize useful information from our experimental findings. From their exposure to this kind of scientific experience, the more than seventy graduate students—at Clark, at Brown, and at Columbia—who completed their work for the Ph.D. degree under his direction learned that hard work and generosity were part of the game, but compromise, never. By the wider community of scholars Graham will be remembered for his high scientific standards and for his dedication to the fields of vision and visual perception.

BIBLIOGRAPHY

KEY TO ABBREVIATIONS

Am. J. Physiol. = American Journal of Physiology
Am. J. Psychol. = American Journal of Psychology
J. Cell Comp. Physiol. = Journal of Cellular and Comparative Physiology
J. Exp. Psychol. = Journal of Experimental Psychology
J. Gen. Physiol. = Journal of General Physiology
J. Gen. Psychol. = Journal of General Psychology
J. Opt. Soc. Am. = Journal of the Optical Society of America
J. Psychol. = Journal of Psychology
Proc. Natl. Acad. Sci. = Proceedings of the National Academy of Sciences
Psychol. Rev. = Psychological Review
Vision Res. = Vision Research

1929

Area, color and brightness difference in a reversible configuration. J. Gen. Psychol., 2:470–83.

1930

With J. P. Nafe. Human intensity discrimination with the Watson–Yerkes apparatus. Journal of Genetic Psychology, 37: 220–31.

An investigation of binocular summation. I. The fovea. J. Gen. Psychol., 3:494–510.

1931

With W. S. Hunter. Thresholds of illumination for the visual discrimination of movement and for the discrimination of discreteness. J. Gen. Psychol., 5:178–90.

An investigation of binocular summation. II. The periphery. J. Gen. Psychol., 5:311–28.

With R. Granit. Comparative studies on the peripheral and central retina. VI. Inhibition, summation, and synchronization of impulses in the retina. Am. J. Physiol., 89:664–73.

1932

With N. Goldman. Intensity and number of cones in foveal stimulation. Am. J. Psychol., 44:275–88.

With H. K. Hartline. Nerve impulses from single receptors in the eye of Limulus. Proceedings of the Society for Experimental Biology and Medicine, 29:613–15.

With H. K. Hartline.   Nerve impulses from single receptors in the eye. J. Cell. Comp. Physiol., 1:277–95.

The relation of nerve response and retinal potential to number of sense cells illuminated in an eye lacking lateral connections. J. Cell. Comp. Physiol., 2:295–310.

1934

Psychophysics and behavior.   J. Gen. Psychol., 10:299–310.

Vision. III. Some neural correlations.   In: *A Handbook of General Experimental Psychology,* ed. by C. Murchison, pp. 829–79. Worcester, Massachusetts, Clark University Press.

1935

With L. A. Riggs.   The visibility curve of the white rat as determined by the electrical retinal response to lights of different wave lengths.   J. Gen. Psychol., 12:279–95.

With H. K. Hartline.   The response of single visual sense cells to lights of different wave lengths.   J. Gen. Physiol., 18:917–31.

With R. Margaria.   Area and intensity–time relation in the peripheral retina.   Am. J. Physiol., 13:299–305.

With E. H. Kemp and L. A. Riggs.   An analysis of the electrical retinal responses of a color-discriminating eye to lights of different wave lengths.   J. Gen. Psychol., 13:275–96.

1937

With R. H. Brown and J. R. Smith.   Brightness discrimination for varying durations of the just discriminable increment.   Psychological Record, 1:229–33.

With C. Cook.   Visual acuity as a function of intensity and exposure-time.   Am. J. Psychol., 49:654–61.

With J. Levine.   The latency of visual after-effects as a function of the intensity of illumination on an adjacent retinal region. Am. J. Psychol., 49:661–65.

1938

With E. H. Kemp.   Brightness discrimination as a function of the duration of the increment in intensity.   J. Gen. Physiol., 21: 635–50.

1939

With R. H. Brown and F. A. Mote, Jr.   The relation of size of stimulus and intensity in the human eye. I. Intensity thresholds for white light. J. Exp. Psychol., 24:555–73.

With N. R. Bartlett. The relation of size of stimulus and intensity in the human eye. II. Intensity thresholds for red and violet light. J. Exp. Psychol., 24:574–87.

1940

With R. M. Gagne. The acquisition, extinction, and spontaneous recovery of a conditioned operant response. J. Exp. Psychol., 26:251–80.

With R. M. Gagne. The effect of an "emotional state" on the initial stages of acquisition in a conditioned operant response. Proc. Natl. Acad. Sci., 26:297–300.

With N. R. Bartlett. The relation of size of stimulus and intensity in the human eye. III. The influence of area on foveal intensity discrimination. J. Exp. Psychol., 27:149–59.

With L. A. Riggs. Some aspects of light adaptation in a single photoreceptor unit. J. Cell. Comp. Physiol., 16:15–23.

1943

With R. N. Berry and W. S. Verplanck. The reversal of discrimination in a simple running habit. J. Exp. Psychol., 32:325–34.

Visual space perception. Federation Proceedings, Federation of American Societies for Experimental Biology, 2:115–2?.

1945

With L. A. Riggs. Effects due to variations in light intensity on the excitability cycle of the single visual sense cell. J. Cell. Comp. Physiol., 26:1–13.

1947

With L. A. Riggs, C. G. Mueller, and F. A. Mote. Photographic measurements of atmospheric boil. J. Opt. Soc. Am., 37:415–20.

1948

With K. E. Baker, M. Hecht, and V. V. Lloyd. Factors influencing thresholds for monocular movement parallax. J. Exp. Psychol., 38:305–23.

With L. A. Riggs, F. A. Mote, and C. G. Mueller. Two devices for evaluating stereoscopic reticle-patterns. Am. J. Psychol., 61: 545–52.

1949

With E. R. Hammer, R. D. Mueller, and F. A. Mote. Stereoscopic settings with reticles providing multiple reference ranges: the perception of spatially repeating patterns. J. Psychol., 27: 209–16.

1950

With F. A. Veniar. The influence of size of test-field surround on visual intensity discrimination. Proc. Natl. Acad. Sci., 36:17–25.
Behavior, perception and the psychophysical methods. Psychol. Rev., 57:108–20.

1951

Visual perception. In: Handbook of Experimental Psychology, ed. by S. S. Stevens, pp. 867–920. New York, John Wiley & Sons.
With P. Ratoosh. Areal effects in foveal brightness discrimination. J. Exp. Psychol., 42:367–75.

1952

With Y. Hsia. Spectral sensitivity of the cones in the dark adapted human eye. Proc. Natl. Acad. Sci., 38:80–85.
Behavior and the psychophysical methods: an analysis of some recent experiments. Psychol. Rev., 59:62–70.

1953

With J. L. Brown, H. Leibowitz, and H. B. Ranken. Luminance thresholds for the resolution of visual detail during dark adaptation. J. Opt. Soc. Am., 43:197–202.
Some observations on psychology in Japan. Transactions of the New York Academy of Sciences, 16:83–87.

1954

With K. Sato. Psychology in Japan. Psychol. Rev., 51:443–64.
With Y. Hsia. Luminosity curves for normal and dichromatic subjects including a case of unilateral color-blindness. Science, 120:780.

1955

With Y. Hsia, and E. Berger. Luminosity functions for normal and dichromatic subjects including a case of unilateral color-blindness. J. Opt. Soc. Am., 45:407.

1957

With Y. Hsia. Luminosity losses in dichromats. Optician, 134: 315–18.

Form perception and sensory processes. In: *Form Discrimination as Related to Military Problems,* ed. by J. W. Wulfeck and J. H. Taylor, pp. 25–27. Washington, D. C., National Research Council.

1958

With Y. Hsia. Spectral luminosity curves for protanopic, deuteranopic and normal subjects. Proc. Natl. Acad. Sci., 43:1011–19.

Sensation and perception in an objective psychology. Psychol. Rev., 65:65–76.

Walter Samuel Hunter, 1889–1954. In: *Biographical Memoirs,* National Academy of Sciences, 1:127–55. New York, Columbia University Press.

With Y. Hsia. The spectral luminosity curves for a dichromatic eye and a normal eye in the same person. Proc. Natl. Acad. Sci., 44:46–49.

Color defect and color theory: studies on normal and color-blind persons including a unilaterally dichromatic subject. Science, 127:675–82.

With Y. Hsia. The discriminations of a normal and color-blind eye in the same person. Proceedings of the American Philosophical Society, 102:168–73.

With E. Berger and Y. Hsia. Some visual functions of a unilaterally color-blind person. I. Critical fusion frequency at various spectral regions. J. Opt. Soc. Am., 48:614–22.

With E. Berger and Y. Hsia. Some visual functions of a unilaterally color-blind person. II. Binocular brightness matches at various spectral regions. J. Opt. Soc. Am., 48:622–27.

With Y. Hsia. Color-blindness and color theory. A.M.A. Archives of Ophthalmology, 60(Part 2):792–99.

1959

With Y. Hsia. Studies of color-blindness: a unilaterally dichromatic subject. Proc. Natl. Acad. Sci., 45:96–99.

Color theory. In: *Psychology: A Study of a Science.* Vol. 1. *Sensory, Perceptual and Physiological Formulations,* ed. by S. Koch, pp. 145–288. New York, McGraw-Hill Book Co.

1960

With Y. Hsia. Luminosity losses in deuteranopes. Science, 131: 417.

A short survey of some leading psychological laboratories in Japan. Columbia University. 36 pp.

1961

With H. G. Sperling, Y. Hsia, and A. H. Coulson. The determination of some visual functions of a unilaterally color-blind subject: methods and results. J. Psychol., 51:3–32.

With Y. Hsia. Some visual functions of a unilaterally dichromatic subject. In: *Visual Problems of Color* (Symposium held at the National Physical Laboratory on September 23–25, 1957), vol. 1, pp. 283–97. New York, Chemical Publishing Company, Inc.

1962

With S. Balaraman and Y. Hsia. The wave length discrimination of some color-blind persons. J. Gen. Psychol., 66:185–201.

With P. Ratoosh. Notes on some interrelations of sensory psychology, perception and behavior. In: *Psychology: A Study of a Science,* ed. by S. Koch, vol. 4, pp. 483–514. New York, McGraw-Hill Book Co.

1963

Simple discriminatory functions: review, summary and discussion. J. Opt. Soc. Am., 53:161–65.

On some aspects of real and apparent visual movement. J. Opt. Soc. Am., 53:1015–25.

1964

With M. Akita, and Y. Hsia. Maintaining an absolute hue in the presence of different background colors. Vision Res., 4:539–56.

1965

With N. R. Bartlett, J. L. Brown, Y. Hsia, C. G. Mueller, and L. A. Riggs. *Vision and Visual Perception.* New York, John Wiley & Sons. 637 pp.

1966

With M. Akita. Maintaining an absolute test hue in the presence of different background colors and luminance ratios. Vision Res., 6:315–23.

With I. M. Siegel, H. Ripps, and Y. Hsia. Analysis of photopic and scotopic function in an incomplete achromat. J. Opt. Soc. Am., 56:699–704.

Robert Sessions Woodworth, 1869–1962. *Biographical Memoirs,* National Academy of Sciences, 39:541–72. New York, Columbia University Press.

1967

With Y. Hsia, and F. F. Stephan. Visual discrimination of a subject with acquired unilateral tritanopia. Vision Res., 7:469–79.

With B. Mates, and R. Shlaer. Two apparatus arrangements for the study of real movement. Psychologia, 10:210–12.

1968

Depth and movement. American Psychologist, 23:18–26.

With J. Pokorny, and R. N. Lanson. The effect of wavelength on foveal grating acuity. J. Opt. Soc. Am., 58:1404–14.

With R. Shlaer. Two apparatus assemblies for the study of real movement. Behavior Research Methods and Instrumentation, 1:18–20.

1969

With Y. Hsia. Saturation and the foveal achromatic threshold. J. Opt. Soc. Am., 59:993–97.

1970

With B. Mates. The effect of rectangle length on velocity thresholds for real movement. Proc. Natl. Acad. Sci., 65:516–20.

With B. J. Gillam. Occurrence of theoretically correct responses during rotation of the Ames window. Perception and Psychophysics, 8:257–60.

William K. Gregory

WILLIAM KING GREGORY

May 19, 1876–December 29, 1970

BY EDWIN H. COLBERT

IN THIS AGE of scientific specialization, many if not most men of authority attain preeminence within some relatively narrow discipline. But William King Gregory, at the time of his death one of the oldest members of the National Academy of Sciences, was distinguished as a zoologist who had spoken influentially on many aspects of vertebrate evolution and structure. He was renowned as a comparative anatomist; as a leading authority on the evolution of the mammalian dentition; as a vertebrate paleontologist; as a widely respected student of the fishes, both fossil and recent; as a contributor of much knowledge concerning the evolution of reptiles, especially the mammal-like reptiles of Permo-Triassic age; as a leader in the study of fossil and recent mammals; as an expert on various mammalian groups, especially the primates; and as a scholar with a worldwide reputation for his contributions to our concepts of the origin and evolution of man. Gregory was in addition a great teacher who trained numerous vertebrate paleontologists and zoologists. At the same time he was instrumental in presenting his subjects to the general public through papers and books and particularly by means of graphic museum exhibits that he conceived and supervised. In short, he was a man of diverse accomplishments.

91

William King Gregory was a native New Yorker who spent almost all of his long life within the metropolis. He was born in Greenwich Village on May 19, 1876, the son of George Gregory, a printer, and Jane King Gregory. He grew up in lower Manhattan, during his early life living with his family in the upper and rear part of a small house, the front of which was occupied by his father's printing shop. As a small boy he attended St. Luke's Primary School, where in his words "the three R's were patiently and persistently taught by the stout and elderly Miss Van Kleek, who wore snake skin wristlets for the gout." After St. Luke's he attended a public school for a few years, but soon was shifted to Trinity School, then located at Broadway and West 45th Street (which today is a part of Times Square). At Trinity he took the "science course" in 1894–1895 to prepare himself for admission to Columbia University.

Gregory began his collegiate education at the Columbia School of Mines, where he was particularly attracted by the course in general zoology, taught by Bashford Dean—a man who was to have great influence upon the course of his life. He soon transferred from the School of Mines to Columbia College. There he majored in zoology and vertebrate paleontology and received a broad training in English, Latin and Greek, French Literature, history, psychology, and philosophy. Dean was his mentor in vertebrate zoology, but very soon he came under the tutelage of Henry Fairfield Osborn, who had recently come to New York from Princeton to help found a department of zoology at Columbia and to establish a department of vertebrate paleontology at the American Museum of Natural History.

In the fall of 1899, while still an undergraduate at Columbia College, Gregory became Professor Osborn's research assistant and demonstrator. This was the beginning of his lifelong association with the American Museum of Natural History and

Columbia University. In 1900 he received his bachelor's degree from Columbia, in 1905 his master's, and in 1910 his doctorate.

Shortly after his appointment as Osborn's assistant, Gregory was married to Laura Grace Foote, a happy union that continued until her death in 1937. In 1938 he married Angela Du Bois. There were no children by either marriage.

To go back a bit, Bashford Dean's researches on fossil and living fishes early stimulated Gregory's interest in these vertebrates. In 1898 he was awarded a Dyckman Traveling Fellowship by the Columbia Department of Zoology, which enabled him to go with Dean to the Hopkins Marine Laboratory at Pacific Grove, California, to study the eggs and embryos of the hagfish *(Bdellostoma)* and the so-called ratfish *(Chimaera)*. This early exposure to the world of fishes led to one of his first scientific papers, "The relations of the anterior visceral arches to the chondrocranium," published in 1904.

Gregory's close association with Osborn developed an early interest in the landliving vertebrates and marked the beginning of his truly remarkable knowledge of all of the backboned animals. Indeed, his paper, "Adaptive significance of the shortening of the elephant's skull," undertaken with the encouragement of Osborn, was published in 1903 and thus preceded his first fish paper. Also in 1903 he published a short note in *Science* entitled "Anent gizzards" and in 1905 a paper, also in *Science,* "The weight of the *Brontosaurus.*" So at an early stage in his career Gregory had made scientific contributions dealing with the several major groups of vertebrates, except for the amphibians. And in 1911 he entered the field of amphibian structure with his paper on the limbs of the Permian labyrinthodont, *Eryops.* In this paper he also took up the problem of the origin of paired limbs from fins, thus demonstrating an interest that was to continue through the rest of his life—namely, the origins of vertebrate structures. In fact, in the preceding year he had embarked upon the field of origins with papers on the origin of mammals, especially as revealed by the homologies of the mammalian auditory ossicles.

With the time-consuming demands imposed by Gregory's work as an assistant to Professor Osborn (and any assistant to Osborn necessarily had a pretty full schedule), combined with his own researches, which already were beginning to produce original published contributions, and with the prosecution of advanced undergraduate and graduate studies in pursuit of the several degrees he was eventually to obtain, it would seem that there would have been little time for other activities. Yet during these busy early years at Columbia and at the American Museum the young Gregory managed to serve as the editor of the *American Museum Journal,* a newly established publication designed to bring the work of the museum to the attention of an interested public. Thus Gregory was the first editor of a periodical that in time evolved into the internationally renowned journal *Natural History.*

These multitudinous, parallel activities of his early adult years established a pattern that was to prevail throughout Gregory's life. He was always to be engaged in varied simultaneous duties and projects. This is illustrated not only by his studies and publications, but also by the posts that he held. He began, of course, as Osborn's assistant, doing much of the detailed research upon which Osborn based his publications, editing these publications in detail (in addition to his editorship of the *American Museum Journal*) and serving as demonstrator and frequently as lecturer to the students in Osborn's Columbia courses. Such activities were formalized at the museum in 1911 when he was appointed to the Scientific Staff and at Columbia in 1916 when he was made a member of the faculty. At the university he rose through the professorial ranks to become a full professor and eventually Da Costa Professor in the Department of Zoology. At the museum he likewise rose through the curatorial ranks to become a full curator, in his later years serving simultaneously in three departments: vertebrate paleontology, comparative anatomy (a department of which he was the founder), and ichthyology. For many years he was also concurrently Chairman of the departments of comparative anatomy and of ichthyology.

Perhaps the department of comparative anatomy at the museum was Gregory's prime professional love. For some three decades he carried on an active program there with the able assistance of Henry C. Raven and, in later years, of Miles Conrad and George Pinkley. Two other fixtures in this department were Helen Ziska, a delightful scientific artist of German origin, and Mrs. C. P. Meadowcroft, his ever-efficient secretary. Such was the organization within which he worked. Some account may now be given of the scientific problems that engaged his attention from about the turn of the century until after the Second World War.

Gregory was above all else a comparative vertebrate anatomist, working with both fossil and recent materials. His particular ability in this field has been nicely stated in a letter from A. S. Romer. "Gregory was essentially an artist by disposition (as was Goodrich of Oxford) and this gave him an invaluable feeling for form, for morphology. Now that I look back on it, he was in my youth the only man in North America who had a knowledge of the basic structure of the skull in lower vertebrates."

Gregory's research studies were frequently of large scope and often of marked significance. He was a pioneer in the study of fossil vertebrates from the viewpoint of functional anatomy—a reflection of his conviction that, for example, bones and muscles in extinct as well as in recent vertebrates should be related to each other. As early as 1915 he published a paper in collaboration with L. A. Adams on the relation between the temporal fossae of the skull and the jaw muscles. In the early 1920s he gave a special course in comparative myology attended by four of his students, A. S. Romer, C. L. Camp, G. K. Noble, and James Chapin, all of whom were to become distinguished scholars in their respective fields. Among the results of this course were the papers by Romer on musculature in various reptiles, including crocodilians and dinosaurs. As has been mentioned, Dr. Gregory was interested in origins—for example, the origin of tetrapod limbs from the paired fins of fishes. He was also interested in evolutionary sequences as shown by anatomical developments through various grades of vertebrate development. Thus he became much involved in the progression from early Paleozoic fishes, through the first landliving tetrapods, the labyrinthodont amphibians, and then through the reptiles, to birds on the one hand and to mammals on the other. This was to culminate during his later years in numerous papers on the progression from fish to man, epitomized in his book of 1929, *Our Face from Fish to Man,* and in his two-volume work, *Evolution Emerging,* published in 1951.

Gregory's work in comparative anatomy went beyond mere description and comparison; he established principles and made generalizations. One of his concepts involved the principle of what he called "habitus" and "heritage" characters, displayed during the evolution of animals. Briefly, he recognized that any particular animal, or any specific phylogenetic line, reveals a complex association of anatomical features—the basic "heritage" characters derived from a long ancestry, combined with the specialized "habitus" characters, as adaptations in response to the many environmental factors to which the organism or its evolutionary line may have been exposed. Thus any particular form, a bat, for example, shows a combination of ancestral and sometimes quite primitive characters (in the bat a basic insectivore pattern of teeth) and advanced and sometimes quite sophisticated specializations (in the bat the adaptation of the forelimbs as wings and the other complex specializations for flight, such as the marvelous echolocation apparatus).

An outgrowth and extension of this concept was Gregory's "palimpsest theory," proposed in 1947 at the end of his long scientific career. In essence, this was another name for his heritage and habitus concept. In Gregory's words "the habitus tends to overlay and obscure more remote heritage features, somewhat as the later writing on a palimpsest hides the partly erased image of the earlier writing." Simpson has pointed out quite rightly that this same principle has in recent years gained prominence and wide acceptance under the name of "mosaic evolution"—with no credit given to Gregory.

Another of Gregory's proposed principles was that of "polyisomerism" and "anisomerism." He had observed that primitive animals commonly display many duplicate, similar structures, which he called polyisomeres. During the course of evolutionary development these parts commonly are reduced in number and differentiated in form, thus becoming anisomeres. This phenomenon he called "Williston's law"—hardly a law, but rather an evolutionary trend.

Gregory's contributions on the origins of vertebrate structures, on the transformation and adaptation of anatomical characters for new functions during evolution from one taxonomic grade to another, on evolutionary sequence among the vertebrates, on the functional anatomy in fossil forms, and on other problems involving the comparative anatomy of the backboned animals, extinct and recent, were not limited to his published scientific contributions. He passed his knowledge on to his students, as we shall see, and he passed it on to the public. His efforts to make the exciting story of vertebrate evolution, with its many ramifications, comprehensible to the layman were concentrated especially in various exhibits displayed in the halls of the American Museum of Natural History.

Two exhibit halls deserve particular mention in this connection. One was the Hall of Fishes, which was developed during the middle years of the 1920s under Gregory's direction.

Here one could see the fishes of the world in all of their variety and complexity, as demonstrated especially by the overwhelming array of teleost or bony fishes. This hall, for so many years of inestimable value to the general public and to students, was to a large degree an expression of Gregory's many years devoted to the anatomy and phylogeny of the fishes. The other exhibit was set forth in a special Hall of Comparative Anatomy where the parallel sequences from fish to man—so long the theme of Gregory's studies—could be followed. The exhibits in this hall comprehended not only the bones, for which much evidence could be displayed from fossil forms, but also the other anatomical systems: muscles, the nervous system, the digestive tract, and so on. And the embryological evidence was also displayed, especially in a handsome panel showing the progress from egg to adult in the various classes of vertebrates. Needless to say, Gregory was ably assisted in the planning and execution of this hall, as he was in so many of his efforts in the field of comparative anatomy, by Harry Raven.

We have seen that Gregory's contact with students began in the early years of the century, when he assisted Professor Osborn in the classroom and in the laboratory. After Osborn had retired from active teaching, Gregory assumed complete responsibility for teaching vertebrate evolution at the graduate level at Columbia University. Actually, the courses were conducted at the American Museum of Natural History, because that was where the materials were available. The collections at the disposal of the students were superb, and the man who lectured on these collections had a superb knowledge of the vertebrates. It is no wonder, therefore, that Gregory trained a large contingent of able vertebrate paleontologists and zoologists, including many of the leaders in these fields in North America and in various foreign countries as well. Numerous distinguished paleontologists and zoologists today have fond memories of the large room at the American Museum where they attended lectures and participated in seminars and of various niches on the fifth floor of that institution where they worked on their theses. An impressive expression of the esteem in which Dr. Gregory was held by those who had studied under him was seen in 1946, on the occasion of his seventieth birthday, when at a dinner attended by many of his former students he was presented with an oil portrait of himself painted by Charles Chapman. A photograph of this portrait is reproduced as the frontispiece of this memoir.

Of course, Dr. Gregory's power to attract able students was the inevitable result of his broad researches in vertebrate paleontology and zoology. But, as has been mentioned, he made many contributions within each class of vertebrates and indeed within lesser taxa as well.

As early as 1907 he published a paper of some length, "The Orders of Teleostomous Fishes," which with subsequent contributions established him as one of the leading authorities on teleost relationships. As a result of his long work on the bony fishes there appeared in 1933 his monograph, *Fish Skulls: A Study in the Evolution of Natural Mechanisms,* published in the *Transactions of the American Philosophical Society.* He continued his studies on the teleosts through many succeeding years, especially with the collaboration of G. Miles Conrad, his colleague in the department of comparative anatomy at the museum. Gregory was however interested in other fishes besides the teleosts, especially the fossil crossopterygians, from which the first amphibians arose.

Of course, he had an interest in the early labyrinthodont amphibians, especially the Permian genus *Eryops,* which demonstrates so nicely labyrinthodont structure. His work on the so-called lower tetrapods was more particularly centered upon the reptiles and, of these, on the mammal-like reptiles or therapsids. This reflected his constant preoccupation with the sequence from fish through mammals and with the transformations that took place in the passage from one vertebrate class to another. Some of the therapsids, so prominent in the fossil faunas of South Africa, obviously were antecedent to early mammals, and these mammalian predecessors always fascinated him. He did much work on the transformations that were involved in the evolution of the mammalian middle-ear bones from the reptilian stapes plus the quadrate and articular bones that formed the reptilian jaw articulation. And he studied numerous transformations in form and proportions within the sequence from therapsid skull bones to mammalian skull bones. Naturally, his encyclopedic knowledge of the dentition in the tetrapods was utilized in these studies of the origin of mammals from reptilian ancestors. In all of this he stressed the role of functional anatomy; thus he published on the musculature of mammal-like reptiles and early mammals, in part in collaboration with Charles Camp. It should be said that Gregory's interest in therapsid reptiles was not confined to the forms directly ancestral to the mammals; he published a monographic study of the skeleton of *Moschops,* one of the large, massive, herbivorous therapsids known as tapinocephalians, so prominent in the lower levels of the Karroo beds of South Africa. Beyond this he published papers on other groups of reptiles, notably on some of the dinosaurs.

His thesis for the doctorate, "The Orders of Mammals," a monograph of more than five hundred pages, published as a Bulletin of the American Museum of Natural History, established him as a foremost authority on mammalian relationships, an eminence he occupied for the rest of his active life. With such a thorough background in mammalian evolution it was only natural that Gregory should address himself in detail to various groups of mammals. His long-term involvement with the primates, from primitive fossil lemurs to man, has been mentioned. Since he was repeatedly investigating the problem of origins, he did a considerable amount of work on those most primitive of placentals, the insectivores, for there could be little doubt but that the earliest primates were direct descendants from insectivore ancestors.

From the early 1920s Gregory delved deeply into marsupial relationships, the result in part of a trip to Australia he made in 1921–1922 with Harry Raven. And at the very bottom of the mammalian ladder he turned his attention to the monotremes. His paper of 1947, published as a Bulletin of the American Museum of Natural History, marshaled the evidence, as he saw it, to show that the monotremes had diverged from an ancestry held in common with the Australian marsupials. It was in this paper that he developed his "palimpsest theory," already cited, showing that although the monotremes retained various characters pointing back to the Triassic mammal-like reptiles known as cynodonts, these features nevertheless were overlain by numerous specializations that today define the monotremes.

In his earlier years, Gregory as Professor Osborn's assistant did a prodigious amount of work on mammals, especially on the extinct titanotheres (early Tertiary herbivores that ecologically preceded the rhinoceroses in a very general way) and on the proboscideans (the mastodonts and elephants and their early ancestors). A considerable portion of what is set forth in Osborn's gigantic two-volume titanothere monograph, published in 1929 by the United States Geological Survey, and in his equally gigantic two-volume Proboscidea monograph, published posthumously in 1942 by the American Museum of Natural History, can be traced back to Gregory. Moreover Gregory had much to do with the writing of Osborn's *Age of Mammals,* published in 1910.

Still other groups of mammals interested Gregory. His papers are too numerous and widely varied to be reviewed here, but particular mention might be made of his study of the civets or viverrids, done in collaboration with Milo Hellman and published in 1939.

Some of his most detailed research, resulting in closely reasoned arguments and elegant demonstrations, was concerned with evolution among the primates. Aside from his comprehensive work on all of the mammals, Gregory's interest in the ancestors of man became manifest as early as 1913, when he published a paper on the relationships of the tupaiids and of the Eocene lemurs, especially the genus *Notharctus*. This was going back right to the beginnings of primate history, for the tupaiids have long been shuttled back and forth between the insectivores and primates by various authorities, and *Notharctus* is certainly one of the earliest well-documented primates. Gregory's interest in *Notharctus* continued, culminating in his classic monograph on this interesting Eocene lemur, published as a Memoir of the American Museum in 1920. It was certainly one of the most detailed studies of a fossil primate ever made.

From about the early 1920s, if not before, until the end of his active career, Gregory was particularly concerned with that portion of primate phylogeny leading to man. It was his contention that early man was descended from brachiating ancestors, not unlike the modern chimpanzee, and he was an early advocate, perhaps the first such, of the theory that the then newly discovered australopithecines of South Africa were more closely related to the hominids than to the anthropoid apes. Gregory's interest in the immediate ancestry of man, and his penetrating studies of this problem, brought him into close association with anthropologists, particularly physical anthropologists, among whom he was regarded as one of their leading advocates.

In connection with his studies of mammals, and especially of primates, and stemming from the early years of the century, when he edited Osborn's book of 1907 on the evolution of mammalian molar teeth, Gregory became increasingly involved through the years with dental evolution. His studies were directed especially along those lines leading to the human dentition, and on this subject he became perhaps the world's leading authority. This work resulted in the publication, in 1922, of his book, *The Origin and Evolution of the Human Dentition* (actually a compendium of papers published originally in the *Journal of Dental Research*), and in his extended summary of molar evolution, *A Half-Century of Trituberculy,* published by the American Philosophical Society in 1934.

The summation of Gregory's research on the vertebrates appeared in the two-volume work, *Evolution Emerging,* already mentioned. This monumental work, which appeared in 1951, was the result of more than a half-century spent with the vertebrates, fossil and recent. As Gregory points out in his preface, Osborn had planned during the last decade of the nineteenth century to write a general book on the evolution of the vertebrates. Some work was done, but then the effort was abandoned. In 1931 Osborn suggested that Gregory revive the project, which he did. The result was a volume of some seven hundred pages of text, outlining vertebrate evolution from its very beginnings to its present stage, with man as the ruler of the earth, supplemented by an equally thick volume of illustrations. As George Gaylord Simpson has said, "It was both the chef d'oeuvre and the swan song of a genius."

Gregory was a most original and assiduous scholar, whose fame rests to a large degree on his numerous important publications. At the same time, he was a collaborator who worked with many other paleontologists and zoologists. Of course, during his early years he worked for and with Osborn, and their collaborative relationships lasted until the time of Osborn's death. It is notable that through all of those years it was a close and friendly relationship, enjoyed by both parties. Osborn was not always an easy man to work with; he was demanding and imperious. Moreover, he did not like to be disputed. But Gregory handled him with remarkable finesse, so that even when they were poles apart, as for example on the subject of primate evolution and the origin of man, there were no hard feelings. To Osborn, Gregory was his "fidus achates"; to Gregory, Osborn was his "imperial mammoth."

Gregory's intimate collaboration with Harry Raven has already been mentioned. He also prosecuted joint studies on functional anatomy in extinct tetrapods with the late Alfred S. Romer, a one-time student, who until his recent death was the dean of vertebrate paleontologists the world around. For many long years Gregory worked closely with W. D. Matthew and with Walter Granger on fossil mammals, and in later years with George Gaylord Simpson, especially on the description of Cretaceous insectivores from Mongolia. There were joint studies and papers with other scholars; special mention should be made of his work with Milo Hellman on the evolution of the human dentition.

Although Gregory was a fine scholar and a prodigious worker, he did not participate in many extensive field studies or expeditions. Most of the vertebrates he studied and described, both fossil and recent, had been collected by other people. Nevertheless, he liked to be out-of-doors, and he enjoyed nature with a sensitivity that bordered on the poetic. He was a willing traveler, and in several instances he was a most active member of important expeditions. His journey to Australia in 1921–1922 with Harry Raven has been mentioned. This was a rather rugged trip into the bush for marsupials. In 1925 he was a member of the *Arcturus* Expedition, led by William Beebe, which explored the Sargasso Sea for marine life. In 1929–1930 he went to Africa with Raven, James H. McGregor, and Earle T. Engel to study gorillas in their native habitat and to collect several specimens for anatomical studies. A delightful by-product of this trip was his book *In Quest of Gorillas*. In 1939 he journeyed to New Zealand with Michael Lerner to study and collect fishes. And in the preceding year he had gone to South Africa with Milo Hellman to study australopithecines in cooperation with Robert Broom and Raymond Dart. Finally, during the closing years of his life he made yearly trips to the Lerner Marine Laboratory in the Bahama Islands.

Gregory formally retired from the American Museum of Natural History in 1944 and from Columbia University in 1945, but he remained active for many years thereafter. He had long owned a home in Woodstock, New York, where he spent his summers. In his later years he and his wife, Angela, gave up their New York City apartment and made the Woodstock house their permanent abode. He died in Woodstock on December 29, 1970.

Dr. Gregory was widely recognized in the scientific community for his achievements. He was elected to the National Academy of Sciences in 1927. He belonged to more than thirty scientific societies, including several foreign ones. Moreover, he was active and held office in many societies. He was for two terms president of the American Association of Physical Anthropologists and was awarded the association's Viking Medal in 1949 for his work in physical anthropology.

Gregory was a truly delightful person. He was quiet, he was modest, he was sincere. Perhaps one of his outstanding characteristics was his enthusiasm—for life and for the world around him. Indeed, the living world had for him the fresh delight that it has for a child. He was a thoroughly objective scientist, but at the same time he could look at an animal or a plant with a feeling of wonder and with a deep appreciation for the intrinsic beauty of natural form and color. These qualities were among the many aspects of his personality that contributed to his great personal charm.

Like many unworldly people he had his foibles. He never seemed to be well organized, yet the fact is that he lived a very full life and carried on many important activities simultaneously. So beneath his apparently absentminded exterior he maintained a complex schedule and brought his numerous projects to completion. He was perhaps not what some people would call a "practical" man; it is hard to imagine him wrestling with the intricacies of a broken-down car or building some piece of furniture; all of which was probably to the good. He could concentrate on the things that interested him—namely, the extinct and recent animals that filled his life.

It was a very full and productive life. His legacy is an amazing collection of publications dealing with vertebrates of all classes, several generations of vertebrate paleontologists and zoologists—his scientific children—and ideas that will live in the annals of vertebrate studies for many years to come.

BIBLIOGRAPHY

KEY TO ABBREVIATIONS

Am. Anthropol. = American Anthropologist
Am. J. Orthodont. = American Journal of Orthodontics
Am. J. Phys. Anthropol. = American Journal of Physical Anthropology
Am. Mus. J. = American Museum Journal
Am. Mus. Nat. Hist. Guide Leafl. Ser. = American Museum of Natural History Guide Leaflet Series
Am. Mus. Novit. =American Museum Novitates
Am. Nat. = American Naturalist
Am. Philos. Soc. Yearb. = American Philosophical Society Yearbook
Anat. Rec. = Anatomical Record
Ann. N.Y. Acad. Sci. = Annals of the New York Academy of Sciences
Biol. Abstr. = Biological Abstracts
Bull. Am. Mus. Nat. Hist. = Bulletin of the American Museum of Natural History
Bull. Geol. Soc. Am. = Bulletin of the Geological Society of America
Bull. N.Y. Acad. Med. = Bulletin of the New York Academy of Medicine
Bull. N.Y. Zool. Soc. = Bulletin of the New York Zoological Society
C.-R. Première Sess. Congr. Int. Sci. Anthropol. Ethnol. = Compte-Rendu de la Première Session, Congrès International des Sciences Anthropologiques et Ethnologiques
Dent. Cosmos = Dental Cosmos
Eugen. News = Eugenical News
Geol. Zentralbl. = Geologisches Zentralblatt
Hum. Biol. = Human Biology
Int. Game Fish Assoc. Yearb. = International Game Fish Association Yearbook
Int. J. Orthod. Dent. Child. = International Journal of Orthodontia and Dentistry for Children
Int. J. Orthod. Oral Surg. Radiogr. = International Journal of Orthodontia, Oral Surgery, and Radiography
J. Dent. Res. = Journal of Dental Research
J. Mammal. = Journal of Mammalogy
J. Morphol. = Journal of Morphology
Lit. Dig. = Literary Digest
Nat. Hist. = Natural History
Neues Jahrb. Miner. Geol. Palaeontol. = Neues Jahrbuch für Mineralogie, Geologie und Palaeontologie
News Bull. Soc. Vertebr. Paleontol. = News Bulletin of the Society of Vertebrate Paleontology
Palaeontol. Zentralbl. = Palaeontologisches Zentralblatt
Pan-Am. Geol. = Pan-American Geologist
Pop. Sci. Mon. =Popular Science Monthly
Proc. Am. Philos. Soc. = Proceedings of the American Philosophical Society
Proc. Linn. Soc. N.Y. = Proceedings of the Linnaean Society of New York
Proc. Natl. Acad. Sci. = Proceedings of the National Academy of Sciences

Q. Rev. Biol. = Quarterly Review of Biology
Rep. Br. Assoc. Adv. Sci. = Report of the British Association for the Advancement of Science
Rev. crit. paleozool. = Revue critique de paleozoologie
Sci. Am. = Scientific American
Sci. Mon. = Scientific Monthly
Sci. Prog. = Science Progress
Trans. N.Y. Acad. Sci. = Transactions of the New York Academy of Sciences
U.S. Geol. Surv. Monogr. = U.S. Geological Survey Monograph

1901

Extracts from the reports of field parties sent by the department of vertebrate paleontology in search of fossil mammals and reptiles, 1900. Am. Mus. J., 1:140–45.

1903

A marine university. Smithsonian Institution Annual Report, 1902, pp. 625–32.
Adaptive significance of the shortening of the elephant's skull. Bull. Am. Mus. Nat. Hist., 19:387–94; Neues Jahrb. Miner. Geol. Palaeontol., 2:471(A).

1904

The relations of the anterior visceral arches to the chondrocranium. Biological Bulletin, 7:55–69.
Anent gizzards. Science, 20:888.

1905

The weight of the *Brontosaurus*. Science, 22:572; Sci. Prog., 1: 457(A).

1906

Department of vertebrate paleontology, explorations of 1905. Am. Mus. J., 6:13–15.
With E. W. Berry. *Prorosmarus alleni,* a new genus and species of walrus from the Upper Miocene of Yorktown, Virginia. American Journal of Science, 21:444–50.
The hailstorm of June 23. Science, 24:115–16.
Notes on a dissected porpoise. Sci. Am., 95:188–90.

1907

The skeleton of the Columbian mammoth. Am. Mus. J., 7:5–6.

The *Naosaurus,* or "ship-lizard." Am. Mus. J., 7:36–41.

The Warren mastodon. Am. Mus. J., 7:90–91.

Editor. *Evolution of Mammalian Molar Teeth to and from the Triangular Type, Including Collected and Revised Researches on Trituberculy and New Sections on the Forms and Homologies of the Molar Teeth in the Different Orders of Mammals,* by H. F. Osborn. New York, Macmillan Inc. ix + 250 pp.

The orders of teleostomous fishes. A preliminary review of the broader features of their evolution and taxonomy. Ann. N.Y. Acad. Sci., 17:437–508.

The place of Linnaeus in the unfolding of science; his views on the class Mammalia. Pop. Sci. Mon., 71:121–30.

1908

Linnaeus as an intermediary between ancient and modern Zoology; his views on the class Mammalia. Ann. N.Y. Acad. Sci., 18: 21–31.

Exhibit illustrating the evolution of the horse. Am. Mus. J., 8: 116–22.

1910

The orders of mammals. I. Typical stages in the history of the ordinal classification of mammals. II. Genetic relations of the mammalian orders: with a discussion of the origin of the Mammalia and of the problem of the auditory ossicles. Bull. Am. Mus. Nat. Hist., 27:1–524. Reviewed in: Nature, 84:216; Am. J. Sci., 30:88.

Genetic relations of the Insectivora to other orders of mammals. Ann. N.Y. Acad. Sci., 19:297–99. (A)

Application of the quadrate–incus theory to the conditions in theriodont reptiles and the genetic relations of the latter to the Mammalia. Science, 31:600; Ann. N.Y. Acad. Sci., 20:404–5 (A).

Notes on the insectivore genus *Tupaia* and its allies. Science, 31: 918–19; Ann. N.Y. Acad. Sci., 20:419 (1911) (A).

The *Tyrannosaurus.* Am. Mus. J., 10:2–8.

1911

The limbs of *Eryops* and the origin of paired limbs from fins. Science, 33:508–9; Ann. N.Y. Acad. Sci., 21:192–93 (1912) (A).

Further notes on the evolution of paired fins. Science, 34:892; Ann. N.Y. Acad. Sci., 21:216 (1912) (A).

1912

A new restoration of a titanothere. Am. Mus. J., 12:15–17.
Notes of the origin of paired limbs of terrestrial vertebrates. Ann. N.Y. Acad. Sci., 21:219–20. (A)
Note on the upper Eocene titanotheroid *Telmatherium* (?) *incisivum* Douglass from the Uinta Basin. Science, 35:546.
Marsupials, insectivores, and primates. Bull. Geol. Soc. Am., 23: 187–96.
Note on the quantitative representation of the factors of evolution. Appendix to: Tetraplasy, the Law of the Four Inseparable Factors of Evolution, by H. F. Osborn. Journal of the Academy of Natural Sciences of Philadelphia, 15:307.
Notes on the principles of quadrupedal locomotion and on the mechanism of the limbs in hoofed animals. Ann. N.Y. Acad. Sci., 22:267–94; Rev. crit. paleozool., 20:46(A).

1913

Critique of recent work on the morphology of the vertebrate skull, especially in relation to the origin of mammals. J. Morphol., 24:1–42; Jahresberichte über die Fortschritte der Anatomie und Entwicklungsgeschichte, Jena, 19:62–64(A).
Crossopterygian ancestry of the Amphibia. Science, 37:806–8.
Homology of the "lacrimal" and of the "alisphenoid" in recent and fossil reptiles. Bull. Geol. Soc. Am., 24:241–46; *ibid.*, 24:118 (A); Geol. Zentralbl., 21:39(A).
Relationship of the Tupaiidae and of Eocene lemurs, especially *Notharctus.* Bull. Geol. Soc. Am., 24:247–52; *ibid.*, 24:117(A); Geol. Zentralbl., 21:37(A).

1914

Comment on "The Auditory Ossicles of American Rodents," by T. D. A. Cockerell, L. I. Miller, and M. Printz. Bull. Am. Mus. Nat. Hist., 33:380.
Convergence and allied phenomena in the Mammalia. Rep. Br. Assoc. Adv. Sci., Birmingham, 1913, 83:525–26.
Exhibition of a fossil skeleton of *Notharctus rostratus,* an American Eocene lemur, with remarks on the phylogeny of the primates. Rep. Br. Assoc. Adv. Sci., Birmingham, 1913, 83:529–30.

Locomotive adaptations in fishes illustrating "habitus" and "heritage." Ann. N.Y. Acad. Sci., 22:267–68.

With H. F. Osborn, A. W. Grabau, W. D. Matthew, and R. Broom. Conference on convergent evolution, including a summary of the recent discussion before the British Association for the Advancement of Science. Ann. N.Y. Acad. Sci., 23:293–99. (A)

The dawn man of Piltdown, England. Am. Mus. J., 14:188–200.

Skeleton of *Notharctus,* an Eocene lemuroid. Bull. Geol. Soc. Am., 25:141. (A)

Phyletic relationships of the Lemuroidea. Bull. Geol. Soc. Am., 25:141–42. (A)

1915

With L. A. Adams. The temporal fossae of vertebrates in relation to the jaw muscles. Science, 41:763–65.

The base of the cranium in anthropoids and man. Ann. N.Y. Acad. Sci., 24:349–51.

Observations on the phylogeny of the higher primates. Bull. Geol. Soc. Am., 26:153. (A)

An American Eocene lemur (*Notharctus* Leidy). Ann. N.Y. Acad. Sci., 24:383–84. (A)

Observations on the Indrisinae and other lemurs. Ann. N.Y. Acad. Sci., 24:388. (A)

Present status of the problem of the origin of the Tetrapoda, with special reference to the skull and paired limbs. Ann. N.Y. Acad. Sci., 26:317–83.

Is *Sivapithecus* Pilgrim an ancestor of man? Science, 42:341–42.

On the relationship of the Eocene lemur *Notharctus* to the Adapidae and to other primates. I. Bull. Geol. Soc. Am., 26:419–25.

On the classification and phylogeny of the Lemuroidea. II. Bull. Geol. Soc. Am., 26:426–46.

With J. T. Nichols. Long Island fishes noted by Mr. J. G. Raynor. Copeia, 1915, 59–60.

1916

Present status of the problem of the origin of birds. Am. N.Y. Acad. Sci., 26:447–48. (A)

With C. R. Eastman and W. D. Matthew. Recent progress in vertebrate paleontology. Science, 43:103–10.

Phylogeny of recent and extinct anthropoids, with special reference to the origin of man. Bull. Am. Mus. Nat. Hist., 35:258–355.

Phylogenetic review of extinct and recent anthropoids, with special reference to the evolution of the human dentition.   Bull. Geol. Soc. Am., 27:149–50. (A)

Preliminary report of the committee on the nomenclature of the skull elements in the Tetrapoda.   Bull. Geol. Soc. Am., 27:152. (A)

Theories of the origin of birds.   Ann. N.Y. Acad. Sci., 27:31–38; *ibid.,* 26:447(A); Rev. crit. paleozool., 21:43(A).

Studies on the evolution of the primates.   I. The Cope–Osborn "theory of trituberculy" and ancestral molar patterns of the primates.   Bull. Am. Mus. Nat. Hist., 35:239–57; Anthropology (Paris), 28:157–59(A); Rev. crit. paleozool., 21:9(A).

Studies on the evolution of primates.   II. Phylogeny of recent and extinct anthropoids, with special reference to the origin of man.   Bull. Am. Mus. Nat. Hist., 35:258–355; Rev. crit. paleozool., 21:9(A).

Note on the molar teeth of the Piltdown mandible.   Am. Anthropol., 18:384–87.

1917

With C. R. Eastman and W. D. Matthew.   Recent progress in vertebrate paleontology.   Science, 45:117–21.

Evolution of the human face.   Chief stages in its development from the lowest forms of life to man.   Am. Mus. J., 17:377–88.   (Reprinted in: Dent. Cosmos, 60:115–125; translation, Egeszsegtudomany, 3:10–12.)

Genetics *versus* paleontology.   Am. Nat., 51:622–35.

With W. Granger.   A revision of the Eocene primates of the genus *Notharctus.*   Bull. Am. Mus. Nat. Hist., 37:841–59.

Second report of the committee on the nomenclature of the cranial elements in the Permian Tetrapoda.   With appendices by R. Broom, D. M. S. Watson and S. W. Williston.   Bull. Geol. Soc. Am., 28:973–86; *ibid.,* 28:210(A).

1918

With W. D. Matthew.   Vertebrate palaeontology.   In: *The American Yearbook,* 1917, pp. 634–36.   New York, D. Appleton & Co.

The structure and mechanism of fishes.   Introduction to: *Fishes of the vicinity of New York City,* by J. T. Nichols, American Museum of Natural History Handbook Series no. 7, pp. 5–17.

The evolution of orthodonty. Dent. Cosmos, 60:417–25. Discussion by H. F. Osborn, M. Hellman, W. K. Gregory. *Ibid.*, 60: 435–37.

With C. L. Camp. Studies in comparative myology and osteology. no. III. Bull. Am. Mus. Nat. Hist., 38:447–563. Reviewed in: Nat. Hist., 19:731–32.

1919

With W. D. Matthew. Vertebrate palaeontology. In: *The American Yearbook,* 1918, pp. 695–96. New York, D. Appleton & Co.

The Galton Society for the study of the origin and evolution of man. Science, 49:267–68.

The evolution of the human face. Nat. Hist., 19:421–25.

The pelvis of dinosaurs: a study of the relations between muscular stresses and skeletal forms. Copeia, 1919, 18–20. (A)

1920

Vertebrate palaeontology. In: *The American Yearbook,* 1919, pp. 681–85. New York, D. Appleton & Co.

Restoration of *Camarasaurus* and life model. Proc. Natl. Acad. Sci., 6:16–17; Geol. Zentralbl., 25:540(A).

Facts and theories of evolution, with special reference to the origin of man. Dent. Cosmos, 62:343–59.

The origin and evolution of the human dentition. A paleontological review. I. Stages of ascent from the Silurian fishes to the mammals of the age of reptiles. J. Dent. Res., 2:89–183.

The origin and evolution of the human dentition. A paleontological review. II. Stages of ascent from the Paleocene placental mammals to the lower primates. J. Dent. Res., 2:215–83.

The origin and evolution of the human dentition. A paleontological review. III. Nature's earlier experiments in evolving large-eyed and short-jawed primates. J. Dent. Res., 2:357–427.

The origin and evolution of the human dentition. A paleontological review. IV. The dentition of the higher primates and their relationships with man. J. Dent. Res., 2:607–717.

On the structure and relations of *Notharctus,* an American Eocene primate. Studies on the evolution of the primates. Part III. Memoirs of the American Museum of Natural History, 3: 49–243.

Studies in comparative myology and osteology. IV. A review of the evolution of the lacrymal bone of vertebrates with special reference to that of mammals. Bull. Am. Mus. Nat. Hist., 42:95–263; Sci. Prog., 16:213(A).

Studies in comparative myology and osteology. V. On the anatomy of the pre-orbital fossae of Equidae and other ungulates. Bull. Am. Mus. Nat. Hist., 42:265–83; Sci. Prog., 16:214(A).

1921

The origin and evolution of the human dentition. A palaeontological review. Part V. Later stages in the evolution of the human dentition; with a final summary and a bibliography. J. Dent. Res., 3:87–228.

Excerpt from letter from Honolulu concerning "Akilolos" (Wrasses). Nat. Hist., 21:555.

Erwin S. Christman, 1885–1921, draughtsman, artist, sculptor. Nat. Hist., 21:620–25.

The origin and evolution of the human dentition. (Quotations from the preface of the book of this title [publ. 1922] which supplement and explain certain features of the comment in the previous publications on the origin and evolution of the human dentition in the J. Dent. Res.) J. Dent. Res., 3:361–66.

Australian mammals and why they should be protected. Australian Museum Magazine, 1:65–74.

1922

Syllabus. Evolution of the human face. Philadelphia, Wagner Free Institute of Science.

The Origin and Evolution of the Human Dentition. Parts I–V. Baltimore, Williams & Wilkins Co. xviii + 548 pp. Note in Anatomischer Anzeiger, 56:303.

On the "habitus" and "heritage" of *Caenolestes.* J. Mammal., 3:106–14.

1923

Erwin S. Christman. (Unsigned.) Nat. Hist., 23:304.

With M. Hellman. Notes on the type of *Hesperopithecus haroldcookii* Osborn. Am. Mus. Novit., no. 53, 16 pp. Reprinted in: J. Dent. Res., 5:9–25; Rev. crit. paleozool., 27:216(A); Neus Jahrb. Miner. Geol. Palaeontol., 2:290(A).

With H. F. Osborn. Authorized interview by H. Weir. Our earliest ancestor—the Dawn Man. McClure's Magazine, 55:12–28.

A forerunner of the horned dinosaurs. Nat. Hist., 23:192.

With E. E. Free. Man—an animal invention. Pop. Sci. Mon., 102(5):32–34, 105–7.

With E. E. Free. How science traces our monkey ancestry. Pop. Sci. Mon., 102(6):28–31, 98–99.

With W. Granger; appendix by C. P. Berkey. *Protoceratops andrewsi*, a pre-ceratopsian dinosaur from Mongolia. Am. Mus. Novit., no. 72, 9 pp.

A Jurassic fish fauna from western Cuba, with an arrangement of the families of holostean ganoid fishes. Bull. Am. Mus. Nat. Hist., 48:223–42.

With R. W. Miner and G. K. Noble. The carpus of *Eryops* and the structure of the primitive chiropterygium. Bull. Am. Mus. Nat. Hist., 48:279–88; Neues Jahrb. Miner. Geol. Palaeontol., 1:276(A); Geol. Zentralbl., 30:444(A); Nature, 112:806(A).

The gorilla's foot. Nature, 112:758, 933.

With M. Hellman. Further notes on the molars of *Hesperopithecus* and *Pithecanthropus*. Bull. Am. Mus. Nat. Hist., 48:509–26; Geol. Zentralbl., 30:253(A).

1924

On design in nature. The Yale Review, 13:334–45. Proc. Linn. Soc. N.Y., nos. 33–36, pp. 08–99(A).

With M. Hellman. Dentition of *Dryopithecus* and the origin of man. Pan-Am. Geol., 42:307–8. (A)

Australia, the land of living fossils. Nat. Hist., 24:4–15.

The gorilla's foot. Nature, 113:421–23, 457–58.

The schoolhouse of the world. Nat. Hist., 24:254–55.

With B. Brown and M. Hellman. On three incomplete anthropoid jaws from the Siwaliks, India. Am. Mus. Novit., no. 130, 9 pp.

A fossil ganoid fish (*Lepidotus* (?) *lacotanus*, new species) from the Lower Cretaceous of South Dakota. Am. Mus. Novit., no. 134, 8 pp.

With G. K. Noble. The origin of the mammalian alisphenoid bone. J. Morphol., 39:435–61; Anat. Rec., 27:204–5(A).

Dryopithecus jaws. Nature, 113:757–58.

1925

Editor. *The Osteology of the Reptiles,* by S. W. Williston. Cambridge, Harvard University Press. xiii + 300 pp.

With C. C. Mook.   On *Protoceratops,* a primitive ceratopsian dinosaur from the Lower Cretaceous of Mongolia.   Am. Mus. Novit., no. 156, 9 pp.

Editor.   *The hall of the age of man,* by H. F. Osborn.   Am. Mus. Nat. Hist. Guide Leafl. Ser., no. 52, 3d ed.   48 pp.

The family tree of man.   In: *The hall of the age of man,* Am. Mus. Nat. Hist. Guide Leafl. Ser., no. 52, 3d ed., pp. 36, 40–48.

Arcturus expedition. (Excerpts from letter.)   Nat. Hist., 25:315–16.

The biogenetic law and the skull form of primitive man.   Am. J. Phys. Anthropol., 8:373–78.

With C. B. Davenport.   Minute on the death of Louis R. Sullivan.   Science, 62:583; also in Nat. Hist., 26:106.

A dissenting opinion.   Proc. Natl. Acad. Sci., 11:751.

1926

With M. Hellman.   The dentition of *Dryopithecus* and the origin of man.   Anthropological Papers of the American Museum of Natural History, 28(Part I):1–123; Rep. Br. Assoc. Adv. Sci., 92:405(A).

Some critical stages in the evolution of the human dental apparatus.   J. Dent. Res., 6:71–100.

Editor, with C. D. Matthew.   Past races of man.   Nat. Hist., 26:227–327.

With J. H. McGregor.   A dissenting opinion as to Dawn Men and Ape Men.   Nat. Hist., 26:270–71.

With M. Hellman.   The crown patterns of fossil and recent human molar teeth and their meaning.   Nat. Hist., 26:300–309.   Reprinted as Part I, Palaeontology of the human dentition.   Int. J. Orthod. Oral Surg. Radiogr., 12:1027–37.

The skeleton of *Moschops capensis* Broom, a dinocephalian reptile from the Permian of South Africa.   Bull. Am. Mus. Nat. Hist., 56:179–251; Bull. Geol. Soc. Am., 31:223(A).

The horse in the tiger's skin.   Bull. N.Y. Zool. Soc., 29:111–33.

With G. G. Simpson.   Cretaceous mammal skulls from Mongolia.   Am. Mus. Novit., no. 225, 20 pp.; Nature, 68:698–99(A).

Palaeontology of the human dentition.   Ten structural stages in the evolution of the cheek teeth.   Am. J. Phys. Anthropol., 9:401–26.   Reprinted in: Int. J. Orthod. Oral Surg. Radiogr., 12:1038–42.

New materials for the study of evolution: a series of primitive fossil rhinoceros skulls *(Trigonias)* from the Lower Eocene of Colorado. Geological Society of America Preliminary List, 49:59.

1927

With F. H. Chapman. In celebration of the seventieth birthday of Henry Fairfield Osborn, August 8, 1927. New York, American Museum of Natural History. 8 pp.

Vertebrate paleontology. *The American Yearbook,* 1926, pp. 911–14.

Mongolia the new world. Part I. Sci. Mon., 24:5–14.

The Mongolian life record. Mongolia the new world. Part II. Sci. Mon., 24:169–81.

Mongolian mammals of the "Age of Reptiles." Mongolia the new world. Part III. Sci. Mon., 24:225–35.

Minute on the death of Dr. Huntington. Eugen. News, 12:33–34.

The Mongolian age of mammals. Mongolia the new world. Part IV. Sci. Mon., 24:337–47.

Missing links of the Gobi Desert. How a handful of fossils has filled a former gap in the evolution tree. Sci. Am., 136:231–32. Quoted in part in: Lit. Dig., 93:15–16.

Did man originate in central Asia? Mongolia the new world. Part V. Sci. Mon., 24:385–401.

New material for the study of evolution: a series of primitive fossil rhinoceros skulls *(Trigonias)* from the Lower Oligocene of Colorado. Bull. Geol. Soc. Am., 38:235.

The present status of the origin of man. Nat. Hist., 27:187. (A)

With R. Kellogg. A fossil porpoise from California. Am. Mus. Novit., no. 269, 7 pp.

The new hall of reptiles and amphibians. Nat. Hist., 27:303.

The palaeomorphology of the human head. Ten structural stages from fish to man. Part I. The skull in norma lateralis. Q. Rev. Biol., 2:267–79; Biol. Abstr., 2:668(A). Reprinted in: Int. J. Orthod. Oral Surg. Radiogr., 14:107–19.

Two views of the origin of man. Science, 65:601–5.

The palaeomorphology of the human head: ten structural stages from fish to man. Bull. N.Y. Acad. Med., 2d ser., 3:525–27. (A)

Dawn man or ape? Sci. Am., 137:230–32.

How near is the relationship of man to the chimpanzee–gorilla stock? Q. Rev. Biol., 2:549–60; Biol. Abstr., 3:391(A).

The origin of man from the anthropoid stem—when and where? Proc. Am. Philos. Soc., 66:439–63. Excerpts reprinted in: Evolution, 2:3–4.

The testimony of man's teeth. Evolution, 1:3–4.

Hesperopithecus apparently not an ape nor a man. Science, 66: 579–81.

1928

The lineage of man. In: *Creation by Evolution,* ed. by F. Mason, pp. 270–92. New York, Macmillan Inc.

Dr. Foote's work. (Letter to Dr. E. H. Bruening.) In: *Bone as a Measure of Development. When and How We Acquired Our Teeth,* by J. S. Foote, Appendix 4. Omaha, Nebraska, Douglas Printing Co.

The body–forms of fishes and their inscribed rectilinear lines. Palaeobiology, 1:93–100.

Were the ancestors of man primitive brachiators? Proc. Am. Philos. Soc., 67:129–50; Eugen. News, 13:54–59.

The upright posture of man: a review of its origin and evolution. Proc. Am. Philos. Soc., 67:339–76.

A tour of the new hall of fishes. Nat. Hist., 28:2–17.

Origin of human limb proportions through change of function. Bull. N.Y. Acad. Med., 2d ser., 4:239–42.

With H. J. Cook. New material for the study of evolution. A series of primitive rhinoceros skulls *(Trigonias)* from the Lower Oligocene of Colorado. Proceedings of the Colorado Museum of Natural History, 8:1–32; Bull. Geol. Soc. Am., 38:235(A); Pan-Am. Geol., 47:239–40(A).

Studies on the body–forms of fishes. Part I. The body–forms of fishes and their inscribed rectilinear figures. Part II. Preliminary review of the evolution of body–forms in fossil and recent fishes. Contributions of the New York Zoological Society, Department of Tropical Research, no. 278; Zoologica, 8:325–421.

Minute on the death of Professor H. H. Wilder. (Unsigned.) Eugen. News, 13:67.

Reply to Professor Wood–Jones's note: Man and the anthropoids. Am. J. Phys. Anthropol., 12:253–56; Biol. Abstr., 6:1197(A).

Bashford Dean, 1867–1928. Science, 68:635–38.

1929

Our Face from Fish to Man. New York, G. P. Putnam's Sons. xl + 295 pp.

Ancyclopoda or Chalicotheroidea. In: *Encyclopaedia Britannica,* vol. 1, p. 893. Chicago, Encyclopaedia Britannica, Inc.

Mammalia. In: *Encyclopaedia Britannica,* vol. 14, pp. 748–54. Chicago, Encyclopaedia Britannica, Inc.

Marsupialia. In: *Encyclopaedia Britannica,* vol. 14, pp. 975–81. Chicago, Encyclopaedia Britannica, Inc.

Monotremata. In: *Encyclopaedia Britannica,* vol. 15, pp. 732–33. Chicago, Encyclopaedia Britannica, Inc.

Perissodactyla. In: *Encyclopaedia Britannica,* vol. 17, pp. 529–31. Chicago, Encyclopaedia Britannica, Inc.

With J. H. McGregor. Primates. In: *Encyclopaedia Britannica,* vol. 18, pp. 485–90. Chicago, Encyclopaedia Britannica, Inc.

Ungulata. In: *Encyclopaedia Britannica,* vol. 22, pp. 699–702. Chicago, Encyclopaedia Britannica, Inc.

The muscular anatomy and the restoration of the Titanotheres. In: *Titanotheres of ancient Wyoming, Dakota, and Nebraska,* by H. F. Osborn. U.S. Geol. Surv. Monogr. 55, 2:703–25.

Principles of leverage and muscular action. In: *Titanotheres of ancient Wyoming, Dakota, and Nebraska,* by H. F. Osborn. U.S. Geol. Surv. Monogr. 55, 2:727–31.

Restudy of the skull of *Portheus molossus* Cope. Bull. Geol. Soc. Am., 40:220(A); Pan-Am. Geol., 51:234(A).

Summary of harmonic and differential allometrons in the skulls and feet and an interpretation of the phylogeny of the Titanotheres. In: *Titanotheres of ancient Wyoming, Dakota, and Nebraska,* by H. F. Osborn. U.S. Geol. Surv. Monogr. 55, 2:828–33.

Is the pro-Dawn Man a myth? Hum. Biol., 1:153–65. Conclusion reprinted in Am. J. Phys. Anthropol., 14:505–6; Biol. Abstr., 4:632–33(A).

The palaeomorphology of the human head. Ten structural stages from fish to man. Part II. The skull in Norma Basalis. Q. Rev. Biol., 4:233–47; Biol. Abstr., 6:1474(A).

With M. Hellman. Paleontology of the human dentition. Family tree of man. Int. J. Orthod. Oral Surg. Radiogr., 15:642–52; Biol. Abstr., 6:2403–4(A).

By H. F. Osborn, with the cooperation of W. K. Gregory, J. H. Mc-
Gregor, and N. C. Nelson. *The hall of the age of man.* Am.
Mus. Nat. Hist. Guide Leafl. Ser., no. 52, 5th ed. 54 pp.
Fossil snapper (family Lutianidae) from the Marianna limestone
of Florida. Bull. Geol. Soc. Am., 40:220(A); Pan-Am. Geol.,
51:233–34(A).
An appreciation of Milo Hellman's work. Int. J. Orthod. Oral
Surg. Radiogr., 15:1067–69, erratum notice, *ibid.*, 16:225.

1930

The animal ancestry of man. In: *Human Biology and Racial Wel-
fare,* ed. by E. V. Cowdry, pp. 53–90. New York, Paul B. Hoeber,
Inc.
A critique of Professor Frederic Wood–Jones's paper: Some land-
marks in the phylogeny of the primates. Hum. Biol., 2:99–108,
erratum notice, *ibid.,* 2:440; Biol. Abstr., 4:2217(A).
A critique of Professor Osborn's theory of human origin. Am. J.
Phys. Anthropol., 14:133–64; Anat. Rec., 45:289–90(A).
The origin of man from a brachiating anthropoid stock. Science,
71:645–50.
Some stages in the adaptive radiation of the teleostome skull. Post-
script. Origin of the V-shaped arrangement of the orobranchial
apparatus of fishes. Copeia, 1930, 56. (A)
Irreversibility of evolution and the origin of man. Am. J. Phys.
Anthropol., 14:84. (A)
Basic patents in evolution. Sci. Am., 143:112–13, 200–202, 286–88.
William Diller Matthew, 1871–1930. Nat. Hist., 30:664–66.
A fossil teleost fish of the snapper family (Lutianidae) from the
Lower Oliogocene of Florida. Bulletin, Florida State Geologi-
cal Survey, no. 5, pp. 7–17.
Memorial of Bashford Dean (1867–1928). In: *Bashford Dean Me-
morial Volume—Archaic Fishes,* ed. by E. W. Gudger, pp. 1–42.
New York, American Museum of Natural History; also in Bull.
Geol. Soc. Am., 41:16–25.
William Diller Matthew, paleontologist (1871–1930). Science, 72:
642–45; excerpt in *Climate and Evolution,* by W. D. Matthew,
2d ed., pp. vii–xi. New York, New York Academy of Sciences.
A comparison of the limbs, hands, and feet of man, anthropoid apes,
and primitive Eocene mammals. Anat. Rec., 45:289–90. (A)

1931

Pleistocene man in Asia. In: *Quest of Glacial Man,* ed. by M. Bentley, pp. 10–11. National Research Council, Reprint and Circular Series, no. 100.

Cope's contributions to ichthyology. In: *Cope: Master Naturalist,* by H. F. Osborn with the cooperation of H. A. Warren, pp. 496–99. Princeton, Princeton University Press.

Letter to Dr. Charles B. Davenport. Eugen. News, 16:16.

Minute on the death of Dr. William Diller Matthew. (Unsigned.) Eugen. News, 16:16–17.

The African anatomical expedition of Columbia University and the American Museum of Natural History. Columbia University Quarterly, 23:79–89; excerpts entitled "In the Land of the Gorilla" reprinted in Evolution, 3:3–4.

With H. F. Osborn. Memorial of William Diller Matthew. Bull. Geol. Soc. Am., 42:55–95.

A review of William Diller Matthew's contributions to mammalian palaeontology. Am. Mus. Novit., no. 473, 23 pp.

Biographical note. Birthdays and research centres. Nature, 127:765.

With M. Mok. How man was created. Pop. Sci. Mon., 118(6): 17–19, 135–38.

With M. Mok. We got our face from a fish. Pop. Sci. Mon., 119(1):22–24, 121–24.

In the land of the gorilla. Evolution, 3:3–4.

With M. Mok. Why some babies are born with tails. Pop. Sci. Mon., 119(2):18–20, 117–19.

With M. Mok. Man is still a monkey. Pop. Sci. Mon., 119(3): 32–34, 114–16.

With M. Mok. How man–apes became men a million years ago. Pop. Sci. Mon., 119(4):22–24, 134–36.

Centenary meeting of the British Association for the Advancement of Science. (Unsigned.) Nat. Hist., 31:675–77.

Certain critical stages in the evolution of the vertebrate jaws. Int. J. Orthod. Oral Surg. Radiogr., 17:1138–48.

1932

J. Leon Williams. (Unsigned.) Nat. Hist., 32:220.

By H. F. Osborn, with the cooperation of W. K. Gregory, J. H. McGregor, and N. C. Nelson. *The hall of the age of man.* Am. Mus. Nat. Hist. Guide Leafl. Ser., no. 52, 6th ed. 54 pp.

Some strange teleost skulls and their derivation from normal forms. Copeia, 1932, 53–60.

The Third International Congress of Eugenics. Nat. Hist., 32: 439–40.

From fish to man. Nat. Hist., 32:440–42.

Progress on the Bashford Dean memorial volume on archaic fishes. Copeia, 1932, 182–83.

1933

Fish skulls: a study of the evolution of natural mechanisms. Transactions of the American Philosophical Society, 23:i–vii, 75–481.

Form factors in types of fish skulls. Science, 73:507(A).

The new anthropogeny: twenty-five stages of vertebrate evolution from Silurian chordate to man. Science, 77:29–40. Brief excerpt reprinted in Monthly Bulletin, Citizen's Forum, vol. 1, no. 3; Biol. Abstr., 8:290(A).

Dr. Henry Fairfield Osborn, retiring president of The American Museum of Natural History. (Unsigned.) Sci. Mon., 36:284–86.

The master builder: Henry Fairfield Osborn. Nat. Hist., 33:251–56.

Nature's wild dog show. Bull. N.Y. Zool. Soc., 36:82–96. Reprinted in: L'Eleveur, Revue Cynegetique et Canine, 1934, no. 2.550, pp. 2–5. Photographs and notes under title "Nature's perpetual wild dog show" reprinted in: *The Illustrated London News,* 184 (Feb. 17, 1934):238–39; excerpts under title "The dog is a native American" reprinted in: Lit. Dig., 117 (Feb. 17, 1934): 19.

Fishes: New models of deep-sea anglers. Nat. Hist., 33:554–55.

With H. C. Raven. The spermaceti organ and nasal passages of the sperm whale *(Physeter catodon)* and other odontocetes. Am. Mus. Novit., no. 677, 18 pp.

Basic patents in nature. Science, 78:561–66.

1934

Man's Place Among the Anthropoids. Oxford, The Clarendon Press. v + 119 pp.

With M. Mellanby. Aspects of dentition. C.-R. Première Sess.

Congr. Int. Sci. Anthropol. Ethnol., pp. 102–4. London, Institut Royal d'Anthropologie.

With F. Lamonte. *The world of fishes: guide to the fish collections of The American Museum of Natural History.* Am. Mus. Nat. Hist. Guide Leafl. Ser., no. 81. 90 pp.

With M. Roigneau. *Introduction to human anatomy: guide to section I of the hall of natural history of man.* Am. Mus. Nat. Hist. Guide Leafl. Ser., no. 86. 82 pp.

Man's place among the primates. C.-R. Première Sess. Congr. Int. Sci. Anthropol. Ethnol., pp. 69–70. London, Institut Royal d'Anthropologie. (A)

The origin, rise, and decline of *Homo sapiens.* Sci. Mon., 39: 481–96.

The comparative aspect of dentition. C.-R. Première Sess. Congr. Int. Sci. Anthropol. Ethnol., pp. 103–4. London, Institut Royal d'Anthropologie. (A)

Polyisomerism and anisomerism in cranial and dental evolution among vertebrates. Proc. Natl. Acad. Sci., 20:1–9.

On the significance of the supra-symphysial depression and groove in the shovel-tusked mastodont. J. Mammal., 15:4–12.

Some new models illustrating the evolution of the human dentition. Int. J. Orthod. Dent. Child., 20:1077–81.

A half century of trituberculy. The Cope–Osborn theory of dental evolution, with a revised summary of molar evolution from fish to man. Proc. Am. Philos. Soc., 73:169–317.

With W. Granger. An apparently new family of amblypod mammals from Mongolia. Am. Mus. Novit., no. 720, 8 pp.

With H. C. Raven. Notes on the anatomy and relationships of the ocean sunfish *(Mola mola).* Copeia, 1934, 145–51.

Evolution of Face from Fish to Man. Russian translation by N. A. Bobrinskii and M. L. Levine. Moscow–Leningrad, Biomedgiz. 156 pp.

Whence came the "dragons of Komodo"? Bull. N.Y. Zool. Soc., 37: 68–90.

Sea serpents. Nat. Hist., 34:327–31.

The Loch Ness "monster." Nat. Hist., 34:674–76.

Some new models illustrating the evolution of the human dentition. Int. J. Orthod. Dent. Child., 20:1077–81.

Polyisomerism and anthropogeny. Hum. Biol., 6:632–36.

Eulogy on the late Dr. Davidson Black. In publications of the Galton Society, American Museum of Natural History, Apr. 16, 1934. Reprinted in: Eugen. News, 19:128–29.

1935

In quest of gorillas. I. On our way to gorilla-land. Sci. Mon., 41:384–95.

In quest of gorillas. II. Tanganyika snapshots. Sci. Mon., 41: 505–29.

Further observations on the pectoral girdle and fin of *Sauripterus taylori* Hall, a crossopterygian fish from the Upper Devonian of Pennsylvania, with special reference to the origin of the pentadactylate extremities of Tetrapoda. Proc. Am. Philos. Soc., 75: 673–90.

On the evolution of the skulls of vertebrates with special reference to heritable changes in proportional diameters (anisomerism). Part I. The skulls of the most primitive known fossil chordates (Ostracoderms). Proc. Natl. Acad. Sci., 21:1–8; Science, 80:548–49(A); Palaeontol. Zentralbl., 10:49(A).

Building a super-giant rhinoceros. Nat. Hist., 35:340–43.

The origin of the human face: a study in paleomorphology and evolution. Dent. Cosmos, 77:344–49.

With W. Granger. A revised restoration of the skeleton of *Baluchitherium,* gigantic fossil rhinoceros of Central Asia. Am. Mus. Novit., no. 787, 3 pp.

Introduction to: Wallace's Line and the distribution of Indo-Australian mammals, by Henry C. Raven. Bull. Am. Mus. Nat. Hist., 68:179–81.

Remarks on the origins of the ratites and penguins, with discussion by R. C. Murphy. Proc. Linn. Soc. N.Y., nos. 45–46, 18 pp. (A)

Nature's sea serpent. Nat. Hist., 35:431–37.

The pelvis from fish to man: a study in paleomorphology. Am. Nat., 69:193–210.

The study of human evolution: a plea for a more synthetic approach. Bulletin of the School of Medicine, University of Maryland, 20: 31–33.

Winged sharks. Bull. N.Y. Zool. Soc., 38:129–33.

With M. Roigneau and others. "Williston's law" relating to the evolution of skull bones in the vertebrates. Am. J. Phys. Anthropol., 20:123–52.

Reduplication in evolution. Q. Rev. Biol., 10:272–90.

The roles of undeviating evolution and transformation in the origin of man. Am. Nat., 69:385–404.

Comparative anatomy notes. Nat. Hist., 36:362–63.

Nature's upstart: *Homo sapiens.* Teaching Biologist, 5:22–25, 30, 31. Reprinted in part in: Columbia Alumni News, 27:3, 16. Reprinted in: Evolution, 4:3–4, 6.

Answers to E. Schaller's questions on evolution. Time, 2:12–13.

(Obituaries of) Henry Fairfield Osborn (1857–1935). Science, 82: 452–54; Nat. Hist., 36:370–73; Sci. Mon., 41:566–69.

1936

In quest of gorillas. III. Kivu, land of Olympian clouds. Sci. Mon., 42:47–61.

In quest of gorillas. IV. Joyous days in the Kivu Country. Sci. Mon., 42:111–28.

In quest of gorillas. V. Elusive giants of the mountains. Sci. Mon., 42:258–79.

In quest of gorillas. VI. Farewell to the Great Lakes. Sci. Mon., 42:325–38.

In quest of gorillas. VII. The Lualaba Showboat. Sci. Mon., 42: 403–20.

In quest of gorillas. VIII. Drums in the forest. Sci. Mon., 42: 517–31.

In quest of gorillas. IX. Congo Queer 'Uns. Sci. Mon., 43:23–32.

In quest of gorillas. X. Cameroon folks. Sci. Mon., 43:130–47.

In quest of gorillas. XI. Gorilla children. Sci. Mon., 43:211–23.

Postscript. In quest of gorillas. XIII. Gorillas, men and sleeping sickness. Sci. Mon., 43:522–40.

Foreword. In: *Apes, Ivory and Jade,* by Kirk Meadowcroft, pp. vii–ix. New York, Richard R. Smith.

Habitus factors in the skeleton of fossil and recent mammals. Proc. Am. Philos. Soc., 76:429–44; Science News Letter, 29:285.

Dr. Merriam's contributions to the development of vertebrate paleontology on the Pacific Coast. Sci. Mon., 42:377–80.

With G. M. Conrad. Pictorial phylogenies of deep sea Isospondyli and Iniomi. Copeia, 1936, 21–36.

With G. M. Conrad. The evolution of the pediculate fishes. Am. Nat., 70:193–208.

The museum of things versus the museum of ideas. Science, 83: 585–88.

(Obituary of) Henry Fairfield Osborn (1857–1935). Proc. Am. Philos. Soc., 76:395–408. Reprinted in: Tributes Paid at Memorial Meetings, Nat. Hist., 37(Suppl.):5–7.

With G. M. Conrad. The structure and development of the complex symphysial hinge-joint in the mandible of *Hydrocyon lineatus* Bleeker, a characin fish. Proceedings of the Zoological Society of London, pp. 975–84.

With M. Hellman and G. E. Lewis. Preliminary report on fossil anthropoid teeth from India collected by the Yale–Cambridge India expedition of 1935. Am. J. Phys. Anthropol., 21(Suppl.):8.

The transformation of organic designs: a review of the origin and deployment of the earlier vertebrates. Biological Reviews of the Cambridge Philosophical Society, 11:311–44.

On the phylogenetic relationships of the giant panda *(Ailuropoda)* to other arctoid Carnivora. Am. Mus. Novit., no. 878, 29 pp.

With W. Granger. Further notes on the gigantic extinct rhinoceros, *Baluchitherium,* from the Oligocene of Mongolia. Publication of the Asiatic Expeditions of The American Museum of Natural History, contrib. no. 135; Bull. Am. Mus. Nat. Hist., 72:1–73; Biol. Abstr., 11:1894(A).

On Doctor Pinkley's brain research. Nat. Hist., 38:361.

On the meaning and limits of irreversibility of evolution. Am. Nat., 70:517–28; Biol. Abstr., 11:1644–45(A); Palaeontol. Zentralbl., 11:68–69(A).

Air conditioning in nature. Nat. Hist., 38:382–84.

1937

With H. C. Raven. *In Quest of Gorillas.* New Bedford, Mass., The Darwin Press. xvi + 241 pp.

With M. Hellman. The evidence of the dentition on the origin of man. In: *Early Man,* ed. by G. G. MacCurdy, pp. 243–56. Philadelphia, J. B. Lippincott Co.; Pan-Am. Geol., 68:71–72(A).

Revised by W. K. Gregory and H. C. Raven. *Introduction to human anatomy: guide to section I of the hall of natural history of man,* by W. K. Gregory and M. Roigneau. Am. Mus. Nat. Hist. Guide Leafl. Ser., no. 86, 2d ed. 76 pp.

The bridge-that-walks. Nat. Hist., 39:33–48.

(Obituary of) Grafton Elliot Smith (1871–1936). Science, 85:66–68.

Reprinted in part under title "Tribute to a Scientist" in New York Times, Jan. 6, 1937.

Supra-specific variation in nature and in classification. IV. A few examples from mammalian paleontology. Am. Nat., 71:268–76.

With G. M. Conrad. The comparative osteology of the swordfish *(Xiphias)* and the sailfish *(Istiophorus)*. Am. Mus. Novit., no. 952, 25 pp.

David Watson. Copeia, 1937, p. 197.

1938

By H. F. Osborn, revised to 1938 by W. K. Gregory and G. Pinkley. *The hall of the age of man.* Am. Mus. Nat. Hist. Guide Leafl. Ser., no. 52, 7th ed. 57 pp.

In praise of natural history. Evolution, 4:9.

With M. Hellman and G. E. Lewis. Fossil anthropoids of the Yale–Cambridge India expedition of 1935. Carnegie Institution of Washington, Publication no. 495. 27 pp.

Man's place among the primates. Palaeobiology, 6:208–13.

With W. Granger. A new titanothere genus from the Upper Eocene of Mongolia and North America. Addendum to: Fossil mammals from Burma in The American Museum of Natural History, by Edwin H. Colbert. Bull. Am. Mus. Nat. Hist., 74: 435–36.

Henry Fairfield Osborn, 1857–1935. In: National Academy of Sciences, *Biographical Memoirs,* 19:53–119. New York, Columbia University Press.

With M. Hellman. Evidence of the Australopithecine man–apes on the origin of man. Science, 88:615–16.

With G. M. Conrad. The phylogeny of the characin fishes. Zoologica, 23:319–60.

1939

With H. Rockwell and F. G. Evans. Structure of the vertebral column in *Eusthenopteron foordi* Whiteaves. Journal of Paleontology, 13:126–29.

With M. Hellman. The South African fossil man–apes and origin of the human dentition. Journal of the American Dental Association, 26:558–64.

With M. Hellman. On the evolution and major classification of the civets (Viverridae) and allied fossil and recent Carnivora: a phylogenetic study of the skull and dentition.   Proc. Am. Philos. Soc., 81:309–92; Palaeontol. Zentralbl., 15:314(A).

With E. H. Colbert.   On certain principles of evolution illustrated in the mammalian orders Perissodactyla and Artiodactyla. Academy of Sciences, URSS, Memorial Volume to A. N. Sewertzoff (1866–1936), 1:97–116. Russian translation, 117–136.

The extinct anthropoid apes and the origin of the human dentition. Mankind, 2(7):223.

With M. Hellman.   Fossil man–apes of South Africa.   Nature, 143:25–26.

With M. Hellman.   The dentition of the extinct South African man– ape *Australopithecus (Plesianthropus) transvaalensis* Broom. A comparative and phylogenetic study.   Annals of the Transvaal Museum, 19:339–73; El Palacio, 47:120(A).

The bearing of Dr. Broom's and Dr. Dart's discoveries on the origin of man. Annual Proceedings. Associated and Technical Societies of South Africa, pp. 25–57.

Biographical sketch of William Diller Matthew, 1871–1930.   In: *Climate and Evolution,* by W. D. Matthew, 2d ed., pp. vii–xii. New York, New York Academy of Sciences.

An evolutionist goes shell hunting.   Nat. Hist., 44:203–12.

The Carnegie Institution of Washington and Dr. Merriam.   Science, 90:466–68.

With G. M. Conrad.   Body–forms of the black marlin (Makaira nigricans marlina) and striped marlin (Makaira mitsukurii) of New Zealand and Australia.   Bull. Am. Mus. Nat. Hist., 76: 443–56.

1940

Relations of preaxial and postaxial borders in paired appendages of rhipidist fishes and their bearing on origin of tetrapod limbs. Bull. Geol. Soc. Am., 51:1971. (A)

New reconstruction of skeleton of *Eusthenopteron* and its bearing on evolution of the paired fins. Bull. Geol. Soc. Am., 51: 1971. (A)

An expedition to study big-game fish.   Sci. Mon., 5:189–90.

An evolutionist looks at the Maoris.   Nat. Hist., 45:133–45.

With M. Hellman.   The upper dental arch of *Plesianthropus transvaalensis* Broom, and its relations to other parts of the skull. Am. J. Phys. Anthropol., 26:211–28; *ibid.*, 27(Suppl.):14(A); Palaeontol. Zentralbl., 16:125(A).

With G. M. Conrad. World-wide hunt for the marlin. Nat. Hist., 45:288–96.

With G. M. Conrad. The sea-god's patchwork. Nat. Hist., 46: 42–51.

Fashion designs in the world of shells. Nat. Hist., 46:160–70.

1941

Evolution of dental occlusion from fish to man. In: *Development of Occlusion,* by W. K. Gregory, B. H. Broadbent and M. Hellman, pp. 1–30. Philadelphia, University of Philadelphia Press.

(Obituary of) Gladwyn Kingsley Noble. (Sept. 20, 1894–Dec. 9, 1940). Science, 93:10–11.

With H. C. Raven. A new restoration of the skeleton of the Devonian lobe-finned fish, *Eusthenopteron foordi* Whiteaves, with remarks on its relationships. Trans. N.Y. Acad. Sci., 3: 146–53.

With H. C. Raven. On the probable mode of transformation of rhipidistian paddle into tetrapod limb. Trans. N.Y. Acad. Sci., 3:153–58.

Family tree of the vertebrates—grandfather fish and his descendants. Am. Mus. Nat. Hist. Guide Leafl. Ser., no. 106. Reprinted in: Nat. Hist., 48:155–65.

With H. C. Raven. Studies on the origin and early evolution of paired fins and limbs. Part I. Paired fins and girdles in ostracoderms, placoderms, and other primitive fishes. Ann. N.Y. Acad. Sci., 42:275–91.

With H. C. Raven. Studies on the origin and early evolution of paired fins and limbs. Part II. A new restoration of the skeleton of *Eusthenopteron* (Pisces Crossopterygii, Devonian, Quebec) with remarks on the origin of the Tetrapod stem. Ann. N.Y. Acad Sci., 42:293–312.

With H. C. Raven. Studies on the origin and early evolution of paired fins and limbs. Part III. On the transformation of pectoral and pelvic paddles of *Eusthenopteron* type into pentadactylate limbs. Ann. N.Y. Acad. Sci., 42:313–27.

With H. C. Raven. Studies on the origin and early evolution of paired fins and limbs. Part IV. A new theory of the origin of the pelvis of tetrapods. Ann. N.Y. Acad. Sci., 42:329–60.

1942

(Biography of) Gladwyn Kingsley Noble (1894–1940). In: Am.

Philos. Soc. Yearb., 1941, pp. 393–97. Philadelphia, American Philosophical Society.

Revised by W. K. Gregory and H. C. Raven. *Introduction to human anatomy: guide to section I, hall of the natural history of man,* by W. K. Gregory and M. Roigneau. Ann. Mus. Nat. Hist. Guide Leafl. Ser., no. 86, 3d ed. 77 pp.

With J. R. Angell. Unveiling of the bust of Henry Fairfield Osborn at the American Museum of Natural History. Science, 95: 470–72.

Unveiling of the bust of Henry Fairfield Osborn and opening of the North American Hall of Mammals at the American Museum of Natural History. Nature, 150:573–75.

1943

The world-wide fraternity of the game fishermen. Int. Game Fish Assoc. Yearb., 1943, pp. 9–11.

The big game fish in science. Int. Game Fish Assoc. Yearb., 1943, pp. 13–15.

With W. Granger. A revision of the Mongolian titanotheres. Bull. Am. Mus. Nat. Hist., 80:349–89.

The earliest known fossil stages in the evolution of the oral cavity and jaws. American Journal of Orthodontics and Oral Surgery, 29:253–76.

Presentation of the Daniel Giraud Elliot medal for 1935 with accompanying Honorarium of $200, to Edwin H. Colbert. Science, 97:433–34.

Environment and locomotion in mammals. Nat. Hist., 51:222–27, 244.

With G. M. Conrad. The osteology of *Luvarus imperialis,* a scombroid fish: a study in adaptive evolution. Bull. Am. Mus. Nat. Hist., 81:225–83.

Is evolution through cooperation enough? Nat. Hist., 52:97.

1944

By H. F. Osborn, revised to 1943 by W. K. Gregory and G. Pinkley. *The hall of the age of man.* Am. Mus. Nat. Hist. Sci. Guide, no. 52, 8th ed. 48 pp.

Australia—the story of a continent. Nat. Hist., 53:360–70, 374, 384.

(Obituary of) Sir Arthur Smith Woodward. News Bull. Soc. Vertebr. Paleontol., 13:11–12.

1945

With F. Weidenreich and J. E. Hill. (Obituary of) Henry Cushier Raven, 1889–1944. Anat. Rec., 92:315–16.

With M. Hellman. Revised reconstruction of the skull of *Plesianthropus transvaalensis* Broom. Am. J. Phys. Anthropol., 3: 267–275.

1946

Award of the Daniel Giraud Elliot Medal (for 1941, to Dr. Theodosius Dobzhansky). Am. Nat., 80:27–29.

With H. C. Raven. Adaptive branching of the kangaroo family in relation to habitat. Am. Mus. Novit., no. 1309, 33 pp.

Pareiasaurs versus placodonts as near ancestors to the turtles. Bull. Am. Mus. Nat. Hist., 86:275–326.

Some critical phylogenetic steps leading to the flight of birds. Proc. Linn. Soc. N.Y., nos. 54–57, pp. 1–15.

"Cat's-eyes" explained. Nat. Hist., 55:310–12.

The roles of motile larvae and fixed adults in the origin of the vertebrates. Q. Rev. Biol., 21:348–64.

1947

The monotremes and the palimpsest theory. Bull. Am. Mus. Nat. Hist., 88:1–52.

With F. LaMonte. *The world of fishes.* Am. Mus. Nat. Hist. Guide Leafl. Ser., no. 122, pp. 1–96.

Minute on the life and scientific labors of Amadeus William Grabau (1870–1946). The Grabau Memorial Volume. Bull. Geol. Soc. China, Nanking, 27:31–34.

1948

Milo Hellman's studies on the evolution of the teeth, jaws, and face. Am. J. Orthod., 34:53–60.

The evolution of some orthodontic systems in nature. Am. J. Orthod., 34:215–34.

Frank Michler Chapman (1864–1945). National Academy of Sciences, *Biographical Memoirs,* 25:111–45. New York, Columbia University Press.

(Obituary of) Milo Hellman (1872–1947): An appraisal of his unifying influence in anthropology, odontology and orthodontia. Am. J. Phys. Anthropol., 6:133–42.

William Letchworth Bryant (1871–1947). In: Am. Philos. Soc. Yearb., 1947, pp. 238–40. Philadelphia, American Philosophical Society.

John Eric Hill (1907–1947). Proceedings of the American Association of Anatomists, 61st Session. Anat. Rec., 101:420.

The significance of the Broom collection of South African fossil vertebrates in the American Museum of Natural History, New York. In: *Robert Broom Commemorative Volume.* Special Publication, Royal Society of South Africa, pp. 17–27. Cape Town, Royal Society of South Africa.

1949

The bearing of the Australopithecinae upon the problem of man's place in nature. Am. J. Phys. Anthropol., 7:485–512.

Franz Weidenreich, 1873–1948. Am. Anthropol., 51:85–90; News Bull. Soc. Vertebr. Paleontol., no. 25, pp. 28–29.

The humerus from fish to man. Am. Mus. Novit., no. 1400, 54 pp.

The bearing of the Australopithecinae upon the problems of man's place in nature. In: *Ideas on Human Evolution,* ed. by William Howells, pp. 105–27. Cambridge, Harvard University Press.

1950

Henry Cushier Raven (1889–1944). In: *The Anatomy of the Gorilla,* by H. C. Raven and others, pp. 1–9. New York, Columbia University Press.

Parallel and diverging skeletal evolution in vertebrates and arthropods. Evolution, 4:164–71.

1951

Evolution Emerging. A Survey of Changing Patterns from Primeval Life to Man. New York, Macmillan Inc. Vol. 1, xxvi + 736 pp.; vol. 2, viii + 1013 pp.

1952

Some critical stages in the evolution of the human back. Am. J. Phys. Anthropol., 10:250. (A)

1955

Pierre Teilhard de Chardin, 1881–1955. News Bull. Soc. Vertebr. Paleontol., no. 44, p. 39.

1958

On interacting casual networks converging towards observed results in evolution. In: *Studies on Fossil Vertebrates,* ed. by T. S. Westoll, pp. 59–70. London, The Athlone Press.

1959

Fish Skulls: A Study of the Evolution of Natural Mechanisms. Laurel, Florida, Eric Lundberg. i–viii, 75–481.

1963

Our Face from Fish to Man. Reprint of 1929 ed. New York, Hafner Publishing Co., Inc. xl + 295 pp.

1965

Our Face from Fish to Man. Reprint of 1929 ed. New York, Capricorn Books. xl + 295 pp.

Donald F. Jones

DONALD FORSHA JONES

April 16, 1890–June 19, 1963

BY PAUL C. MANGELSDORF

IF THERE were a Nobel prize in agriculture as there is in medicine, it would undoubtedly have been awarded many years
ago to Donald F. Jones for his part in the development of hybrid corn.* This is an achievement in applied genetics that has
sparked an agricultural revolution in the United States. It has
affected agricultural production in many other parts of the
world as well, including the countries of Latin America, where
corn is the principal source of food, and those of southern
Europe, where corn is an important crop. To this monumental
achievement Dr. Jones made four distinct contributions.

Jones's most practical contribution was the invention in
1917 of the double-cross method of hybrid seed production.
George H. Shull had shown previously that self-pollination in
corn, a naturally cross-pollinated plant, resulted in the isolation
of inbred strains that were uniform and true breeding. Following Johanssen, he called these "pure lines." They were much
less vigorous than the open-pollinated varieties from which they
had been derived. However, when two such lines were crossed,
the F_1 hybrids were uniform, like their inbred parents, but
much more vigorous and in some cases more productive than

* Since this was written, a notable contribution to agriculture has been
recognized by the award in 1970 of the Nobel Peace Prize to Dr. Norman E.
Borlaug for his work on the breeding of highly productive new dwarf varieties
of wheat for the underdeveloped regions of the globe.

the original open-pollinated varieties. Shull recognized that he had discovered a revolutionary new method of corn breeding, and he made determined efforts to persuade agronomists to adopt and practice it, but with little success. Shull's method of crossing two inbred strains had one serious shortcoming: The hybrid seed was borne on the weak, unproductive plants of the inbred strains used as the female parents. Since production was low, the hybrid seed was costly—too expensive for the average farmer to afford. Edward M. East, who independently of Shull, had observed the effects of inbreeding and crossbreeding in corn, doubted that the crossing of inbred strains to produce hybrid seed would ever become practical.

East, who had participated for several years in the famous experiments at the University of Illinois on selection for chemical composition of corn, initiated a corn-breeding program at the Connecticut Agricultural Experiment Station in New Haven in 1905. When East moved to the Bussey Institution of Harvard as a professor in 1909 he was succeeded by Herbert K. Hayes, who had been his assistant in New Haven and later became his graduate student at Harvard. When Hayes accepted a position at Minnesota, Jones, then a graduate student at Harvard, took charge under East's direction of the Connecticut corn program. He moved to New Haven early in 1915.

During his first year at New Haven Jones did little more than maintain the experiments that East and Hayes had initiated. But later, impressed by the weakness of the inbred strains and their feeble production of grain and by the vigorous production of their single crosses, he decided to try crossing two of the single crosses. Thus in 1917 he crossed the single cross of two strains of Chester's Leaming with a single cross of two strains of Burr White. Grown in 1918 this cross, which later came to be known as a "double cross," yielded more than either of its single-cross parents and considerably more than the best open-pollinated varieties.

Jones recognized that double crosses offered a means of producing hybrid seed corn at a cost within the means of progressive farmers. This fact was then quickly recognized by other corn breeders, including Henry Wallace, H. K. Hayes, and F. D. Richey. Within a few years corn-breeding programs, including the isolation of inbred strains and testing of single and double crosses, had been initiated by the U.S. Department of Agriculture and many of the state experiment stations. By 1933 hybrid corn was in commercial production on a substantial scale, and the USDA began to collect statistics on it. By 1949, 78 percent of the total U.S. corn acreage was planted in hybrid corn. By 1959, more than 95 percent was in hybrid corn, and the average yield of corn in the United States was double that of 1929.

Ironically, it turns out that Jones was not the first to make double crosses in corn. At the Heterosis Conference held in Ames, Iowa, in 1950 Shull reported that he had made a number of such crosses in 1910 and grown the hybrids in 1911. One of these crosses yielded considerably more than any of the single crosses. Shull, however, apparently saw no particular significance in the fact at that time; in 1950 he asked no credit for making double crosses before Jones and reported it only as a historical fact.

Ironically, too, once the use of double crosses established the production of hybrid corn on a highly successful scale, corn breeders found that, by developing more vigorous inbred strains than those isolated by Shull, East, and Jones, it was possible to employ single crosses instead of double crosses in the production of hybrid seed corn. Today much of the hybrid corn in the United States is represented either by single crosses or by three-way crosses, the latter being crosses of single crosses by inbred strains.

It is obvious that hybrid corn, which has revolutionized the production of corn in the United States and other parts of the world, is a method of exploiting hybrid vigor or heterosis. Thus heterosis must be considered, along with replication of the hereditary material (DNA) and photosynthesis, one of the three principal biological phenomena underlying the practice of agriculture. What, then, is the genetic basis of heterosis?

In the same year, 1917, that Jones made his first double cross, which solved the problem of hybrid seed corn production, he published a theory explaining the phenomenon of heterosis. He was at that time twenty-seven years old. Jones's theory applied the concept of chromosomal linkage of Morgan and his students to the earlier concrete explanation of hybrid vigor by Keeble and Pellew. These last two had explained the increased height of a cross of two varieties of peas over their parents in Mendelian terms. It was linkage that explained why it was not possible to combine in one race the favorable dominant factors of both parents.

Jones's theory probably gave as much stimulus to hybrid corn breeding as did his double-cross method of seed production. Hybrid corn became a practical reality when his method of seed production made it feasible and his theory of heterosis made it plausible. This combination was difficult for even the most conservative agronomists to resist. Seldom in the history of agriculture has one man made two such significant contributions, one in theory and the other in practice.

A third contribution to hybrid corn production was one in which I had the privilege of participating. It involves a method of employing cytoplasmic male sterility, of a type first described in corn by Marcus M. Rhoades, to avoid the operation of emasculation, commonly known as "detasseling," in the seed-production fields. Detasseling has been called the "peskiest and most expensive part of producing hybrid seed corn." Before cytoplasmic sterility was employed to avoid it, some one hundred and twenty-five thousand workers were engaged on the peak day of the season in removing tassels from corn plants.

By employing cytoplasmic male sterility, it was possible to eliminate as much as two thirds of the detasseling operation. To ensure fertility in the farmer's crop, sterile hybrids were mixed with fertile hybrids, involving the same inbred strains, produced in the conventional way.

Jones made still another contribution to hybrid corn production when he employed fertility-restoring genes to overcome the cytoplasmic sterility in the farmer's crop. This method employs hereditary factors in the cytoplasm to make corn sterile when sterility is a distinct asset and uses hereditary factors on the chromosomes to make it fertile when fertility is essential. A patent on the method of using genetic restorers in hybrid-seed-corn production was issued to Jones in 1956. It was the first patent on a genetic technique to be granted in the United States. The validity of the patent was challenged by the seed corn industry, but finally, after long and extensive litigation, an amicable agreement was reached: The patent's validity was generally accepted, and royalties on its use were paid.

For many years the method of employing cytoplasmic male sterility to avoid the operation of detasseling and using fertility-restoring genes to overcome this sterility in the farmer's crop was phenomenally successful. It not only drastically reduced the labor required in producing hybrid seed but also eliminated the reduction in yield of hybrid seed caused by the removal of one or more leaves in the detasseling operation. The method has probably been a factor also in making possible on an extensive scale the replacement of double crosses by higher-yielding single crosses. There is a danger—susceptibility to plant diseases—inherent in growing these genetically uniform hybrids, as Jones pointed out in an article in *American Naturalist* in 1958. But their use, combined with increased applications of fertilizer, to which the new hybrids were responsive, has undoubtedly contributed to the spectacular increase in average yields in the decade 1959–1969. This is shown in the following table, which also demonstrates the remarkable progress that has occurred between 1929 and 1969 in increasing yields of corn in the United States.

Acre Yields of Corn in the United States

Year	Percent Hybrid Corn	Bushels per Acre	Percent Increase over Previous Decade
1929	0	25.7	
1939	22.9	29.7	16
1949	78.3	37.8	27
1959	94.8	51.5	36
1969	99+	80.0	55

Eventually, however, the method became, at least for several years, the victim of its own success. In 1969 there were reports that corn hybrids carrying the Texas cytoplasmic male sterility, the type almost universally employed, were becoming susceptible to the southern corn blight fungus, *Helminthosporium maydis*. Since susceptibility to a disease determined by the cytoplasm had never previously been observed in the United States, these reports were met with skepticism on the part of some plant pathologists. In 1970, however, the blight, apparently a new mutant strain, spread over the entire eastern half of the United States. It caused a reduction in corn yields for the country as a whole of about 13 percent. Many fields in the southern states, where the infection occurred early in the season, suffered losses of 50 percent or more. Single and three-way crosses suffered greater damage from the blight than double crosses, as Jones some twenty years earlier had warned that they would when faced with a new hazard. The use of fertility-restoring genes proved not to be a factor in the susceptibility of corn hybrids to the blight. As soon as other types of cytoplasmic male sterility can be introduced into commercial hybrids, it is probable that the method will again be commonly employed.

In the meantime the blight, despite its destructive effects on the 1970 corn crop, has had one beneficial result. It has focused new attention on the importance of genetic diversity in the world's major food crops. The new dwarf varieties of wheat and rice that are revolutionizing the agriculture of underdeveloped countries have, in the case of each of these crops, dwarfing genes in common, although they are diverse in their remaining heredity. These common genetic loci may, like the universally used cytoplasmic male sterility in corn, become susceptible to new mutant pathogens with disastrous results in countries and regions already overpopulated. Recognizing this danger, the National Academy of Sciences in 1970 came forward with a proposal to study not only the problem of the corn blight, but also the genetic vulnerability of major food crops in general. The study was financed in large part by Research Corporation, to which Dr. Jones assigned his patent on the use of fertility-restoring genes, and with particular appropriateness by the Donald F. Jones Fund, which represents the corporation's share of the net proceeds from the Jones patent. The results of this study, published in 1972 in a volume entitled *Genetic Vulnerability of Major Crops,* emphasized the fact that "most major crops are impressively uniform and impressively vulnerable." Thus Donald F. Jones has left a heritage that continues to affect in tangible ways the course of applied genetics to which, while living, he made such notable contributions.

Jones's conviction that selection in self-fertilized lines is one of the most effective plant breeding methods that can be practiced in cross-pollinated plants, and his interest in exploiting heterosis was not confined to corn. During the period from 1921 to 1926, when I served as his assistant, he undertook breeding programs in numerous field and horticultural crops, including such diverse crops as alfalfa and asparagus, and strawberries and squashes. Later, when it became apparent that the use of cytoplasmic sterility in corn was becoming a resounding success, he encouraged breeders of other field crops to search for forms of cytoplasmic male sterility in the species to which they were giving attention. The success of hybrid corn also led to the exploitation of hybrid vigor in animals, especially chickens, pigs, and cattle.

Jones's research was by no means confined to practical plant breeding. His interest in theoretical genetics was as keen as his concern with crop improvement. I have mentioned his theory of heterosis. For a number of years he studied and wrote extensively on somatic segregation, especially in its relation to various kinds of atypical growths. Another subject to which he gave attention was sex differentiation in maize and other plants. In this connection he succeeded in converting maize—which is normally monoecious, having both sexes on the same plant, into a dioecious form having the two sexes on separate plants. From this he concluded that monoecism may be an intermediate step between perfect flowers and dioecism.

Donald Forsha Jones was born near Hutchinson, Kansas, on April 16, 1890. He was the second of four children of Oliver Winslow Jones and Minnie Wilcox Bush Jones. Both parents were descendants of New England families. The Winslow in Jones's father's name traces back to Kenelm Winslow, who came to Plymouth, Massachusetts, in 1629. His maternal ancestors were among the early settlers who founded Hartford, Connecticut. Jones, in one biographical sketch, has been aptly called "a Yankee from Kansas."

At the time of their marriage both parents were schoolteachers. The family subsequently moved to Mulvane, Kansas, and later to Wichita, where the father continued as a teacher and a school principal. Their home, a small farm on the outskirts of Wichita, had ample space for gardening and for a horse, a cow, a pig, and a flock of chickens. Donald and his older brother, Kenneth, later a professor at Northwestern University Medical School, had a newspaper delivery route for several years that required their getting up before daylight, hitching the horse to the buggy, and completing their deliveries in time to have breakfast at home. The family garden became Donald's special responsibility, and he tried to grow some of virtually everything. His boyhood interest in gardening was to persist throughout his life. He was an ardent and talented gardener. Even after a day's work in the experimental corn field during the summer months he was not too tired to spend the evening in his own garden. His gardening included a wide variety of vegetables, small fruits, and ornamentals, all of which responded to his gardening skill. Many of the popular articles on horticulture that he wrote were based on his own firsthand gardening experience.

After completing his secondary school education, Jones attended Kansas State Agricultural College, where he majored in horticulture. His college years apparently were neither particularly inspiring nor enjoyable, and he was not regarded as an outstanding student. However, one of the honors that he cherished most in his later years was an honorary degree, Doctor of Science, awarded to him in 1947 by his alma mater.

Graduating from college in 1911, he took a position at the Arizona Experiment Station, where one of his principal jobs was pollinating alfalfa flowers in a breeding program. He once spoke disparagingly of his role in this position as "taking the place of the bumble bee." While there he read the recently published bulletin by East and Hayes, "Heterozygosis in Evolution and Plant Breeding." Having already observed the effects of inbreeding on alfalfa, he found this publication of unusual interest, and he wrote to East inquiring about the possibility of doing graduate work at Harvard under East's direction. In the meantime, however, he took a position at Syracuse University, where he spent the year 1913–1914 teaching and working toward the master's degree. He enrolled as a graduate student at Harvard in the fall of 1914. In February 1915 he moved to New Haven to take charge under East's supervision of the plant-breeding program, which had been initiated by East in 1905 at the Connecticut station. For the next several years he divided his time between New Haven and Cambridge

Jones remained at the Connecticut Agricultural Experiment Station for the rest of his professional life, and this continuity of effort was undoubtedly one factor in his lifelong productiveness in research and publication. His technical scientific publications cover a period from 1915 to ·964 and include approximately one hundred titles. In addition he wrote many popular and semipopular articles covering a wide variety of subjects for the farm and garden press. When I joined him as a graduate assistant in 1921, he advised me also to write for these media, partly in the interest of informing the general public on new developments in agricultural science and partly as practical experience in writing, which for me it proved indeed to be.

An inveterate reader as well as a prolific writer, Jones, during the winter months, usually spent his mornings writing and reading scientific literature. His evenings at home, except during the summer when he worked in his garden until darkness, were most commonly spent in reading. Among his favorite subjects were biography and history. Even his luncheon periods were devoted partly to reading. Alternating in reading aloud to each other, he and I, in the years between 1921 and 1926, went through various works, including Darwin's *Voyage of the Beagle*.

One of the most unusual aspects of Jones's career was his close and congenial collaboration for a number of years with Edward M. East, his graduate-school mentor. The two men were quite different in temperament. Henry Wallace once described East as "sardonic, explosive, genial, intolerant, charming, stimulating." Jones was modest, soft-spoken, patient, retiring, slow to anger, tolerant, and wise. What they did have in common were keen intellects, and each admired that of the other. When Jones proposed his theory of dominant-linked factors to account for heterosis, East was so impressed that he asked his student, then still in his twenties, to join him in writing the book that he had for several years been planning on the effects of inbreeding and crossbreeding. The product of their joint efforts, *Inbreeding and Outbreeding: Their Genetic and Sociological Significance,* is one of the classics in the history of genetics. A joint paper of East and Jones, "Genetic Studies on the Protein Content of Maize," published in 1917, showed how effective selection in self-fertilized lines can be in changing the characteristics of a population. This paper was also one of the first to describe a method of breeding now known as "recurrent selection." The method has proved to be quite effective, not only in changing chemical composition but also in improving the combining ability of inbred strains. Both men were intellectually stimulating. I have always counted it rare good fortune to have had both as mentors, one in my work as a graduate assistant and the other in my graduate studies.

Like many another Yankee, Jones was almost instinctively inventive. His inventions ranged from the double cross, which made the production of hybrid seed corn practical, to innumerable small devices around his laboratory and home. One of his students once remarked that if a rootless corn plant were to turn up in his cultures, Jones would find some good use for it. This he never did, but he found an immensely practical use for cytoplasmic male sterility and for the genetic fertility-restoring factors. The latter had been in part responsible for the failure of a number of earlier corn breeders to make use of cytoplasmic sterility in avoiding detasseling.

Also from the program in applied genetics that Jones directed for some forty years came one of the important recent developments in corn improvement, the breeding of high-lysine hybrid corns. This development owes its beginning to a mutant, *opaque-2*, that affects the composition of the endosperm. Dr. Jones's associate, Dr. Ralph Singleton, had found the mutant in a New England variety of white flint corn in the early 1920s and had determined its genetic linkage relations. Jones continued to maintain a stock of *opaque-2* in hopes that this unusual characteristic would some day prove useful. His hope was realized when one of his former students, Oliver Nelson of Purdue University, with his colleague Edwin Mertz, showed that the endosperm of *opaque-2* contains about twice as much lysine and tryptophan—amino acids in which maize is notoriously deficient—as normal corn. *Opaque-2* is now the subject of numerous breeding programs in the United States and the countries of Latin America to increase the useful protein content of maize. Already, nutritional trials in Colombia have shown that advanced cases of kwashiorkor in children can be cured with a diet in which the sole source of protein is *opaque-2*. Jones was indeed a man of many dreams with a remarkable ability to make his dreams come true.

An effective worker in advancing the science of genetics, Jones served in several capacities. Before the Genetics Society of America was organized, he was secretary of the Genetics Section sponsored jointly by the Botanical Society of America and the American Society of Zoologists. Later, in 1934, he was vice president of the Genetics Society and president in 1935. He was editor of the *Proceedings of the Sixth International Congress of Genetics*, held at Ithaca, New York, in 1932. He was the second editor of *Genetics* and served from 1926–1935, longer than any other editor except George H. Shull, its founder, and during the especially exciting period of genetic research when the chromosome theory of heredity was becoming firmly established.

In Jones's later years, in addition to his duties at the Connecticut Station, he was a lecturer in genetics at Yale University and at the University of Connecticut. He was Sprague Memorial Lecturer at Michigan State College in 1935; research fellow at California Institute of Technology in 1935–1936 and again in 1946–1947; and visiting professor at the University of Washington in 1953.

Jones was the recipient of many honors. He was elected to the American Academy of Arts and Sciences in 1934, to the National Academy of Sciences in 1939, and to honorary membership in the Societa Italiana Genetica Agraria in 1955. I have already mentioned the honorary degree that he received from his alma mater in 1947. The accompanying citation reads:

"As a major contributor to the development of hybrid corn . . . he has conferred immense benefits upon a hungry world. As research scientist, teacher, and leader in scientific societies, he has inspired his colleagues and students by . . . his extraordinary achievements . . ."

The New England Council and the Governors of New England made him a charter member of the "Fellowship of Agricultural Adventurers," saying that,

"with an imagination which delved below and soared above the findings of his predecessors, he translated the learning of the laboratory into the fruitfulness of the field."

He was awarded gold medals by the Massachusetts Horticultural Society and the American Farm Bureau. In addition he was given awards by the Connecticut State Confederation of Women's Clubs, the American Seed Trade Association, the Connecticut State Grange, the New York Farmers' Club, and the Botanical Society of America.

Dr. Jones died at his home in Hamden, Connecticut, on June 19, 1963. He is survived by his wife, Eleanor March Jones, a son, Loring M. Jones, and a daughter, Mrs. Margaret Owen.

BIBLIOGRAPHY

Prepared by Carolyn A. Staehly

KEY TO ABBREVIATIONS

Am. J. Bot. = American Journal of Botany
Am. Nat. = American Naturalist
Biol. Bull. = Biological Bulletin
Bot. Gaz. = Botanical Gazette
Conn. Agric. Exp. Stn. Bull. = Connecticut Agricultural Experiment Station Bulletin
Conn. Agric. Exp. Stn. Circ. = Connecticut Agricultural Experiment Station Circular
Conn. Agric. Exp. Stn. Rep. = Connecticut Agricultural Experiment Station Report
J. Am. Soc. Agron. = Journal of the American Society of Agronomy
J. Hered. = Journal of Heredity
Proc. Natl. Acad. Sci. = Proceedings of the National Academy of Sciences
Proc. ——— Int. Congr. Genet. = Proceedings of the ——— International Congress of Genetics
Sci. Mon. = Scientific Monthly
Seventh Int. Manage. Congr. = Seventh International Management Congress

1915

Illustration of inbreeding. Maize self–pollinated for three generations produces one-fourth albino plants—abnormality isolated and bred out of part of the stock. J. Hered., 6:477–79.

1916

With S. L. Mason. Inheritance of congenital cataract. Am. Nat., 50:119–26.

With S. L. Mason. Further remarks on the inheritance of congenital cataract. Am. Nat., 50:751–57.

Natural cross-pollination in the tomato. Science, 43:509–10.

With H. K. Hayes. The effects of cross- and self-fertilization in tomatoes. Conn. Agric. Exp. Stn. Rep., 1916, pp. 305–18.

With H. K. Hayes. First generation crosses in cucumbers. Conn. Agric. Exp. Stn. Rep., 1916, pp. 319–22.

With H. K. Hayes, W. L. Slate, Jr., and B. G. Southwick. Increasing the yield of corn by crossing. Conn. Agric. Exp. Stn. Rep., 1916, pp. 323–47.

With H. K. Hayes. The purification of soy bean varieties. Conn. Agric. Exp. Stn. Rep., 1916, pp. 348–53.

1917

Linkage in *Lycopersicum*. Am. Nat., 51:608–21.

Dominance of linked factors as a means of accounting for heterosis. Proc. Natl. Acad. Sci., 3:310–12.

Dominance of linked factors as a means of accounting for heterosis. Genetics, 2:466–79.

1918

The effect of inbreeding and crossbreeding upon development. Proc. Natl. Acad. Sci., 4:246–50.

The effects of inbreeding and crossbreeding upon development. Conn. Agric. Exp. Stn. Bull. 207. 100 pp.

Bearing of heterosis upon double fertilization. Bot. Gaz., 65:324–33.

Segregation of susceptibility to parasitism in maize. Am. J. Bot., 5:295–300.

Review of *Plant Genetics* by J. M. Coulter and M. C. Coulter, University of Chicago Press, 214 pp. Science, 48:346–47.

1919

With C. A. Gallastegui. Some factor relations in maize with reference to linkage. Am. Nat., 53:239–46.

Selection of pseudo-starchy endosperm in maize. Genetics, 4:364–93.

With E. M. East. *Inbreeding and Outbreeding: Their Genetic and Sociological Significance.* Philadelphia, J. B. Lippincott Co. 285 pp.

Hybrid vigor and its meaning. Scientific American, 121:230–31, 239–41.

1920

With W. O. Filley. Teas' hybrid catalpa. J. Hered., 11:16–24.

A paraffine ruler for drawing curves. Science, 51:245.

Selection in self-fertilized lines as the basis for corn improvement. J. Am. Soc. Agron., 12:77–100.

Heritable characters of maize. IV. A lethal factor—defective seeds. J. Hered., 11:161–67.

Selective fertilization in pollen mixtures. Biol. Bull., 38:251–89.

With E. M. East. Genetic studies on the protein content of maize. Genetics, 5:543–610.

Sterility in animals and plants.   Hereditary lethal factors which stop development when received from both parents.   Scientific American Monthly, 2:117–19.

1921

With E. M. East.   Round Tip tobacco—a plant "made to order." J. Hered., 12:51–56.

Connecticut Round Tip tobacco—a new type of wrapper leaf. Conn. Agric. Exp. Stn. Bull. 228, pp. 285–92.

The indeterminate growth factor in tobacco and its effect upon development.   Genetics, 6:433–44.

Collins's remarks on the vigor of first generation hybrids.   Am. Nat., 55:457–61.

Meeting of the geneticists interested in agriculture.   Science, 53: 429–31.

1922

Hybridization in plant and animal improvement.   Sci. Mon., 14: 5–23.

Selective fertilization as an indicator of germinal differences.   Science, 55:348–49.

Indirect evidence from duplex hybrids bearing upon the number and distribution of growth factors in the chromosomes.   Am. Nat., 56:166–73.

The productiveness of single and double first generation corn hybrids.   J. Am. Soc. Agron., 14:242–52.

Selective fertilization and the rate of pollen–tube growth.   Biol. Bull., 43:167–74.

1923

Review of *The Outline of Genetics, with Special Reference to Plant Material,* by M. C. Coulter, University of Chicago Press.   Bot. Gaz., 75:427–28.

1924

Selective fertilization among the gametes from the same individuals. Proc. Natl. Acad. Sci., 10:218–21.

With W. L. Slate, Jr. and B. A. Brown.   Corn in Connecticut. Conn. Agric. Exp. Stn. Bull. 259, pp. 381–470; also as Storrs (Conn.) Agric. Exp. Stn. Bull. 124, pp. 307–96.

Methods of seed corn production being revised. J. Hered., 15: 291–98.

The attainment of homozygosity in inbred strains of maize. Genetics, 9:405–18.

The origin of flint and dent corn. J. Hered., 15:417–19.

1925

With P. C. Mangelsdorf. The improvement of naturally cross-pollinated plants by selection in self-fertilized lines. I. The production of inbred strains of corn. Conn. Agric. Exp. Stn. Bull. 266, pp. 345–418.

Heritable characters of maize. XXIII. Silkless. J. Hered., 16: 339–41.

Genetics in Plant and Animal Improvement. The Wiley Agricultural Series. New York, John Wiley & Sons, Inc. 568 pp.

1926

With P. C. Mangelsdorf. Crossed corn. Conn. Agric. Exp. Stn. Bull. 273, pp. 151–87.

Hybrid vigor and tumors in mice. Am. Nat., 60:482–84.

With P. C. Mangelsdorf. The expression of Mendelian factors in the gametophyte of maize. Genetics, 11:423–55.

1927

Manifestations of impotence in a plant propagated by seed. Memoirs of the Horticultural Society of New York, 3:299–303.

1928

Like father like son-in-law. Sci. Mon., 26:557–60.

Burbank's results with plums. J. Hered., 19:359–71.

Selective Fertilization. Chicago, University of Chicago Press. 163 pp.

1930

With W. R. Singleton. Canada–Leaming corn. Conn. Agric. Exp. Stn. Bull. 310, pp. 185–95.

With W. R. Singleton. Heritable characters of maize. XXXV. Male sterile. J. Hered., 21:266–68.

1931

With W. R. Singleton. Spanish Gold early yellow sweet corn. Conn. Agric. Exp. Stn. Circ. 75, pp. 23–30.

Dioecious maize. Science, 73:432.

With L. C. Curtis. Testing vegetables for Connecticut. Results for 1931. Conn. Agric. Exp. Stn. Circ. 82, pp. 13–24.

Efforts to increase food resources. In: *Biology in Human Affairs,* ed. by E. M. East, pp. 318–63. New York, McGraw–Hill Book Co.

1932

The interaction of specific genes determining sex in dioecious maize. Proc. 6th Int. Congr. Genet., 2:104–7.

Editor. Proc. 6th Int. Congr. Genet., vols. 1 & 2.

1934

Unisexual maize plants and their relation to dioecism in other organisms. Proc. Natl. Acad. Sci., 20:39–41.

Unisexual maize plants and their bearing on sex differentiation in other plants and in animals. Genetics, 19:552–67.

With W. R. Singleton. Crossed sweet corn. Conn. Agric. Exp. Stn. Bull. 361, pp. 487–536.

1935

The similarity between fasciations in plants and tumors in animals and their genetic basis. Science, 81:75–76.

With W. R. Singleton. The improvement of naturally cross-pollinated plants by selection in self-fertilized lines. II. The testing and utilization of inbred strains of corn. Conn. Agric. Exp. Stn. Bull. 376, pp. 649–91.

Somatic segregation due to hemizygous and missing genes and its bearing on the problem of atypical growth. Proc. Natl. Acad. Sci., 21:90–96.

With W. R. Singleton and L. C. Curtis. The correlation between tillering and productiveness in sweet corn crosses. J. Am. Soc. Agron., 27:138–41.

With E. Huntington. The adaptation of corn to climate. J. Am. Soc. Agron., 27:261–70.

A multiple mosaic in maize. J. Hered., 26:191–92.

With E. Huntington. Further comments on adaptation of corn to climate. J. Am. Soc. Agron., 27:682–83.

1936

Segregation of color and growth-regulating genes in somatic tissue of maize. Proc. Natl. Acad. Sci., 22:163–66.

Tumors in *Drosophila melanogaster* resulting from somatic segregation. Science, 84:135.

Mutation rate in somatic cells of maize. Proc. Natl. Acad. Sci., 22:645–48.

Atypical growth. Am. Nat., 70:86–92.

With W. R. Singleton. Sweet corn inbreds. Conn. Agric. Exp. Stn. Circ. 112, pp. 49–58.

1937

Somatic segregation in relation to atypical growth. Proceedings of the American Philosophical Society, 77:411–16.

Somatic segregation and its relation to atypical growth. Genetics, 22:484–522.

The life and work of Luther Burbank. Spragg Memorial Lectures on Plant Breeding, Michigan State College, East Lansing, Michigan, pp. 57–76.

1938

Crops and forests: their production, protection and use. Seventh Int. Manage. Congr., Washington, D.C. Agriculture Section, Session II, pp. 25a and 25b. (A critique prepared by D. F. Jones, Rapporteur)

Utilization of plant resources. Seventh Int. Manage. Congr., Washington, D.C. Agriculture Section, Session II, pp. 27–29.

Translocation in relation to mosaic formation in maize. Proc. Natl. Acad. Sci., 24:208–11.

Nuclear control of cell activity. Science, 88:400–401.

1939

Sex intergrades in dioecious maize. Am. J. Bot., 26:412–15.

Continued inbreeding in maize. Genetics, 24:462–73; Russian translation, IArovizatsiià, 2:23–32, 1940.

With W. R. Singleton. The Shelton and Hebron strawberries. Conn. Agric. Exp. Stn. Circ. 137. 4 pp.

With W. R. Singleton. Early sweet corn hybrids—Spancross, Marcross, and Carmelcross. Conn. Agric. Exp. Stn. Circ. 138, pp. 5–11.

1940

Nuclear changes affecting growth. Am. J. Bot., 27:149–55.

With W. R. Singleton. The improvement of naturally cross-pollinated plants by selection in self–fertilized lines. III. Investigations with vegetatively propagated fruits. Conn. Agric. Exp. Stn. Bull. 435, pp. 325–47.

1941

Somatic segregation. Botanical Review, 7:291–307.

An investigation of growth in plants. Science, 93:40.

Natural and induced changes in chromosome structure in maize endosperm. Proc. Natl. Acad. Sci., 27:431–35.

With W. R. Singleton. Sweet corn hybrids—Lexington, Lincoln and Lee. Conn. Agric. Exp. Stn. Circ. 148, pp. 45–51.

1942

Chromosome degeneration in relation to growth and hybrid vigor. Proc. Natl. Acad. Sci., 28:38–44.

1943

Review of *Producer of Better Fruits and Fairer Flowers (Luther Burbank—Plant Magician)*. Journal of the New York Botanical Garden, 44:286–87.

Chromosome degeneration. J. Hered., 34:104.

1944

Equilibrium .in genic materials. Proc. Natl. Acad. Sci., 30:82–87.

Growth changes in maize endosperm associated with the relocation of chromosome parts. Genetics, 29:420–27.

1945

Edward Murray East (1879–1938). In: National Academy of Sciences, *Biographical Memoirs*, 23:217–42.

Heterosis resulting from degenerative changes. Genetics, 30:527–42.

The importance of degenerative changes in living organisms. Science, 102:209.

With W. R. Singleton and O. E. Nelson, Jr. The improvement of naturally cross-pollinated plants by selection in self-fertilized lines. IV. Combining ability of successive generations of inbred sweet corn. Conn. Agric. Exp. Stn. Bull. 490, pp. 453–98.

1947

Effect of temperature on the growth and sterility of maize. Science, 105:390–91.

The nature of gene action as shown by cell-limited and cell-diffusible gene products. Proc. Natl. Acad. Sci., 33:363–65.

1948

Induced and naturally occurring mutations. In: Proceedings, Auburn Conference on the Use of Radio-active Isotopes in Agricultural Research, 1:120–23. Alabama Polytechnic Institute.

With W. R. Singleton and H. L. Everett. Sweet-dent silage. Conn. Agric. Exp. Stn. Circ. 165. 14 pp.

1949

With H. L. Everett. Hybrid field corn. Conn. Agric. Exp. Stn. Bull. 532. 39 pp.

1950

The interrelation of plasmagenes and chromogenes in pollen production in maize. Genetics, 35:507–12.

1951

The cytoplasmic separation of species. Proc. Natl. Acad. Sci., 37:408–10.

With P. C. Mangelsdorf. The production of hybrid corn seed without detasseling. Conn. Agric. Exp. Stn. Bull. 550. 21 pp.

The induction of cytoplasmic pollen sterility and the restoration of fertility in maize. Genetics, 36:557(A).

1952

Plasmagenes and chromogenes in heterosis. In: *Heterosis,* ed. by John W. Gowen, pp. 224–35. Ames, Iowa State College Press.

1954

Gene and cytoplasm interaction in species separation. Proc. 9th Int. Congr. Genet., pp. 1225–27. Caryologia. Vol. VI, Suppl.

1956

Genic and cytoplasmic control of pollen abortion in maize. In: *Genetics in Plant Breeding,* Brookhaven Symposia in Biology, 9:101–12.

1957

Gene action in heterosis. Genetics, 42:93–103.

With H. T. Stinson, Jr. and U. Khoo. Transmissible variations in the cytoplasm within species of higher plants. Proc. Natl. Acad. Sci., 43:598–602.

With H. T. Stinson, Jr. and U. Khoo. Pollen restoring genes. Conn. Agric. Exp. Stn. Bull. 610. 43 pp.

1958

Heterosis and homeostasis in evolution and in applied genetics. Am. Nat., 92:321–28.

1959

Basic research in plant and animal improvement. Proc. 10th Int. Congr. Genet., 1:172–76.

1960

The genotype as the sum of plasmatype and chromotype. Am. Nat., 94:181–83.

Remington Kellogg

REMINGTON KELLOGG

October 5, 1892–May 8, 1969

BY FRANK C. WHITMORE, JR.

WITH BIBLIOGRAPHY COMPILED BY JANE KNAPP

REMINGTON KELLOGG, retired assistant secretary of the Smithsonian Institution and director of the United States National Museum, died of a heart attack on May 8, 1969, in his seventy-seventh year, at his home in Washington, D.C. He had been recuperating from a broken pelvis suffered in a fall on the ice the previous January, but, except for this period, he had been constantly and productively engaged in research at the national museum for more than forty-nine years. Retirement, which came in 1962, brought him welcome relief from administrative duties and an opportunity to intensify his study of fossil marine mammals. The years 1962 to 1969 were among his most productive.

Arthur Remington Kellogg, as he was christened (he early dropped "Arthur" from his name), was born in Davenport, Iowa, on October 5, 1892, the son of Clara Louise (Martin) and Rolla Remington Kellogg. He was descended from colonial stock on both sides of the family. One ancestor, Sergeant Joseph Kellogg, came from England in 1651, settling first in Farmington, Connecticut, and finally at Hadley, Massachusetts, in 1661. Sergeant Kellogg helped to defeat the Connecticut Indian tribes at Turner's Falls, Massachusetts, in 1676.

Kellogg's paternal grandfather taught Latin and Greek in high school in Davenport, Iowa. His father was a printer who

159

at one time or another was owner of several printing shops. Remington's mother was a school teacher before her marriage. The Kelloggs moved to Kansas City, Missouri, when Remington was six years old.

Of his early years Dr. Kellogg said, "I do not recall that I disliked any particular study. Westport High School in Kansas City was considered at the time to be an academic rather than a manual training high school. The courses given were in accordance with a regular schedule of four years of English, history, mathematics, science, and Latin. . . .

"From the fourth grade onward while attending public grade and high schools most of my spare time outside of school hours was devoted to studying wild life in the nearby woods, and by the time I graduated from grade school I had prepared a small collection of mounted birds and mammals."

Before completing his high school studies, Kellogg had decided to attend a university where there were natural history collections. This interest led him to the University of Kansas, the training ground for many famous naturalists. In order to save enough money for college, Remington found it necessary to find employment as a salesman in a dry-goods store, as a worker in the smokehouse of a packing plant, and as a cement worker on a construction crew. In his first years at the university he cooked his own meals and delivered papers. He sold trunks as a traveling salesman during the summer after freshman year. At the university he concentrated first in entomology; later he changed his field to mammals. From 1913 to 1916 he was a taxonomic assistant for mammals under Charles D. Bunker, curator of birds and mammals in the Museum of Natural History at the university. His first paper, published in 1914, resulted from this museum work. Bunker took Kellogg to his cabin, where he instructed him in skinning and preserving vertebrate specimens. In Kellogg's senior year, when an instructor died, he helped give a class in ornithology. He received his A.B. in January 1915 and his M.A. in 1916.

In Kellogg's freshman year there began a lifelong friendship with Alexander Wetmore. In 1911, Wetmore joined the Bureau of Biological Survey, U.S. Department of Agriculture, and helped Kellogg in getting summer jobs with the survey, conducting field surveys of plant and animal life in the West. The two men worked closely together for many years in the Smithsonian Institution, first as curators and later in administrative positions, when Wetmore was secretary of the Smithsonian and Kellogg was director of the United States National Museum. Another admired friend of undergraduate days was Edward A. Preble of the Biological Survey. Preble was an editor and frequent contributor to the magazine *Nature* (not to be confused with the British journal), then published in Washington, D.C. Among many wildlife monographs he published a study of the fur seals of the Pribilof Islands.

Immediately after graduation, in the winter of 1915–1916, Kellogg worked for the Biological Survey in southeastern Kansas and, in the following summer, in North Dakota. Of this assignment he said, "I remember the first year I went out to Wahpeton, North Dakota, the first day the chief of the survey took me out and we walked all over the area. Then he said, 'Well, I'm leaving. You know all about it.' From then on I was alone. I had to cover everything—plants and animals—and write a report. It didn't faze me a bit—I guess I didn't know any better."

While at the University of Kansas, Kellogg made his first acquaintance with marine mammals, in the form of skeletons of white whale, porpoise, walrus, and seal. In the fall of 1915, at the end of his summer's fieldwork, the Biological Survey paid his way to Washington, D. C. He made a tour of museums in the eastern United States, which undoubtedly gave him further opportunity to examine whales, pinnipeds, and sirenians. At about this time he made his decision to study the evolution of marine mammals, and in the fall of 1916 he entered the University of California at Berkeley to concentrate in zoology. At Berkeley, Kellogg met several men who became lifelong friends and in various ways influenced his professional growth. Perhaps the most revered of these was David Starr Jordan, ichthyologist and president of Stanford. Joseph Grinnell, director of the Museum of Vertebrate Zoology at the University of California, stimulated Kellogg's interest in ornithology. Chester Stock, a fellow graduate student and later professor of vertebrate paleontology at California Institute of Technology, shared many hours of discussion of evolution.

The most lasting influence resulting from the Berkeley years was that of John C. Merriam. Kellogg was given a teaching fellowship and was invited by Merriam to study the fossil record of the seals, sea lions, and walruses whose remains had been found in Pacific Coast Tertiary formations. This project resulted in Kellogg's first important papers on marine mammals (1921 and 1922), both dealing with fossil pinnipeds. With the thoroughness, coupled with deceptively modest titles, that was to characterize his published work throughout his career, the second of these, entitled "Pinnipeds from Miocene and Pleistocene Deposits of California," incorporated a critical review of the literature of fossil pinnipeds of the world. This work remains today the base upon which modern research on fossil pinnipeds begins.

In the summer of 1917, Kellogg again did fieldwork for the Biological Survey. He went to Montana and then to California, where he studied the *Microtus californicus* group of meadow mice. A monograph resulting from this work was published in 1918.

Graduate work was interrupted by service in World War I.

On December 11, 1917, Kellogg enlisted in the 20th Engineer Battalion at San Francisco, and on February 19, 1918, he sailed from Hoboken for France. By a stroke of luck for a naturalist, Kellogg was transferred in May 1918 to the Central Medical Department Laboratory at Dijon, where he was promoted to sergeant and found himself under the command of Major E. A. Goldman, one of the last of the general field naturalists. One of their major assignments was rat control in the trenches and at the base ports. During his service in France, Kellogg observed and collected birds and small mammals and sent collections to Joseph Grinnell at Berkeley and Charles D. Bunker at the University of Kansas. His notebook contains almost daily observations from November 17, 1918, to February 23, 1919. The climax of this period was a motor trip that he took between January 29 and February 23 with Major Goldman and Lt. A. C. Chandler from Dijon to Toul and "such other places in depts. of Meurthe-et-Moselle, Meuse, and Ardennes as is necessary to carry out instructions of Chief Surgeon, in connection with preparation of medical history of war." During the period of this reconnaissance, his notebook lists thirty species of birds and five of small mammals.

Upon his return to Berkeley, Kellogg gave a talk to the Northern Division of the Cooper Ornithological Club entitled "Experiences with Birds of France," and in 1919 he published, with Francis Harper, who had also been in the Army in France, a Christmas day bird census made at Is-sur-Tille in the Department of Côte d'Or, where the Army Medical Laboratory was situated.

In June 1919 Kellogg returned to the United States. He was discharged from the Army at Newport News, Virginia, on July 2 and returned immediately to Berkeley to complete the residence requirements for the Ph.D. He transferred from zoology to vertebrate paleontology under Merriam, resumed his teaching fellowship for a semester, and then, on January 1, 1920, was appointed assistant biologist in the Biological Survey, with headquarters in Washington, D. C.

While at Berkeley, Kellogg had met a fellow student, Marguerite E. Henrich, a native Californian. They were married in Berkeley on December 21, 1920, and set up their home in Washington, where, with many interludes of travel, they were to spend their entire married life.

For the next eight years Kellogg performed varied assignments, in field and laboratory, for the Biological Survey. He was well suited to such work by inclination and training and by a tremendously retentive memory and systematic use of the literature. All his life he was an inveterate reader and maker of reference cards, with annotations, filed taxonomically, by subject, and by author.

Much of Kellogg's work with the Biological Survey had to do with the feeding habits of hawks and owls, which entailed both field observation and the examination of hundreds of pellets. Observations were also made of the feeding habits of diving ducks, which were suspected of depleting trout populations. In a travel authorization issued in 1920, Kellogg is referred to as assistant in economic ornithology.

Between 1920 and 1927, a great deal of time was devoted to the drudgery of examining pellets and stomach contents from owls and hawks. These data were published (1926) in H. L. Stoddard's *Report on Cooperative Quail Investigation* and in his book, *The Bobwhite Quail;* also in Alfred O. Gross (1928), *Progress Report of the New England Ruffed Grouse Investigations Committee.*

Concurrently with his ornithological work, Kellogg spent much time studying toads, mainly museum specimens, including examination of stomach contents. In 1922 he published a Biological Survey circular, one of a number that he wrote, on the toad, and during that year he planned to revise the taxonomy of the toads of North and Middle America. The entire project was not completed, but it did result in an important monograph, *Mexican tailless amphibians in the United States National Museum* (1932).

Another dietary study was made of alligators. In the 1920s, there was a controversy over whether alligators should be protected from indiscriminate hunting, and Kellogg was given the task of finding out how predatory they actually were. He published a technical bulletin of the U.S. Department of Agriculture, *The Habits and Economic Importance of Alligators*, in 1929.

At about the time Kellogg joined the Biological Survey, his professor, John C. Merriam, was appointed president of the Carnegie Institution of Washington. Merriam arranged an appointment for Kellogg as a research associate of the Carnegie Institution, a position he held from 1921 to 1943. Annual research grants from the institution helped Kellogg to carry on research on marine mammals concurrently with his extensive projects for the Biological Survey. It was decided that an investigation of the earliest known predecessors of the typical cetaceans, the Archaeoceti, found in older Tertiary rocks, would be supported by a grant. In October 1929, Kellogg went to Choctaw and Washington Counties, Alabama, to collect zeuglodont material to supplement the archaeocete collections in the National Museum. The monograph resulting from this study, *A Review of the Archaeoceti,* published in 1936, is a landmark in cetology.

Merriam's increased administrative duties left him little time for paleontology, and he encouraged Kellogg to begin a project that Merriam had long had in mind: the study of the marine mammals of the Calvert Cliffs in Maryland. Beginning in the early 1920's, Kellogg devoted many weekends to collecting, adding significantly to the collections of his predecessors, William Palmer and Frederick W. True. By the time of Kellogg's death, the collection of fossil marine mammals in the National Museum was probably the best in the world.

The most fascinating aspect of marine mammals is the way in which existing mammalian organs have been modified for life in the sea. Kellogg decided to make this theme the basis for his doctoral thesis, which, because of the war and other matters, had yet to be written. Using the literature, but also drawing heavily on his own original studies, he wrote "The History of Whales—Their Adaptation to Life in the Water" (1928), for which he was awarded the Ph.D. by the University of California. This paper is still the best summary of the subject.

In 1928, Kellogg transferred to the U.S. National Museum as assistant curator of mammals under Gerritt S. Miller, Jr. He became curator in 1941. With his transfer to the Smithsonian, he was able to devote more time to study of marine mammals. He has described the course of his research as follows:

"In the earlier stages the marine mammal studies were largely descriptive, but as they progressed the importance of fossil cetaceans for geological correlation became apparent. As a collateral investigation, the recorded occurrences of migrating whales in the several oceans were collated. These observations confirmed the belief, more recently supported by whale marking, that the Recent whalebone whales make seasonal migrations from tropical calving grounds to the food banks located on or near the colder waters of the Arctic and Antarctic regions. The location of fossil remains tends to confirm the conclusion that the precursors of present day whalebone whales followed similar migration routes, and that similar types of fossilized skeletal remains occur in geological formations of corresponding age on the old shores that bordered these oceans.

"Examination of fossilized cetacean skeletons excavated in sedimentary strata deposited on ancient beaches, estuaries and river deltas revealed that although these air breathing mammals had been adapted for habitual aquatic existence, no funda-

mentally new structures had been added in the course of geologic time, and that the functioning of the entire body is
conditioned by adjustments of old organs to an exclusive life
in the water" (McGraw-Hill, *Modern Men of Science,* 1968,
pp. 283–84).

The Archaeoceti—the most primitive of the three suborders
of whales, dating from Eocene and early Oligocene time—are
well represented in fossil collections. So also are whales from
the Miocene Epoch, a period of tremendous evolutionary radiation of Cetacea. Much less well known are the Oligocene ancestors of modern whale types.

While he was treating the Archaeoceti systematically, Kellogg simultaneously worked on the description of Miocene
Cetacea from both coasts of North America. This study was
of major concern to him from the time of his description of
the humpback whale *Megaptera miocaena,* in 1922, to his last
paper, "Cetothere Skeletons from the Miocene Choptank Formation of Maryland and Virginia," published the week after
his death.

The difference in Kellogg's approach to the Archaeoceti and
the Miocene Cetacea is significant and proper. The Archaeoceti are unified by primitive characteristics that permit standard
taxonomic treatment, whereas the variation among the Miocene
forms is such that Kellogg, rightly, usually refused to assign
genera to families or to express opinions as to their relationships
to modern forms. At the same time his meticulous treatment of
both specimens and literature clarified many a taxonomic problem, even though it was as yet insoluble because of paucity of
data. An example is his treatment of the Squalodontidae
(1923), published under the title "Description of Two Squalodonts Recently Discovered in the Calvert Cliffs, Maryland,
and Notes on the Shark-Toothed Cetaceans." All genera assigned to the family are recorded and are either accepted,
reassigned, or placed in limbo as insufficiently known. This last

course was often preferred by him over the formal declaration of a *nomen nudum* because the number of available specimens was so small that he felt it wise to wait for further information before making such decisions. The squalodont paper remained the definitive work on that group until Rothausen, in 1968, built upon it in his "Die systematische Stellung der europäischen Squalodontidae" (*Paläont. Zeitung,* 42, 1/2, pp. 83–104).

Kellogg was not always taxonomically so cautious, however. In "Miocene Calvert Mysticetes Described by Cope" (1968) he declared a number of Cope's genera, based on mandibular fragments, to be *nomina nuda.*

Although Kellogg avoided formal taxonomic assignment to higher categories of most of the Miocene Cetacea that he described, he often discussed relationships, paleoecology, and geographic distribution. The great mass of his work on Miocene forms is indispensable for all workers on cetacean evolution: It not only furnishes them with clear and accurate information, including many evolutionary ideas, but also leaves them free of premature taxonomic assignments that would only have to be undone. This attribute of his work is particularly noticeable in his treatment of the Miocene porpoises. The Miocene produced many porpoises of modern type, undoubtedly including both forerunners and members of the modern families. At this state of evolution, however, the distinctions between families are subtle, and it is easy to be misled by obvious characteristics that probably result from parallelism or convergence. While describing or analyzing a number of genera—*Eurhinodelphis, Zarhachis, Kentriodon, Phocageneus, Schizodelphis, Hadrodelphis,* and others—he left their assignment to higher taxa for future workers. At the time of his death, he was reviewing the Miocene porpoises.

The publication of "The History of Whales" established Kellogg as an authority in the field of cetology, and soon thereafter, in 1930, a new and important phase of his life began. In

April of that year he went to Berlin as a delegate to a conference of experts on whaling matters held under the auspices of the League of Nations. This was the first of a series of conferences on international regulation of whaling, including the Washington conference of 1946, which formulated the International Convention providing for the establishment of the International Whaling Commission. In 1937, Kellogg was appointed by the State Department as United States delegate to the International Conference on Whaling at London, which resulted in the protocol of 1937, prohibiting the killing of all right and gray whales and establishing minimum legal lengths for commercial kinds of whales. The protocol of 1938 established a "sanctuary for two years for baleen whales in a sector of the Antarctic Ocean . . . and absolute protection of all whales against pelagic whaling in the North Atlantic sector of the Arctic Ocean." Kellogg was chairman of the American delegation to the conferences of 1944 and 1945 and was chairman of the Washington conference of 1946. He was United States commissioner on the International Whaling Commission from 1949 until 1967, vice-chairman of the commission from 1949 to 1951, and chairman from 1952 to 1954.

J. L. McHugh, Kellogg's successor as United States Commissioner, has evaluated his work in the International Whaling Commission:

"Although the United States had long since ceased to be a major whaling nation, it continued to exert a substantial influence in world whaling matters, largely through the efforts of Remington Kellogg. He was Head of United States Delegations to the first 16 meetings of the International Whaling Commission and attended his last meeting of that body, the 16th, at Sandefjord, Norway, in June 1964. By this time, scientific evidence of the alarming condition of the stocks of blue and humpback whales in the Antarctic was indisputable, and the Commission had already recommended, and the member nations had adopted, a complete ban on killing those species in the Southern Ocean. The scientists also had presented evidence that the fin whale resource in this region was overexploited, and that the catch quota for the Antarctic must be substantially reduced to prevent a continuation of this overharvesting. Dr. Kellogg fought very hard at the Sandefjord meeting to obtain agreement on a rational catch limit on Antarctic whaling, based on the scientific evidence. He returned from that disastrous meeting deeply discouraged by the failure of the Commission to act responsibly, and pessimistic about the future of world whale resources. It was unfortunate that illness prevented him from participating in subsequent meetings of the Commission, for the bitter controversy of the 1964 meeting, which almost destroyed the Commission, led eventually to a reversal of its do-nothing record. Since 1965, although this has not been widely recognized, a number of positive steps have been taken to place world whaling under rational scientific control. Although it has not solved all of its problems the Commission has come a long way toward meeting its responsibilities since 1964. Remington Kellogg remained interested in the affairs of the Commission until his death, although illness prevented active participation, and his influence is still felt in many ways."

An important by-product of the 1930 trip to Europe was the opportunity to study fossil whales in museums in Berlin, Munich, Stuttgart, Vienna, Padua, Bologna, Florence, Turin, Brussels, Haarlem, Amsterdam, and London. Whales of Miocene age have been found in sedimentary basins in Belgium, Austria, and Italy, and observation of the European specimens was essential to the attempt to establish the worldwide pattern of Miocene whale distribution. Understandably, specimens described in Europe and America had almost always been given different names, yet the habits of whales today indicate the probability that Miocene genera and even species ranged widely over the oceans. Kellogg's discussion with European specialists led to lifelong friendships; notable was his relationship with Ernst Stromer von Reichenbach in Munich.

Detailed comparisons with European specimens are frequent in Kellogg's papers and yet, as in his approach to taxonomy, he was conservative in suggesting trans-Atlantic relationships.

Kellogg's position in the Division of Mammals of the National Museum naturally involved him in work on groups other than marine mammals. He published an annotated list of West Virginia mammals in 1937, one of Tennessee mammals in 1939, and (with Wetmore) one of the mammals of Shenandoah National Park in 1947. He produced several studies of fossil and subfossil mammals from caves and archeological sites and in 1942 led a party in excavating Pleistocene mammals in Rampart Cave, near Boulder Dam on the Colorado River. He collaborated with his old commanding officer, E. A. Goldman, in 1940 in naming ten new white-tailed deer from North and Middle America and, in 1944, in a review of the spider monkeys.

The advent of World War II brought new responsibilities to the Smithsonian. In 1943, as a participant in "the program for the furtherance of cultural relations with scientists of the Latin-American republics," Kellogg was one of three museum officials to visit Brazil. This three-month assignment was an experience that he remembered happily: He observed field stations and laboratories engaged in the study of tropical diseases, with particular reference to Brazilian mammals believed to be carriers of disease. In 1944 and 1945, he added to the literature of disease transmission with two papers on the macaque monkey and with two on rodents in the South Pacific. In August 1947, he again visited Brazil as the delegate of the United States to the International Commission for the Establishment of the International Hylean Amazon Institute.

Through the period of his service in the Division of Mammals, Kellogg had collaborated with his predecessor as curator, Gerrit S. Miller, Jr., in the tremendous project of listing the North American Recent mammals. He carried on this work after Miller's death, and the 954-page volume was published by the U.S. National Museum in 1955.

In May 1948, Kellogg was appointed director of the U.S. National Museum, and in February 1958 he was appointed assistant secretary of the Smithsonian Institution. He got a chuckle out of the fact that when he retired, in 1962, he was replaced by three appointees: an assistant secretary, the director of the National Museum, and the director of the Museum of Natural History. The period of Kellogg's administrative appointments was an active one for the Smithsonian: Almost all the exhibit halls in the Museum of Natural History were modernized; the scientific staff of the museum was enlarged, and many new directions of research were entered; and the new Museum of History and Technology was built. Despite the demands of these and many other activities, Kellogg managed to spend part of each day in research on fossil marine mammals.

Over the years, in addition to activities closely related to his research, Kellogg served on many bodies devoted to the advancement of science and the public interest. He was a member of the board of governors of the Crop Protection Institute; vice-chairman of the Division of Biology and Agriculture, National Research Council; and a member of the advisory committee, Chemical–Biological Coordination Center. He was a member of the Pacific Science Board; the Board of Directors, Canal Zone Biological Area; the Advisory Board, Arctic Research Laboratory; the Committee on Research and Exploration, National Geographic Society; and the Research and Development Board, Department of Defense. He was President, American Society of Mammalogists; and President, Paleontological Society of Washington. He was a correspondent of the Academy of Natural Sciences of Philadelphia, a trustee of the

National Parks Association, a fellow of the Geological Society of America, a foreign fellow of the Zoological Society of London, and a member of Sigma Xi, the American Academy of Arts and Sciences, and the American Philosophical Society. In 1947, he was given a citation for distinguished service by the University of Kansas. He was elected to the National Academy of Sciences in 1951.

In 1962, when he retired, Dr. Kellogg moved to an office in the vertebrate paleontology area in the newly built east wing of the National Museum of Natural History. He organized the collection of fossil marine mammals, which had perforce been neglected during his years of administration. Then he plunged into the study of the Miocene marine mammals of Maryland; as always, he brought into this work comparisons based on his wide studies. Between 1965 and 1969 he published nine major contributions to the study of fossil marine mammals. He was working hard, but he was never too busy to discuss paleontology with his colleagues, visiting students, or children who had found a porpoise vertebra on a Chesapeake Bay holiday.

A longtime friend, Edward P. Henderson, wrote, after reading this memorial:

"The above outlines the accomplishments of this man, but neglects the unusual personality which those who were associated with him knew so well. He was recognized by all to be able in many fields, he accepted nothing as being true until it was proven, and usually he accented the negative side of all that was submitted to him, because he wanted more than one reason for accepting anything as a fact or policy. It is impossible to describe with words the expression on his face as he exploded into a few choice sentences often sprinkled with 'Kelloggical' profanity and a well-known grin.

"His door was always open not only to the professional colleagues but to all levels of the staff, and all who came could present their case."

Dr. Kellogg is survived by his wife of nearly fifty years. He was the last of his immediate family, his younger sister and brother preceding him in death.

Mrs. Kellogg has presented Dr. Kellogg's library on marine mammals, including the bookcases that he built for his home, to the Smithsonian Institution, where it forms the nucleus of the Remington Kellogg Library of Marine Mammalogy. His books on land mammals were presented to the University of Kansas. In his will, Dr. Kellogg expressed his intent to establish a fund for the advancement of knowledge of fossil marine mammals. Such a fund, bearing Kellogg's name, has been established by Mrs. Kellogg at the Smithsonian Institution; the National Geographic Society and friends of Dr. Kellogg have also contributed to it. A memorial fund has also been established at the Museum of Paleontology, University of California, Berkeley, through the generosity of Dr. Leslie E. Wilson and the late Edith P. Wilson. This fund is used to support research on the Cetacea by qualified graduate students.

BIBLIOGRAPHY

KEY TO ABBREVIATIONS

Am. Mus. Novit. = American Museum Novitates

Biol. Abstr. = Biological Abstracts

Carnegie Inst. Wash. Contrib. Palaeontol. = Carnegie Institution of Washington, Contributions in Palaeontology

Carnegie Inst. Wash. Publ. = Carnegie Institution of Washington Publication

Carnegie Inst. Wash. Year Book = Carnegie Institution of Washington Year Book

Geol. Soc. Am. Mem. = Geological Society of America Memoir

J. Mammal. = Journal of Mammalogy

Harv. Univ. Mus. Comp. Zool. Bull. = Harvard University Museum of Comparative Zoology Bulletin

Proc. Biol. Soc. Wash. = Proceedings of the Biological Society of Washington

Proc. U.S. Natl. Mus. = Proceedings of the U.S. National Museum

Smithson. Inst. Ann. Rep. = Smithsonian Institution Annual Report

Smithson. Inst. Explor. Field-Work = Smithsonian Institution Explorations and Field-Work

Smithson. Inst. Misc. Collect. = Smithsonian Institution Miscellaneous Collections

Univ. Calif. Dep. Geol. Bull. = University of California Department of Geology Bulletin

Univ. Calif. Publ. Zool. = University of California Publications in Zoology

U.S. Dep. Agric. Bur. Biol. Surv. Circ. = U.S. Department of Agriculture Bureau of Biological Survey Circular

U.S. Natl. Mus. Bull. = U.S. National Museum Bulletin

1914

On the retention of *Neotoma campestris* Allen as a separate subspecies from *Neotoma floridana baileyi* Merriam. University of Kansas Museum of Natural History, Zoology Series, Publication 1(1):3–6.

1918

A revision of the *Microtus californicus* group of meadow mice. Univ. Calif. Publ. Zool., 21(1):1–42.

1919

With Francis Harper. Is-sur-Tille, Département of Côte d'Or, France. In: *Nineteenth Christmas Bird Census.* Bird-Lore, 21(1): 49.

1921

The American chameleon and its care. U.S. Dep. Agric. Bur. Biol. Surv. Circ. Bi-565, pp. 1–3. (mimeographed).

Quotation. In: Remains of a fossil phocid from Plattsburg, New York, by S. C. Bishop. J. Mammal., 2 (3):170.

A new pinniped from the Upper Pliocene of California. J. Mammal., 2(4):212–26.

With J. C. Merriam and associates. *Continuation of Paleontological Researches.* Carnegie Inst. Wash. Year Book no. 20, pp. 447–51.

1922

Change of name. Proc. Biol. Soc. Wash. 35:78.

Pinnipeds from Miocene and Pleistocene deposits of California. Univ. Calif. Dep. Geol. Bull. 13(4):23–132.

A study of the California forms of the *Microtus montanus* group of meadow mice. Univ. Calif. Publ. Zool., 21(7):245–74.

A synopsis of the *Microtus mordax* group of meadow mice in California. Univ. Calif. Publ. Zool., 21(8):275–302.

Are moles held in check by blacksnakes? U.S. Golf Association, Green Section Bulletin, 2(5):157–59.

Description of the skull of *Megaptera miocaena*, a fossil humpback whale from the Miocene diatomaceous earth of Lompoc, California. Proc. U.S. Natl. Mus., 61:1–18.

The toad. U.S. Dep. Agric. Bur. Biol. Surv. Circ. Bi-664, pp. 1–7. (mimeographed).

1923

With John C. Merriam and associates. *Continuation of Paleontological Researches.* Carnegie Inst. Wash. Year Book no. 21, pp. 398–400.

Description of two squalodonts recently discovered in the Calvert Cliffs, Maryland, and notes on the shark-toothed cetaceans. Proc. U.S. Natl. Mus., 62:1–69.

Description of an apparently new toothed cetacean from South Carolina. Smithson. Inst. Misc. Collect., 76(7):1–7.

1924

With John C. Merriam and associates. *Continuation of Paleonto-*

logical Researches. Carnegie Inst. Wash. Year Book no. 22, pp. 351–53.

Description of a new genus and species of whalebone whale from the Calvert Cliffs, Maryland. Proc. U.S. Natl. Mus., 63:1–14.

A fossil porpoise from the Calvert formation of Maryland. Proc. U.S. Natl. Mus., 63:1–39.

With John C. Merriam and associates. *Continuation of Paleontological Researches.* Carnegie Inst. Wash. Year Book no. 23, pp. 293–96.

Tertiary pelagic mammals of eastern North America. Geological Society of America Bulletin, 35:755–66.

1925

A fossil physeteroid cetacean from Santa Barbara County, California. Proc. U.S. Natl. Mus., 66:1–8.

Two fossil physeteroid whales from California. In: *Additions to the Tertiary History of the Pelagic Mammals on the Pacific Coast of North America.* Carnegie Inst. Wash. Contrib. Palaeontol. Publ. 348, pp. 1–34.

Fossil cetotheres from California. In: *Additions to the Tertiary History of the Pelagic Mammals on the Pacific Coast of North America.* Carnegie Inst. Wash. Contrib. Palaeontol. Publ. 348, pp. 35–56.

A new fossil sirenian from Santa Barbara County, California. In: *Additions to the Tertiary History of the Pelagic Mammals on the Pacific Coast of North America.* Carnegie Inst. Wash. Contrib. Palaeontol. Publ. 348, pp. 57–70.

New pinnipeds from the Miocene diatomaceous earth near Lompoc, California. In: *Additions to the Tertiary History of the Pelagic Mammals on the Pacific Coast of North America.* Carnegie Inst. Wash. Contrib. Palaeontol. Publ. 348, pp. 71–96.

Structure of the flipper of a Pliocene pinniped from San Diego County, California. In: *Additions to the Tertiary History of the Pelagic Mammals on the Pacific Coast of North America.* Carnegie Inst. Wash. Contrib. Palaeontol. Publ. 348, pp. 97–116.

On the occurrence of remains of fossil porpoises of the genus *Eurhinodelphis* in North America. Proc. U.S. Natl. Mus., 66:1–40.

With John C. Merriam and associates. *Continuation of Paleontological Researches.* Carnegie Inst. Wash. Year Book no. 24, p. 357.

The relationships of the Tertiary cetaceans of Jugo-Slavia to those of eastern North America. Exemplar e Xeniis Gorjanovic-Krambergerianis, pp. 1–8, Zagreb.

1926

Supplementary observations on the skull of the fossil porpoise *Zarhachis flagellator* Cope. Proc. U.S. Natl. Mus., 67:1–18.

Report on examination of one thousand and ninety-eight Marsh Hawk pellets. In: *Report on Cooperative Quail Investigation: 1925–1926.* With preliminary recommendations for the development of quail preserves, ed. by H. L. Stoddard, p. 39. Quail Study Fund for Southern Georgia and Northern Florida.

Report of Remington Kellogg. In: *Continuation of Paleontological Researches,* by John C. Merriam and associates. Carnegie Inst. Wash. Year Book no. 25, pp. 405–6.

Facts about snakes. U.S. Dep. Agric. Bur. Biol. Surv. Circ. Bi-855. 9 pp. (mimeographed).

1927

Kentriodon pernix, a Miocene porpoise from Maryland. Proc. U.S. Natl. Mus., 69:1–55.

With W. K. Gregory. A fossil porpoise from California. Am. Mus. Novit. no. 269, pp. 1–7.

Study of the skull of a fossil sperm-whale from the Temblor Miocene of southern California. Carnegie Inst. Wash. Publ. no. 346, pp. 1–23.

Fossil pinnipeds from California. Carnegie Inst. Wash. Publ. no. 346, pp. 25–37.

Report on researches by Remington Kellogg. In: *Continuation of Paleontological Researches,* by John C. Merriam and associates. Carnegie Inst. Wash. Year Book no. 26, p. 366.

1928

The history of whales—their adaptation to life in the water. Quarterly Review of Biology, 3(1):29–76; 3(2):174–208.

Poisonous snakes of the United States. U.S. Dep. Agric. Bur. Biol. Surv. Circ. Bi-571, 15 pp. (mimeographed).

Toads destroy many harmful insects and should be protected. U.S. Department of Agriculture Yearbook, pp. 620–22.

An apparently new *Hyla* from El Salvador. Proc. Biol. Soc. Wash., 41:123–24.

Programme of the final public examination for the degree of doctor of philosophy. University of California, Graduate Division, 6 pp.

Vertebrates in the marine Tertiary formations of western Oregon. In: *Stratigraphic Relations of Western Oregon Oligocene Formations,* ed. by H. G. Schenck. Univ. Calif. Dep. Geol. Bull., 18(1):1–50.

Determinations of the food of 95 snowy owls and of 139 goshawks. In: *Progress Report of the New England Ruffed Grouse Investigations Committee,* by A. O. Gross. Boston, Massachusetts Fish and Game Commission. 8 pp.

Report of researches by Remington Kellogg. In: *Continuation of Paleontological Researches.* Carnegie Inst. Wash. Year Book no. 27, pp. 386–87.

History of the cetacean fore limb. Exhibition representing results of research activities. Carnegie Institution of Washington, December 14, pp. 15–16.

1929

Extinct ocean-living mammals from Maryland. Smithson. Inst. Explor. Field-Work, 1928, Publ. 3011, pp. 27–32.

What is known of the migrations of some of the whalebone whales. Smithson. Inst., Ann. Rep., 1928, Publ. 2997, pp. 467–94.

A new fossil toothed whale from Florida. Am. Mus. Novit. no. 389. 10 pp.

Report of researches by Remington Kellogg. In: *Continuation of Paleontological Researches,* by John C. Merriam and associates. Carnegie Inst. Wash. Year Book no. 28, pp. 389–90.

A new cetothere from southern California. Univ. Calif. Dep. Geol. Bull. 18(15):449–57.

The habits and economic importance of alligators. U.S. Department of Agriculture Technical Bulletin no. 147, pp. 1–36.

1930

With others. Preliminary draft convention for the regulation of whaling. League of Nations Economic Committee. Report to the Council on the work of the thirty-second session. Official no. C353.M.146.1930. II, pp. 8–11.

Report of researches by Remington Kellogg. In: *Continuation of Paleontological Researches,* by John C. Merriam and associates. Carnegie Inst. Wash. Year Book no. 29, pp. 397–98.

1931

Pelagic mammals from the Temblor formation of the Kern River region, California. Proceedings of the California Academy of Sciences, 19(12):217–397.

Whaling statistics for the Pacific Coast of North America. J. Mammal., 12(1):73–77.

Ancient relatives of living whales. Smithson. Inst. Explor. Field-Work, 1930, Publ. 3111, pp. 83–90.

Whales. U.S. Congress, Senate, Special Committee on Wild Life Resources, Hearings on the conservation of whales and other marine mammals, 72d Congr., 1st sess., pp. 6–9.

The last phase in the history of whaling. Whales. U.S. Congress, Senate, Special Committee on Wild Life Resources, Hearings on the conservation of whales and other marine mammals, 72d Congr., 1st sess., pp. 20–29; also in: Lewis Radcliffe, Economics of the whaling industry with relationship to the convention for the regulation of whaling. U.S. Congress, Senate, Special Committee on the Conservation of Wild Life Resources, 73d Congr., 2d sess., pp. 57–66.

Report on examination of 1098 Marsh Hawk pellets from Leon County, Florida. In: *The Bobwhite Quail. Its Habits, Preservation and Increase,* by H. L. Stoddard. New York, Charles Scribner's Sons. xxix + 559 pp.

Obituary notice of David Starr Jordan. J. Mammal., 12(4):445.

Obituary notice of James Williams Gidley. J. Mammal., 12(4): 445–46.

Report of researches by Remington Kellogg. In: *Continuation of Paleontological Researches,* by John C. Merriam and associates. Carnegie Inst. Wash. Year Book no. 30, p. 450.

1932

A Miocene long-beaked porpoise from California. Smithson. Misc. Collect., 87 (2):1–11.

Notes on the spadefoot of the western plains *(Scaphiopus hammondii).* Copeia, no. 1, p. 36.

Mexican tailless amphibians in the United States National Museum. U.S. Natl. Mus., Bull. 160. iv + 224 pp.

New names for mammals proposed by Borowski in 1780 and 1781. Proc. Biol. Soc. Wash., 45:147–48.

Researches by Remington Kellogg. In: *Continuation of Paleontological Researches,* by John C. Merriam and associates. Carnegie Inst. Wash. Year Book no. 31, p. 330.

1933

The last phase in the history of whaling. U.S. Congress, Senate Committee Print, 73d Congr., 2d sess., pp. 57–66.

Protective measures needed to perpetuate the supply of whales off the coasts of North America, as recommended by the Committee on Marine Mammals. U.S. Congress, Senate Committee Print, 73d Congr., 2d sess., pp. 67–68.

Obituary notice of Barton Warren Evermann. J. Mammal., 14(4): 394.

Researches by Remington Kellogg. In: *Continuation of Paleontological Researches,* by John C. Merriam and associates. Carnegie Inst. Wash. Year Book no. 32, pp. 328–29.

1934

With Earl L. Packard. A new cetothere from the Miocene Astoria formation of Newport, Oregon. Carnegie Inst. Wash. Contrib. Palaeontol. Publ. 447, pp. 1–62.

The Patagonian fossil whalebone whale, *Cetotherium moreni* (Lydekker). Carnegie Inst. Wash. Contrib. Palaeontol. Publ. 447, pp. 63–81.

A new cetothere from the Modelo formation at Los Angeles, California. Carnegie Inst. Wash. Contrib. Palaeontol. Publ. 447, pp. 83–104.

Description of periotic bones of *Schizodelphis bobengi.* In: *A Specimen of a Long-Nosed Dolphin from the Bone Valley Gravels of Polk County, Florida,* by E. C. Case, vol. 4, no. 2, pp. 105–113. Ann Arbor, University of Michigan, Museum of Palaeontology Contributions.

The search for extinct marine mammals in Maryland.   Smithson. Inst. Explor. Field-Work, 1933, Publ. 3235, pp. 15–17.

Researches of Remington Kellogg.   In: *Continuation of Paleontological Researches,* by John C. Merriam and associates.   Carnegie Inst. Wash. Year Book no. 33, p. 311.

1935

Savage, Thomas Staughton (1804–1880).   In: *Dictionary of American Biography,* vol. 16, pp. 391–92.

Researches of Remington Kellogg.   In: *Continuation of Paleontological Researches,* by John C. Merriam and associates.   Carnegie Inst. Wash. Year Book no. 34, p. 316.

1936

Henry Fairfield Osborn. (Obituary note)   J. Mammal., 17(1):84.

Sigurd Risting. (Obituary note)   J. Mammal., 17(1):84.

Mammals from a native village site on Kodiak Island.   Proc. Biol. Soc. Wash., 49:37–38.

The whaling treaty act.   U.S. Congress, House of Representatives, Committee on Foreign Affairs, Hearings on S.3413.   74th Congr., 1st sess., Feb. 11, 18, 25, March 3, 7, and 10, 1936.   160 pp.

Researches of Remington Kellogg.   In: *Continuation of Paleontological Researches,* by. J. C. Merriam and associates.   Carnegie Inst. Wash. Year Book no. 35, p. 321.

A review of the Archaeoceti.   Carnegie Inst. Wash. Publ. 482. xv + 366 pp.

1937

Comments on whale vertebra from Escalante Point.   In: *Gold-Bearing Deposits on the West Coast of Vancouver Island between Esperanza Inlet and Alberni Canal,* by M. F. Bancroft, Canada Geological Survey Memorandum 204, no. 2432.   34 pp.

With others.   International Agreement for the Regulation of Whaling.   With Final Act of the Conference.   Misc. no. 4, London, His Majesty's Stationery Office, June 8, 1937.   Cmd. 5487, 12 pp.; also in Confidential Document, U.S. Congress, Senate, 75th Congr., 1st sess., Executive U, pp. 6–14, July 31, 1937; U.S. Congress, Senate, Congressional Record, 75th Congr., 1st sess, August 5, 81(150):10672, 10674.

With Herschel V. Johnson. Report of the delegates of the United States to the International Whaling Conference, London, May 24–June 8. Confidential Document, U.S. Congress, Senate, 75th Congr., 1st sess., Executive U, July 31, pp. 14–19.

Annotated list of West Virginia mammals. Proc. U.S. Natl. Mus., 84(3022):443–79.

Researches of Remington Kellogg. In: *Continuation of Paleontological Researches,* by J. C. Merriam and associates. Carnegie Inst. Wash. Year Book no. 36, pp. 339–40.

1938

With others. Regulation of whaling. Agreement between the United States of America and other powers, and final act of the conference. Department of State, Treaty Series no. 933, pp. 1–12.

With A. S. Pearse. Mammalia from Yucatan caves. Carnegie Inst. Wash. Publ. 491, pp. 301–4.

With others. Protocol amending the International Agreement of June 8, 1937, for the Regulation of Whaling. With Final Act of the Conference, London, June 24. Misc. no. 6, London, His Majesty's Stationery Office, June 24, 1938. Cmd. 5827. 13 pp.

Adaptation of structure to function in whales. In: *Cooperation in Research.* Carnegie Inst. Wash. Publ. 501, pp. 649–82.

Researches of Remington Kellogg. In: *Continuation of Paleontological Researches,* by J. C. Merriam and associates. Carnegie Inst. Wash. Year Book no. 37, pp. 352–53.

1939

Annotated list of Tennessee mammals. Proc. U.S. Natl. Mus., 86(3051):245–303.

Report of the delegates of the United States to the International Whaling Conference, London, June 14–24, Protocol, and Final Act. Executive Report no. 1, U.S. Congress, Senate, 76th Congr., 1st sess., Feb. 23. 27 pp.

With others. Regulation of whaling. Protocol between the United States of America and other powers amending the International Agreement for the Regulation of Whaling signed in London June 8, 1937 (Treaty Series no. 933), with certificate of extension and Final Act of Conference. Department of State, Treaty Series, no. 944, pp. 1–14.

A new red-backed mouse from Kentucky and Virginia. Proc. Biol. Soc. Wash., 52:37–39.

Cetacean studies in Europe. Smithson. Inst. Explor. Field-Work, Publ. 3525, pp. 41–46.

With E. A. Goldman. The status of the name *Dorcephalus crooki* Mearns. J. Mammal., 20(4):507.

Studies on the history and evolution of whales. Carnegie Inst. Wash. Year Book no. 38, pp. 311–12.

1940

Whales, giants of the sea. National Geographic Magazine, 77(1): 35–90.

With E. A. Goldman. Ten new white-tailed deer from North and Middle America. Proc. Biol. Soc. Wash., 53:81–89.

Studies on the history and evolution of whales. Carnegie Inst. Wash. Year Book no. 39, pp. 294–95.

1941

On the cetotheres figured by Vandelli. Museu de Mineralogía e Geología da Universidade de Lisboa, Bolletim, Ser. 3a, nos. 7–8, pp. 3–12.

On the identity of the porpoise *Sagmatias amblodon.* Field Museum of Natural History, Zoology Series Publ. 511, vol. 27, pp. 293–311.

Palaeontology, early man, and historical geology. In: *Report of John C. Merriam.* Carnegie Inst. Wash. Year Book no. 40, pp. 316–33.

1943

Notes and measurements of the skull. In: *A Second Specimen of True's Beaked Whale,* Mesoplodon mirus *True, from North Carolina,* by H. H. Brimley. J. Mammal., 24(2):200–203.

Tertiary, Quaternary, and Recent marine mammals of South America and the West Indies. Proceedings, Eighth American Scientific Congress, Washington, 3:445–73.

Past and present status of the marine mammals of South America and the West Indies. Smithson. Inst. Ann. Rep., 1943, Publ. 3719, pp. 299–316.

1944

Mammals. In: *A Field Collector's Manual in Natural History,* prepared by members of the staff of the Smithsonian Institution, Publ. 3766. iv + 118 pp.

With Lloyd V. Steere. Report of the delegation of the United States to the International Whaling Conference held at London, January 4, 13, 19 and 31, 1944. Confidential Document, U.S. Congress, Senate, 78th Congr., 2d sess., Executive D, pp. 11–17. Made public June 8, 1944.

A new macaque from an island off the east coast of Borneo. Proc. Biol. Soc. Wash., 57:75–76.

With E. A. Goldman. Review of the spider monkeys. Proc. U.S. Natl. Mus., 96:1–45.

Fossil cetaceans from the Florida Tertiary. Harv. Univ. Mus. Comp. Zool. Bull., 94(9):433–71.

1945

Macaques. In: *Primate Malaria,* ed. by S. D. Aberle. Office of Medical Information, Division of Medical Sciences, National Research Council. Washington, D.C., National Academy of Sciences. iii + 171 pp.

Two rats from Morotai Island. Proc. Biol. Soc. Wash., 58:65–68.

A new Australian naked-tailed rat *(Melomys).* Proc. Biol. Soc. Wash., 58:69–71.

Two new Philippine rodents. Proc. Biol. Soc. Wash., 58:121–24.

1946

Three new mammals from the Pearl Islands, Panama. Proc. Biol. Soc. Wash., 59:57–62.

Problems related to marine animals. In: *A Program of Desirable Scientific Investigations in Arctic North America,* ed. by R. F. Flint, pp. 43–44. Montreal, Arctic Institute of North America.

Mammals of San José Island, Bay of Panama. Smithson. Inst. Misc. Collect. 106(7):1–4.

With Ira N. Gabrielson. Report of the delegation of the United States to the International Whaling Conference, held at London, November 20, 21, 22, 23, and 26, 1945. U.S. Congress, Senate, 79th Congr., 2d sess., Executive I, pp. 13–16; also in Executive Report no. 9, pp. 15–18.

A century of progress in Smithsonian biology. Science, 104:132–41.

1947

With Ira N. Gabrielson and William E. S. Flory. Report of the delegation of the United States to the International Whaling Commission held at Washington, D.C., November 20 through December 2, 1946. U.S. Congress, Senate, 80th Congr., 1st sess., Executive I, April 8, 1947, pp. 28–35.

With Victor B. Scheffer. Occurrence of *Stenella euphrosyne* off the Oregon Coast. Murrelet, 28(1):9–10.

With A. Wetmore. A preliminary list of the mammals of the Shenandoah National Park. U.S. National Park Service (mimeographed circular), 6 pp.

Scientists and deep sea resources. University of Kansas, Graduate Magazine, 46(8):6–8.

International commission for the establishment of an International Hylean Amazon Institute. U.S. Department of State Bulletin, 17(436):891–92.

1949

Regulation of whaling. U.S. Congress, Senate, Subcommittee of the Committee on Interstate and Foreign Commerce, Hearings on S.2080. 81st Congr., 1st sess., July 20, 1949, pp. 32–40.

1955

With Gerrit S. Miller, Jr. List of North American Recent mammals. U.S. Natl. Mus. Bull. 205, pp. xii–954.

Three Miocene porpoises from the Calvert Cliffs, Maryland. I. *Lophocetus pappus,* new species. II. *Pelodelphis gracilis,* new genus, new species. III. Identity of *Tretosphys gabbii* (Cope). Proc. U.S. Natl. Mus., 105:101–54.

1956

The International Whaling Commission. Papers presented at the International Technical Conference on the Conservation of the Living Resources of the Sea, Rome, 18 April to 10 May 1955. United Nations Publication, Sales no. 1956. II.B.1., pp. 256–61.

What and where are the whitetails? In: *The Deer of North America. The White-Tailed, Mule and Black-Tailed Deer, Genus Odocoileus, Their History and Management,* ed. by Walter P. Taylor, pp. 31–55. The Stackpole Co. and Wildlife Management Institute.

Table I: Distribution and supposed age relationships of New Zealand cetaceans. In: *Provisional Correlation of Selected Cenozoic Sequences in the Western and Central Pacific,* by Preston E. Cloud, Jr. Proceedings, Eighth Pacific Science Congress, 2:555–76.

1957

With Frank C. Whitmore, Jr. Marine mammals. In: *Treatise on Marine Ecology and Paleoecology,* ed. by Joel W. Hedgpeth. Geol. Soc. Am., Mem. 67, 1:1223–25.

With Frank C. Whitmore, Jr. Mammals. In: *Treatise on Marine Ecology and Paleoecology,* ed. by Joel W. Hedgpeth. Geol. Soc. Am., Mem. 67, 2:1021–24.

Two additional Miocene porpoises from the Calvert Cliffs, Maryland. Proc. U.S. Natl. Mus., 107:279–337.

1959

Description of the skull of *Pomatodelphis inaequalis* Allen. Harv. Univ. Mus. Comp. Zool. Bull., 121(1):3–26.

Introduction. Symposium, *Systematics, Present and Future,* Society of Systematic Zoologists, Washington, December 29, 1958. Systematic Zoology, 8(2):59.

1960

Mammals and how they live. In: *Wild Animals of North America,* ed. by A. Severy, chap. 1, pp. 13–35. Washington, D.C., National Geographic Society.

The rise of modern mammals. In: *Wild Animals of North America,* ed. by A. Severy, chap. 2, pp. 37–51. Washington, D.C., National Geographic Society.

Whales, giants of the sea. In: *Wild Animals of North America,* ed. by A. Severy, chap. 28, pp. 366–93. Washington, D.C., National Geographic Society.

1961

Antarctic whales. In: *Science in Antarctica.* Part 1: *The Life Sciences in Antarctica,* chap. 14, pp. 115–28. Washington, D.C., National Academy of Sciences–National Research Council.

1965

Fossil marine mammals from the Miocene Calvert formation of Maryland and Virginia. Part 1. A new whalebone whale from the Miocene Calvert formation. U.S. Natl. Mus. Bull. 247, pp. 1–45.

Fossil marine mammals from the Miocene Calvert Formation of Maryland and Virginia. Part 2. The Miocene Calvert sperm whale *Orycterocetus.* U.S. Natl. Mus. Bull. 247, pp. 47–63.

1966

Fossil marine mammals from the Miocene Calvert formation of Maryland and Virginia. Part 3. New species of extinct Miocene Sirenia. U.S. Natl. Mus. Bull. 247, pp. 65–98.

Fossil marine mammals from Miocene Calvert formation of Maryland and Virginia. Part 4. A new odontocete from the Calvert formation of Maryland. U.S. Natl. Mus. Bull. 247, pp. 99–101.

1968

Fossil marine mammals from Miocene Calvert formation of Maryland and Virginia. Part 5. Miocene Calvert mysticetes described by Cope. U.S. Natl. Mus. Bull. 247, pp. 103–32.

Fossil marine mammals from Miocene Calvert formation of Maryland and Virginia. Part 6. A hitherto unrecognized Calvert cetothere. U.S. Natl. Mus. Bull. 247, pp. 133–61.

Fossil marine mammals from Miocene Calvert formation of Maryland and Virginia. Part 7. A sharp-nosed cetothere from the Miocene Calvert. U.S. Natl. Mus. Bull. 247, pp. 163–73.

Fossil marine mammals from Miocene Calvert formation of Maryland and Virginia. Part 8. Supplement to description of *Parietobalaena palmeri*. U.S. Natl. Mus. Bull. 247, pp. 175–97.

1969

Cetothere skeletons from the Miocene Choptank formation of Maryland and Virginia. U.S. Natl. Mus. Bull. 294, pp. 1–40.

Mervin J Kelly

MERVIN JOE KELLY

February 14, 1894–March 18, 1971

BY JOHN R. PIERCE

IN PREPARING this memoir of a remarkable man, I now regret that I did not have a closer association with him. During his life, I regarded Mervin Kelly as an almost supernatural force. While I saw him many times in the course of my work at Bell Laboratories, usually with others, and a few times in his home, I did not seek him out for fear of being struck by lightning. Thus I have had to rely on other sources for some aspects of his life and personality. In quoting directly from such sources, I have in some cases eliminated passages or inserted explanatory material in brackets; I have not otherwise altered the writer's text.

In trying to organize the material in a sensible way, I have put Kelly's character and work first; then his ideas concerning research and technology; and following these, a brief biographical sketch; a list of honors, awards, and memberships; and a bibliography.

THE MAN AND HIS WORKS

Mervin Kelly had great intelligence and great force. His work with R. A. Millikan at the University of Chicago gave him a lasting appreciation of the rarity and importance of first-rate scientists and first-rate research. He himself did creditable physical research. Later at the Western Electric Company and at the Bell Laboratories (which was not formed until 1925), he did early and important work on vacuum tubes, including research, development, and manufacture. His group increased the life of telephone repeater (amplifier) tubes from 1,000 to 80,000 hours and led by 1933 to a transmitting tube for transatlantic telephony and broadcasting with an unprecedented power of 100,000 watts, later to a tube with a power of 250,000 watts.

It is clear, however, that Kelly's greatest contribution lay in creative technical management. It is no more than just to say that Kelly made Bell Laboratories the foremost industrial laboratory in the world. He recognized and inspired good men and good work. He assessed and drove to completion important technical potentialities and opportunities. He shaped and managed a complex organization. And, he inspired the confidence and won the support of the management of AT&T and of the operating telephone companies of the Bell System. As Frederick R. Kappel, former board chairman of AT&T said after Kelly's death:

"He was a great fellow for the Bell System. Mervin was always and forever pushing the operating management, and the heads of AT&T as well, to get on with new things. His aggressiveness got him in a lot of hot arguments, but I always sat back and said, 'Give it to them, Mervin, that's what we need.' Every place needs a fireball or sparkplug, and he was it."

Kelly was not only a sparkplug; he combined determination and showmanship. Twice he submitted his resignation to the president of AT&T, stating that important work at Bell Laboratories was not being adequately funded. In each case, he got the funds. Surely, he was sincere, but he was dramatic as well.

Kelly's potentials as a manager and organizer were not recognized immediately. It is said that H. D. Arnold kept him for a long time at a low administrative level because he distrusted his judgment. One contemporary said that Kelly always had a reason for his actions, but one might not agree with the reason. Oliver Buckley is quoted as having once said that when Kelly was made director of research in 1936, those who were put directly under him were men who could take his personality and so protect those at lower levels. Yet, it became clear that Kelly's very positive virtues outweighed any shortcomings. He was made executive vice president in 1944 and president in 1951.

Certainly, Kelly had a temper that frightened many. When provoked he would turn dark red, but a moment later he would be normal again. Harald Friis, who admired Kelly greatly, notes that at a large conference "He [Kelly] got excited and made what I thought were derogatory remarks about my boys. I got mad as a hornet and could not sleep for several nights. A few days later I ran into Mervin at Murray Hill. He was smiling and asked why I looked so gloomy, and took me into Bown's office. I reminded him of the meeting and said, 'I got mad about what you said about my boys and would have shot you if I had had a gun.' "

Others were less disturbed by Kelly's temper. Estill Green describes his experience as vice president in charge of systems engineering in these mellow words:

"A few years in close association with Mervin were the happiest time of my life. For years on end I had believed I needed insulation from the high voltage. Yet when I was directly exposed to it, I never experienced a serious shock, and I rejoiced to observe how the high potential overpowered inertia and loose thinking and prejudice.

"I learned never to oppose him when he had the bit in his teeth. Next morning I could remark casually, 'Mervin, there are some aspects of that matter discussed in yesterday's conference that you may not be fully aware of.' He would listen, and generally modify his position, to a minor or sometimes major extent."

This willingness to rectify an error was a quality particularly valuable in one so quick and positive as Kelly. Kelly thought he could judge a man after a few moments of conversation. Though he had a high batting average, sometimes he was mistaken. He made very confident technical judgments and they, too, could be wrong. Yet, he was fair and honest and always willing to admit a mistake.

Kelly was courageous in breaking with tradition, but very determined in having his own way. It did not bother him to break Bell Laboratories regulations. But when he laid down the law, he expected to be heard and obeyed, whether it was a matter of lax working hours of management or staff, the neatness of premises, or the nature and direction of technical programs. While he would listen to advice, his judgments were his own, not a consensus. When he addressed groups of Bell Laboratories people, he often spoke with his eyes closed. Clearly, he was looking inward for inspiration and not outword for acceptance. On one occasion, an executive spoke somewhat contrary to a pronouncement Kelly made. I said to the man sitting next to me, "The moving finger writes, and having writ. . . ." I was correct; the executive was not demolished, he was merely disregarded.

Yet, Kelly was universally respected and admired by the most competent and touchy men who worked under him. They received an interested and fair hearing, and he remembered what they told him. His memory was indeed phenomenal. After someone had shown and explained his work, Kelly would remember everything a year later.

Kelly worked harder than he felt others should. As Kappel said, "When Mervin was an advocate for something, there was no shortchanging of his energy to get the job done." More than once, Kelly drove himself to the point of exhaustion.

In the end, Kelly judged people and programs by real accomplishment. His integrity was absolute. I believe that he never thought in any terms other than what was right and what was just.

Kelly's greatest accomplishments lay in the Bell Laboratories. He valued talent sincerely, as his warm biographical sketch of C. J. Davisson shows. He wanted, found, appreciated, and encouraged the sort of men who invented the transistor. William Shockley has said, "Kelly's stimulus to look for new devices useful in the telephone business, plus exposure to new theories about rectification mechanisms in copper oxide, led me to invent a structure that would have worked as a transistor."

When the transistor had been invented, Kelly recognized its worth. As a foreign member of the Swedish Academy of Sciences, he pressed for the award of the Nobel Prize to Bardeen, Brattain, and Shockley. And, for years at Bell Laboratories nothing was any good unless it was "new art" (solid state).

Kelly fostered or launched ambitious programs in nationwide dialing, in automation of maintenance and testing, in microwave communication, in coaxial cable transmission, in transoceanic cables, and in electronic switching. All were timely, and, in the end, all were successful.

In 1943 Kelly outlined a branch-laboratory concept. This eventually led to the establishment of laboratories for final development at manufacturing locations of Western Electric. This proved important in several ways. It linked final development and its procedures and personnel closely to those responsible for the manufacture of new devices and systems. It prevented too large a concentration of personnel in a few central locations. It gave a desirable measure of responsibility and independence to work in various well-defined fields of development.

Kelly valued training as well as talent. When he found, after World War II, that university instruction in engineering was not fresh and deep enough for the graduates to cope with current communications problems, he inaugurated in 1948, within Bell Laboratories, a Communications Development Training Program (known as C.D.T., and as "Kelly College"). C.D.T. emphasized, as he said, "increasing depth in the physics, chemistry, and mathematics essential to modern technology, with advanced courses in communications and electronic technology." The courses were taught partly by university faculty members.

Yet, Kelly looked toward universities as the normal channels of education. He wrote:

"While it is probably always worthwhile for a laboratory to give some orientation courses to new members of technical staff, I believe that much of the training of our graduate course would have greater value if done at the university in academic surroundings. The problem of deeper and more basic training for the young engineers who wish a career in creative technology is a problem of importance to national strength. It needs a more positive attack."
and also:

"We must all keep in mind though that the first and most important responsibility of the universities is the training of scientists and engineers in adequate volume to meet our country's needs."

In furtherance of these beliefs, Kelly arranged for Bell Laboratories-supported fellowships in physics, electronics, and communication to be established at a number of universities.

In 1957 C.D.T. was changed in this direction when New York University opened a graduate center at Bell Laboratories. As engineering education caught up with the postwar world, emphasis changed to oncampus training, including doctoral programs, and to specialized communication courses given within Bell Laboratories.

While the Bell Laboratories' work in common carrier communication was closest to Kelly's heart, he recognized the country's need for advanced military systems. It was his influence and driving force that made Bell Laboratories so active and productive in radar during the war and later in antisubmarine warfare and antiaircraft and antimissile missiles. Yet, Kelly was no militarist. In 1954 he wrote, "It is a tragedy of our times that our nation's primary concern is with security." He tried as best he could to help the nation meet what he saw as a most urgent need, both in individual articles and speeches and as a member of various defense advisory bodies. He was chairman of the Subcommittee on Research Activities in the Department of Defense and related Defense agencies that reported to the Hoover Commission on organization of the Executive Branch in 1955.

Kelly also served on a number of committees advisory to the Department of Commerce and in this connection played an important part in frustrating the move to dismiss Allen Astin, the Director of the Bureau of Standards, for the honest and straightforward testing of a commercial battery additive that showed the product to be ineffective. As Detlev Bronk, then President of the National Academy of Sciences, tells the story:

"[In 1953] I heard of the impending dismissal of Allen Astin by the Secretary of Commerce, Sinclair Weeks. I called Eisenhower, or perhaps Sherman Adams. Eisenhower asked me to see Weeks. When I told him that I did not know the man, he said, 'Don't worry, he'll know you by the time you get there.' I then said to Eisenhower that because Mervin Kelly was a member [of the Statutory Advisory Committee to the Bureau of Standards], I should wish to have him accompany me. Eisenhower said, 'It is up to you to straighten out this job. I'm used to having good staff work, and apparently I'm not getting it.'

"Mervin was superb with his usual very forceful manner, arguing strongly for the integrity of the Bureau, and I insisting that the National Academy would surely back Kelly and his Advisory Committee in strong support of Astin. I recall [Weeks] asking, 'What can I do?' We told him that there was just one thing to do and that was to reappoint Astin. Weeks objected that it would be political suicide. I recall saying, 'I am no politician, but I don't think you are correct, Mr. Secretary.' To which Mervin added, 'We all make so many mistakes, that for a man in public office to make a mistake and admit it will, I am sure, earn him good marks politically'." Weeks reappointed Astin. Moreover, Kelly's conduct so impressed Weeks that he appointed Kelly Chairman of the Department of Commerce's Statutory Visiting Committee, a post that he held for some nine years.

According to Bronk and others, Kelly also played a leading role in the location of the new Engineering Society's building in New York, in providing a sensible procedure for deciding where it should be, and in campaigning to raise millions of dollars from industry to help build it. He also played an important role as a trustee of the Atoms for Peace awards. Of this, J. R. Killian says, "He took a very active part in the work of the board, and his judgment was excellent and his policy views broad." Kelly was also a Member and Life Member Emeritus of the Corporation of the Massachusetts Institute of Technology. Killian says, "I will always remember visiting a number of companies along with him and his persuasive and forceful presentation of the need for corporate contributions in the support of science and engineering and private education." Kelly raised millions for MIT and for other causes.

Kelly's retirement from the Bell Laboratories in 1959 marked the end of an era, for his qualities were unique. One of Kelly's friends and admirers put it thus:

"Why did I like Mervin? He was no fake, a real man, true to himself. He drove himself for the betterment of the labs and expected others to do likewise. He always listened and observed what was said and had the technical know-how to assess it and have it put to use.

"Why did I feel that his successor should be different? No one else could be like Mervin and get away with it. He was the backbone and the strength that has made BTL what it is today."

After Kelly retired from Bell Laboratories, he acted as a consultant to a number of companies, but chiefly to International Business Machines Incorporated. In this capacity, his energy and enthusiasm were no less than in his leadership of Bell Laboratories, but he wisely realized that his role was that of counsellor to the management, including Thomas Watson, Jr., the chairman of the board, and not that of a boss. According to E. R. Piore, vice president and chief scientist of IBM:

"He traveled to all technical locations in IBM that stretch across this country north and south and east and west and which are located in six countries in Europe. Once in the laboratory, he would [as he used to do at Bell Laboratories] spend time with the people at the bench, stimulating discussion and thinking, constantly evaluating the person and the program. Thus he acquired possibly more than any other person, a judgment of men, of programs, and the methods in use. This quality of conversing with the man at the bench, making the man feel at home with Kelly, in no way inhibited him with similar conversations with men up the ladder, including Tom Watson, Jr., and the rest of the group that had oversight over the whole IBM enterprise. Thus he would report to me after his trip and report to Tom Watson also. Mervin was not making a career for himself in IBM. Thus he never fought for his convictions but quietly gave his views—strong, moderate, or negative. This is one reason why his influence was great whether talking to me or to those above me. These conversations dealt with technology, people and management.

"His evaluation and identification of people had a profound effect on their careers. He was after the best technical people, and recommended that they be placed in jobs of ever-increasing responsibility. I would judge that this was his greatest accomplishment in IBM.

"There were areas of great technological deficiencies in our laboratories. Mervin was most helpful in smelling them out and articulating the need for correction. Without his presence this would have taken longer."

Some remarks of G. R. Gunther-Mohr are illuminating:

"My first encounter with Dr. Kelly was at the annual research meetings [which Piore used to hold]. He sat there smoking endlessly and often seemed asleep, yet it was clear he was not from the incisive questions he would ask. He never, however, gave the audience a real view of his thinking. We expected higher management was benefiting.

"He had the respect of a wide variety of people. I had the opportunity to accompany him in a trip to Allentown. It was impressive to see how no one talked down to him technically, but took him on as a participant.

"I believe we all miss his presence greatly. I do, especially since in the later years of his association with IBM, I got to know him better. He never retired and was mentally alert even when he had great difficulty in moving about. He was never sentimental about anything, including himself, but clear eyed, hard headed and positive."

Continually pressing for higher achievement, Kelly always prized and promoted ability wherever he found it. Conversely, he was uniformly impatient with mediocrity and almost ruthlessly intolerant of incompetence. His frequently awesome aspect in business did not, however, carry over into private life.

He entertained frequently and was a genial and gracious host. But it was among close friends of long standing that other traits emerged, including an essential simplicity and boyishness that scientists sometimes exhibit. He was an enthusiastic, though not expert, bridge player. For one thing, a consuming desire to be dealt thirteen of a suit tended to impair his concentration on the game. Then, too, there were other distractions.

As he played, he would sit, drumming his fingers on the table, meanwhile singing, not quite under his breath, folk songs that reflected his Missouri background. One of his favorites was "Upon a pole a polecat sat, He didn't know where he was at."

Kelly had a deep love of music, particularly chamber music. A side consequence of this, plus his innate generosity, was the help he rendered the Summit (N.J.) School of Music. This school could not have survived without the sacrifice of time and energy (and some of his own income) that Kelly gave it for years, no matter how busy he was. The Director of the school was an able musician with no financial acumen. Kelly supervised everything about the school that related to money—budgets, tax returns, etc. He even succeeded in setting funds aside so the Director would have some income after retirement.

During one period Kelly did a great deal for Overlook Hospital in Summit, N.J. When Christ Church in Millburn had great trouble with acoustics, he concerned himself deeply with the problem and brought in highly qualified people to help. After his retirement, when the Kellys' longtime housemaid planned to return with her husband to her native region in Germany, Kelly provided funds for the move. When the couple realized that they preferred the United States, he took care of that move, too.

Kelly loved flowers and gardening. During the growing season, he began work in the garden at 5 a.m. In one year he planted 5,000 bulbs, and the garden included some 20,000 tulips, hyacinths and narcissus. After Kelly's death, his wife, Katherine, asked the gardener, "Why doesn't the garden look the same? You still work in it." The gardener replied, "No one loves it anymore." Katherine liked the garden, but she did not need it.

THE PHILOSOPHER OF RESEARCH AND TECHNOLOGY

Kelly had clear and concrete ideas concerning the importance of scientists and engineers, of research and development, and of the organization and management of technical enterprises. His views were important to him. He expressed them persuasively and with remarkable clarity. In justice to him, I believe that they should be reviewed in this memoir.

Kelly had no doubt as to the place of science and technology in man's life. He wrote: "So completely have they dominated the pattern of our growth that when the man in the street speaks of 'progress,' he usually means scientific and technological progress."

Kelly was equally clear concerning the source of such progress: "Basic research is the foundation on which all technologic advances rest."

What is the source, the generating force behind new ideas? Kelly said: "But with all the needed emphasis on leadership, organization and teamwork, the individual has remained supreme—of paramount importance. It is in the mind of a single person that creative ideas and concepts are born."

Where should basic research be carried out? Kelly noted that " . . . the academic community has been the principal home of basic research for more than a century. . . ." However, he looked toward industry for substantial contributions to research: "The author believes that at least 10 per cent of most research and development budgets can be profitably employed in basic research. Any company that has 50 or more members of professional staff, that will dedicate 10 per cent of them to basic research, can build a strong, productive, and profitable effort."

If research is to be carried out in an industrial laboratory, that laboratory must have some management. Concerning the management of laboratories and, indeed, of technological manufacturing organizations, Kelly had firm words. In a conference on higher technological education held in London in 1950, he noted that:

"The industrial research laboratory directed by men trained in the research methods of science had its beginnings in my country in the first decade of this century. Dr. F. B. Jewett of the Bell System and Dr. W. R. Whitney of the General Electric Company were among the first men trained as pure scientists with a working knowledge of the scientific research method. The laboratories they founded have become two of the great industrial laboratories of our country."

With respect to Bell Laboratories he proudly said:

"There have been four presidents of Bell Telephone Laboratories, for example, since it was established in 1925. All were trained to the doctorate level in science and had won their spurs in research." In the London conference on technological education, Kelly said concerning the United States:

"Now substantially all members of manufacturing engineering organizations are engineering graduates and the top few levels of management of manufacture are largely filled by engineering graduates."

While Kelly recognized basic research as the source of all technological advances, he understood that a complicated technological process lies between discovery and use. He wrote:

"There has been so much emphasis on industrial research and mass-production methods in my country, that even our well-informed public is not sufficiently aware of the necessary and most important chain of events that lies between the initial step of basic research and the terminal operation of manufacture. In order to stress the continuity of procedures from research to engineering of product into manufacture and to emphasize their real unity, I speak of them as the single entity 'organized creative technology'."

Using the Bell Laboratories as an example of organized technology, Kelly delineated three areas that preceded the manufacture of complicated technological systems:

"The first includes all of the research and fundamental development. This is our non-scheduled area of work. It provides the reservoir of completely new knowledge, principles, materials, methods, and art that are essential for the development of new communications systems and facilities.

"The second we call 'systems engineering'. Its major responsibility is the determination of the new specific systems and facilities development projects—their operational and economic objectives and the broad technical plan to be followed. 'Systems engineering' controls and guides the use of the new knowledge obtained from the research and fundamental development programs in the creation of new telephone services and the improvement and lowering of cost of services already established.

"The third encompasses all specific development and design of new systems and facilities. The work is most carefully programmed in conformity with the plan established by the systems engineering studies. Our research and fundamental development programs supply the new knowledge required in meeting the objectives of the new specific devleopments."

In addition to these three technical areas, Kelly referred to another, the management of buildings, shops, and services:

"The nonscientific duties of management should be minimized for all levels of the research supervision. Through proper organization, direct responsibility for people can be limited to scientists and their aides. Budget preparation, management of shops, services, secretaries and typists, for example, can be done by an intimately associated professional management staff of non-scientists. There should be the very minimum of diversion of the attention of the research leadership and the individual researchers from their scientific programs. This can be accomplished by organizational structures and operations fashioned to free all scientists from nonresearch supervisory duties which, at the same time, provide excellent and economical service in all areas that support the direct scientific endeavor."

While Kelly speaks here of research, he applied this plan to systems engineering and development as well.

Kelly's threefold organization of technological endeavor differed from other existing or possible organizations in a number of ways.

Besides research, Kelly classed fundamental development as unscheduled work. He understood that the demonstration of a useful device or a system that embodied really new ideas was uncertain and unpredictable and that things must be carried into practical operation before they could be evaluated.

Kelly's separation of systems engineering from research and development, eventually as a separate vice-presidential area, had roots in a much earlier pattern of system studies in the Department on Development and Research of AT&T, which was transferred to Bell Laboratories in 1934. But, when in 1948 Kelly established Systems Engineering under George W. Gilman, who chose the name, he added a new prerogative: systems engineers were to go beyond planning and to assume a cooperative status with development in the conduct and reporting on projects. Some systems engineers looked on this as a responsibility to control the course of development.

Concerning the three functions into which he divided technological endeavor, Kelly made a number of observations. About research, he said:

"Inspired and productive research in industry requires men of the same high quality as is required for distinguished pure research in our universities.

"They must be given freedoms that are equivalent to those

of the research man in the university." Elsewhere he wrote:

"A universal and invariant requirement for building an enduring and successful basic research endeavor in industry is its complete segregation into a single organizational unit or at most with adjacent and closely related applied research."
and:

"Only one who is expert in research can wisely establish the environment, the freedoms, the salary levels and the programs of research." After research, and close to it, came fundamental development:

"Staff members for fundamental development are drawn from our research groups by selecting those having technologic and engineering aptitudes and interests who prefer to move into development and by recruitment from among the most promising of the graduate students of our schools of applied science, such as Massachusetts and California Institutes of Technology."

Kelly's concept of fundamental development is well illustrated by the course followed at Bell Laboratories after the invention of and publication concerning the transistor:

"In accord with our policy of concentrating the efforts of our scientists on research, we immediately formed a closely associated fundamental development group to acquire that body of technological knowledge essential to the development and design of transistors for the many specific communications applications that would certainly follow."

Concerning Systems Engineering, Kelly said:

"Approximately 10% of our scientific and technical staff are allotted to systems engineering. Its staff members must supply a proper blending of competence and background in each of the three areas that it contacts: research and fundamental development, specific systems and facilities development, and operations. It is therefore, largely made up of men drawn from these areas who have exhibited unusual talents in analysis and the objectivity so essential to their appraisal responsibility."

"Systems engineering has intimate knowledge of the telephone plant and its operation and maintains close contact with engineers of the operating organization.

"Systems engineering also maintains close association with our research and fundamental development work.

"Typical examples of recent systems engineering studies that have led to development and standardization are: television transmission over coaxial cables, a broadband microwave radio repeatered communication system, a mobile radio subscriber telephone system, and a new subscriber telephone set."

Kelly illustrated an ideal relation between systems engineering, research and development by the case of the NIKE antiaircraft missile:

"For example, the programming study on the NIKE missile system established that basic knowledge and art were available for the development of a system that would meet the service requirements except for a particular area of radar technology. This area was at once subjected to a research and exploratory development attack. The project was not undertaken until this deficiency was eliminated by new knowledge from research. The NIKE missile system now in production meets the requirements initially agreed upon and in its technical character is in close correspondence with the plan of the initial study.

"I am familiar with large military systems developments where this approach is absent, where research and exploration are intermingled with specific development, probably with the intent of gaining time. Actually, time has been lost."

As to development, Kelly said:

"In the development area most of our recruits have a training of four or five years in electrical, mechanical or chemical engineering. A few trained to the doctorate level are added each year. Their number is limited by the number trained to this level who are initially interested in development and design as a career.

"We hold the view that in the development and design of electronics of today and certainly of tomorrow, more than four or five years of training are required." And:

"The work of specific systems and facilities development is closely programmed. Its projects are organized in the patterns that the studies of systems engineering prescribe."

Kelly goes on to say that development, while a continuous operation, is done in three distinct stages: first the laboratory model; after tests and modifications, the preproduction model, which is field tested; and finally, the final design for manufacture (by Western Electric).

Kelly's concept of "organized creative technology," embracing research, fundamental (or exploratory) development, systems engineering, and final development for manufacture is persuasive. His concept of the place of basic research in industry is inspiring and appealing. What, however, are we to make of these in practice?

There seems to be no avoiding Kelly's conclusion that industrial progress is based on the results of basic research. We can note that basic research is sometimes inspired by technological invention. Thermodynamics was inspired by the steam engine. But, whatever its inspiration, basic research lies behind the whole of modern technology. Kelly felt strongly that much basic research should be carried out in industrial laboratories.

During Kelly's career at Bell Laboratories, he experienced (despite the years of the Depression) the relatively stable support derived from the provision of a service as opposed to the manufacture of products for the market place. The exception to this was defense work, but this was done during periods of close cooperation between government and industry in the national crises of World War II and the Korean War. These were circumstances far more favorable to research, or at least to the dedicated effort of first-rate men, than is work in a manufacturing industry where markets as well as revenues fluctuate.

Further, in Kelly's time the effect on science of some government actions and attitudes was less clear than it is today. The consequences to science of antitrust actions that sever service from manufacture (in aircraft and airlines, for example), that render successful companies insecure in their operations and in cooperative relations with universities, and that prevent cooperative research toward common needs, were not yet clear. Further, in Kelly's time the attitude of government toward both science and industry was on the whole friendly and cooperative. Today, the attitude of government has, in many areas, become at once hostile, highly demanding, and minutely dictatorial through statutory and bureaucratic means.

Thus, Kelly may have overestimated the amount and quality of research that could in the future be expected from industry, and perhaps from the nation.

Some of Kelly's ideas concerning the organizational form most suitable for "organized creative technology" have hazards as well as power. The autonomy of research, the prerogatives of systems engineering, and the separation of the management of nontechnological functions from the technological management depend for their success on inspired leadership.

When leadership is uninspired or inadequate, it is easy for research to drift away from the overall purpose of an organization. It is easy for the rest of the organization to disregard research. It is easy for systems engineers to become stale and to lose their feel for the actual state of research on one hand and the current realities of development, manufacture, and operation on the other. It is easy for a large staff organization concerned with buildings, facilities, shops, libraries, and even computer services to put organizational order and budgetary neatness ahead of the real needs and problems of scientists and engineers.

Above all, a technological organization must have the leadership to see and pursue real opportunities and real needs. In an address to a naval research conference, Kelly said:

"The first, and perhaps the most important, factor is the

program itself. What shall it contain? What can be discarded at once, and what shall be eliminated after limited exploration? How can comprehensive coverage with freedom from gaps be assured? In an endeavor so broad in scope and requiring such a highly functional organization for its operation, how can unneeded duplication be prevented, and duplication that is worthwhile, though usually small in volume, be provided?"

Such overall planning and programming is possible only when one point that Kelly made concerning the leadership or management of research and technology is held to. Leaders or managers must be technologically trained and technologically competent. Only thus can decisions be based on insight and understanding rather than on salesmanship and hearsay. And, leadership is most effective when it is strong and decisive.

A man with Kelly's energy and insight could by his own knowledge, perception, and authority avoid organizational pitfalls and bridge organizational gaps, but it was no easy matter, even for him.

Mervin Kelly had a large and optimistic view of the place of science and technology in man's world. He had a clear and persuasive plan for its organization. The success of Bell Laboratories vindicated his ideas in a general way. But, the world is complicated and changeable, and even the most experienced and wisest man cannot catch it eternally in a few, clear, understandable words, or in a great many words, for that matter. Kelly's words are wise and worthy of consideration, but they are less than the man and what he accomplished.

BIOGRAPHICAL SKETCH

Mervin Kelly's great-great-grandfather came from Northern Ireland to Virginia. The family proceeded by way of Indiana to Missouri, where Mervin's father, Joseph Fenimore Kelly, went to teach school at the age of 17. There he met and married Mervin's mother, Mary Etta Evans, whose Welsh parents were Missouri farmers.

Mervin Joe Kelly was born on February 14, 1894, at Princeton, Missouri. His father was then principal of the high school at the Mercer County seat. Shortly thereafter he bought a hardware and farm implement business at Gallatin, Missouri. There Mervin received his grade and high school education, graduating as class valedictorian at the age of 16.

During his school years, Mervin worked at various odd jobs during the summers. He kept the store books for his father and had a newspaper delivery route. By the time he was 16, he had saved just enough money for tuition at the Missouri School of Mines and Metallurgy, at Rolla. His ambition was to become a mining engineer, a career that would take him to far-off places. "I was really pretty lucky to go to Rolla," he once recalled. "In those days, not too many youngsters got to go to college." To make ends meet, he took a job with the State Geological Survey, which allowed him to sleep in a room over its headquarters. Working nights and weekends, he managed to earn $18 a month cataloging and numbering mineral specimens.

Mervin was a brilliant student, particularly in chemistry and physics. At the end of his sophomore year at Rolla, he was appointed an assistant in chemistry, for tuition and $300 a year. The next summer he worked in a Utah copper mine. This changed his mind about metallurgy, and on returning to Rolla he switched to a general science course. The heads of the chemistry and mathematics departments volunteered to give him special instruction. When he graduated from Rolla in 1914 with a B.S. degree and honors in science, Kelly decided that he wanted "to make a life in academic research."

Kelly taught physics and studied mathematics at the University of Kentucky, receiving his master's degree in 1915. On November 11, 1915, he married Katharine Milsted, a Rolla girl. He once called her his "most candid critic."

The Kellys went to the University of Chicago and he received his Ph.D. in 1918. While at Chicago he was an assistant to Professor Robert A. Millikan, and he participated in the famous oil drop experiments for measuring the charge of the electron. From his work with Millikan, he developed the conviction that it was necessary to undertake basic investigations of nature in order to be able to manipulate nature in a practical way.

When World War I came, Frank B. Jewett, who later became the first president of Bell Laboratories, offered Kelly a $2100 a year job as a research physicist in the Engineering Department of the Western Electric Company. His initial work was in providing practical vacuum tubes.

In 1925 the research and development work of Western Electric was incorporated separately as Bell Telephone Laboratories. Kelly worked as a physicist until 1928, as director of vacuum tube development from 1928 until 1934, and as development director of transmission instruments and electronics during 1934–1936.

In 1936 he was appointed director of research. He became executive vice president in 1944 and president in 1951. On January 1, 1959, he was named chairman of the board of directors. He retired from Bell Laboratories on March 1, 1959.

Kelly served on the board of directors of Bell Laboratories from 1944 until his retirement and was a director of the Sandia Corporation, a subsidiary of the Western Electric Company, from 1952 through 1958. In addition, he was a director of the Prudential Insurance Company of America, Bausch and Lomb Optical Company, Tung–Sol Electric, Incorporated, and the Economic Club of New York. He acted as a consultant to the International Business Machines Corporation, Bausch and Lomb, Ingersoll–Rand Company, and the Kennecott Copper Corporation.

Mervin Joe Kelly died on March 18, 1971, at Port Saint Lucie, Florida, where he had a second home, at the age of 77.

THE FOLLOWING INDIVIDUALS, through personal communications, provided material for this biographical sketch: Richard M. Bozorth, Harald T. Friis, Detlev W. Bronk, James R. Killian, Emmanuel R. Piore, G. R. Gunther-Mohr, and Estill I. Green. Other information was obtained from Bell Laboratories; Harald T. Friis, *Seventy-five Years in an Exciting World,* San Francisco Press; and William Shockley, *Bell Laboratories Record,* Vol. 50, December 1972.

AWARDS, HONORS, MEMBERSHIPS

AWARDS

Presidential Certificate of Merit, 1947
Medal of the Industrial Research Institute, 1954
Christopher Columbus International Communication Prize, 1955
Air Force Exceptional Service Award, 1957
James Forrestal Memorial Medal, 1957
Air Force Association Trophy Award, 1958
John Fritz Medal, 1959
Mervin J. Kelly Award of the American Institute of Electrical Engineers, initial award, 1960
The Golden Omega Award, 1960
The Hoover Medal, 1961
Centennial Medal of Honor, University of Missouri at Rolla, 1970

HONORARY DEGREES

University of Missouri, D.Eng., 1936
University of Kentucky, D.Sc., 1946
University of Pennsylvania, LL.D., 1954
New York University, D.Eng., 1955
Polytechnic Institute of Brooklyn, D.Eng., 1955
University of Lyons, Doctor Honoris Causa, 1957
Wayne State University, D.Eng., 1958
Case Institute of Technology, D.Sc., 1959
University of Pittsburgh, D.Sc., 1959
Princeton University, D.Eng., 1959

MEMBERSHIPS

National Academy of Sciences
American Philosophical Society
American Academy of Arts and Sciences
Royal Academy of Sciences (Sweden)
American Physical Society (Fellow)
Acoustical Society of America (Fellow)
Institute of Electrical and Electronic Engineers (Fellow)
Sigma Xi
Eta Kappa Nu
Tau Beta Pi
Rochester Museum of Arts and Sciences
University Club of New York
Baltusrol Golf Club of Springfield, N. J.

BIBLIOGRAPHY

KEY TO ABBREVIATIONS

Bell Lab. Rec. = Bell Laboratories Record
Bell Syst. Monogr. = Bell System Monograph
Bell Syst. Tech. J. = Bell System Technical Journal
Bell Teleph. Mag. = Bell Telephone Magazine
Electr. Eng. = Electrical Engineering
J. Franklin Inst. = Journal of the Franklin Institute
Phys. Rev. = Physical Review
Phys. Today = Physics Today
Proc. I.R.E. = Proceedings of the Institute of Radio Engineers

1919

With R. A. Millikan and V. H. Gottschalk. Effect upon the atom of the passage of an alpha ray through it. Proceedings of the National Academy of Sciences, 5:591–92.

1920

With R. A. Millikan and V. H. Gottschalk. Nature of the process of ionization of gases by alpha rays. Phys. Rev., 5:157–77.
The valency of photo-electrons and the photo-electric properties of some insulators. Phys. Rev., 15:260–73; also in J. Franklin Inst., 190:916–17.

1926

Manufacture of vacuum tubes. Bell Lab. Rec., 2(4):137–44.

1932

Vacuum tubes and photoelectric tube developments for sound picture systems. Journal of the Society of Motion Picture Engineers, 18:761–81; also in Motion Picture Projectionist, 5:15–20; Bell Syst. Monogr. B-694; Eastman Kodak Monthly Abstract Bulletin, 19:255(1933); Wireless Engineer, 10:571(1933).
With C. H. Prescott, Jr. The caesium–oxygen–silver photoelectric cell. Bell Syst. Tech. J., 11:334–67; also in Transactions of the Electrochemical Society, 62:297–322; Bell Syst. Monogr. B-681; Bell Lab. Rec., 12:34–39(1933); Radio Revisita, 18:443–45(1933); International Projectionist, 6:27(1933).

1934

With A. L. Samuel. Vacuum tubes as high frequency oscillators.

Electr. Eng., 53:1504–17; also in Bell Syst. Tech. J., 14:97–134 (1935); Bell Syst. Monogr. B-839(1935).

1943

The American engineer. The Bridge of Eta Kappa Nu, September; also in Bell Lab. Rec., November, p. 122(A).

1945

Science as a force in our civilization, past, present, and future. (Talk presented before Science Club) Kearnygram, 18:1–2. (A)
Discussion on the future of industrial research. In: *The Future of Industrial Research*. New York, Standard Oil Development Co.
Radar and Bell Laboratories. Bell Teleph. Mag., 24:221–55.

1947

Our country's preparedness research and development program—a cooperative undertaking of our military, university and industrial laboratories. (Address given at Navy Research Conference, Wash., D.C., November 18–19) Published in pamphlet form.

1949

Radar Systems and Components; with an Introduction by M. J. Kelly, pp. 1–8. New York, D. Van Nostrand Co. 1042 pp.

1950

Bell Telephone Laboratories—an example of an institute of creative technology. Proceedings of the Royal Society (London), Series A, 203:287–301; also Bell Syst. Monogr. 1794.

1951

Educational patterns in U.S. and England. Journal of Engineering Education, 41:358–61; also Bell Syst. Monogr. 1836.
Education requirements for development engineers in electronic and communication technology. (Paper presented at Institute of Radio Engineers Convention, New York City, March 19–22) Proc. I.R.E., 39:299. (A)
The Institutes for Basic Research—their contribution to national strength. (Address at the dedication of the Institutes for Basic Research, The University of Chicago, May 16) Published as a pamphlet entitled "Applied Research is Not Enough."

Dr. C. J. Davisson. Bell Syst. Tech. J., 30(Part I):779–85; also Bell Syst. Monogr. B-1876.

1952

Communications and electronics. Elecr. Eng., 71:965–69; also Bell Syst. Monogr. 2026.

1953

First five years of the transistor. Bell Teleph. Mag., 32(2):73–86; also Bell Syst. Monogr. 2130.

Research and development problems of engineering management in the electronics industry. (Paper presented at Institute of Radio Engineers Convention, New York City, March 23–26) Proc. I.R.E., 41:425; also Bell Syst. Monogr. 2070 (A).

Air defense: Kelly vs. "summer study" group. Fortune, 48:40. (A)

Kelly committee report, a summary. Phys. Today, 6:4–11.

The contribution of industrial research to national security. (Presented at American Association for the Advancement of Science, Boston, Mass., December 29) Bell Syst. Monogr. 2181; also published in pamphlet form.

1954

Russian threat and our attitude toward it. New Jersey Bell, 27:10–13.

With A. T. Waterman and J. C. Ward, Jr. Scientific research and national security. Scientific Monthly, 78:214–24.

The interactions of applied science and technology for the civilian economy and for national security—a case study. (Eighth annual address in the Charles M. Schwab Memorial Lectureship, delivered in New York City, May 26, 1954, at the 62nd General Meeting of the American Iron and Steel Institute) Published in pamphlet form.

1955

As told to D. Robinson. Should your child be an electronic engineer? Prepared originally as an advertisement for New York Life Insurance Co. Reprinted in pamphlet form.

With Sir G. Radley, G. W. Gilman, and R. J. Halsey. A transatlantic telephone cable. Communication and Electronics, 17:124–36; also in Electr. Eng., 74:192–97; Bell Syst. Monogr. 2434.

Aiding academic programs in fields of science. Bell Teleph. Mag., 34:194–99.

With others. Subcommittee report on research activities in the Department of Defense and defense related agencies. Prepared for the Commission on Organization of the Executive Branch of the Government. Published in pamphlet form.

Training programs of industry for graduate engineers. Electr. Eng., 74:866–69; also Bell Syst. Monogr. 2512.

1956

Research and development. Engineers Joint Council, Proceedings of the Second General Assembly, Panel on the Hoover Commission Reports—a Review of the Engineering Aspects, p. 52.

A scientist's look at our developing military strength. (Address given at the Cleveland Council on World Affairs, February 8) Indiana Bell Highlights, August 20, pp. 4–6. Reprinted in pamphlet form.

Contributions of research to telephony—look at past and glance into future. J. Franklin Inst., 261:189–200; also Bell Syst. Monogr. 2590. Reprinted in pamphlet form.

Record of profitable research at Bell Telephone Laboratories. Proceedings of the National Industrial Research Conference, July, pp. 3–11; also Bell Syst. Monogr. 2663.

Our developing military strength—a scientist's view. Signal, September–October, pp. 26, 28–29, 77.

Advances in communications. Age of Science Magazine, Yale University, December, p. 106.

1957

With Sir G. Radley. Transatlantic communications—an historical resume. Bell Syst. Tech. J., 36:1–5; also Bell Syst. Monogr. 2710.

The work and environment of the physicist yesterday, today, and tomorrow. Phys. Today, 10:26–31. Also published in pamphlet form.

Factors promoting productivity in research and development at Bell Telephone Laboratories. (Address presented at the National Meeting of the American Chemical Society, September 13) Reprinted in pamphlet form.

Girding for the nuclear age. In: Brainpower Quest, ed. by A. A. Freeman. New York, Macmillan Inc. 242 pp.

The trends of telecommunications as affected by solid state electronics instrumentation. (Address given at Symposium on Radio Links, Rome, June 5) Published in symposium proceedings.

The nation's research and development—their deficiencies and means for correction. Proceedings of the American Philosophical Society, 101(4):386–91.

Our woeful lag in basic research. Part I. *New York Herald Tribune*, October 25. Part II. *New York Herald Tribune*, October 27.

The nation's need for greater scientific and technical strength—means for its attainment. Institute of Radio Engineers, Transactions of the Professional Group on Engineering Management, M-4(4):122–27.

1958

The transistor—ten years of progress. Bell Lab. Rec., 36:190–91.

Career of H. S. Black, 1957 Lamme Medalist. Electr. Eng., August.

The first decade of the transistor. Bell Teleph. Mag., 37(2):24–38.

Some essentials for national strength. (Address before the National Security Industrial Association's 1958 James Forrestal Memorial Award Dinner) Published in 1959 in pamphlet form.

1959

Development of the nation's scientific and technical potential. (Presented at John Fritz Medal Award ceremony, American Institute of Electrical Engineers Winter General Meeting, February) Electr. Eng., April.

Basic research. An unpublished document. Appears to have been intended as a chapter in a handbook on the management of industrial research.

1961

Response of the medalist. (Address presented at M. J. Kelly Medal Award ceremony, American Institute of Electrical Engineers Winter General Meeting, February) Electr. Eng., April.

1962

The role of the engineer in a world of change. (Technical paper presented at the Design Engineering Conference and Show, Chicago, Ill., April 30–May 3) Design News, June 27. (A)

CHARLES CHRISTIAN LAURITSEN *

April 4, 1892–April 13, 1968

BY WILLIAM A. FOWLER

CHARLES CHRISTIAN LAURITSEN, Danish-born physicist, became, in his later years, an elder statesman in science for the defense forces and government of his adopted country, the United States. Through his own work, through the work of the laboratory that he established, and through students and colleagues, he exercised a profound influence on nuclear physics and its applications in astronomy over a span of four decades. During and after World War II he turned his attention to the scientific and technological needs and capabilities of the United States in national defense. By active and continuous engagement for thirty years as participant, adviser, and consultant in the national scientific defense effort, he contributed to the interplay between science and government that is so essential to both.

Charles Lauritsen was born in Holstebro, Denmark, on April 4, 1892. He graduated in architecture from the Odense Tekniske Skole in 1911 and emigrated in 1917 to find his fortune in America. After various undertakings, from designing naval craft in Boston to professional fishing off the Florida coast, he went to Palo Alto in 1921 to work on ship-to-shore radio for Federal Telegraph. There his interest turned to designing radio receivers, and, together with several enthusiastic

---

* This biography, without the bibliography, appeared earlier in the *Year Book of the American Philosophical Society*, 1969.

partners, he started producing them in a rented garage. In 1923 he went to St. Louis to become chief engineer for the Kennedy Corporation and started making those fifty-pound, ten-tube radio sets that brought music and entertainment to tens of thousands of American households.

In 1926 Robert Andrews Millikan gave a lecture in St. Louis that opened Lauritsen's eyes to a new world. Six years earlier Millikan had become head of a small college in Pasadena, California, which at about the same time took the name, the California Institute of Technology. This was the new world where graduate research in physics was pre-eminent. A certain uneasiness about the future of the radio business, together with the enthusiasm inspired by Millikan, led him to move his wife, Sigrid, and a ten-year-old son, Thomas, to Southern California.

In Pasadena, he found much to his surprise that you could get paid—though not handsomely—for working at a place like Caltech, and he settled down to work. He signed up for the courses of Epstein and Smythe and Tolman and Bowen and Zwicky and Bateman and started to rebuild his intellectual capital. More than that, he went to Millikan and asked for a doctoral research project. What was interesting Millikan in the fall of 1926 was the cold-emission effect: pulling electrons out of metals by high electric fields. If one put in the experimental numbers, it appeared to be easier to get electrons out than the theory would allow, considering that they had to be pulled over a quite formidable potential barrier at the surface. Would Lauritsen look into it? Lauritsen was able to show that the field emission was quite insensitive to temperature and displayed a simple exponential dependence on field strength that agreed very well with a theory developed by Oppenheimer on the basis of quantum-mechanical barrier penetration.

In 1929 Lauritsen received his Ph.D. in physics from the California Institute, with which he remained associated for the rest of his life. He became assistant professor of physics in

1930, associate professor in 1931, professor in 1935, and professor emeritus in 1962.

Field emission, vacuum tubes, and the availability of a million-volt cascade transformer led Lauritsen to x rays. He built a series of x-ray tubes operating up to 750 kilovolts. Three-quarters of a million volts was a considerable step forward in the technology of the time. The largest medical x-ray tubes then available were fragile overgrown glass bulbs rated for 200 kilovolts and worth their weight in gold. It seemed natural, then, to explore whether the bigger tubes offered any new opportunities in medicine, particularly in the treatment of deep-seated malignant tumors. This idea proved quite interesting to Albert Soiland, a distinguished radiologist in Los Angeles, and after some preliminary experiments with animals, treatment of patients with "super-voltage" x rays began in the old High Voltage Laboratory at the California Institute in October 1930. In the following year, Millikan interested W. K. Kellogg in improving the facilities, and the Kellogg Radiation Laboratory was funded and built. Lauritsen was elected a Fellow of the American College of Radiology in 1931, at which time he received the college's Gold Medal.

In 1932 Cockroft and Walton in Cambridge, England, announced that man-made machines could be used to disintegrate nuclei. Lauritsen had a laboratory ready to enter this new and exciting field. H. R. Crane, now professor of physics at the University of Michigan, was still a graduate student under Lauritsen. The x-ray therapy had been transferred from the High Voltage Laboratory to Kellogg. The two immediately converted one of the old x-ray tubes in the High Voltage Laboratory into a positive-ion accelerator using a bottle of helium gas and a primitive ion source. One of the first projects, published in September 1933, was the artificial production of neutrons by bombarding beryllium targets with simple quartz fiber electroscope that Lauritsen had developed for the x-ray work, now furnished with a lining of paraffin. Neutrons had been detected by Chadwick from studies of the rare but potent radiations produced by bombarding beryllium with alpha particles from radium. The discovery that neutrons could now be made "artificially" with machines, in numbers many orders of magnitudes greater than using natural sources, revolutionized neutron physics.

Not long after the discovery that neutrons could be produced using helium ions, G. N. Lewis of Berkeley supplied Lauritsen with a sample of heavy water and Lauritsen and Crane soon found how to augment this supply by electrolyzing ordinary water. They discovered that deuterons produced neutrons even more copiously than helium ions. In addition, in 1934 they were the first to find that deuteron bombardment produced radioactive nuclei as well as neutrons. This was first published by Lauritsen, Crane, and W. W. Harper in early 1934. From carbon there was produced a ten-minute activity that yielded the same positrons that Carl Anderson had discovered in the cosmic radiation in 1932. Lauritsen soon found the annihilation radiation that resulted when a positron met a matching electron. He performed a pretty experiment, remarkably convincing in its simplicity. He placed a graphite target, bombarded side up, on top of one of his sensitive electroscopes and measured a certain discharge rate. He then placed a thin absorber, previously shown not to be radioactive, on top of the target—the discharge rate doubled. The explanation was indeed quite simple. The positrons were created in a thin surface layer of the target slab. The half moving downward were annihilated in the target adjacent to the electroscope and the resulting annihilation radiation discharged the electroscope. When the absorber was not in place, the half moving upward escaped into the atmosphere and were eventually annihilated at some distance from the electroscope—too far, in fact, to affect the discharge rate. The absorber placed on top of the target stopped the upward moving positrons, which then produced a discharge rate practically identical to the downward moving ones—thus, the doubling. To an observer not acquainted with the nature of the radiation, it seemed very mysterious. When explained, the experiment became a simple demonstration of the annihilation phenomenon.

Lauritsen loved experimental work in the laboratory, and he passed this along to his graduate research students. I was one of the first of his students. He taught us everything from how to run a lathe to how to design and build electroscopes, ion sources, cloud chambers, magnetic spectrometers, electrostatic analyzers, and high voltage accelerators. But most of all he taught us how to do experiments—in simple, direct, but very elegant ways.

It was always the case that Lauritsen saw through to the heart of any problem. Whereas most of us tend to overdesign apparatus and to use redundant procedures in our experiments, Lauritsen delighted in designing inexpensive and simple devices that would make the experiment and its theoretical interpretation as straightforward as possible. He delighted too in convincing us in his logical manner that his suggestions were the right ones. When agreement had been reached, he got perhaps his greatest satisfaction in going to the lathe and turning out the most difficult parts and pieces himself. But withal he always taught us why he did thus and so and we learned, insofar as we were able, something of his marvelous insight into how to *do* physics, as he so frequently expressed it.

Lauritsen was primarily an experimentalist, but it was his close personal relationship with theorists that broadened and deepened the experiences of his students. This continued throughout his lifetime, but it was especially true before World War II when what we now call classical nuclear physics was in its golden age. It was truly golden for all the students in Kellogg because first of all there was Charles Lauritsen, one of the great men in the field, along with Rutherford and Cockcroft and Lawrence and Tuve, but also there were his two great and eminent friends Richard Tolman and Robert Oppenheimer.

They were giants—all three in their different ways—but all three truly great men. It was exciting and even awe-inspiring to listen to their discussions about our experiments and what the experimental results meant in terms of the nuclear theory of that time. Tolman and Oppenheimer were delighted with the discoveries in nuclear physics that came out of Lauritsen's laboratory—the discovery of resonance in proton-induced reactions; the first production of high-energy gamma rays, neutrons, and radioactivity with accelerators; the discovery of the "mirror" nuclei as well as the proof of the annihilation of positrons, among many other firsts. Oppenheimer played a key role in elucidating the significance of "mirror" nuclei such as $^{11}C-^{11}B$, $^{13}N-^{13}C$, $^{15}O-^{15}N$, and $^{17}F-^{17}O$. The laboratory measurements on the positron emission between these pairs showed that the beta decay energy increased uniformly up the series. At Oppenheimer's suggestion a calculation showed that the energy increase was entirely due to the coulomb interactions between the protons in these nuclei and that the intrinsic nuclear interactions between pairs of protons and pairs of neutrons were identical, thus establishing the charge symmetry of the nuclear forces. At a later date Lauritsen and his students and collaborators went on to show that the excited states of "mirror" nuclei were identical in energy, except for well-defined effects due to particle emission. This was part of a comprehensive study of the excited states of all the light nuclei undertaken in Lauritsen's laboratory.

Lauritsen was also a close friend of H. P. Robertson who left Caltech for Princeton in 1929 but returned in 1948. They both had a broad range of interests in the physical sciences, from nuclei to galaxies, and they also shared a common interest in the interrelationship of science and society. In addition

Lauritsen was instrumental in bringing R. F. Christy, one of Oppenheimer's students, to Caltech in order to provide theoretical guidance in the nuclear research.

One of Lauritsen's most significant discoveries was that of the capture of protons by carbon with the emission of gamma radiation. This process, called radiative capture, was a matter of considerable theoretical controversy until Niels Bohr introduced the concept of long-lived compound nuclei in connection with the radiative capture of neutrons.

The full significance of Lauritsen's discovery did not come until 1939 when Bethe at Cornell and Von Weizsäcker in Germany independently suggested that hydrogen could be converted into helium in stars by means of a catalytic process involving the isotopes of carbon and nitrogen that came to be called the CN-cycle. The first reaction in the cycle is the radiative capture of protons by ^{12}C. The second and third reactions involve similar capture by ^{13}C and ^{14}N. The fourth reaction is the emission of alpha particles in the interaction of protons with ^{15}N in which ^{12}C is the residual nucleus thus closing the cycle. Lauritsen also studied this reaction.

Bethe and Critchfield suggested another process, the proton–proton chain, by which hydrogen could be converted directly into helium in stars. Bethe thought that the CN-cycle was the dominant process in the sun and that the pp-chain predominated only in somewhat cooler stars than the sun. It is now known from measurements in Lauritsen's laboratory that the pp-chain dominates in the sun and that the CN-cycle takes over in stars somewhat hotter than the sun. Even so, it was quite clear in 1939 that problems in the application of nuclear physics to astronomy could only be solved by detailed and accurate measurements of nuclear reaction rates.

A start was made in this direction, mainly the construction of a 2-million-volt electrostatic accelerator capable of high-resolution direct-current operation, but World War II put a stop to all nondefense related research and teaching. At the end of the war Lauritsen had to decide the future direction of research in his laboratory. He did not hesitate, and under his direction the laboratory staff enthusiastically returned to the field of low-energy, light-element nuclear physics. It was resolved to spend a good part of the effort on the study of those nuclear reactions thought to take place in stars. Lauritsen was encouraged in this by Ira Bowen, who became director of the Mount Wilson and Palomar Observatories early in 1946. Bowen held a series of informal seminars in his home, where physicists and astronomers discussed problems of mutual interest over beer and pretzels. In 1948 Jesse L. Greenstein came to Caltech to lead the work in astronomy, and his interests, particularly in the abundances of the elements in stars, stimulated much of the experimental research.

Studies of the hydrogen-burning processes in main sequence stars such as the sun began in earnest in 1946. Two additional electrostatic accelerators were built, and in 1958 the Office of Naval Research funded the purchase and installation of a tandem accelerator capable of accelerating protons to 13-million-electron-volts energy in the new Alfred P. Sloan Laboratory of Mathematics and Physics. On the basis of laboratory observations made with these accelerators and with auxiliary electrostatic analyzers and magnetic spectrometers designed by Lauritsen and of theoretical calculations on stellar structure and evolution, it is possible to predict with considerable accuracy, for example, the flux of neutrinos from the sun at the surface of the earth. Attempts are now under way to detect these neutrinos, the observation of which will mark a culminating stage in one phase of the work that Lauritsen originated and encouraged in his laboratory.

In the decade of the 1950s the big question was "How does helium burn in stars?" The question was solved in 1957 when the energy, angular momentum, parity, and decay modes of the

7.65-million-electron-volt excited state of ^{12}C were determined in the laboratory. It is through this state that the Salpeter–Hoyle process, $3\,^4He \rightarrow \,^{12}C$, occurs in helium burning in red giant stars.

In his later years, when he personally became more and more involved in national defense matters, Lauritsen encouraged the staff of his laboratory to continue experimental work in nuclear astrophysics and to use the laboratory accelerators in other fields. Beam foil spectroscopy for the study of atomic transition probabilities and proton channeling for the study of properties of the solid state were introduced. These developments were a mark of Lauritsen's broad and far-ranging interests in all aspects of nuclear physics and its applications.

In the summer of 1940, Lauritsen went to Washington to join the newly formed National Defense Research Committee as vice chairman of the section on Armor and Ordnance under Tolman. His principal work in the initial stages of this effort lay in organizing the development of proximity fuses and artillery rockets and in promoting the interest of the armed services in the exploitation of scientific research in the war effort. One of the earliest substantive results of this work was the establishment of a group at the Department of Terrestrial Magnetism for the development of the proximity fuse under Merle Tuve. Lauritsen participated actively in the work of this group during the latter part of 1940 and early 1941, until the development of bomb and rocket fuses had reached the service test phase and the shell fuse development was well under way.

At this point, partly as a result of a visit to England, Lauritsen concluded that a major effort on artillery rockets was needed. Under the aegis of the Office of Scientific Research and Development, he set up a project for that purpose at the California Institute of Technology in the summer of 1941. This project, which he directed all through the war, made a number of major advances in rocket technology and developed some dozens of service weapons, many of which were adopted and used by the armed services. Among these were the "Mousetrap" antisubmarine rocket, the 4.5-inch Beach Barrage Rocket, and the 3.25-inch, 5.0-inch, and 11.75-inch aircraft rockets. A large part of the success of this effort may be ascribed to the close relations that Lauritsen maintained with the services. Through these connections, he was able to appreciate, and sometimes to anticipate, tactical requirements and to insure that the newly developed weapons were properly introduced into use. On many occasions he participated in the training programs and advised field commanders in the early phases of service applications. Thus, for example, he led a mission to England in 1944 to introduce U.S. Air Force pilots to the 5.0-inch aircraft rocket; these pilots made effective use of their training in the Saint-Lo breakthrough after D-day.

With the rocket development project well under way, Lauritsen turned his attention in 1944 to the atomic bomb project. During 1944 and 1945, he spent a considerable fraction of his time at Los Alamos with Oppenheimer, participating in the technical steering committee and in the scientific development work. Some parts of the development were carried out in Pasadena, again under his direction.

Late in the war, when it became apparent that a continuing development and test facility would be needed by the armed services, he persuaded the navy to establish the Naval Ordnance Test Station at Inyokern, California. He took an active part in the planning of this facility and supported its work over the years, both informally and as a member of its Advisory Board. In recognition of his contribution to the war effort, he was awarded the Medal for Merit by President Truman in 1948.

Possibly the most far-reaching of Lauritsen's endeavors was his early influence on the establishment of the Office of Naval Research, an organization that played an important part in the recovery of scientific research after the war, and whose operation set the pattern for broad federal support of science in this country. Together with Captain R. D. Conrad, of the Office of Research and Inventions of the United States Navy, and with other members of the scientific community, he helped to lay down the ground rules for the Office of Naval Research and to bring it into being. He served the Office of Naval Research for many years on its Advisory Committee and through informal consultation with its administrators. He was the first recipient of the Conrad Award for Scientific Achievement in 1958.

Starting in 1950, Lauritsen took an active part in a number of major scientific study projects, carried out at the request of the armed services. Among these were Project Hartwell, 1950; Project Charles, 1950–1951; Project Michael, 1951; Project Vista, 1951–1952; and the Lincoln *Ad Hoc* Study Group for Continental Defense, 1951–1953.

At the time of the Korean War, he traveled to Korea for the Weapons Systems Evaluation Group to observe the Inchon landings and generally to evaluate the role of new-weapons development in that action. He continued these activities through his membership in a number of scientific advisory boards, where he was involved in both scientific development and tactical problems embracing the whole spectrum of defense activities.

Lauritsen also became heavily involved in the scientific and military aspects of the ballistic-missile development program. He served on the Panel on Weapons Technology for Limited Warfare for the President's Scientific Advisory Committee, the Strategic Weapons Panel and other advisory groups for the Department of Defense, the U.S.–U.K. Ballistic Missile Scientific Advisory Committee, the Advisory Committee on the Intercontinental Ballistic Missile, the Air Force Space Study Committee, the Minuteman Flexibility and Safety Group for the U.S. Air Force, the Advisory Board, Pacific Missile Board for the U.S. Navy, and the *Ad Hoc* Committee on the Role of the

Army in Space for the U.S. Army. As their names suggest, these activities were directed to the scientific evaluation of national needs and capabilities in the currently most conspicuous example of the effect of science and technology on national defense. In his participation in this work, Lauritsen's understanding of both the detailed scientific considerations and the broad tactical and strategic problems made an invaluable contribution to the sound conception and to the ultimate success of these programs.

Lauritsen received many honors in his lifetime. In addition to those already mentioned he was elected to the Royal Society of Copenhagen in 1939 and was made Kommandor of Dannebrog by the King of Denmark in 1953. He was elected president of the American Physical Society in 1951 and was awarded the Tom W. Bonner Prize of the Society in 1967. He became a member of the National Academy of Sciences in 1951 and of the American Philosophical Society in 1954. The library of the Aerospace Corporation, which he was instrumental in founding, was dedicated to Lauritsen in 1968. The degree of Doctor of Laws was conferred upon him by the University of California at Los Angeles in 1965.

Charles Christian Lauritsen was an eminent research scientist and teacher. More than one hundred graduate students have received their doctoral degrees in the laboratory he founded, many under his direct supervision. He authored or co-authored approximately one hundred papers. He gave unstintingly of his time and effort to the scientific aspects of the national defense of his adopted country. He was a man of great integrity and character and his influence on his students, his colleagues, and his times is immeasurable.

IN PREPARING this biography of Charles Lauritsen I have made abundant use, in some cases *verbatim,* of notes and papers by his son, Thomas Lauritsen. I am grateful for permission to do this.

BIBLIOGRAPHY

KEY TO ABBREVIATIONS

Am. J. Roentgenol. Radium Ther. = American Journal of Roentgenology and Radium Therapy
Phys. Rev. = Physical Review
Phys. Rev. Lett. = Physical Review Letters
Rev. Sci. Instr. = Review of Scientific Instruments

1928

With R. A. Millikan. Relations of field-currents to thermionic-currents. Proceedings of the National Academy of Sciences, 14:45.
With R. D. Bennett. A new high potential x-ray tube. Phys. Rev., 32:850.

1929

With R. A. Millikan. Dependence of electron emission from metals upon field strength and temperature. Phys. Rev., 33:598.
Electron emission from metals in intense electric fields. Ph.D. thesis. California Institute of Technology. Unpublished.

1930

With B. Cassen. High potential x-ray tube. Phys. Rev., 36:988.
Spectrum of the radiation from a high potential x-ray tube. Phys. Rev., 36:1680.

1931

With C. Packard. The biological effect of high voltage x-rays. Science, 73:321.

1933

With R. Crane. A high potential porcelain x-ray tube. Rev. Sci. Instr., 4:118.
With R. Crane. A combined tesla coil and vacuum tube. Rev. Sci. Instr., 4:497.
Energy considerations in high voltage therapy. Am. J. Roentgenol. Radium Ther., 30:380.
Energy considerations in medium and high voltage therapy. Am. J. Roentgenol. Radium Ther., 30:529.

With H. R. Crane and A. Soltan.   Nouvelle source artificielle de neutrons.   Comptes Rendus, 197:913.

With H. R. Crane and A. Soltan.   Artificial production of neutrons. Phys. Rev., 44:507.

With H. R. Crane and A. Soltan.   Production of neutrons by high speed deutons.   Phys. Rev., 44:692.

With H. R. Crane.   On the production of neutrons from lithium. Phys. Rev., 44:783.

1934

With H. R. Crane.   Gamma rays from lithium bombarded with protons.   Phys. Rev., 45:63.

With H. R. Crane.   Disintegration of beryllium by deutons.   Phys. Rev., 45:226.

With H. R. Crane.   Gamma rays from carbon bombarded with deutons.   Phys. Rev., 45:345.

With H. R. Crane.   Radioactivity from carbon and boron oxide bombarded with deutons and the conversion of positrons into radiation.   Phys. Rev., 45:430.

With J. Read.   An investigation of the Klein–Nishina formula for x-ray scattering in the wave-length region 50 to 20 X-units. Phys. Rev., 45:433.

With H. R. Crane.   Disintegration of boron by deutons and by protons.   Phys. Rev., 45:493.

With H. R. Crane.   Further experiments with artificially produced radioactive substances.   Phys. Rev., 45:497.

With H. R. Crane.   Transmutation of lithium by deutons and its bearing on the mass of the neutron.   Phys. Rev., 45:550.

With J. R. Oppenheimer.   On the scattering of the ThC″ gamma-rays.   Phys. Rev., 46:80.

With H. R. Crane, L. A. Delsasso, and W. A. Fowler.   High energy gamma-rays from lithium and fluorine bombarded with protons. Phys. Rev., 46:531.

With H. R. Crane.   Evidence of an excited state in the alpha-particle.   Phys. Rev., 46:537.

With H. R. Crane, L. A. Delsasso, and W. A. Fowler.   Gamma-rays from boron bombared with deutons.   Phys. Rev., 46:1109.

With H. R. Crane. Gamma-rays from artificially produced nuclear transmutations. *Papers and Discussions of the International*

Conference on Physics, London. Vol. 1. *Nuclear Physics,* p. 130. London, Physical Society.

With H. R. Crane and W. W. Harper. Artificial production of radioactive substances. Science, 79:234.

1935

On the relation between the roentgen and the erythema dose. Am. J. Roentgenol. Radium Ther., 33:235.

With H. R. Crane. The masses of Be^8, Be^9, and B^{11} as determined from transmutation data. Phys. Rev., 47:420.

With H. R. Crane, L. A. Delsasso, and W. A. Fowler. Gamma rays from the disintegration of beryllium by deuterons and protons. Phys. Rev., 47:782.

With H. R. Crane, L. A. Delsasso, and W. A. Fowler. The emission of negative electrons from boron bombarded by deuterons. Phys. Rev., 47:887.

With H. R. Crane, L. A. Delsasso, and W. A. Fowler. The emission of negative electrons from lithium and fluorine bombarded with deuterons. Phys. Rev., 47:971.

With H. R. Crane, L. A. Delsasso, and W. A. Fowler. Gamma rays from nitrogen bombarded with deuterons. Phys. Rev., 48:100.

With H. R. Crane, L. A. Delsasso, and W. A. Fowler. Gamma rays from boron bombarded with protons. Phys. Rev., 48:102.

With H. R. Crane, L. A. Delsasso, and W. A. Fowler. Cloud chamber studies of the gamma-radiation from lithium bombarded with protons. Phys. Rev., 48:125.

With L. A. Delsasso and W. A. Fowler. Protons from the disintegration of lithium by deuterons. Phys. Rev., 48:848.

1936

With W. A. Fowler and L. A. Delsasso. Radioactive elements of low atomic number. Phys. Rev., 49:561.

1937

With L. A. Delsasso and W. A. Fowler. Energy absorption of the gamma-radiation from $Li^7 + H^1$. Phys. Rev., 51:391.

With L. A. Delsasso and W. A. Fowler. Gamma-radiation from fluorine bombarded with protons. Phys. Rev., 51:527.

With W. A. Fowler. Radioactive alpha-particles from $Li^7 + H^2$. Phys. Rev., 51:1103.

With T. Lauritsen. Simple quartz fiber electrometer. Rev. Sci. Instr., 9:51.

1938

With W. A. Fowler and E. R. Gaerttner. Gamma radiation from boron bombarded by protons. Phys. Rev., 53:628.

The development of high voltage x-ray tubes at the California Institute of Technology. Radiology, 31:354.

Geometrical factors in the measurement of radiation in roentgens. British Journal of Radiology, 11:471.

With W. E. Stephens. A short ion path high voltage tube. Rev. Sci. Instr., 9:51.

1939

With E. R. Gaerttner and W. A. Fowler. The gamma radiation from boron bombarded by deuterons. Phys. Rev., 55:27.

With W. B. McLean, R. A. Becker, and W. A. Fowler. Short range alpha-particles from $F^{19} + H^1$. Phys. Rev., 55:769.

With W. B. McLean, R. A. Becker, and W. A. Fowler. Short range alpha-particles from $F^{19} - H^1$. Phys. Rev., 55:796.

With W. A. Fowler. Pair emission from fluorine bombarded with protons. Phys. Rev., 56:840.

With W. A. Fowler. Low energy gamma-radiation from lithium bombarded with protons. Phys. Rev., 56:841.

1941

With T. Lauritsen and W. A. Fowler. Application of a pressure electrostatic generator to the transmutation of light elements by protons. Phys. Rev., 59:241.

With J. F. Streib and W. A. Fowler. The transmutation of fluorine by protons. Phys. Rev., 59:253.

1942

With R. A. Becker and W. A. Fowler. Short range alpha-particles from fluorine bombarded with protons. Phys. Rev., 62:186.

1947

With S. Rubin and W. A. Fowler. Angular distribution of the Li^7 (p, γ) γ reaction. Phys. Rev., 71:212.

With R. F. Christy, E. R. Cohen, W. A. Fowler, and T. Lauritsen. The conservation of momentum in the disintegration of Li^8. Phys. Rev., 72:698.

With W. A. Fowler and T. Lauritsen. Electrostatic analyzer for 1.5-Mev protons. Rev. Sci. Instr., 18:818.

1948

With W. A. Fowler and T. Lauritsen. Gamma radiation from light nuclei under proton bombardment. Phys. Rev., 73:181.

With T. Lauritsen, W. A. Fowler, and V. K. Rasmussen. Excited states of B^{10}. Phys. Rev., 73:636.

With W. A. Fowler and T. Lauritsen. Gamma radiation from excited states of light nuclei. Reviews of Modern Physics, 20:236.

With T. Lauritsen. A null-reading fluxmeter. Rev. Sci. Instr., 19:916.

With T. Lauritsen. Vacuum fittings. Rev. Sci. Instr., 19:919.

With T. Lauritsen and W. A. Fowler. Energy levels of light nuclei. Nucleonics, 2:18.

1949

With T. Lauritsen and V. K. Rasmussen. Doppler broadening of a gamma-ray line. Phys. Rev., 75:199.

With A. V. Tollestrup and W. A. Fowler. Energy release in beryllium and lithium reactions with protons. Phys. Rev., 75:428.

With R. G. Thomas, S. Rubin, and W. A. Fowler. Beryllium-proton reactions and scattering. Phys. Rev., 75:1612.

With W. A. Fowler. Gamma radiation from light nuclei under proton bombardment. Phys. Rev., 76:314.

With W. A. Fowler and A. V. Tollestrup. Investigations of the capture of protons and deuterons by deuterons. Phys. Rev., 76:1767.

A portable roentgenmeter for field use. Rev. Sci. Instr., 20:964.

1950

With V. K. Rasmussen, W. F. Hornyak, and T. Lauritsen. Nuclear pairs and gamma radiation from excited states of O^{16}. Phys. Rev., 77:617.

With A. Tollestrup and W. A. Fowler. Nuclear mass determinations from nuclear Q-values. Phys. Rev., 78:372.

With C. Y. Chao, A. V. Tollestrup, and W. A. Fowler. Low energy alpha-particles from fluorine bombarded by protons. Phys. Rev., 79:108.

With T. Lauritsen. A radiation meter for disaster use. Science, 112:137.

With C. W. Snyder, S. Rubin, and W. A. Fowler. A magnetic analyzer for charged-particles from nuclear reactions. Rev. Sci. Instr., 21:852.

1951

With A. B. Brown, C. W. Snyder, and W. A. Fowler. Excited states of the mirror nuclei Li7 and Be7. Phys. Rev., 82:159.

With C. W. Li, W. Whaling, and W. A. Fowler. Masses of light nuclei from nuclear disintegration energies. Phys. Rev., 83:512.

1952

With A. Schardt and W. A. Fowler. The disintegration of N^{15} by protons. Phys. Rev., 86:527.

1953

With A. A. Kraus, Jr., A. P. French, and W. A. Fowler. Angular distribution of gamma rays and short range alpha particles from N^{15} (p, a γ) C^{12}. Phys. Rev., 89:299.

With W. D. Waters and W. A. Fowler. The elastic scattering of protons by lithium. Phys. Rev., 91:917.

1954

With F. Mozer and W. A. Fowler. Inelastic scattering of protons by Li7. Phys. Rev., 93:829.

With R. W. Peterson, C. A. Barnes, and W. A. Fowler. Low excited states of F^{19}. I. Proton inelastic scattering. Phys. Rev., 94:1075.

With J. Thirion and C. A. Barnes. Low excited states of F^{19}. II. Lifetime measurements. Phys. Rev., 94:1076.

With R. W. Peterson and W. A. Fowler. Flourine-plus-proton reactions. Phys. Rev., 96:1250.

1957

With F. B. Hagedorn, F. S. Mozer, T. S. Webb, and W. A. Fowler. The elastic scattering of protons by N^{14}. Phys. Rev., 105:209.

With H. J. Martin, W. A. Fowler, and T. Lauritsen. Angular correlations in the F^{19} (p, a γ) O^{16} reaction. Phys. Rev., 106: 1260.

With C. W. Cook, W. A. Fowler, and T. Lauritsen. B^{12}, C^{12} and the red giants. Phys. Rev., 107:508.

1958

With C. W. Cook, W. A. Fowler, and T. Lauritsen. High energy alpha particles from B^{12}. Phys. Rev., 111:567.

With T. Lauritsen, C. A. Barnes, and W. A. Fowler. Angular correlation of alpha particles from decay of Li^8. Phys. Rev. Lett., 1:326.

With C. A. Barnes, W. A. Fowler, H. B. Greenstein, and M. E. Nordberg. Nature of the Li^8 beta-decay interaction. Phys. Rev. Lett., 1:328.

Clarence Cook Little

CLARENCE COOK LITTLE

October 6, 1888–December 22, 1971

BY GEORGE D. SNELL

D R. CLARENCE COOK LITTLE died December 22, 1971, in Ellsworth, Maine, at the age of eighty-three. A leader in education, in the national effort to understand and control cancer, and in the development of mammalian genetics, Dr. Little inspired in the many people who knew him not only admiration but warm personal friendship. He is survived by his wife, Beatrice, two sons, two daughters, and nine grandchildren.

Dr. Little was born in Brookline, Massachusetts, October 6, 1888. He was a member of an old Boston family and a descendent of Paul Revere. His boyhood was spent on the family estate in Brookline, where a variety of animals and pets, including his own mice and prize pigeons, provided an early exposure to biology. He was educated at Noble and Greenough School and Harvard College and continued at Harvard as a graduate student in mammalian genetics under Dr. William E. Castle, who pioneered in the application of Mendelian principles to mice and rabbits. During his senior year at Harvard, Pete, as he was known by his college friends, was captain of the track team. Dr. Castle related later how this handsome team captain signed up for his genetics course and soon had persuaded most of the team to sign up with him.

While still a graduate student at Harvard, Dr. Little became interested in studies being carried out by Professor Tyzzer at

241

Harvard Medical School on the inheritance of susceptibility and resistance to tumor transplants in mice. This work led him to prepare a paper, published in *Science,* describing a type of multifactor inheritance that anticipated present concepts of histocompatibility genetics. Little's major research interests—transplantation, the cancer problem, and mammalian and especially murine genetics—were established during this period.

Following the award of his D. Sc. in 1914, Dr. Little held various positions at Harvard: secretary to President Lowell, assistant dean of the college, and acting marshall. With the entrance of the United States into the First World War, he enlisted in the army and trained at Plattsburgh, New York. Subsequently he was assigned to administrative duty in Washington with the Signal Corps, later to become the U.S. Air Force. He was discharged in 1918 with the rank of Major. After his war service, Dr. Little spent three years at the Station for Experimental Evolution in Cold Spring Harbor, New York, serving during the last year as assistant director.

Throughout this period Dr. Little maintained his interest in mammalian genetics and cancer. He published numerous papers and even during the war saw to it that his animal colony was maintained. Perhaps his most lasting contribution was the establishment of the first inbred strains of mice. Inbreeding had been extensively studied in corn, and Jennings had examined mathematically the expected increase in homozygosis. The mouse was a logical choice for inbreeding experiments with a mammal, perhaps, in fact, an especially fortunate choice, since wild populations of mice form small colonies with considerable inbreeding so that the accumulation of deleterious recessive genes is restricted. But successful establishment of a homozygous strain required careful selection from a colony of adequate size. Dr. Little's pioneer inbreeding efforts resulted in two highly successful inbred strains, the dilute brown (DBA) strain, begun when he was still at Harvard, and the black

(C57BL) strain, started at Cold Spring Harbor. The genetic uniformity of these and the dozens of other lines subsequently produced in many laboratories makes them a research tool of major importance. The C57BL strain heads the list in popularity—worldwide annual use certainly exceeds one million mice. The DBA strain is not far behind.

The time was less propitious for another project that Dr. Little undertook at Cold Spring Harbor. In collaboration with Halsey Bagg he attempted to induce mutations in mice with X rays. Hermann Muller was to win the Nobel Prize in 1946 for a similar experiment with *Drosophila,* but with mice the number of gametes that it was feasible to test was too small; also the X-ray dose used was probably too low. Two variants appeared, but at least one of these also turned up in the controls.

In 1922, at the age of thirty-three, Dr. Little became president of the University of Maine. He was at this time the youngest college president in the country. Perhaps his most successful innovation during the three years that he held this office was the establishment of Freshman Week. This was held prior to the opening of college and was "designed to instruct all freshmen in methods of study, in choice of courses, and in the aims and value of college work as well as to give an opportunity for the study of the individual freshman in order to recognize, measure, and in so far as possible begin to utilize his particular abilities, and to avoid or to bolster up his weaknesses." The success of this institution is attested to by its permanence and its imitation by other universities. Although there was some growth in the university plant during Dr. Little's term of office, he was not as successful in obtaining money from the legislature as he had hoped to be.

One of Dr. Little's stipulations in accepting the University of Maine presidency was that he have funds and facilities to continue his biological research. Several young men whom he interested in biology during this period remained associated with him for years. He also succeeded in establishing at Bar Harbor, Maine, a summer laboratory on the site where The Jackson Laboratory was later to be built.

After three years at the University of Maine, Dr. Little was offered and accepted the presidency of the University of Michigan. His appointment provided "an unprecedented $5000 for research assistance," testimony to his determination to continue his research. He was later able to add substantial support from outside sources. Again his tenure of office was marked by innovation and attempted innovation. A Freshman Week was introduced; a School of Forestry and a Department of Postgraduate Medicine were established; the first faculty research fund was created, and research expanded substantially. A plan to enroll all freshmen and sophomores in a separate University College under its own dean encountered a barrage of faculty criticism and was dropped. Lack of funds rather than active opposition was principally responsible for the demise of a plan for the erection of dormitories housing a few instructors or professors as well as students and designed to serve as small residential colleges.

The latter plan was typical of Dr. Little's interest in the welfare of the undergraduate. A representative group of students met regularly in his home. He worked successfully for better intramural athletic facilities that could serve the student body as a whole. Less popular in some quarters was a ban on liquor in fraternity houses and, with some exceptions, on the use of autos by students.

But probably nothing stirred up more controversy than Little's views on birth control. He spoke out for this boldly and repeatedly. Many people were not ready for such frank talk, and some bitter criticism resulted. The official history of the university refers to his presidency as a "stormy term" and "brilliant but tactless," but in retrospect it appears that his successes were substantial and his failures prophetic.

The year 1929 was a turning point in Dr. Little's life. In January of that year he submitted his resignation to the Regents of the University of Michigan. He also was divorced from his first wife after eighteen years of marriage and three children. Doubtless his divorce had something to do with his break with the university, as did the antagonism he had aroused in some quarters among the faculty. Perhaps he had decided also that his talent lay in pioneering and not in routine administration. With financial help from the Jackson and Ford families of Detroit and Mount Desert Island, he turned to his first love, research, and set out to create in Bar Harbor a laboratory for the study of mammalian genetics and cancer. When Roscoe B. Jackson, one of the major donors, died, the laboratory was named in his honor.

The laboratory was staffed by a group of six young men and one woman who had worked with "Prexy," as he was still called, during his years as college president. The first major project undertaken by the staff was a study of the genetics of tissue transplantation. Crosses were made between the now highly inbred strains of mice, and data gathered on the growth of transplantable tumors in the parental and various hybrid generations. The existence of multiple genes for susceptibility and resistance, subsequently called histocompatibility genes, was thereby established. Another project took advantage of the great difference in mammary tumor incidence between some of the inbred strains. In a cross between high and low strains, it was found that tumor incidence of the first hybrid generation was determined by the maternal parent. Subsequent foster nursing experiments implicated some agent transmitted through the mother's milk. Dr. Little at the time was under the influence of the antivirus school of thought—the word virus was taboo, as at least one young staff member discovered—but other laboratories picked up the work and proved the existence of a mammary tumor virus.

In these early days, the research at the laboratory, despite its substantial success, was not carried on in easy circumstances. Nineteen twenty-nine was the year when the stock market broke. After a brief honeymoon, the deepening depression cut off sources of support. The research continued, but on a curtailed basis while the staff turned to fishing, gardening, and canning to provide food. It was at this time that the laboratory initiated the sale of its inbred strains to other investigators, an activity that ultimately became both a major service to researchers all over the world and a much needed source of uncommitted income.

The depression finally passed. Dr. Little initiated a program of modest expansion that ultimately was to change the character of the laboratory considerably, but for the first two decades of its existence its small size and location in "down-east" Maine permitted a mode of life that he and his associates found much to their liking. Dr. Little was an enthusiastic outdoorsman, a knowledgeable ornithologist, and an accomplished fisherman. The Maine countryside provided an ideal setting for these interests. He raised a strain of dachshunds that his father had first brought to this country and was in demand as a judge at dog shows. The life at the laboratory was kept informal. During the winter there were monthly parties, with games and refreshments, in which all employee families participated. If the games lagged, which they seldom did, Dr. Little could always liven the occasion with some good stories. In the warmer seasons there might be a laboratory picnic at which he could still display his prowess in a footrace. World War II took a number of workers away from the laboratory and led to a greatly increased production of mice suitable for the study of tropical diseases, but the research went on, even though curtailed.

It was during this same early period that Dr. Little started a program of summer training in research for precollege and college students. This program was ultimately to expand considerably. Its numerous alumni, many of them now physicians or engaged in biological research, still refer fondly to Dr. Little as "Prexy."

With the end of the war the laboratory seemed headed for a period of substantial expansion when disaster struck a second time. The main laboratory building was largely destroyed in the forest fire of 1947 that burnt part of the town of Bar Harbor and many summer estates and hotels. The mice were wiped out excepting a few in a fireproof section of the building. Resisting pressure from friends to relocate at some major research center, Dr. Little, with the enthusiastic agreement of the staff, determined to rebuild in Bar Harbor. Part of the staff moved to temporary quarters in other laboratories, part to a remodeled barn on a summer estate that had been donated earlier. The inbred strains of mice flooded back from laboratories around the world, and potential grantors heard, as they never would have otherwise, of their essential value to hundreds of researchers. Within two and one half years the laboratory was housed in far better quarters than it had enjoyed before the fire, and Dr. Little was able to see the staff expand and the research grow and diversify.

One project in which Dr. Little took particular pleasure was the Behavior Study, centered in the barns of the estate already mentioned. Because of the favorable location and Dr. Little's knowledge of genetics and of dogs, Alan Gregg of the Rockefeller Foundation planned with him the creation of a center for the study of behavioral genetics. The project was started with colonies of several breeds of dogs, but inbred mice were later included with considerable profit. Dr. Little followed the project with interest and found time to study the segregation of canine coat color genes in the second and third generation hybrids of the various breeds.

The founding and direction of a laboratory would have been enough of a career for most men, but Dr. Little found the time and energy for additional major undertakings. In 1929 he became managing director of the American Cancer Society and retained this position till 1945. In the fall of 1930 he traveled extensively throughout western Europe, studying methods of cancer research and care. He was impressed by the long-term view of European cancer workers and urged the desirability of a cancer research program in the United States with similar orientation. He also stressed the need for better facilities for cancer patients and for doctor education in cancer detection and care. In 1935, with these goals substantially attained, he led in the organization of the Women's Field Army, dedicated to lay education concerning cancer. This had a tremendous influence in changing the public attitude toward cancer and in encouraging early diagnoses.

Dr. Little's recognized scientific accomplishments and ability as a leader, his impressive good looks, his warm personality, and his talents as a public speaker and raconteur naturally led him into other positions and activities. He was twice president of the American Association of Cancer Research and was influential in creating *Cancer Research* as its official journal. At one time or another he also served as president of the American Eugenics Society, the American Birth Control League, and the American Euthanasia Society. He was for years a warden in the Bar Harbor Episcopal Church. He was in demand as a speaker and always drew a good audience at local affairs, including the occasional church service at which he gladly filled in for the rector. In 1937 Dr. Little was appointed as one of the six original members of the National Advisory Cancer Council, a body created by the act of Congress that established the National Cancer Institute. The council played an influential role in setting the policies for cancer research in this country. There were considerable differences of opinion within the council. Dr. Little appears to have been one of the active supporters of the grants-in-aid and peer-review systems that have done so much to further biomedical research in this country.

In 1954, shortly before his retirement as director of The Jackson Laboratory, Dr. Little accepted a position as scientific director of the Tobacco Industrial Research Committee, a position he held until his death. Because of the link between cigarette smoking and cancer, already suspected at the time, he was widely criticized for accepting this position. Doubtless there were many reasons back of his decision. It did have at least two positive aspects. It gave him continuing opportunity, and probably considerable freedom, to influence biomedical research through the disbursement of funds; by providing an outlet for his still considerable energies, it enabled him to make a complete break with the laboratory, giving his successor a free hand.

Dr. Little was a member of the American Academy of Arts and Sciences and the National Academy of Sciences, to which he was elected in 1945, as well as of various scientific societies. He was the recipient of numerous honorary degrees. The Clarence Cook Little Hall at the University of Maine, the Clarence Cook Little Science Building at the University of Michigan, and most recently the Clarence Cook Little Library and Conference Center at The Jackson Laboratory were named in his honor.

In both science and education, Dr. Little was perhaps more the originator than the exploiter of new developments. He preferred the broad view to attention to detail. But despite his diversity of interests, he found the time to be a productive scientist. He was the author of 188 papers, three books on cancer directed primarily at the layman, and a book on coat color in dogs. Of his scientific achievements, perhaps four stand out: the development of inbred strains of mice and the demonstration of their value in medical and biological research; the formulation of the genetic theory of susceptibility and resistance to tissue transplants; the discovery of the milk-transmitted murine mammary tumor incitor; and the establishment, with Rockefeller Foundation initiative and support, of a study of the genetics of behavior. Of necessity, Dr. Little's personal participation in these projects decreased as his executive duties increased. But if his varied administrative responsibilities narrowed his own opportunities for scientific exploration, he used them, with warmth and wisdom, to open the doors so that younger men could reach for new horizons. Perhaps this was his greatest contribution.

BIBLIOGRAPHY

KEY TO ABBREVIATIONS

Am. J. Cancer = American Journal of Cancer
Am. J. Roentgen Radium Ther. = American Journal of Roentgenology and Radium Therapy
Am. Nat. = American Naturalist
Ann. Clin. Med. = Annals of Clinical Medicine
Bull. Am. Soc. Control Cancer = Bulletin of the American Society for the Control of Cancer.
Cancer Res. = Cancer Research
J. Am. Med. Assoc. = Journal of the American Medical Association
J. Cancer Res. = Journal of Cancer Research
J. Exp. Med. = Journal of Experimental Medicine
J. Exp. Zool. = Journal of Experimental Zoology
J. Genet. = Journal of Genetics
J. Hered. = Journal of Heredity
J. Natl. Cancer Inst. = Journal of the National Cancer Institute
Occas. Publ. Am. Assoc. Adv. Sci. = Occasional Publication of the American Association for the Advancement of Science
Proc. Natl. Acad. Sci. = Proceedings of the National Academy of Sciences
Proc. Soc. Exp. Biol. Med. = Proceedings of Society for Experimental Biology and Medicine
Sci. Mon. = Scientific Monthly
Sigma Xi Q. = Sigma Xi Quarterly

1909

With W. E. Castle. The peculiar inheritance of pink eyes among colored mice. Science, 30:313–14.

1910

With W. E. Castle. On a modified Mendelian ratio among yellow mice. Science, 32:868–70.

1911

The "dilute" forms of yellow mice. Science, 33:896–97.
The influence of heredity and of environment in determining the coat colors in mice. Science, 34:563.

1912

Preliminary note on the occurrence of a sex-limited character in cats. Science, 35:784–85.
Yellow and agouti factors in mice not "associated." Am. Nat., 46: 491–93.

1913

Yellow and "agouti" factors in mice.   Science, 38:205.

Experimental studies of the inheritance of color in mice.   Carnegie Institution of Washington Publication, 179:11–102.

With J. C. Phillips.   A cross involving four pairs of Mendelian characters in mice.   Am. Nat., 47:760–62.

1914

"Dominant" and "recessive" spotting in mice.   Am. Nat., 48:74–82.

Coat color in pointer dogs.   J. Hered., 5:244–48.

A possible Mendelian explanation for a type of inheritance apparently non-Mendelian in nature.   Science, 40:904–6.

1915

A note on multiple allelomorphs in mice.   Am. Nat., 49:122–24.

The inheritance of black-eyed spotting in mice.   Am. Nat., 49: 727–40.

Cancer and heredity.   Science, 42:218–19.

The inheritance of cancer.   Science, 42:494–95.

1916

With E. E. Tyzzer.   Further experimental studies on the inheritance of susceptibility to a transplantable carcinoma (JWA) of the Japanese waltzing mouse.   Journal of Medical Research, 33: 393–427.

The relation of heredity to cancer in man and animals.   Sci. Mon., 3:196–202.

The occurrence of three recognized color mutations in mice.   Am. Nat., 50:335–49.

With E. E. Tyzzer.   Studies on the inheritance of susceptibility to a transplantable sarcoma (J.W.B.) of the Japanese waltzing mouse.   J. Cancer Res., 1:387–89.

1917

Evidence of multiple factors in mice and rats.   Am. Nat., 51:457–80.

The relation of yellow coat color and black-eyed white spotting of mice in inheritance.   Genetics, 2:433–44.

The use of vasectomized male mice as indicators.   Proc. Natl. Acad. Sci., 3:186–88.

1918

Color inheritance in cats with special reference to the colors black, yellow, and tortoise-shell. J. Genet., 8:279–90.

1919

A note on the fate of individuals homozygous for certain color factors in mice. Am. Nat., 53:185–87.

Some factors influencing the human sex ratio. Proc. Soc. Exp. Biol. Med., 16:127–30.

With E. E. Jones. The inheritance of coat color in Great Danes. J. Hered., 10:309–20.

1920

Alternative explanations for exceptional color classes in doves and canaries. Am. Nat., 54:162–75.

Is there linkage between the genes for yellow and for black in mice? Am. Nat., 54:267–70.

Note on the occurrence of a probable sex-linked lethal factor in mammals. Am. Nat., 54:457–60.

With L. C. Strong. Tests for physiological differences in transplantable tumors. Proc. Soc. Exp. Biol. Med., 18:45–48.

A note on the human sex ratio. Proc. Natl. Acad. Sci., 6:250–53.

Factors influencing the growth of a transplantable tumor in mice. J. Exp. Zool., 31:307–26.

The heredity of susceptibility to a transplantable sarcoma (J.W.B.) of the Japanese waltzing mouse. Science, 51:467–68.

1921

Report of the committee on genetic form and nomenclature. Am. Nat., 55:175–78.

Evidence for sex-linked lethal factors in man. Proc. Soc. Exp. Biol. Med., 18:111–15.

Non-disjunction of the fourth chromosome of *Drosophila*. Science, 53:167.

1922

With B. W. Johnson. The inheritance of susceptibility to implants of splenic tissue in mice. I. Japanese waltzing mice, albinos, and their F_1 generation hybrids. Proc. Soc. Exp. Biol. Med., 19:163–67.

Relation between research in human heredity and experimental genetics. Sci. Mon., 14:401–14.

1923

Congenital and acquired predisposition and heredity. Abt's Pediatrics, 1:171–256.

With H. J. Bagg. The occurrence of two heritable types of abnormality among the descendants of x-rayed mice. Am. J. Roentgen Radium Ther., 10:975–89.

Inheritance of a predisposition to cancer in man. Eugenics, Genetics, and Family, 1:186.

With E. E. Jones. The effect of selection upon a Mendelian ratio. Genetics, 8:1–26.

1924

With H. J. Bagg. Hereditary and structural defects in the descendants of mice treated with Roentgen-ray irradiation. American Journal of Anatomy, 33:119–45.

With L. H. Snyder and M. Schneider. A report of a histological study of the eyes and gonads of mice treated with a light dosage of x-rays. Am. Nat., 58:383–84.

The genetics of tissue transplantation in mammals. J. Cancer Res., 8:75–95.

With L. C. Strong. Genetic studies on the transplantation of two adenocarcinomata. J. Exp. Zool., 41:93–114.

With H. J. Bagg. The occurrence of four inheritable morphological variations in mice and their possible relation to treatment with x-rays. J. Exp. Zool., 41:45–91.

With J. M. Murray and W. T. Bovie. Influence of ultra-violet light on nutrition in poultry. Maine Agricultural Experiment Station Bulletin, 320:141–64.

1925

Inaugural address of the president of the University of Michigan. School and Society, 22:1–16.

1926

Preparation and practice in medical education. Ann. Clin. Med., 4:781–87.

A discussion of certain phases of sterility. Ann. Clin. Med., 5:1–4.

Genetic investigations and the cancer problem. Commonwealth Review, 8:130–36.

1927

Preliminary report on a species cross in rodents, *Mus musculus* × *Mus wagneri*. Papers of Michigan Academic Sciences, Arts and Letters, 8:393–99.

Notes on a species cross in mice and on an hypothesis concerning the quantitative potentiality of genes. Science, 66:542–43.

1928

Report of Committee on Formal Education of the American Eugenics Society, Inc. New Haven, The Society.

Agents modifying the germ plasm. Surgery, Gynecology and Obstetrics, 46:155–58.

Shall we live longer and should we? (president's address) Proceedings of 3d Race Betterment Conference (January), pp. 5–14. Battle Creek, Michigan, Race Betterment Foundation.

Evidence that cancer is not a simple Mendelian recessive. J. Cancer Res., 12:30–46.

Opportunities for research in mammalian genetics. Sigma Xi Q., 16:16–35.

Opportunities for research in mammalian genetics. Sci. Mon., 26:521–34.

1931

Education in cancer. Am. J. Cancer, 15:280–83.

The present status of the cancer problem. Annals of Surgery, 93:11–16.

The effects of selection on eye and foot abnormalities occurring among the descendants of x-rayed mice. Am. Nat., 65:370–75.

The role of heredity in determining the incidence and growth of cancer. Am. J. Cancer, 15: 2780–89.

With R. A. Hicks. The blood relationship of four strains of mice. Genetics, 16:397–421.

1932

With B. W. McPheters. The incidence of mammary cancer in a cross between two strains of mice. Am. Nat., 66:568–71.

With B. W. McPheters. Further studies on the genetics of abnormalities appearing in the descendants of x-rayed mice. Genetics, 17:674–88.

Cancer survey of St. Louis and St. Louis County, Missouri, 1931. Journal of the Missouri Medical Association, 29:249–75.

1933

Individuality and the hereditary process in mammals. Recordings of the Genetic Society of America, 2:65.

With B. W. McPheters. Hound-eared mice. J. Hered., 24:157–58.

Variability and individuality. Science, 77:195–97.

The relation of the American Society for the Control of Cancer to radiologists. Am. J. Roentgen Radium Ther., 30:723–26.

Not dead but sleeping. J. Hered., 24:149–50.

The challenge of cancer. Maine Medical Journal, 24:165–68.

The existence of non-chromosomal influence in the incidence of mammary tumors in mice. Science, 78:465–66.

1934

How to educate women to recognize breast tumors. Bull. Am. Cancer Soc., August, 3 pp.

Inheritance in Toy Griffons. J. Hered., 25:198–200.

With P. Weir. The incidence of uterine cancer in Jews and Gentiles. J. Hered., 25:277–80.

The relation of coat color to the spontaneous incidence of mammary tumors in mice. J. Exp. Med., 59:229–50.

The bearing of genetic work with transplanted tumors on the genetics of spontaneous tumors in mice. Am. J. Cancer, 22:578–85.

Education and cancer control. International Journal of Medicine and Surgery, 47:49–50.

White cats and deafness. Nature, 133:215.

1935

With S. G. Warner. Failure to transmit carcinogenic agents from the pregnant mouse embryos *in utero*. Proc. Soc. Exp. Biol. Med., 32:866–69.

With W. S. Murray. The genetics of mammary tumor incidence in mice. Genetics, 20:466–96.

With W. S. Murray. Further data on the existence of extra-chromosomal influence on the incidence of mammary tumors in mice. Science, 82:228–30.

With A. M. Cloudman. A laboratory test of "Hoxin" as a claimed cancer "cure." J. Am. Med. Assoc., 104:1815.

Some recent advances in cancer research. Sigma Xi Q., 23:128–34.

1936

Applications of biology to human affairs. J. Hered., 27:317–18.

With A. M. Cloudman. The genetics of tumor formation in mice, in relation to the gene T for brachyury. J. Genet., 32:487–504.

Charles Velmar Green. Science, 83:543.

With W. S. Murray. Extrachromosomal influence in relation to the incidence of mammary and non-mammary tumors in mice. Am. J. Cancer, 27:516–18.

The present status of our knowledge of heredity and cancer. J. Am. Med. Assoc., 106:2234–35.

The constitutional factor in the incidence of mammary tumors. Am. J. Cancer, 27:551–55.

Genetics in relation to carcinoma. Proceedings of the Staff Meeting of the Mayo Clinic, 11:782–83.

1937

The genetics of spontaneous mammary carcinoma in mice. Occas. Publ. Am. Assoc. Adv. Sci., 4:17–21.

With A. M. Cloudman and J. J. Bittner. The relationship between the histology of spontaneous mouse tumors and the genetic constitution of the animals in which they arise. Occas. Publ. Am. Assoc. Adv. Sci., 4:37–41.

The social significance of cancer. Occas. Publ. Am. Assoc. Adv. Sci., 4:242–45.

Biology of cancer. Proceedings of Annual Congress on Medical Education, February 15–16, pp. 12–14.

With J. J. Bittner. The transmission of breast and lung cancer in mice. J. Hered., 28:117–21.

With A. M. Cloudman. The occurrence of a dominant spotting mutation in the house mouse. Proc. Natl. Acad. Sci., 23:535–37.

1938

Influence of intrinsic factors on development of tumors in mice. University of Wisconsin, Symposium on Cancer, pp. 20–31. Madison, University of Wisconsin Press.

With J. H. Mowat. Effect of choline chloride on oestrus cycle of mice. Proc. Soc. Exp. Biol. Med., 39:211–12.

Recent advances in research on biology of cancer. Journal of Medicine, 18:567–72.

With S. P. Reimann. Dialogue on the relations of genetics and experimental embryology to neoplasia. American Journal of Clinical Pathology, 8:109–19.

Fundamental cancer research. Report of a committee appointed by the Surgeon General. Public Health Report, 53:2121–30.

1939

With W. S. Murray and A. M. Cloudman. The genetics of non-epithelial tumor formation in mice. Am. J. Cancer, 36:431–50.

With W. S. Murray. Chromosomal and extrachromosomal influence in relation to the incidence of mammary tumors in mice. Am. J. Cancer, 37:536–52.

Civilization against Cancer. New York, Farrar & Rinehart, Inc. 150 pp.

Some contributions of the laboratory rodents to our understanding of human biology. Am. Nat., 73:127–38.

With W. S. Murray and A. M. Cloudman. The genetics of non-epithelial tumor formation in mice. Am. Nat., 73:467–69.

With G. W. Woolley and E. Fekete. Mammary tumor development in mice ovariectomized at birth. Proc. Natl. Acad. Sci., 25:277–79.

Hybridization and tumor formation in mice. Proc. Natl. Acad. Sci., 25:452–55.

1940

Cancer control: early is the word. Medical Annals of the District of Columbia, 9:97–98.

Hospitals and cancer. Hospitals, 14:109–10.

Deadly disease number 3—cancer. Hygeia, 18:316.

Criteria for genetic susceptibility to tumor formation in mice. Acta Unio Internationales Contra Cancrum, 5:15–24.

With J. Pearsons. The results of a "functional test" in a strain of mice (C57 black) with a low breast tumor incidence. Am. J. Cancer, 38:224–33.

With G. W. Woolley and E. Fekete. Differences between high and low breast tumor strains of mice when ovariectomized at birth. Proc. Soc. Exp. Biol. Med., 45:796–98.

1941

Indications of progress in cancer control through education. Bull. Am. Soc. Control Cancer, 23:2–3.

The genetics of spontaneous tumor formation. In: *Biology of the Laboratory Mouse,* ed. by G. D. Snell, pp. 248–78. New York, McGraw-Hill Book Co.

The genetics of tumor transplantation. In: *Biology of the Laboratory Mouse,* ed. by G. D. Snell, pp. 57–61. New York, McGraw-Hill Book Co.

Value of research with animals. Quarterly Review of New York City Cancer Commission, July–October, pp. 57–61.

A review of progress in the study of the genetics of spontaneous tumor incidence. J. Natl. Cancer Inst., 1:727–36.

Program for research on the biology of human cancer. J. Natl. Cancer Inst., 2:133–37.

With G. W. Woolley and E. Fekete. Effect of castration in the dilute brown strain of mice. Endocrinology, 28:341–43.

With G. W. Woolley and L. W. Law. Occurrence in whole blood of material influencing the incidence of mammary carcinoma in mice. Cancer Res., 1:955–56.

With E. Fekete and A. M. Cloudman. Some effects of the gene W^v (dominant spotting) in mice. Proc. Natl. Acad. Sci., 27: 114–17.

With E. Fekete and G. W. Woolley. Histological changes following ovariectomy in mice. I. dba High tumor strain. J. Exp. Med., 74:1–8.

1942

Value of research with animals. Bull. Am. Soc. Control Cancer, 24:7–10.

With E. Fekete. Observations on the mammary tumor incidence in mice born from transferred ova. Cancer Res., 2:525–30.

With J. M. Spangler and J. M. Murray. Genetics of the susceptibility of mice to a transplantable melanoma. J. Natl. Cancer Inst., 3:123–30.

1943

Cancer research. Bull. Am. Soc. Control Cancer, 25:113–15.

With G. W. Woolley and L. W. Law. Increase in mammary carcinoma incidence following inoculations of whole blood. Proc. Natl. Acad. Sci., 29:22–24.

With G. W. Woolley and E. Fekete. Gonadectomy and adrenal neoplasms. Science, 97:291.

1944

Facing the challenge of a new era. Hospitals, 18:23–25.

Editor. *Cancer, A Study for Laymen.* New York, Farrar & Rinehart, Inc. 122 pp.

Parental influence on incidence of cancer. J. Am. Med. Assoc., 125:93–97.

Cancer prevention clinic. Hospitals, 18:29.

1945

With H. McDonald. Abnormalities of the mammae in the house mouse. J. Hered., 36:285–88.

Don't neglect cancer. Mississippi Doctor, 22:191.

With G. W. Woolley. The incidence of adrenal cortical carcinoma in gonadectomized female mice of the extreme dilution strain: I. Observations on the adrenal cortex. Cancer Res., 5:193–202.

With G. W. Woolley. The incidence of adrenal cortical carcinoma in gonadectomized female mice of the extreme dilution strain: II. Observations on the accessory sex organs. Cancer Res., 5: 203–10.

With G. W. Woolley. The incidence of adrenal cortical carcinoma in gonadectomized male mice of the extreme dilution strain. Cancer Res., 5:211–19.

With E. Fekete. Histological study of adrenal cortical tumors in gonadectomized mice of the ce strain. Cancer Res., 5:220–26.

With G. W. Woolley. The incidence of adrenal cortical carcinoma in gonadectomized female mice of the extreme dilution strain: III. Observations on adrenal glands and accessory sex organs in mice 13 to 24 months of age. Cancer Res., 5:321–27.

With G. W. Woolley. The incidence of adrenal cortical carcinoma in male mice of the extreme dilution strain over one year of age. Cancer Res., 5:506–10.

With E. M. Vicari. "Lipid–steroid" fractions of mouse adrenal lipids. Proc. Soc. Exp. Biol. Med., 58:59–60.

1946

Some aspects of cancer research. Alexander Blain Hospital Bulletin, 5:1–7.

Parental influence of mammary tumor incidence. Surgery, 19:25–31.

With G. W. Woolley. Transplantation of an adrenal cortical carcinoma. Cancer Res., 6:712–17.

With G. W. Woolley. Prevention of adrenal cortical carcinoma by diethylstilbestrol. Proc. Natl. Acad. Sci., 32:239–40.

1947

With H. J. Muller and L. H. Snyder. *Genetics, Medicine and Man.* Ithaca, Cornell University Press. 158 pp.

The genetics of cancer in mice. Biological Review, 22:315–43.

With K. P. Hummel. A reverse mutation to a "remote" allele in the house mouse. Proc. Natl. Acad. Sci., 33:42–43.

1948

Halsey Joseph Bagg. Anatomical Record, 100:397.

Genetics in cocker spaniels. J. Hered., 39:181–85.

1949

Biological research in cancer. Chicago Medical Society Bulletin, 52:7–12.

With K. P. Hummel. Studies on the mouse mammary tumor agent. I. The agent in blood and other tissues in relation to the physiologic or endocrine state of the donor. Cancer Res., 9:129–34.

With K. P. Hummel. Studies on the mouse mammary tumor agent. II. The neutralization of the agent by placenta. Cancer Res., 9:135–36.

With K. P. Hummel. Studies on the mouse mammary tumor agent. III. Survival and propagation of the agent in transplanted tumors and in hosts that grew these tumors in their tissues. Cancer Res., 9:137–38.

1951

James B. Murphy, 1884–1950. Cancer Res., 11:296.

Genetics in cancer. American Journal of Obstetrics and Gynecology (Supplement) , 61A:64–68.

Genetics and the cancer problem. In: *Genetics in the 20th Century,* ed. by L. C. Dunn, pp. 431–72. New York, Macmillan Inc.

With K. P. Hummel, M. Eddy and B. Rupple. Young produced from ovaries subjected to endocrine imbalance. Proc. Natl. Acad. Sci., 37:666–69.

1952

With G. W. Woolley and M. M. Dickie. Adrenal tumors and other pathological changes in reciprocal crosses in mice. I. Strain DBA × strain CE and the reciprocal. Cancer Res., 12:142–52.

With E. Fekete and F. L. Richardson. The influence of blockage of the nipples on the occurrence of hyperplastic nodules in the mammary glands of C3H mice. Cancer Res., 12:219–21.

1953

With G. W. Woolley and M. M. Dickie. Adrenal tumors and other pathological changes in reciprocal crosses in mice. II. An introduction to results of four reciprocal crosses. Cancer Res., 13:231–45.

1954

Genetics, Biological Individuality, and Cancer. Stanford, Stanford University Press. 115 pp.

With L. C. Stevens. Spontaneous testicular teratomas in an inbred strain of mice. Proc. Natl. Acad. Sci., 40:1080–87.

1957

The Inheritance of Coat Color in Dogs. Ithaca, Comstock Publishing Associates. 194 pp.

The problem of cancer. In: *Proceedings of the 3d National Cancer Conference* (1956), pp. 469–72. Philadelphia, J. B. Lippincott Co.

Four-ears, a recessive mutation in the cat. J. Hered., 48:57.

The yellow Siamese cat. J. Hered., 48:57–58.

1958

Biological aspects of cancer research. J. Natl. Cancer Inst., 20: 441–64.

Coat color genes in rodents and carnivores.   Quarterly Review of Biology, 33:103–37.

1959

Genetics of neoplasia. In: *Physiopathology of Cancer,* 2d ed., ed. by F. Homburger, pp. 127–51.   New York, Paul B. Hoeber, Inc.

With K. P. Hummel.   Comparison of the virulence of the mammary tumor agent from four strains of mice.   J. Natl. Cancer Inst., 23:813–21.

Francisco Duran-Reynals, bacteriologist.   Science, 129:881–82.

1961

Some phases of the problem of smoking and lung cancer.   New England Journal of Medicine, 264:1241–45.

1963

With K. P. Hummel.   Comparative virulence of the mammary tumor agent from different sources; qualitative and quantitative differences.   J. Natl. Cancer Inst., 30:593–604.

John Joseph Bittner, 1904–1961.   Oncologia, 16:354–56.

1964

The relation of age to the incidence of cancer of certain sites. Proc. Natl. Acad. Sci., 52:865–69.

1965

Trends in reported incidence of cancer by age in Connecticut and in New York State (1935–1960).   Proc. Natl. Acad. Sci., 54: 1779–85.

1967

With W. S. Murray.   Genetic studies of carcinogenesis in mice. J. Natl. Cancer Inst., 38:639–56.

1969

With W. S. Murray.   Reproductive effectiveness in crosses between five inbred strains of mice.   J. Natl. Cancer Inst., 42:219–25.

C. N. H. Long

CYRIL NORMAN HUGH LONG

June 19, 1901–July 6, 1970

BY O. L. K. SMITH AND J. D. HARDY

CYRIL NORMAN HUGH LONG, the elder son of John Edward and Rose Fanny (Langdill) Long, was born on June 19, 1901, in a village in Wiltshire, England. Most of his youth, however, was spent near Manchester, where his family had settled in the industrial town of Wigan. He spoke of his childhood often, as if it were of some special importance to the rest of his life.

Mr. John Long was the son of an impressive Color Sergeant in the Scots' Guards. He had shown great academic promise as a boy, but for some reason failed to pursue the life of a scholar or scientist, to which he might have been well suited, and instead entered government service, becoming a Tax Surveyor. As such he was known for his rigid honesty and retiring disposition. On the other hand, he pursued at home a lively interest in history and literature, and his creative energies poured forth in a number of hobbies. Wearing a white coat he experimented in the making of perfumes and jams or inlaid delicate woodwork. He collected rare books and knew some authors personally, notably Joseph Conrad. It may be imagined that his son inherited unusual intellectual ability, versatility, curiosity, and manual dexterity from his father, who encouraged him to be a serious student and to become a scientist. It also seems likely that the Long family set high standards for both moral character and achievement.

265

Mrs. Long was more of a companion to her two boys than their father. Cyril, as he was then known, often mentions in his diaries (1914–1917) "going out with mother," perhaps to the library, sometimes to tea or even the theater. He was said to resemble her physically, and it may have been the gentle good nature and flexibility inherited from her that were to distinguish him in later life in the role of teacher and administrator. The Longs were conservative people, and one can only speculate as to how much they might have felt the effects of changing times in England at the turn of the century, but it is worthy of note that they were living near the city of Dickens' *Hard Times,* the cradle of a great liberal tradition, during a period of social reform and of expanding interest in education. Intellectual life in Edwardian England as a whole, moreover, as has been pointed out recently by J. B. Priestley, had some unique qualities that influenced its youth—first, a distinct optimism that Priestley has termed "an atmosphere of hopeful debate" and, second, a peculiar climate "in which English genius, talent and generosity of mind could flourish."

As to his own education, Dr. Long was fond of describing to his American grandsons the Wigan Grammar School, where he and his brother Reggie began their studies, as a strict old-fashioned British boys' school. It was then directed by a Reverend Chambres, a scholar himself, who had the gift of interesting others in learning. Classes were small, especially in the upper grades, and the group became quite competitive, doing well in their outside examinations. Cyril was developing a keen interest in history and soon became known for his exceptional memory and ability to write good essays. The latter he afterward attributed to early experience with corporal punishment, but memories of hard work and even canings seem to have been mellowed by those of the headmaster's charming wit and of pleasant holidays. For the legendary Mr. Chambres, after a strenuous academic term, would take his boys on a bicycle or camping trip at his own retreat in Wales rather than seek relaxation for himself. These were pleasant days. Even World War I was remote, although the boys did participate in some civilian volunteer activities and Cyril's first experience in a hospital was probably that of writing letters for wounded soldiers.

Little guessing that his love of sports was to have an unexpected part in his future, Cyril was a skillful and enthusiastic player of soccer or cricket after school. In fact, his father sometimes had to remind him to return home to study. Like most boys, he also loved such robust activities as "tenting," hiking, or bicycle tours. Wet days found him building models or in the library reading—Jules Verne or historical novels, for he was naturally too precise to enjoy literature as an art. His boyhood diaries give glimpses, too, of the early development of certain other familiar aspects of their writer's personality. Facts and figures, such as cricket scores, everyone's term grades, cash flow "in" at a birthday and "out" afterward, are carefully recorded in a boyish hand, observation without comment, much as in the laboratory notebooks that followed in later years. His growing interest in stamp collecting and photography shows the scientist's taste for doing things by himself and also for arranging things each in its own place. No wonder that he became addicted to crossword puzzles in later life. Stamps continued to interest him for many years, so that his final collection was of such high value that eventually it was lost through an unsolved burglary in 1968. He became a skillful and artistic photographer, producing both landscapes and portraits of professional quality. It is interesting to note in view of later events that at the age of fifteen he was already developing his own pictures. He was generally well liked and had several close friends, typically from among the top-ranking students at school. He was always friendly, but most attracted to those with the keenest minds. He said in his mature years that his membership in the American Philosophical Society gave him great pleasure because of the variety of distinguished scholars it brought together.

Cyril continued to do well in school, in such subjects as English, mathematics, French and Latin, geography, Bible, and history. He placed fourth in his class in 1917. In that year, however, he also discovered chemistry, in which he rose immediately to the top of the class. Perhaps it was only natural talent and previous experience in the darkroom that accounted for this new interest, but many years later, when considering the selection and training of young scientists, he wrote of the primary importance of contact with inspiring teachers, "I was attracted at an early age to chemistry, largely by my own fortunate contact in an English school with a science master, who . . . was not a distinguished investigator, but had an enthusiasm for his subject, and a way of teaching it that was so effective that a large number of his students have become scientists." Thus it was that Long embarked upon what he later called the "exciting life adventure" of science. On completion of grammar school he enrolled immediately in the Honours School of Chemistry at nearby Manchester University.

His choice, according to a description by J. F. Fulton, was "a school with a long and distinguished record, especially in the training of men. Founded by Dalton early in the 19th century, such chemists as Sir William Roscoe and Carl Schorlemmer later added great lustre to the school, Schlorlemmer's chair being the first in organic chemistry in England. In the 20th century it helped to produce men like W. H. Perkin, Waynflete Professor of Chemistry at Oxford and his successor at Oxford, Robert Robinson who was appointed in 1930. Long had part of his training under Robinson but principally under . . . Arthur Lapworth."

Years later, when Long had become a champion of accelerated education for talented young American scientists, he wrote that in the British universities "in order to accommodate those students who enter the University solely for the purpose of obtaining competence in a particular field the Honors Schools are provided. To my mind this is an excellent way to recruit scientists, and while it is true that they may emerge somewhat deficient in what is called a liberal arts education, they are likely to be exceedingly competent in their area of study. You may also be sure that only those who want to do nothing else but pursue their life work in a particular field will be attracted to such an exacting course of study."

Long might have become a different sort of young man if he had gone to Cambridge, which was at first considered, but he seems to have been satisfied to commute to Manchester and to live at home with father and mother. At any rate he obtained a thorough training in both inorganic and organic chemistry, prepared his first two publications on the subject of the Friedel-Crafts reaction, and received his Bachelor of Science degree with first class honors in chemistry in 1921. Now twenty years of age, he was apparently well on the way to a career as an organic chemist when something unexpectedly set him off in quite a different direction. His own version of what happened is as follows:

"During my years in the School of Chemistry I had become interested in organic chemistry, particularly in that of carbohydrates, and had thought that I might devote myself to this subject after graduation. However, one day in 1921, I was asked to see A. V. Hill, the newly appointed Professor of Physiology at the University. He told me that he was working on the physical and chemical changes underlying muscular contraction, and that the latter was associated with the breakdown of glycogen to lactic acid. He needed the assistance of a chemist to follow these changes both in animals and in the blood of humans who were exercising. I must say that my first reaction was not too enthusiastic, I had had but little experience in biology, and in those days the efforts of the so-called biochemists were not held in too high regard by many of their colleagues in pure chemistry. I was used to dealing with substances that could be crystallized, whose physical constants and chemical properties were predictable. The heterogeneous, messy and unknown properties of extracts of cells or of blood which this investigation required me to analyze seemed to offer nothing but a struggle against large odds. Nevertheless, as Professor Hill talked about the enormous possibilities for the understanding of living processes that the methods of chemistry and physics were able to offer, I began to be caught up in his enthusiasm and vision. I accepted the great opportunity he offered me and in due course wondered why I had not had the sense to see for myself the challenge and excitement that these 'messes' offered to young students of chemistry and physics; that they were indeed the only keys that would unlock the mysteries of living cells and organisms. . . .

"When I began my work with Hill and his colleague Lupton, I soon began to suspect that their interest in me had not been entirely due to my extensive training in chemistry. I was at that time an enthusiastic player of football, field hockey, and cricket and this interest was soon put to practical uses by my superiors for I found myself running up and down stairs, or round the professor's garden while at intervals healthy samples of blood were withdrawn from my arms. When I had recovered from my exertions I was asked to sit down and analyze these for lactic acid."

Professor Hill's story is a little different and gives Long credit for more initiative:

"Long came and joined me in 1922 in Manchester. It was his own idea. He had just got a first class degree in chemistry there and I think he possessed a microscope which set him thinking about biology. . . .

"Long was a charming fellow to work with—there was quite a party of us—and enjoyed attempts to break world records of rate of oxygen consumption during a total oxygen debt after severe exercise to which my colleagues and I were rather addicted."

Hill's reputation must have preceded him to Manchester, and in view of later patterns of behavior it seems quite likely that Long got up courage to seek him out. He knew the use of a microscope well, for they had studied one at Wigan Grammar School, and he had taken bacteriology as an undergraduate. He was, in addition, probably familiar with some other biology courses offered the chemists. The classical work done in 1907 by F. G. Hopkins and W. Fletcher (who had been Hill's tutor at Cambridge), describing the production of lactic acid from glycogen during contraction of the isolated frog muscle, must have excited his curiosity, especially since he was already interested in the chemistry of carbohydrates.

Although neither account mentions it specifically, Long's next course of study took him to the medical school at Manchester where, having received a scholarship, he began his work in October of 1921. We now know that although he was studying for his M.Sc., Hill encouraged him to qualify also for the medical examinations because he could see his young associate's "mind was already bending towards medicine."

In the meanwhile the conversion of Long the chemist to Long the physiologist took place rapidly and, after receiving his master's degree from Manchester in 1923, he continued on with Hill to join Starling's department at University College, London, for the next two years. Of this move he wrote: "[There was] freedom in those days to take advantage of unexpected opportunities and to choose one's own course. Today's young scientist may find himself working in a very limited area. . . . There are tremendous pressures on him, mainly financial ones, to stay within a specialized area. When I was a Demonstrator in physiology [at University College] in London, my salary was equivalent to only $250 a year, but I was free to work in any area of physiology that interested me. I think it would be impossible to duplicate my career today."

Eight papers were published by Long alone or in collaboration with Hill and others on correlating what was then known about the chemistry and physiology of isolated muscle with what could be observed after exercise in the whole animal, particularly man, and later on about more clinical aspects of the same subject. It is interesting to note that this early work was also carried out under the watchful eye of Walter Fletcher, by now director of the Medical Research Council, and that the papers were usually submitted to the exacting Professor J. N. Langley of Cambridge (owner and editor of the *Journal of Physiology*), who wouldn't have hesitated to return them completely written over in red pencil! A further connection with Cambridge was made during a summer when Long worked in Joseph Barcroft's laboratory.

The years with Hill were important, too, not only for acquiring technical training, but also for leading to the development of a philosophy. The growth of biological science in England at the turn of the century owed much to the Cambridge school of physiologists, under Michael Foster and later Langley, where Hill had received his own training. Under Fletcher's supervision Hill had worked in an odoriferous, unglamorous cellar side by side with Lucas and others, for the physiology laboratory at Cambridge in those days was crowded with many "giants per square foot." Thus it is not surprising to find Long assimilating some progressive ideas about science and education. Always a staunch adversary of Victorian utilitarianism, he quoted Sir Edward Appleton in 1955—"Knowledge and insight are sufficient reward in themselves"—to express a view that has not enjoyed universal popularity as the century progressed. Also, Long began to believe, as Hill and Hopkins did, that the greatest discoveries are made from astute observation as a matter of chance—"things just happen" rather than being planned. Further, he believed that the function of the scientific mind is, simply as it says in the dictionary, to revise "accepted conclusions in the light of newly discovered facts." All of this means that the most important piece of equipment in the laboratory is the scientist himself, and it demands that the scientist be given, as Long would say, the minimum of requirements and the maximum opportunity. This was the state that suited his own temperament so well. It might also be observed that such individualized endeavors thrive best in a climate of friendship and the strong personal bonds that were to provide an important ingredient in the course of Long's own career.

Leaving his home district and parents for the first time may have been difficult for Long, but once settled in London he soon made many new friends. A gala farewell party a few years later at the Astoria tells of their high regard for him, and his fondness for his companions is recorded in many snapshots showing them in the laboratory, enjoying parties, or boating together. It was not long before his interests widened, and his responsibilities were increased when it became evident that their colleague Harvey Lupton was dying of cancer. Interestingly enough, a letter from Lupton from the nursing home suggests that some of their techniques for studying exercise in man be applied to diabetic patients.

It is not unlikely that Long was himself already thinking about the subject that was ever after on his mind: the syndrome of diabetes and how the various endocrine glands play upon metabolism during its development. He had a great admiration for Ernest Starling, and it is possible that his interest in diabetes dates from 1924 when a photograph of Long was taken with a dog depancreatized by the professor (Banting's and Best's discovery of insulin was still only three years old and was receiving much attention throughout the world). Having appreciated the advantages of applying chemistry to physiology, Long again began to apply what he knew of one discipline to another, clinical medicine. The result was "The Metabolism of the Diabetic Individual During and After Muscular Exercise," written with K. S. Hetzel from the Department of Medicine. About this time he discovered Graham Lusk's *The Science of Nutrition,* which was to influence his work for many years to come. He was also seeing a great deal of his friend Alan Parkes, who was studying medicine. Their discussions together led to another clinical paper, on fetal reabsorption, Parkes's interest at the time.

Accordingly, A. V. Hill arranged an opportunity for Long to return to his medical studies: "In 1925 Jonathan Meakins, Professor of Experimental Medicine at McGill University, Montreal, asked me if I could recommend somebody to join his team there. This led to Long going to McGill where he continued experimental studies in the intervals during his study of clinical medicine."

During the next two years Long held the post of lecturer in medical research in the Department of Biochemistry at McGill. Upon receiving his M.D.C.M. degree, in 1928, he took charge of the medical laboratory at the Royal Victoria Hospital for the Department of Medicine, becoming assistant professor of medical research at McGill in 1929. Writing of the talented and kindly Meakins in an obituary in 1959 he said, "My acceptance of this opportunity was perhaps the most fortunate decision I have made in my scientific career." While it would have been easy for Long to enjoy moderate fame (a contemporary newspaper article refers to him as a "noted physiologist"), he had detected in the McGill offer, quite apart from the opportunity to get his medical degree, some of his favorite ingredients. First of all, Dr. Meakins had written that there would be "no interference on the part of others" with one's own laboratory work. In addition, Dr. Meakins, who had lately arrived himself as the first full-time chief of medicine at McGill, had some interesting new ideas about the future of medicine. His position included the directorship of the University Clinic, which, as it turned out, was "one of the earliest attempts to integrate the rapidly developing basic medical sciences into the fabric of internal medicine." Nowadays, when the sick enjoy daily the fruits of such collaboration, it is hard to believe that the concept of a laboratory where the clinician could work side by side with the pure scientist was, in 1925, a revolutionary idea. As might be expected, Long's previous success as a chemist venturing into other fields made him quick to appreciate the potential of the new facilities at the Royal Victoria Hospital. Finally, might he not find congenial and stimulating companions in the new world?

He was not disappointed. Mrs. Meakins met him at the ship, installing him as a houseguest until he could get settled. Indeed, his laboratory notebook was hardly interrupted by its trip across the Atlantic. While the publications of the next seven years covered a variety of topics as Long gained knowledge of medicine and collaborated with others on the staff, it is interesting to note that throughout he was still preoccupied with the fate of lactic acid in health and disease and the neuroendocrine control of carbohydrate metabolism. "These were fruitful and exciting days," he wrote, "as we pursued our particular interests and at the same time exchanged ideas and talked shop among ourselves and clinicians and medical students who gradually began to drop in." Typically, he became treasurer of the Fund for Afternoon Tea, a daily social function that attracted a variety of stimulating associates and was to become a ritual in all his future laboratories.

Hill came to visit and later reported to Long's proud father, "He is extremely happy and doing very well indeed. . . . All his colleagues seem to love him and they have great hopes for his future. He seems to be taking to his clinical work like a fish to water." Hill also tells how Long's playful colleagues asked him questions they knew he couldn't answer on his final medical examinations, filling him with "dismay," only to announce later that he had "passed with Aggregate Honours!" Certainly his ability was appreciated. Dean Charles Martin was able to describe him in a recommendation as "excellent teacher, pleasing and stimulating personality, fertile mind, original work speaks for itself."

The easy informality on the new continent apparently agreed well with Long. Perhaps that is why he became "Hugh" instead of "Cyril" to his new friends. The "heartily democratic" manners (according to Priestley) of the people from manufacturing towns like Manchester during the early twentieth century may explain why Long later adapted more readily to life in the United States than do many of the British and why he seemed happily disinterested in class distinctions. He gained some reputation for youthful gaiety among his fellow medical students, although one can hardly imagine his having much time for such things considering the burden of work he carried at the time. He was changing, too, becoming more teacher than student, more leader than follower, and guiding his first graduate students.

One must agree with Yale colleague John Fulton that "his educational career has been peculiarly felicitous," for he now superimposed on his basic chemical and physiological *modus operandi* the clinical point of view, which became his permanent outlook, although he was not to enter the practice of medicine. He was always the medical man first, and a quietly compassionate one, sometimes exasperating his more zealous, less humanitarian associates. Years later (1950) his final admonition to the medical educators of Japan was to remember "the doctor is the servant of the sick and must endeavor to get him well."

It may be pointed out here that Long's first ties in the United States were with the clinical societies (he was president of the American Society of Clinical Investigation in 1944) and that he soon became known for his ability to restate the problems of disease more clearly to physicians in biochemical or physiological terms. Driven by the curiosity that earlier had sent him to Hill, the young medical student, unabashed, had struck up a correspondence with some famous figures—Carl Cori, W. B. Cannon, and Graham Lusk himself. It was with some annoyance that he received a typical reply from Lusk in which this hero casually discounted Long's meticulous results as due to a leaky apparatus! Nevertheless he had gained enough confidence in his own accomplishments to present a paper to Manchester University for a D.Sc., which was bestowed on him in 1932, shortly before he left McGill.

Dr. Meakins was to make one further contribution to Long's happiness, that of introducing him to Hilda Jarman, who was to become his wife. Having encountered a group of attractive young women from Calgary starting out on a holiday abroad, and knowing Long was on his way home to England for a visit by the same ship, Meakins couldn't resist arranging what developed into a shipboard romance. The wedding was at the bride's summer home in Vancouver in 1928. Hilda Long, an attractive, intelligent, and practical person, was to have an unusual appreciation of her husband's important contributions to science and human welfare. In addition, she shared his enjoyment of the social side of life, and she was to bestow gentle concern and friendship in the future on hundreds of his students and associates.

Although those who knew Long were convinced of his future success, the newly formed George S. Cox Research Institute at the University of Pennsylvania would perhaps have seemed an unlikely spot from which to make an important scientific discovery when he left McGill to become its director in 1932. The new arrivals were greeted by a modest suite of rooms, walls bare except for a plaque advising the occupants that the purpose of the institute was to "find a cure for diabetes." "A rather overwhelming assignment for a young man," Long recalled later. Undaunted he immediately set about exploiting the advantages of this position as he saw them: great freedom, continued close contact with clinical medicine without, however, direct responsibility for patient care, and, finally, the stimulating association with physiologists A. N. Richards and Detlev W. Bronk, friends of his in the preclinical science departments. (The Longs had renewed ties with physiologists in 1929 when returning from a trip to England by the same ship that brought Hill and all the other noted Europeans to attend the International Physiological Congress in Boston.) His responsibilities in the laboratory, moreover, were to be shared with a skillful clinician from the department of medicine, Francis Lukens.

In spite of evidence to the contrary it was generally agreed in those days that all the symptoms of diabetes mellitus were simply due to the underutilization of sugar because of an insufficient supply of insulin. Although Long came from a school that upheld the pancreatic origin of diabetes, he immediately appreciated the importance of the discovery a few years before by Bernardo Houssay that the removal of the pituitary gland produced a remarkable amelioration of experimental diabetes, clearly demonstrating the participation of at least one extrapancreatic factor in the diabetic syndrome. Thinking of the task ahead, Long and Lukens remembered the clinical observation that diminished function of the cortical portion of the adrenal gland lowers the blood sugar. Knowing also that removal of the pituitary is followed by adrenal atrophy, they set about investigating the possible role of the adrenal cortex in the Houssay preparation.

By early 1934 Dr. Lukens was able to prepare cats not only pancreatectomized but having both adrenals removed as well. To the two scientists' delight, the first such cat lived eleven days, or about twice as long as the usual diabetic cat; its blood sugar values were actually lower than normal in spite of its receiving no insulin whatsoever. They knew immediately that they were on the right track.

Long said afterwards, "Our feelings of achievement and excitement in those spring days now nearly 30 years ago [*sic*], when we saw those cats alive and well long after their controls had died, are still very vivid in my mind. It is one of the great though far too infrequent rewards of research to realize that you have made a lasting, albeit small contribution to knowledge. To be privileged to do so is an experience that remains with you long after your work has been expanded and incorporated in the greater achievements of your successors."

A short note appeared in *Science* in June 1934; as news of their discovery spread in the months that followed, Long and Lukens carefully extended and confirmed their observations. The evidence suggested that (1) the amelioration of diabetes in their animals was because the cortex of the adrenal had been removed, not the medullary or "nervous" portion of the gland as had usually been suggested and (2) that indeed the lessening after adrenalectomy of the copious amounts of sugar in the body so typical of diabetes might best be attributed after all to a reduction in sugar production from other sources, notably body protein. These conclusions have since been confirmed many times, not only in Long's own laboratory, as more highly purified hormones became available, but also, as the years have passed, by the work of others throughout the world.

At the time, however, these were conclusions that might not be accepted joyfully by all. The history of the study of diabetes is one of intermittent bitter contests, often unfortunately sparked by speculation on inconclusive evidence. But Long, by temperament and training, was never inhibited by old ideas. On the contrary, he delighted in the assumption of a new point of view, refuting erroneous work and bolstering his arguments with sound facts. He was an instant success as a speaker, sharp in debate but modest as he faced the first imposing scientific meetings. His success prompted a new friend (also a biochemist turned physician), J. P. Peters of Yale, to write, "I hear about your talks at every corner from those who have been stimulated by them. It was good to have someone with a really objective attitude discuss an endocrine subject."

Long's most important contribution, then, was not that he and Lukens had "cured diabetes" by adrenalectomy—for such a naïve idea was never entertained—but rather that the syndrome of diabetes itself was reconsidered in the light of newer knowledge of the parts played by the pituitary and other ductless glands in the events that follow pancreatectomy in animals. Long gave substance to the concept that the "balance of the endocrine glands" was related to the "diseases of metabolism." In 1936 he proposed to the American College of Physicians that "the clinical condition that follows hypo- or hyperfunction of an endocrine organ is not merely due to the loss or plethora of that particular internal secretion but is a result of the disturbance of the normal hormonal equilibrium of the body"—still, almost forty years later, perhaps the most important single idea in endocrine research.

The rooms of the new institute in Philadelphia were well filled now. Working in the laboratory were Lukens, Gerald Evans, and a young physiology student, Edith Fry, as well as other students and visitors. Long's "office" was a desk at the end of a corridor where he received the distinguished guests who came to observe, C. H. Best and H. M. Evans as well as Professor Houssay. He received invitations from many places, including one to visit Elliot Joslin in Boston. Professor of Medicine Alfred Stengel wrote him later that those four years at the Cox were nothing short of "a brilliant performance."

It was inevitable that Long would attract the attention of those seeking a candidate for the chair at Yale University vacated recently by the death of the celebrated biochemist

CYRIL NORMAN HUGH LONG

Lafayette Mendel. As a result of the efforts of Peters, who was specializing in diabetes in the Department of Medicine, and of the distinguished neurophysiologist John Fulton, Long moved to New Haven in the fall of 1936 as professor of physiological chemistry. Although Fulton's report for the committee praised his teaching and administrative ability, which had already become evident at the Cox Institute, it is most interesting for its evaluation of his scientific work. It states that Long has "perhaps more than any other contributed to the disentanglement of the confusion that reigned between the functions of the various endocrine glands and . . . metabolism and had put this on a sound scientific basis."

For his part, Long wrote this rather interesting acceptance to Dean Stanhope Bayne-Jones: "Not only my own future but also that of the subjects in which I am interested are to be best served by accepting your invitation." Privately he felt some trepidation. He was only thirty-five years old, and his accomplishments were unknown to many outside his field. Nevertheless, as A. V. Hill correctly predicted in a congratulatory letter, he need not have feared to follow the famous Professor Mendel, for his own interdisciplinary training uniquely fitted him for the needs of the future.

Long remained at Yale until his retirement thirty-three years later, first as professor and chairman of the Department of Physiological Chemistry, receiving the appointment as Sterling Professor in 1938. (His department, renamed the Department of Biochemistry in 1952, was the first department of biochemistry in the United States.) Later, Long became chairman of the Department of Physiology, having twice assumed responsibility also for the Department of Pharmacology as interim chairman, as well as serving as chairman of the university's Division of Biological Sciences. From 1947 to 1952 he served as dean of the School of Medicine, having already been acting dean briefly in 1943. From the first he took an active part in the affairs of the School of Medicine and joined in the life of the Yale community, being immediately well liked and respected. His department published fifty-seven papers in 1937–1938 and entered into many new outside activities under his leadership.

Long's years at Yale saw changes in the university, some the result of World War II, others economic and social, but it was fortunate perhaps that his early years and a good part of his deanship corresponded with the presidency of Charles Seymour. They had much in common, and Cambridge-educated Seymour appreciated his British colleague. Furthermore, the Seymour administration was noted for its enthusiastic support of science in general, a fact that on at least one occasion kept Long at Yale. Long participated in the overall reorganization of the teaching of biology at the university and gave promise that he would be as inventive and unconventional in administration as he had been in the laboratory. He became an ardent supporter of plans to unify the basic science departments of the university so that undergraduates, graduate students, and medical students would be enrolled side by side, perhaps not even deciding what degree to take until a later date. These plans were carried out only in part. He consistently urged the support of unusually gifted students, to free them from required work and from pressures (mainly financial) to finish quickly, and to allow each to chart his own course. Admittedly, the champions of such freedom were to suffer mounting frustrations in the mid-century United States as the young scientist became more and more lost in vast impersonal projects, often entirely taken out of private hands by the government.

Long found much to do at Yale in the thirties and forties and much to admire, chiefly those elements introduced previously under that dynamic innovator in medical education, Milton C. Winternitz, dean from 1920 to 1935. The so-called "Yale system," with its emphasis on individual achievement and self-reliance, was of course very much Long's own style. His arrival coincided with a period of modernization of teaching in the preclinical years in which he took an active part. He worked assiduously for his belief that the chemistry and physics of cellular function were the future of medicine and must be taught to the students on an advanced level. Fortunately he was also wary of teaching too many facts: "independence of thought and a capacity to form judgments will be required of the physician all his life, while techniques and the interpretation of information are always changing" and "the secret of success in medicine is an enquiring mind. Take nothing for granted, see and find out for yourself" rather than rely on the authorities, who don't, after all, have a "monopoly on all future ideas."

Long usually participated in the teaching of courses in his departments and also continued to meet with small groups of students until his retirement. Sometimes, he admitted, these conferences lapsed into an unscientific discussion of baseball, for he was still an avid sports fan. He once declined a strictly research post because "teaching is an important task." Of lecturing he admitted in 1942, "Indeed I can honestly say that since I have started to teach I have worked harder at elementary biochemistry than I ever did when a student." The fruits of this labor were lectures, later covering endocrinology, that were attended by such large audiences that around 1950 they had to be moved to a special auditorium. His lectures may have been a shock to the neophyte for whom they were intended, however, because of his preoccupation with the history of endocrinology and various unorthodox points of view. Surprisingly, the sense of humor that animated his private conversations, often making him a genial host or welcome arrival at a dull party, almost never surfaced in his formal lectures. In this he was in marked contrast to some of his lively contemporaries at the school. Perhaps he wished merely to emphasize the seriousness with which those of his training viewed their task. His interest in medical education was not a transient one, and he followed the careers of the medical students after graduation. He was proud of their high marks in National Board Examinations and celebrated their other achievements as much as he did those of junior members in his own departments. He took particular satisfaction in the large numbers of both groups of former students who became professors and department chairmen at other schools throughout the country, for he thought that the most important responsibility of the school to the community was to provide leadership in teaching and research. That his own leadership should ultimately be recognized by the endowment of a chair in his name at Yale devoted to endocrinology and metabolism was therefore one of the most gratifying of the many honors he received. One cannot consider the list of his former students, moreover, without being impressed by the large number of professional women whom he encouraged and trained, starting with his first graduate student in Montreal, Eleanor Venning. At that time women were not accepted universally in the laboratory nor as physicians.

Maintaining high standards in education and research had not been easy during World War II, and the pressures of the postwar period on medical schools were combined with mounting economic problems. Thus when Long was asked to become dean in 1947, the School of Medicine was facing a grave crisis. In fact, there were rumors that it might close entirely—hardly happy circumstances under which the new dean was to take office! Needless to say, the school did not close, largely because of extraordinary efforts to reach a compromise on the question of how to relieve the university of the responsibility for the entire deficit of the New Haven Hospital, which was becoming an alarming drain on Yale's educational funds. Dean Long was one of the architects of that agreement and was responsible as well for numerous other improvements in service and economy, notably the centralization of clinical laboratories.

While the most striking accomplishment of Long's term as dean was the lowering of the school's deficit by one-half, there were many other advances, for example: 1) the broadening of the responsibility of the School of Medicine in the community both by the offering of postgraduate medical education and by the initiation of measures to establish the school as the medical center of Connecticut, and 2) the improvement of personal relationships within the school itself. Perhaps this latter was due to the sincere attempts to reach a consensus among the faculty on important questions without overlooking anyone's private opinion, an awesome task considering what strong personalities were involved. It would have been an impossible one without the maximum of mutual respect that fortunately seems to have prevailed. In describing Long's term of office one of his former colleagues singled out his sympathy for a fellow department chairman's problems (for the deanship was only a part-time job in those days), his availability in spite of "onerous burdens," and his continued interest in the care of patients, particularly where basic research applied to clinical problems.

For the future Long hoped for medical curriculum revisions, including a forward-looking expansion of the sections on epidemiology and public health. He was the first dean to express concern for the health of the medical students then living in tenements and pointed out the urgent need for a modern dormitory. Although it made newspaper headlines, one of his more radical proposals to provide more and younger doctors never gained acceptance by the university. The proposal was for a cooperative program between the School of Medicine and Yale College to grant the M.D. degree after only five years of study instead of the usual eight. Similar plans are now being adopted by many medical schools throughout the country.

Since the school had been on the brink of disaster, it is amazing to hear from Long's professor of surgery that the five years of his deanship were "thoroughly happy years professionally, perhaps in part because we were both new in our respective positions with high hopes for the School and a minimum of accumulated frustrations." Another associate described the hospital crisis thus: "I am impressed with the stimulation, fun and pleasure that both Hugh and I got out of our administrative responsibilities. I recognize that this is almost inconceivable today. . . ." Perhaps, after all, what he gave to that difficult term of office was a little of the "atmosphere of hopeful debate."

No description of those days of stringent economy would be complete without reference to the semblance of a gracious social life that the Longs and their friends somehow continued to bring to Cedar Street. Thus the traditional afternoon teas popular since the Winternitz days at the medical school were enthusiastically continued. Faculty wives presided, and the refreshments were provided by funds raised annually at a gala ball arranged by the students. It all required some effort, but succeeded in bringing the medical community together in ways that were not entirely academic.

When Long's term elapsed, in 1952, he left with relief, for he believed the deanship should be a full-time job. At this time he moved from biochemistry to the physiology department where he served as chairman until 1964, remaining as Sterling Professor until he became emeritus in 1969. There, he could be found in an office typical of his Yale days. It was, like himself, a blend of old and new styles. Visitors sat upright on ancient, durable chairs that scraped on bare floors because elaborate furnishings were considered extravagant. Shiny office machinery, on the other hand, had been selected from the latest models. One saw him over a very neat but undistinguished desk, hair prematurely white since the thirties above a rather long, thin face with sharp, closely set dark eyes and a slightly deviated nose, the result of his athletic past. An adroit practitioner of the art of conversation, he was a restless talker, leaning back gently in his chair to pick a book from the shelf, or pacing about the room, stopping periodically to assume a characteristic pose—bent at the waist, one hand on hip, the other busy with pencil or chalk.

Although administrative responsibilities took more and more of the actual work out of Long's hands, there can be no doubt that he continued to play a large part in the direction of his laboratories at Yale. He enjoyed the company of his co-workers and sought them out to discuss problems. His special flair for the application of a new or unusual method to an old question continued to characterize his work, and he drove his young associates to thorough calculation and recalculation, interpretation and reinterpretation. At the same time, like Gowland Hopkins, he had the tolerance for youth and inexperience that is a mark of greatness, the ability to listen patiently to salvage something worthwhile from the most inept presentation. The audiences were always amazed at his respect for the value of the older medical literature, of which he had an encyclopedic knowledge. Final evidence over the years that he maintained full command of his subject is found in the series of sparkling, unbiased review articles and talks with which he inspired a new generation of endocrinologists. He developed a worldwide audience, and in recognition of his accomplishments was elected to the National Academy of Sciences in 1948. He participated actively in a number of professional societies, but served none more faithfully than the Endocrine Society, of which he was president in 1947–1948.

The central theme of Long's research remained the endocrine control of metabolism, which is "far more complex than appeared possible a few years ago." On the basis of work carried out with Miss Fry, who had come with him from Philadelphia, and a medical student, B. Katzin, he was able to describe quantitatively for the first time the biological properties of the adrenal cortical hormones, and a classic paper was published on this subject in *Endocrinology* in 1940. The availability of more highly purified hormones and the use of partially depancreatectomized rats made possible the demonstration of exacerbation of the diabetes previously attenuated by adrenalectomy. This work, moreover, definitely established the effects of the glucocorticoids on protein as well as on carbohydrate metabolism, laying the foundation for future studies on the popular topic, the therapeutic effects of cortisone and related drugs on man. Reexamination of the possible hypophyseal factors participating in the diabetic syndrome also led toward the isolation of prolactin (with A. White), of adrenocorticotrophic hormone (with G. E. Sayers), and of growth hormone by Alfred and Jane (Russell) Wilhelmi; furthermore, the development of the adrenal ascorbic acid bioassay for pituitary adrenocortical hormones in Long's laboratory and the resulting studies of the latter continued for many years to constitute some of his most important contributions. During World War II his group, under Frank Engel, investigated the role of the catabolic effects of the adrenal cortex in hemorrhagic shock. Afterward the laboratory returned to diabetes and related topics, particularly obesity, and continued the search for the nature of the effects of the adrenal cortical hormones on intermediary metabolism. The work of Long's later years, moreover, is distinguished by a surprisingly youthful originality. For example, undaunted by the most formidable procedures devised by physiologists, he described with T. Hiroshige in 1964 a procedure for the "visceral preparation" in the rat.

With students in all parts of the globe, with activities in remarkably varied professional societies, and with the wide recognition he received for his achievements in basic science, Hugh Long was destined to have more than a local influence on the course of medical science in his time. Some measure of this was a consequence of the service he gave to the government of his adopted country, which urgently needed him as a consultant during World War II. His desire for citizenship in the United States was granted in 1942. The story is told that, according to his usual custom, he came to the examination for naturalization very well prepared. When asked some minor questions about American history, he astounded his audience with a twenty-minute scholarly talk on the subject.

No native-born American scientist gave his energies more willingly to the task of advising the government on medical research. Long worked under various government offices starting in 1937, when he had first joined the Endocrine Research Committee of the National Research Council. His post as deputy chief of the Division of Physiology of the Office of Scientific Research and Development assured permanent contact with physiologists and took him to visit many of their laboratories (for example in 1943) where a great deal of the best work in endocrine research was then in progress. While primarily concerned with subjects relating to the endocrine glands, his involvement broadened as he became more experienced in the administration of medical research and education.

Long had witnessed at close range the postwar surge of public interest in research in medicine, which was responsible in part, it must be admitted, for the success of laboratories like his own. He had, nevertheless, several opportunities to survey the less fortunate effects of government support of science and of medical research. Among them he cited the tendency of the government to focus funds on the eradication of certain diseases, diverting doctors from teaching and the practice of medicine and neglecting the general support of institutions engaged in the discovery and training of the gifted new scientists necessary for more basic research.

Long took some memorable trips abroad in the interest of medical education. The first was as leader of a harrowing (because of the outbreak of the Korean War) but successful advisory mission to Japan in 1950. In 1965 he joined a similar mission to Egypt for the Agency for International Development. An invitation to return to Japan for the Atomic Bomb Casualty Commission was also gratefully accepted, since he was an enthusiastic tourist and had ties in both Japan and Hawaii. He took a rare sabbatical to assist in the founding of a new medical school in Honolulu in 1964.

Such assignments were rewarding in new associations, ideas, and friendships, but were time-consuming and exhausting and performed at considerable sacrifice. Following one trip to Washington in October of 1960, after a strenuous summer of meetings abroad, Long entered the hospital with a severe myocardial infarction. He recovered in time, however, to receive in person an honorary degree from McGill University in June of the next year. He lived almost ten years longer, a life sometimes dissatisfying professionally as the elements of his philosophy were inevitably challenged, but full of honor and never dull. Upon reaching the age of retirement, in 1969, he was appointed a fellow of the John B. Pierce Foundation's Yale-affiliated laboratory, where he continued his research in the endocrine control of metabolism as related to environmental physiology. Although suffering increasing physical limitations he took pleasure as usual from work, friendship, and family life, for he was always happiest at home or traveling abroad with his two daughters. His close relationship with them is more evidence of his extraordinary strength and discipline when one considers the heavy demands of his work during the years of their childhood. One of his proudest moments was when his younger daughter, Diana, received her Ph.D. in the History of Science and Medicine from Yale. After his daughters married and he became the delighted grandfather of six grandchildren, summers in Maine continued to unite him with his children. There, while fishing with a young grandson on a beautiful summer day, his heart finally stopped, ending a remarkable career.

In accounting for a life so full of meaning and accomplishment one is struck in the first place not only with the optimism but also the good will, tolerance, and mutual enjoyment with which this older generation, particularly in Britain, endowed its scientific work. It was before, as Priestley observes, "we had to move into a world largely alien to the English temperament." Second, while the old world was small enough for individuals to have importance, it was large enough to accommodate the freedom that Long so valued and used to such advantage in his own career. At every crossroad he consistently chose freedom over security and material gain. Third, much of Long's success, both in the laboratory and as an administrator, stemmed from his breadth of knowledge, his appropriate choice and effective promotion of the original, neglected ideas of others. He was a nonspecialist with the broader understanding possible before the current necessity of specialization. While today, because of overwhelming advances in the body of scientific knowledge itself, there is "more emphasis on the accumulation of facts than on the ability to comprehend them (D. W. Bronk)," it seems highly unlikely that Long and Lukens would ever have fully appreciated the relationship of the endocrine glands to the biochemical changes of diabetes mellitus if they had not had wide experience in clinical medicine. Fourth, in Hugh Long's day there was more leisure for maturing, more time for contemplation and, finally, no one was ashamed, in the words of A. N. Whitehead, to take "an active interest in the simple occurrences of life for their own sake."

FOR ASSISTANCE in the preparation of this biographical memoir, the authors are particularly indebted to G. B. Darling, A. V. Hill, G. E. Lindskog, T. W. Shaw, A. W. Snoke, and to the Long family, who generously provided the complete memorabilia, including the collection now at the American Philosophical Society, Philadelphia. Quotations from current books are from:

Bronk, D. W., in *Britannica Yearbook of Science and the Future,* Chicago, Encyclopedia Britannica, Inc., 1971.

Hill, A. V., *Trials and Trails in Physiology,* London, Edward Arnold (Publisher) Ltd., 1965.

Priestley, J. B., *The Edwardians,* New York, Harper & Row Publishers, 1970.

CHRONOLOGY AND MEMBERSHIPS

1901	Born June 19, Nettleton, Wiltshire, England
1918	Wigan Grammar School
1921	B.Sc., Manchester University; M.Sc., 1923; D.Sc., 1932
1923–1925	Demonstrator in Physiology, University College, London
1925–1932	Lecturer and Assistant Professor of Medical Research, McGill University
1928	M.D., C.M., McGill University
1928	Married to Hilda Gertrude Jarman. Children: Barbara Rosemary (Mrs. Richard P. Simons), Diana Elizabeth (Mrs. David D. Hall).
1928–1932	In charge, Medical Laboratories, Royal Victoria Hospital, Montreal
1932–1936	Director, George S. Cox Medical Research Institute, and Assistant Professor of Medicine, University of Pennsylvania
1942	Became an American citizen
1936–1970	Yale University: Chairman, Department of Physiological Chemistry, 1936–1951; Professor of Physiological Chemistry, 1936–1938; Sterling Professor of Physiological Chemistry, 1938–1951; Director of Graduate Studies, Department of Physiological Chemistry, 1937–1948; Chairman, Department of Pharmacology, 1939–1941, 1952–1953; Chairman, Division of Biological Sciences, 1939–1942; Fellow, Calhoun College, 1940–1970; Dean, School of Medicine, 1947–1952; Chairman, Department of Physiology, 1951–1964; Sterling Professor of Physiology, 1951–1969; Director of Graduate Studies, Department of Physiology, 1952–1961.
1936	M.A. (Hon.), Yale University
1946	Sc.D. (Hon.), Princeton University
1948	Army–Navy Certificate of Appreciation
1950	Squibb Award, Endocrine Society
1951	Banting Memorial Medal of the American Diabetes Association
1955–1956	Fellow, John S. Guggenheim Memorial Foundation

1956   Schering Scholar, Endocrine Society
1959   Modern Medicine Award
1959   Scientific Award of the Pharmaceutical Manufacturers
            Association
1961   Sc.D. (Hon.), McGill University
1962   M.D. (Hon.), University of Venezuela
1964   Medal of Hiroshima University (Japan)
1964   Visiting Professor, University of Hawaii
1964   Faculty of Medicine plaque, Tokyo University
1966   C.N.H. Long Professorship established, Yale University
1969–1970   Fellow, John B. Pierce Foundation
1970   Died July 6

Member American Diabetes Association, American Philosophical
Society, American Physiological Society, American Society for
Clinical Investigation, Argentine Society of Biology, Association
of American Physicians, The Biochemical Society (Great Britain),
British Diabetic Association, Connecticut Diabetes Association
Inc., Connecticut State Medical Society, Endocrine Society, Fulton
Society, Horseshoe Club (London), International Brain Research
Association, Interurban Clinical Club, National Academy of Sci-
ences of the United States of America, Peripatetic Club, Physio-
logical Society (Great Britain), Society for Experimental Biology
and Medicine, Yale Medical Society. Editorial Board of *American
Journal of Physiology, Endocrinology, Journal of Applied Physi-
ology, Physiological Reviews, Proceedings of the Society for Ex-
perimental Biology and Medicine, Yale Journal of Biology and
Medicine.* Board of Governors, *Methods in Medical Research.*
Committee member or Consultant for Armed Forces Institute of
Pathology, Atomic Bomb Casualty Commission, Atomic Energy
Commission, Armed Forces Quartermaster's Food and Container
Institute, Department of Health, Education and Welfare, Insti-
tute for Defense Analyses, National Research Council, National
Science Foundation, Office of Scientific Research and Develop-
ment, President's Scientific Advisory Committee, United States
Army, United States Public Health Service. Fellow, American
Academy of Arts and Sciences and College of Physicians of
Philadelphia.

Articles and obituaries about Dr. Long are to be found in *Yale Medicine 1*, 12, 1966; *Yale J. Biol. Med. 41*, 95, 1968; *Year Book of the American Philosophical Society*, 1970, p. 143; *Endocrinology 88*, 537, 1971; and *Nature 229*, 356, 1971.

BIBLIOGRAPHY

KEY TO ABBREVIATIONS

Am. J. Med. Sci. = American Journal of the Medical Sciences
Am. J. Physiol. = American Journal of Physiology
Ann. Intern. Med. = Annals of Internal Medicine
Ann. N.Y. Acad. Sci. = Annals of the New York Academy of Science
Ann. Rev. Physiol. = Annual Review of Physiology
Biochem. J. = Biochemical Journal
Can. J. Biochem. = Canadian Journal of Biochemistry
Cold Spring Harbor Symp. Quant. Biol. = Cold Spring Harbor Symposium on Quantitative Biology
Ergeb. Physiol. = Ergebnisse der Physiologie
Fed. Proc. = Federation Proceedings
Jap. J. Physiol. = Japanese Journal of Physiology
J. Biol. Chem. = Journal of Biological Chemistry
J. Endocrinol. = Journal of Endocrinology
J. Exp. Med. = Journal of Experimental Medicine
J. Physiol. (Lond.) = Journal of Physiology (London)
Proc. Assoc. Res. Nerv. Ment. Dis. = Proceedings of the Association for Research in Nervous and Mental Disease
Proc. ——— Congr. Int. Diabetes Fed. = Proceedings of the ——— Congress of the International Diabetes Federation
Proc. ——— Int. Congr. Endocrinol. = Proceedings of the ——— International Congress on Endocrinology
Proc. —— Int. Congr. Physiol. = Proceedings of the —— International Congress of Physiology
Proc. ——— Meet. Endocr. Soc. = Proceedings of the ——— Meeting of the Endocrine Society
Proc. R. Soc. (Lond.), Ser. B = Proceedings of the Royal Society (London): Biological Sciences
Proc. Soc. Exp. Biol. Med. = Proceedings of the Society for Experimental Biology and Medicine
Recent Prog. Horm. Res. = Recent Progress in Hormone Research
Yale J. Biol. Med. = Yale Journal of Biology and Medicine

1923

With A. V. Hill and H. Lupton. Lactic acid in human muscle. Proceedings of the Physiological Society. J. Physiol. (Lond.), 57:xliv–xlv.

With H. Lupton. The removal of lactic acid during recovery from muscular exercise in man. Proceedings of the Physiological Society. J. Physiol. (Lond.), 57:lxvii–lxviii.

1924

With A. V. Hill and H. Lupton. The effect of fatigue on the relation between work and speed, in the contraction of human arm muscles. J. Physiol. (Lond.), 58:334–37.

The lactic acid in the blood of a resting man. J. Physiol. (Lond.), 58:455–60.

With A. S. Parkes. On the nature of foetal reabsorption. Biochem. J., 18:800–805.

With A. V. Hill and H. Lupton. Muscular exercise, lactic acid, and the supply and utilization of oxygen. Parts I–III. Proc. R. Soc. (Lond.), Ser. B, 96:438–75.

With K. Furusawa, A. V. Hill, and H. Lupton. Muscular exercise, lactic acid, and the supply and utilization of oxygen. Parts VII–VIII. Proc. R. Soc. (Lond.), Ser. B, 97:155–76.

With A. V. Hill and H. Lupton. Muscular exercise, lactic acid, and the supply and utilization of oxygen. Parts IV–VI. Proc. R. Soc. (Lond.), Ser. B, 98:84–138.

1925

With A. V. Hill. Muscular exercise, lactic acid, and the supply and utilization of oxygen. Ergeb. Physiol., 24:43–51.

With L. N. Katz. A comparison of the lactic acid contents of the mammalian heart and skeletal muscle after stimulation and in rigor mortis. Proceedings of the Physiological Society. J. Physiol. (Lond.), 60:iii–iv.

With L. N. Katz. Lactic acid in mammalian cardiac muscle. Part I. The stimulation maximum. Proc. R. Soc. (Lond.), Ser. B, 99:8–20.

With H. J. G. Hines and L. N. Katz. Lactic acid in mammalian cardiac muscle. Part II. The rigor mortis maximum and the normal glycogen content. Proc. R. Soc. (Lond.), Ser. B, 99:20–26.

With L. N. Katz and P. T. Kerridge. Lactic acid in mammalian cardiac muscle. Part III. Changes in hydrogen-ion concentration. Proc. R. Soc. (Lond.), Ser. B, 99:26–27.

1926

Muscular exercise, lactic acid, and the supply and utilization of oxygen. Part XIV. The relation in man between the oxygen intake during exercise and the lactic acid content of the muscles.

Proc. R. Soc. (Lond.), Ser. B, 99:167–72.

With K. S. Hetzel. The metabolism of the diabetic individual during and after muscular exercise. Proc. R. Soc. (Lond.), Ser. B, 99:279–306.

1927

With J. Meakins. Oxygen consumption, oxygen debt and lactic acid in circulatory failure. Journal of Clinical Investigation, 4:273–93.

1928

The effect of anesthesia on the recovery process in mammalian skeletal muscles. J. Biol. Chem., 77:563–79.

1930

With G. R. Brow. Biochemical changes in the heart during anesthesia. Current Research in Anesthesia and Analgesia, 9:193–97.

With J. Beattie and G. R. Brow. The hypothalamus and the sympathetic nervous system. In: *The Vegetative Nervous System,* vol. IX, pp. 249–316. Proc. Assoc. Res. Nerv. Ment. Dis., New York, Dec. 27 and 28, 1928. Baltimore, The Williams & Wilkins Co.

With J. Beattie and G. R. Brow. Physiological and anatomical evidence for the existence of nerve tracts connecting the hypothalamus with spinal sympathetic centres. Proc. R. Soc. (Lond.), Ser. B, 106:253–75.

With G. R. Brow and J. Beattie. Irregularities of the heart under chloroform. Journal of the American Medical Association, 95:715–16.

With R. Grant. The recovery process after exercise in the mammal. I. Glycogen resynthesis in the fasted rat. J. Biol. Chem., 89: 553–65.

1931

With E. M. Hill and D. Slight. Plasma fats in some cases of mental depression. J. Biol. Chem., 92:lxxxi–lxxxii.

1932

With F. L. Horsfall, Jr. The recovery process after exercise in the mammal. II. The conversion of infused d-lactic acid into muscle glycogen. J. Biol. Chem., 95:715–33.

With E. M. Venning. The alleged increase in plasma fats after the injection of epinephrine. J. Biol. Chem., 96:397–404.

With G. T. Evans. Glycogen content of the rat heart. Proc. Soc. Exp. Biol. Med., 30:186–89.

1933

With E. G. Fry. The effect of vagotomy on muscle glycogen resynthesis. Am. J. Med. Sci., 185:884.

With F. D. Lukens and E. G. Fry. Glycogen restoration after exercise in depancreatized cats. Am. J. Med. Sci., 186:153.

With D. Slight. Plasma lipoids in mental depression. American Journal of Psychology, 13:141–50.

1934

With F. D. W. Lukens. Observations on adrenalectomized depancreatized cats. Science, 79:569–71.

With F. D. W. Lukens. Observations upon hypophysectomized–depancreatized cats. Proc. Soc. Exp. Biol. Med., 32:326–28.

With F. D. W. Lukens. Observations on a dog maintained for five weeks without adrenals or pancreas. Proc. Soc. Exp. Biol. Med., 32:392–94.

1935

With F. D. W. Lukens. Observations on adrenalectomized–depancreatized and hypophysectomized–depancreatized cats. J. Biol. Chem., 109:lvi–lvii.

With F. D. W. Lukens. Effect of adrenalectomy and hypophysectomy upon experimental diabetes in the cat. Proc. Soc. Exp. Biol. Med., 32:743–45.

Recent advances in carbohydrate metabolism with particular reference to diabetes mellitus. Ann. Intern. Med., 9:166–74.

With J. B. Collip, R. L. Katz, and D. L. Thomson. Acute fatty liver following partial hepatectomy. Canadian Medical Association Journal, 33:689.

1936

With F. D. W. Lukens. The effects of adrenalectomy and hypophysectomy upon experimental diabetes in the cat. J. Exp. Med., 63:465–90.

With F. D. W. Lukens and E. G. Fry. The effect of adrenalectomy and hypophysectomy upon the fatty infiltration of the liver following total pancreatomy in the cat. Am. J. Physiol., 116:96.

Disturbances of the endocrine balance and their relation to diseases of metabolism. Ann. Intern. Med., 9:1619–27.

The interrelationships of the glands of internal secretion concerned with metabolism. (Newbold Lecture) Am. J. Med. Sci., 191: 741–59.

With F. D. W. Lukens. The effects of hypophysectomy and adrenalectomy upon pancreatic diabetes. Transactions of the Association of American Physicians, 51:123–28.

The relation of the anterior pituitary to carbohydrate metabolism. Proc. Assoc. Res. Nerv. Ment. Dis., 17:276–86.

1937

With F. D. W. Lukens and F. C. Dohan. Adrenalectomized depancreatized dogs. Proc. Soc. Exp. Biol. Med., 36:553–54.

Studies on the "diabetogenic" action of the anterior pituitary. Cold Spring Harbor Symp. Quant. Biol., 5:344–56.

With S. Zuckerman. Relation of the adrenal cortex to cyclical changes in the female accessory reproductive organs. Nature, 139:1106–7.

The interrelationships between the pituitary, pancreas and adrenal glands. In: *Practitioners Handbook,* chap. III, pp. 20–32. New York, D. Appleton & Company.

The influence of the pituitary and adrenal glands upon pancreatic diabetes. Harvey Lectures, 1936–1937, pp. 194–228.

With A. White and H. R. Catchpole. A crystalline protein with high lactogenic activity. Science, 86:82–83.

With A. White. Intermediary carbohydrate metabolism. Ergeb. Physiol., 40:164–203.

1938

With B. Katzin. Effect of adrenal cortical hormone on carbohydrate stores of fasted hypophysectomized rats. Proc. Soc. Exp. Biol. Med., 38:516–18.

With B. Katzin. The effect of the adrenal cortical hormone on the liver and muscle glycogen of normal fasting mice and rats. Am. J. Physiol., 123:113–14.

With E. G. Fry and K. W. Thompson. The effect of adrenalectomy and adrenal cortical hormones upon pancreatic diabetes in the rat. Am. J. Physiol., 123:130–31.

With R. A. Shipley. I. The relation of ketonaemia to ketonuria in the rat. II. A method for the assay of the ketogenic activity. III. The nature of the ketogenic principle. Biochem. J., 32: 2242–56.

The adrenal cortex and carbohydrate metabolism. Sigma Xi Quarterly, 26:175–86.

1939

Diabetes mellitus in the light of our present knowledge of metabolism. (Hatfield Lecture) Transactions & Studies of the College of Physicians of Philadelphia, 7:21–46.

With E. G. Fry and H. B. Ritter. The aggravation of pancreatic diabetes by adrenal cortical extract. Am. J. Physiol., 126:497.

With H. C. Harrison. The effect of anterior pituitary extract on the metabolism of fasting normal and adrenalectomized rats. Am. J. Physiol., 126:526–27.

With B. Katzin. The effect of adrenal cortical extract on the carbohydrate and protein metabolism of the rat. Am. J. Physiol., 126:551.

With K. W. Thompson and B. F. Lyons. The effect of hypophysectomy on the hypercholesterolemia of the thyroidectomized dogs. Am. J. Physiol., 126:643–44.

1940

Recent research on the control of metabolism by the endocrine glands. Journal of the American Dietetic Association, 16:395–406.

With B. Katzin and E. G. Fry. The adrenal cortex and carbohydrate metabolism. Endocrinology, 26:309–44.

With H. C. Harrison. The distribution of ketone bodies in tissues. J. Biol. Chem., 133:209–18.

With H. C. Harrison. Effects of anterior pituitary extracts in the fasted rat. Endocrinology, 26:971–78.

Evidence for and against control of carbohydrate metabolism by the hypothalamus. Association for Research in Nervous and Mental Disease, Research Publications, 20:486–500.

1941

With J. R. Brobeck. The influence of hypothalamic lesions on pancreatic diabetes. Am. J. Physiol., 133:224.

With K. W. Thompson. The effect of hypophysectomy upon hypercholesterolemia of dogs. Endocrinology, 28:715–22.

With C. A. Elvehjem and E. V. McCollum. Nutrition. In: *The Endocrine Control of Metabolism,* pp. 13–33. University of Pennsylvania Bicentennial Conference. Philadelphia, University of Pennsylvania Press.

1942

Pituitary hormones influencing growth in higher animals. Cold Spring Harbor Symp. Quant. Biol., 10:91–103.

Carbohydrate metabolism. In: *Diseases of Metabolism,* chap. II, pp. 19–72. 1st ed. Philadelphia, W. B. Saunders Co.

Etiology, diabetes mellitus. In: *Diseases of Metabolism,* chap. XVI, pp. 711–21. 1st ed. Philadelphia, W. B. Saunders Co.

With W. R. C. Golden. The influence of certain hormones on the carbohydrate levels of the chick. Endocrinology, 30:675–86.

A discussion of the mechanism of action of adrenal cortical hormones on carbohydrate and protein metabolism. Endocrinology, 30:870–83.

Metabolic functions of the endocrine glands. Ann. Rev. Physiol., 4:465–502.

With E. G. Fry and M. Miller. The "corticomimetic" action of stilbestrol on carbohydrate and protein metabolism. Endocrinology, 30:S1029–30.

With A. White and R. W. Bonsnes. Prolactin. J. Biol. Chem., 143:447–64.

With W. R. C. Golden. Absorption and disposition of glucose in the chick. Am. J. Physiol., 136:244–49.

The endocrine control of carbohydrate metabolism and its relation to diabetes in man. Proceedings of the American Diabetes Association, 2:99–115.

1943

With G. Sayers, M. A. Sayers, and A. White. Effect of pituitary adrenotropic hormone on cholesterol content of rat adrenal glands. Proc. Soc. Exp. Biol. Med., 52:200–202.

The growth and metabolic hormones of the anterior pituitary. Ann. N.Y. Acad. Sci., 43:383–426.

With J. Tepperman and F. L. Engel. A review of adrenal cortical hypertrophy. Endocrinology, 32:373–402.

With J. Tepperman and F. L. Engel. Effect of high protein diets on size and activity of the adrenal cortex in the albino rat. Endocrinology, 32:403–9.

With F. L. Engel and M. G. Winton. Biochemical studies on shock. I. The metabolism of amino acids and carbohydrate during hemorrhagic shock in the rat. J. Exp. Med., 77:397–410.

With J. R. Brobeck and J. Tepperman. Experimental hypothalamic hyperphagia in the albino rat. Yale J. Biol. Med., 15: 831–53.

With J. Tepperman and J. R. Brobeck. The effects of hypothalamic hyperphagia and of alterations in feeding habits on the metabolism of the albino rat. Yale J. Biol. Med., 15:855–73.

With V. C. Dickerson and J. Tepperman. The role of the liver in the synthesis of fatty acids from carbohydrate. Yale J. Biol. Med., 15:875–92.

With J. R. Brobeck and J. Tepperman. The effect of experimental obesity upon carbohydrate metabolism. Yale J. Biol. Med., 15: 893–904.

With G. Sayers and A. White. Preparation and properties of pituitary adrenotropic hormone. J. Biol. Chem., 149:425–36.

1944

With G. Sayers, M. A. Sayers, E. G. Fry, and A. White. The effect of the adrenotrophic hormone of the anterior pituitary on the cholesterol content of the adrenals. Yale J. Biol. Med., 16: 361–92.

With G. Sayers, M. A. Sayers, and H. L. Lewis. Effect of adrenotropic hormone on ascorbic acid and cholesterol content of the adrenal. Proc. Soc. Exp. Biol. Med., 55:238–39.

With J. A. Russell and F. L. Engel. Biochemical studies on shock. II. The role of the peripheral tissues in the metabolism of protein and carbohydrate during hemorrhagic shock in the rat. J. Exp. Med., 79:1–7.

With F. L. Engel and H. C. Harrison. Biochemical studies on shock. III. The role of the liver and the hepatic circulation in the metabolic changes during hemorrhagic shock in the rat and the cat. J. Exp. Med., 79:9–22.

With J. A. Russell and A. E. Wilhelmi. Biochemical studies on shock. IV. The oxygen consumption of liver and kidney tissue from rats in hemorrhagic shock. J. Exp. Med., 79:23–33.

1945

With H. N. Harkins. Metabolic changes in shock after burns. Am. J. Physiol., 144:661–68.

With G. Sayers, M. A. Sayers, and T.-Y. Liang. The cholesterol and ascorbic acid content of the adrenal, liver, brain and plasma following hemorrhage. Endocrinology, 37:96–110.

With A. E. Wilhelmi, J. A. Russell, and M. G. Engel. Some aspects of the nitrogen metabolism of liver tissue from rats in hemorrhagic shock. Am. J. Physiol., 144:674–82.

With A. E. Wilhelmi, J. A. Russell, and F. L. Engel. The effects of hepatic anoxia on the respiration of liver slices *in vitro*. Am. J. Physiol., 144:683–92.

With E. G. Fry. Effect of epinephrine on adrenal cholesterol and ascorbic acid. Proc. Soc. Exp. Biol. Med., 59:67–68.

With M. A. Sayers, G. Sayers, M. G. Engel, and F. L. Engel. Elevation of plasma amino nitrogen as an index of the gravity of hemorrhagic shock. Proc. Soc. Exp. Biol. Med., 60:20–22.

With H. C. Harrison. The regeneration of liver protein in the rat. J. Biol. Chem., 161:545–57.

1946

Biochemical changes associated with the activity of the adrenal cortex. Bulletin of the Johns Hopkins Hospital, 78:317–21.

With G. Sayers, M. A. Sayers, and T.-Y. Liang. The effect of pituitary adrenotrophic hormone on the cholesterol and ascorbic acid content of the adrenal of the rat and the guinea pig. Endocrinology, 38:1–9.

With M. A. Sayers and G. Sayers. The standardization of hemorrhagic shock in the rat: observation on the effects of transfusions of whole blood and some blood substitutes. Am. J. Physiol., 147:155–64.

With J. A. Russell. Amino nitrogen in liver and muscle of rats in shock after hemorrhage. Am. J. Physiol., 147:175–80.

With A. E. Wilhelmi and M. G. Engel. The influence of feeding on the effects of hepatic anoxia on the respiration of liver slices *in vitro*. Am. J. Physiol., 147:181–90.

1947

The conditions associated with the secretion of the adrenal cortex. Fed. Proc., 6:461–71.

Recent studies on the function of the adrenal cortex. Bulletin of the New York Academy of Medicine, 23:260–82.

The relation of cholesterol and ascorbic acid to the secretion of the adrenal cortex. Recent Prog. Horm. Res., 1:99–122.

1948

Presidential address at thirtieth annual meeting of the Association for the Study of Internal Secretions. Endocrinology, 43:89–96.

With H. Gershberg. The activation of the adrenal cortex by insulin hypoglycemia. Journal of Clinical Endocrinology, 8:587–88.

With A. E. Wilhelmi. Metabolic changes associated with hemorrhage. Ann. N.Y. Acad. Sci., 49:605–21.

1949

The adrenal gland, a regulatory factor. In: *The Chemistry and Physiology of Growth,* chap. X, pp. 266–84. Princeton, Princeton University Press.

With G. B. Pinchot and V. P. Close. Adrenal changes produced in rats by infection with *B. tularense* and *B. coli.* Endocrinology, 45:135–42.

Factors regulating the adrenal cortical secretion. In: *Pituitary–Adrenal Function,* pp. 24–30. Washington, D.C., American Association for the Advancement of Science.

Report of the Dean of the School of Medicine, Yale University.

1950

With W. V. McDermott, E. G. Fry, and J. R. Brobeck. Release of adrenocorticotrophic hormone by direct application of epinephrine to pituitary grafts. Proc. Soc. Exp. Biol. Med., 73:609–10.

With H. Gershberg, E. G. Fry, and J. R. Brobeck. The role of epinephrine in the secretion of the adrenal cortex. Yale J. Biol. Med., 23:32–51.

With W. V. McDermott, E. G. Fry, and J. R. Brobeck. Mechanism of control of adrenocorticotrophic hormone. Yale J. Biol. Med., 23:52–66.

Problems in planning medical education. Connecticut State Medical Journal, 14:313–15.

With H. Mankin, J. A. F. Stevenson, J. R. Brobeck, and D. Stetten, Jr. The turnover of body fat in obesity resulting from hypothalamic injury studied with the aid of deuterium. Endocrinology, 47:443–47.

1951

With M. J. Oesterling. Adrenal cholesterol in the scorbutic guinea pig. Science, 113:241–42.

With J. C. Opsahl and E. G. Fry. Chronic gonadotrophin, ACTH, and the adrenalhyaluronidase relationship. Yale J. Biol. Med., 23:399–406.

With J. C. Opsahl. Identification of ACTH in human placental tissue. Yale J. Biol. Med., 24:199–209.

The endocrine regulation of carbohydrate metabolism and its application to the problems of diabetes mellitus. Proceedings of the Royal College of Physicians and Surgeons of Canada, Sept. 28 and 29.

The adrenal mechanism in relation to shock. Symposium on Shock at the Army Medical Service Graduate School, May 7, pp. XII-1–XII-16.

1952

The endocrine control of the blood sugar. (Banting Lecture—American Diabetes Association) Diabetes, 1:3–11.

The endocrine control of the blood sugar. (Banting Lecture, London) Lancet, February 16, pp. 325–29.

Regulation of ACTH secretion. Recent Prog. Horm. Res., 7:75–105.

With W. W. Winternitz. Participation of adrenal cortex in alterations in carbohydrate metabolism produced by epinephrine. Proc. Soc. Exp. Biol. Med., 81:683–85.

The role of epinephrine in the secretion of the adrenal cortex. In: Ciba Foundation Colloquia on Endocrinology, vol. IV, p. 139. London, Churchill & Co.

1953

Regulation of ACTH secretion. Annual Lectures, National Institute of Arthritis and Metabolic Diseases, May 25, pp. 73–87.

Influence of the adrenal cortex on carbohydrate metabolism. In: *Ciba Foundation Colloquia on Endocrinology,* vol. VI, p. 136. London, Churchill & Co.

The adrenals and growth hormone diabetes. In: *Experimental Diabetes and Its Relation to Clinical Medicine,* p. 172. Oxford, Blackwell.

1954

The hormones and metabolism. In: *Symposium on Problems of Gerontology,* pp. 106–19. Nutrition Symposium Series, no. 9. New York, The National Vitamin Foundation.

1955

Closing remarks. In: *The Hypophyseal Growth Hormone, Nature and Actions,* ed. by R. W. Smith, Jr., O. H. Gaebler, and C. N. H. Long, chap. 30, pp. 573–76. International symposium. New York, McGraw-Hill Book Co.

With F. Ulrich. The effects of propylthiouracil and thyrotropic hormone on the uptake of radioactive thallium by the rat thyroid. Yale J. Biol. Med., 27:371–78.

With W. W. Winternitz and R. Dintzis. The effect of adrenal cortical hormones on the carbohydrate metabolism of the liver. Yale J. Biol. Med., 27:381–83.

With D. Abelson and F. Ulrich. Identification of 20 beta-hydroxyhydrocortisone in rat plasma after administration of hydrocortisone. Proc. Soc. Exp. Biol. Med., 89:386–88.

The selection, care and preservation of research scientists. Pediatrics, 15:203–10.

With A. Brodish. Blood ACTH estimation by a cross-circulation technique. Fed. Proc., 14:18. (A)

1956

Pituitary–adrenal relationships. Ann. Rev. Physiol., 18:409–32.

With A. Brodish. Changes in blood ACTH under various experimental conditions studied by means of a cross-circulation technique. Proc. 20th Int. Congr. Physiol., p. 260, Brussels. (A)

With E. G. Fry. The function of ocular and kidney transplants of pituitary tissue in the hypophysectomized rat. Proc. 20th Int. Congr. Physiol., p. 324, Brussels. (A)

With A. Brodish. A technique of cross-circulation in the rat which permits accurate control of blood volume transfers. Yale J. Biol. Med., 28:644–49.

With A. Brodish. Estimation of blood ACTH by means of a cross-circulation technique. Yale J. Biol. Med., 28:650–56.

With F. Ulrich. Effects of stress on serum C^{14} levels in rats following administration of hydrocortisone-4-C^{14} and corticosterone-4-C^{14}. Endocrinology, 59:170–80.

With A. Brodish. Changes in blood ACTH under various experimental conditions by means of a cross-circulation technique. Endocrinology, 59:666–76.

1957

Studies on experimental obesity. J. Endocrinol., 15:vi–xvi.

With M. F. M. Bonnycastle. The rate of discharge of adrenocorticotrophic hormone as determined by timed hypophysectomy in the rat. Can. J. Biochem., 35:929–33.

With W. W. Winternitz and R. Dintzis. Further studies on the adrenal cortex and carbohydrate metabolism. Endocrinology, 61: 724–41.

With A. Brodish. Evidence of an ACTH-releasing neurohumor in peripheral blood. Proc. 39th Meet. Endocr. Soc., p. 31. (A)

1958

With A. Brodish. Mechanism of inhibition of ACTH release by hydrocortisone. Proc. 40th Meet. Endocr. Soc., p. 38. (A)

With J. R. Paul. John Punnett Peters. In: *Biographical Memoirs,* vol. 31, pp. 347–75. Washington, D.C., National Academy of Sciences.

The adrenal cortex and carbohydrate metabolism. Proc. 3d. Congr. Int. Diabetes Fed., pp. 6–7. Dusseldorf. Stuttgart, Georg Thieme Verlag. (A)

Recent observations on the role of the adrenal cortex in carbohydrate metabolism. Proc. 3d. Congr. Int. Diabetes Fed., pp. 41–47. Dusseldorf. Stuttgart, Georg Thieme Verlag.

1959

With O. K. Smith. Acute effects of adrenalectomy and hydrocortisone on glucose tolerance of diabetic and eviscerated rats. Proc. 41st Meet. Endocr. Soc., p. 54. (A)

1960

With A. Brodish. Characteristics of the adrenal ascorbic acid response to adrenocorticotrophic hormone (ACTH) in the rat. Endocrinology, 66:149–59.

With E. G. Fry and M. F. M. Bonnycastle. The effect of cortisol on carbohydrate deposition and urea nitrogen excretion in adrenalectomized rat. Proc. First Int. Congr. Endocrinol., Copenhagen, ed. by F. Fuchs, no. 411, p. 819. (A)

With O. K. Smith. The effect of adrenalectomy and cortisol on alloxan diabetic rats. Proc. First Int. Congr. Endocrinol., Copenhagen, ed. by F. Fuchs, no. 651, p. 1293. (A)

With O. K. Smith and E. G. Fry. Actions of cortisol and related compounds on carbohydrate and protein metabolism. In: *Metabolic Effects of Adrenal Hormones*, pp. 4–24. Ciba Foundation Study Group no. 6. London, Churchill & Co.

Medical science and the future. Yale J. Biol. Med., 33:227–34.

1962

With O. K. Smith. Some recent studies on the adrenal cortex and carbohydrate metabolism. In: *The Human Adrenal Cortex*, pp. 268–93. Edinburgh & London, E. & S. Livingstone, Ltd.

With A. Brodish. ACTH-releasing hypothalamic neurohumor in peripheral blood. Endocrinology, 71:298–306.

With A. Arimura. The influence of a small dose of vasopressin upon the pituitary–adrenal activation in the rat. Jap. J. Physiol., 12:411–22.

With A. Arimura. Effect of intracarotid injection of pitressin, pitocin, epinephrine and acetyl choline on ACTH release in rats. Jap. J. Physiol., 12:423–28.

With A. Arimura. Influence of various vaso-active materials upon the hypophyseal portal vessels of rats: observation *in situ*. Jap. J. Physiol., 12:429–32.

1964

With T. Hiroshige. Effect of insulin on the visceral organism in the rat. Fed. Proc., 23:461. (A)

With T. Hiroshige. Effect of dexamethasone on gluconeogenesis in the visceral organism. Proc. 46th Meet. Endocr. Soc., p. 100. (A)

With T. Hiroshige. The preparation, maintenance and use of a visceral organism for metabolic studies in the rat. Yale J. Biol. Med., 37:75–92.

1965

With T. Hiroshige. Effect of dexamethasone and insulin on gluco-neogenesis in the adrenalectomized-diabetic visceral organism. Proc. 23d Int. Congr. Physiol., Tokyo, p. 259.

With O. K. Smith. The effects of cortisol on the eviscerated adrenalectomized–diabetic rat. Proc. 47th Meet. Endocr. Soc., p. 128. (A)

1967

With O. K. Smith. Effect of cortisol on the plasma amino nitrogen of eviscerated adrenalectomized–diabetic rats. Endocrinology, 80:561–66.

In memoriam: Jane A. Russell. Endocrinology, 81:689–92.

1970

With C. Rosendorff and J. Mooney. Sites of action of leucocyte pyrogen in the genesis of fever in the conscious rabbit. Fed. Proc., 29:523, no. 1547. (A)

1971

With O. K. Smith. Renal gluconeogenesis in eviscerated diabetic rats. Proceedings of the National Academy of Sciences, 68: 1618–22.

W. C. Mendenhall

WALTER CURRAN MENDENHALL

February 20, 1871–June 2, 1957

BY THOMAS B. NOLAN

IN THE SCANTY biographical material that he provided the Academy following his election, Walter Curran Mendenhall listed as his occupations, "Farmer, student, and geologist." To these he might well have added, "explorer, administrator, and public servant." He will be remembered, by all who knew him, for the latter as well as for his accomplishments as a scientist and administrator. He would probably have felt that his greatest contributions, both to science and to the country, were effected through his devotion to absolute integrity. His insistence on the maintenance of the highest standards was evidenced in all the varied activities of the federal scientific agency with which he was associated for nearly fifty years.

Mendenhall was born in Marlboro, Stark County, Ohio, on February 20, 1871. The small community was a Quaker cultural and religious center. His father, William King Mendenhall, was a descendent of William Mendenhall who emigrated from England with William Penn. The Mendenhalls lived in Pennsylvania as farmers until the middle of the nineteenth century, when the paternal grandfather, Robert, moved to the farming community near Alliance, Ohio. He was remembered by his grandson as a "large man, well proportioned," who was "well-balanced, social, often selected by

311

neighbors as a trustee, etc." The father too, was tall, though slight, and was recalled as "social, and humorous."

The mother, Emma Pierce Garrigues, was of Quaker descent; her family had moved from Pennsylvania to Ohio at about the same time as the Mendenhalls. She and William King Mendenhall were second cousins. She began teaching school when she was fourteen years old and continued teaching for some years after marriage. Her son characterized her as "steady, stable, self controlled, retiring, and fond of reading." These phrases could equally well have been applied to the son, though he inherited his physical characteristics and his humor from his father.

Mendenhall's early schooling started in the country school at Marlboro, but was completed (through high school) in Portland, Oregon. There he lived for several years with the family of his mother's brother, Samuel Parker Garrigues, whom he characterized as "merchant, kindly, good business man." He then returned to Ohio and taught school for a short time before entering Ohio Normal University (now Ohio Northern University) at Ada.

While still an undergraduate, Mendenhall had been employed, initially as a teamster and laborer, by the U.S. Geological Survey, assisting M. R. Campbell with a study of the Appalachian coal fields. Campbell, some thirteen years older, had been a family friend and must have been largely responsible for Mendenhall's decisions to enter the field of geology and to affiliate with the U.S. Geological Survey—two decisions that determined the remainder of Mendenhall's long career.

There seems to be no indication of other factors that led to these decisions, as there is no evidence in Mendenhall's family background or in his schooling of what became so profound an interest in earth history. Even in a letter that he wrote in early 1893 to Senator Brice of Ohio, asking him to intercede with Major Powell (Director of the U.S. Geological Survey at that time) in his behalf, there seems to have been no particular interest in geology. He wrote, characteristically emphasizing a concern on performance, "You may rest assured that if I should secure the appointment it would fall to one who fully appreciates the opportunities it offers for study, and who would go out to *work* and make the most of those opportunities, and not for a summer's vacation."

Mendenhall graduated from Ohio Normal in 1895 with the degree of B.S. and immediately entered full-time work with the U.S. Geological Survey—again as assistant to Campbell in a continuation of the coal basin studies. Except for leaves of absences in 1896–1897 for a year of graduate work at Harvard and in 1899–1900 for a year of study at Heidelberg, Germany, Mendenhall remained a member of the Survey until his retirement February 28, 1943.

The young man from Ohio quickly impressed his colleagues and superiors in the U.S. Geological Survey. His first publication in 1896, as junior author with Campbell, grew out of their geologic exploration in the southern extension of the Pennsylvania coal fields. Such early joint authorship was unusual and must have indicated the prompt recognition, by his colleagues and superiors in the Survey, of his competence and energy—both physical and mental.

These qualities were of prime importance in his assignments during the next several years, for he was one of the small number of Survey geologists selected to carry out explorations—geographic as well as geologic—in the vast little-known area of Alaska. On the first of these, in the summer of 1898, he was attached to a military expedition; however, on succeeding trips in 1900, 1901, and 1902, the projects were under Survey auspices without direct military support.

Except for the field season of 1899, when he was an assistant to George Otis Smith in a mapping project in the central

Cascade Mountains of Washington, Mendenhall spent the years through 1902 in exploratory work in Alaska. His first assignment, as geologist to Military Expedition No. 3 was a reconnaissance from Resurrection Bay to the Tanana River. The discoveries of gold in the Klondike in 1896–1897 generated a demand for knowledge of possible routes to the mineralized areas in interior Alaska, and this expedition of 1898 was directed to seek information on possible wagon or railroad routes inland from the coast. Mendenhall's route, as it turned out, proved to be the one that was eventually followed in part by the Alaska Railroad, as well as passing through the area later colonized in the Matanuska Valley. In his report, Mendenhall notes that "in two months and two days after leaving [the present site of Anchorage], having travelled in the interim about 670 miles, [he had] mapped topographically and geologically some 400 miles of hitherto unexplored country."

The two seasons of 1900 and 1901 were in even more remote country, northwest of the Yukon River, between it and Norton and Kotzebue sounds. The 1901 expedition, from Fort Hamlin to Kotzebue Sound, covered between 1100 and 1200 miles; it led him to observe that "exploring expeditions in high latitudes . . . are limited in time, and hence . . . certain sacrifices must be made to the paramount necessity of gaining ground. Work under these conditions cannot be uniform in quality. Observations made while the observer is struggling ahead at the end of a tracking line, or bending all his energies to the prevention of disaster in the wild waters of a gorge, or perhaps zigzagging up a 1000 foot climb with 90 pounds on his back, are not always as complete as is desirable. It is hoped, however, that such conditions have not resulted in other inaccuracy than that due to incompleteness."

One understands Mendenhall's uncharacteristic note of apology in the above quotation on reading that one phase of the expedition involved an 18-mile portage of boats and equipment over a summit that reached elevations of 1500 feet above the Yukon and Kobuk drainages. More characteristic is the expressed concern over maintenance of quality of his observations.

The final Alaskan season of 1902 was spent in the Copper River region, where Mendenhall and F. C. Schrader developed knowledge of the geologic framework and provided a sound appraisal of the economic potentiality of a region that was being vigorously explored for base metals deposits as well as gold. Typically, he presented what must have been an unpopular conclusion in respect of the inflated claims, so often made during the period, of the mineral potential of the new territory. He and Schrader wrote,

"We regret our inability to present as encouraging a report for the section as has been made by the prospectors. . . . The opinion is forced upon me that the assay returns which have led prospectors to believe that platinum exists in commercial quantities . . . must have been faulty. We do not believe that the metal . . . exists in the Nadina field. . . . Samples of the rock that was supposed to carry the tin . . . proved not to carry the metal."

The explorations in Alaska were followed by a series of assignments of a very different sort. In 1903, Mendenhall was asked to undertake a study of the groundwater resources of southern California. He continued work there until 1908, and during these five years produced a series of reports on the supplies of water available both in the California coastal plain areas southward from Los Angeles and in the San Joaquin Valley.

The rapid development of irrigation in southern California after about 1900 had resulted in the essentially complete appropriation of the surface waters and in a significant decrease in both the amount of artesian water available and in the areas from which artesian flow could be obtained.

The reports prepared as a result of the five years in California anticipate to a remarkable extent three elements that were characteristic of Mendenhall's later career as an administrator and public servant: a deep feeling of individual responsibility in the public interest; an acute awareness of the practical aspects of development of natural resources; and, above all, the need for thorough and detailed understanding of natural processes, and for the research that would provide the basis for this understanding.

During his first year in California he recognized the problems, and dangers, of uncontrolled and rapid development. In a report prepared at that time he wrote, "if . . . it is . . . understood that each additional plant installed . . . is at the expense of those already in existence, it is better [to curtail new developments] . . . than to . . . [obtain] a temporary increase in industrial activity."

This early recognition of the need for conservation, which preceded by several years the 1908 White House Conference, was expanded in later reports: "A strong public sentiment, therefore, should be created, which will under all circumstances oppose the careless use of artesian wells," and an even more present day expression of concern, "The promoting and speculative spirit, the desire to get rich overnight, to control large holdings, and to avoid personal labor, will have to be superseded by a willingness to be satisfied with sure but moderate returns, to be content with small farm units, and to attain personal independence through individual efforts."

This concern for the public interest characteristically was accompanied by a recognition of the practical aspects of irrigation farming. F. H. Newell in a preface to one of Mendenhall's reports of this period wrote, "The author has had consistently in mind . . . the needs of the practical irrigator and the questions which must arise in disputes concerning title to percolating waters." The reports contained thorough discussions of such matters as pumping costs, sound irrigation practices and the like.

Throughout the series of reports prepared in this period is the emphasis on the need for an adequate scientific understanding of the geology and hydrology of the natural resource. He wrote, "Obviously a resource which has become as important to the continued welfare of so rich a district is worthy of careful study." Mendenhall became one of the earliest students of the principles of groundwater hydrology. He introduced quantitative elements into his discussions of the available supplies, as well as emphasis on the geologic factors. Some of the earliest estimates of "safe yield" from the groundwater reservoirs were presented, as well as such modern concepts as the possibility of constructing check dams as a mechanism for recharging the underground aquifers.

One of the last of the projects undertaken during this period was a study of "Some Desert Watering Places in Southeastern California and Southwestern Nevada" instigated by the mining boom of the early 1900s in this area. One earthy piece of advice —which is still valid for portions of the West—concerned the then rather frequent misfortune that befell the casual prospector:

"With some persons . . . the faculty of getting lost amounts to genius. They are able to accomplish this wherever they are. The only suitable advice for them is to keep out of the desert. There are safer places in which to exercise their talents."

The groundwater work in California was Mendenhall's last systematic geologic fieldwork. He was transferred to the headquarters of the U.S. Geological Survey in Washington on July 1, 1908, to become Geologist in Charge, Underground Water Investigations. This marked the beginning of his career as a scientific administrator which was to continue for thirty-five years through the rest of his professional life.

As the supervisor of the Survey's groundwater work, the concepts and techniques he had so skillfully and successfully utilized in southern California were now applied over a much wider area. Mendenhall was an extremely effective supervisor—

leading, but not dominating, and generating loyalty and high performance in the men and women in his units.

After four years as chief of groundwater studies, Mendenhall was asked to assume the chairmanship of the Land Classification Board, of which he had been a member since 1908. With his transfer, the Board became the Land Classification Branch (now the Conservation Division of the Survey), and Mendenhall's responsibilities now included supervision of regulatory activities, as well as the scientific ones that had characterized his previous position. Major functions of the Branch were to identify mineral lands for withdrawal from entry pending their proper classification, to classify the public lands for mineral or water potential, and to determine values as a basis for transfer to private ownership. After passage of the Mineral Leasing Act in 1920 the functions of the Branch were expanded to include the administration of that Act.

At that time there were five major operating Branches or Divisions of the U.S. Geological Survey; Mendenhall had served in four. He had begun his career in the Geologic Branch; his Alaskan work was under the direction of what was to become the Alaskan Division; his California assignment was in the hydrology unit that became the Water Resources Division; and he chaired the Land Classification Branch, the predecessor of the Conservation Division. Only the Topographic Branch had been omitted from this broad range of experience, although the Alaskan exploratory trips had in fact involved essentially as much topographic, as geologic, mapping.

In November 1922, Mendenhall returned to his first organizational unit, the Geologic Branch, as Chief Geologist. In this position he succeeded David White, who had requested relief from administrative work to resume his own paleobotanical work. Mendenhall further developed the high standards established by his predecessors, among whom were White, G. K. Gilbert and Waldemar Lindgren. Gilbert, who had been a member of one of the four exploratory Surveys that were merged to form the Geological Survey in 1879, was in many respects, the scientific mentor of Mendenhall. Even after his death in California in 1918, Mendenhall's Survey career was deeply influenced by his memories of Gilbert.

Mendenhall was especially insistent on maintaining high standards, through close control of the employment of young geologists for the Survey. Under his leadership, the U.S. Civil Service entrance examination for Junior Geologists became a nationwide measure of excellence, and practically all universities encouraged their students to take it, regardless of their ultimate job objectives. The relatively few, in those days, who were given employment in the Survey found an environment that was stimulating in the extreme. A clue to his success in recruiting employees of high quality is the disproportionate number of geologists of that vintage on the staff of the Survey who became members of the Academy.

Viewed in the context of the times, Mendenhall's record as Chief Geologist is even more impressive. The years following World War I were times of considerable stress. Funding was low in the aftermath of the war, and the applied work of the Survey during the War, together with the great expansion of the petroleum industry, resulted in a large number of resignations by the more experienced Survey geologists to enter industry. Maintaining high standards while rebuilding the geologic staff required full use of his administrative talents.

Increasingly too, he was called on to act as Director during the absences of George Otis Smith, and when Smith resigned at the end of 1930 to become Chairman of the Federal Power Commission, Mendenhall was named Acting Director. The following year he was appointed by President Herbert Hoover to be the fifth Director of the Survey. He continued to serve in this capacity until his retirement, after two Presidential extensions, February 28, 1943.

In accepting the appointment as Director, Mendenhall out-lined his concept of the responsibilities of the position in a memorandum to the then-Secretary of the Interior, Ray Lyman Wilbur. He wrote, "Insofar as my part in Survey affairs may be effective, it will be directed toward fostering closely coordi-nated team work, to the end that the products of Survey activi-ties shall continue to be of high quality,—since quality is essen-tial to permanent value—and as useful in the public service and in the advancement of geologic and engineering science as we can make them. We hope that our ideals will continue to be what we hope they are now, sane and practical ideals; that we shall not dissipate energy pursuing perhaps temporarily at-tractive, but impracticable dreams. . . . We shall hope . . . to continue to devote our energies to the advancement of useful knowledge and the permanent welfare of our fellow citizens through our scientific and engineering services."

The changing national climate, however, made achievement of these goals difficult. Mendenhall was faced with a succession of events for the next twelve years that tested his abilities and determination to the limit.

With Secretary Wilbur's assistance, he had initiated a pro-gram as Chief Geologist with what was then regarded as ade-quate funding, "for fundamental research in geologic sciences." But financial constraints during the years of the Great Depres-sion not only put an end to this enlarged program, but resulted in progressively decreased appropriations that required curtail-ment of staff and fieldwork, as well as other drastic economies. The Survey's appropriations, during the years from 1932 to 1935, were cut almost in half.

Mendenhall continued as Director after the change in ad-ministration that resulted from the election of Franklin Roose-velt to succeed Herbert Hoover as President. The Survey Direc-torship had been regarded as nonpolitical from the beginning, even though the position was a Presidential appointment subject to Senate confirmation. All but King, the first Director, who served only two years, had served under both Republican and Democratic administrations. Efforts were made to replace Mendenhall, when the new President was inaugurated, but these happily failed, at least partly as a result of the support volunteered on his behalf. C. K. Leith and Isaiah Bowman, both members of the Academy, were especially active in the representations that were made. One of the expressions of support, made by a midwestern university professor, was typical of the regard in which he was held; it was addressed to the newly appointed Secretary of the Interior Harold L. Ickes:

". . . an unsolicited expression of the exceptional regard in which . . . Dr. Mendenhall is held by his associates in the geological profession. In my own experience I have known no man in whom personal ambition was so completely subordinated to devotion to the public welfare or in whom sound judgment, fairness, complete honesty and kindliness were so combined with technical knowledge and administrative capacity of the highest order."

In addition to this very personal problem, the depression seriously affected planning for the Sixteenth International Geological Congress. Mendenhall had been selected to serve as General Secretary of the Congress, which was originally planned to be held in Washington in 1932, and which was to be preceded and followed by an extensive series of excursions to all parts of the country. Traditionally, these quadrennial International Congresses were substantially subsidized by the host government. But the United States Congress did not make funds available, and Mendenhall was forced to postpone the sessions until 1933 to provide opportunity to seek financial support from other sources, especially the Geological Society of America. But in spite of all this, the gathering, under his leadership, was successfully held, and was attended by a large and distinguished group of geologists from all over the world.

Finally, the increasing tensions in Europe culminating in the entry of the United States into World War II in 1941, progressively affected the normal work of the Survey. Beginning as early as 1939, the mapping, water, and mineral resource activities were more and more oriented towards national defense matters. In spite of his Quaker background and beliefs, Mendenhall wholeheartedly supported this shift in emphasis as one that was required by a public agency. In a congressional hearing during this period he affirmed that, "The effort of every individual and of every agency must be thrown completely into the war effort."

The transition from peacetime to war work was successfully accomplished largely through Mendenhall's effective and loyalty-inspiring leadership. The U.S. Geological Survey's contribution to the war effort was substantial. The degree to which he was personally responsible for this performance was recognized by two Presidential extensions as Director after he reached the normal retirement age of seventy.

For the more than fourteen years after retirement Mendenhall lived quietly at his home in Chevy Chase, Maryland, near the Chevy Chase Club where he enjoyed golf games with his old friends. A major disappointment during this time was caused by a fire in his home that destroyed material he had accumulated on the history of the early exploratory surveys of the West. He had planned to prepare an account of this history, for which he would have been ideally qualified. In fact, he had started to develop the subject in his presidential address before the Geological Society of America. He concluded that address with a statement that reflected his dedication to the science of geology:

". . . it seems to me that geology in developing to its present full stature has come to fill that desirable dual role, of a rich culture and a very practical science. Cultivated for its own sake, it is one of the finest of disciplines, which opens to its disciples vast concepts of time and process, and eons of pre-human history, leading back toward remote and fascinating beginnings of things on earth. Practically applied, it is one of the most useful of sciences, because the materials with which it deals include a large proportion of those things derived from the earth, out of which our civilizations are builded. Mankind in a century or more has obtained glimpses of its value in both fields, but who can doubt that, measured by what the future has in store, they will prove to have been glimpses only."

Mendenhall was a member of many scientific and professional societies, including the National Academy of Sciences (to which he was elected in 1932), the Geological Society of America (president in 1936), the American Institute of Mining and Metallurgical Engineers and the American Association of Petroleum Geologists (in both of which he held Honorary Memberships).

Among his honors were Honorary Sc.Ds from the Colorado School of Mines in 1928 and University of Wisconsin in 1932. He received the Penrose Medal of the Society of Economic Geologists in 1944.

Mendenhall was survived by his widow, Alice M. Boutell Mendenhall, whom he married on September 20, 1915, and two daughters, Margaret Boutell Smith and Alice Curran Mendenhall.

I have drawn extensively on two memorials prepared by contemporaries of Mendenhall, which were written shortly after his death. It is perhaps appropriate to close this account with the summary appraisals made by each of them. D. F. Hewett, writing in *Science* (vol. 126, pp. 603–04, September 27, 1957) observed, "In the science of geology, where progress depends on myriad observations, . . . Mendenhall approved of discussion but disliked arguments. Quite unemotional himself, he was suspicious of fervor. Many who knew him well agree that one of his outstanding qualities was integrity in thought and action and none who knew him ever suspected him of having a selfish purpose." M. M. Leighton (*Bulletin of the American Association of Petroleum Geologists,* vol. 42, pp. 682–95, March, 1958) wrote, "He prized humility for himself, yet with it came distinction."

BIBLIOGRAPHY

KEY TO ABBREVIATIONS

Geol. Soc. Am. Bull. = Geological Society of America Bulletin
Natl. Geogr. Mag. = National Geographic Magazine
Sci. Mon. = Science Monthly
U.S. Geol. Surv. Bull. = U.S. Geological Survey Bulletin
U.S. Geol. Surv. Prof. Pap. = U.S. Geological Survey Professional Paper
U.S. Geol. Surv. Water-Supply Pap. = U.S. Geological Survey Water-Supply
  Paper.

1896

With M. R. Campbell. Geologic section along the New and
  Kanawha Rivers in West Virginia. U.S. Geological Survey,
  17th Annual Report, Part 2, pp. 473–511.

1900

A reconnaissance from Resurrection Bay to the Tanana River,
  Alaska, in 1898. U.S. Geological Survey, 20th Annual Report,
  Part 7, pp. 265–340, maps.
With G. O. Smith. Tertiary granite in the Northern Cascades.
  Geol. Soc. Am. Bull., 11:223–30; Science, 11:144(A).

1901

A reconnaissance in the Norton Bay Region, Alaska, in 1900. In:
  *Reconnaissances in the Cape Nome and Norton Bay Regions,
  Alaska, in 1900,* by A. H. Brooks and others, pp. 187–218. Wash-
  ington, D.C., U.S. Geological Survey Special Publication.

1902

Reconnaissance from Fort Hamlin to Kotzebue Sound, Alaska.
  U.S. Geol. Surv. Prof. Pap. 10, 68 pp., maps.
Notes on the geology of the Klondike. Science, 15:389.

1903

With F. C. Schrader. The mineral resources of the Mount Wrangell
  District, Alaska. U.S. Geol. Surv. Prof. Pap. 15, 71 pp., maps.
The Christochina Gold Field, Alaska. U.S. Geol. Surv. Bull. no.
  213, pp. 71–75.

With F. C. Schrader. Copper deposits of the Mount Wrangell Region, Alaska. U.S. Geol. Surv. Bull. no. 213, pp. 141–48.

The Wrangell Mountains, Alaska. Natl. Geogr. Mag., 14:395–407.

A Carboniferous section in the Upper Copper River Valley, Alaska. Science, 17:25–26. (A)

1905

Geology of the Central Copper River Region, Alaska. U.S. Geol. Surv. Prof. Pap. 41, 133 pp., maps.

Development of underground waters in the Eastern Coastal Plain Region of Southern California. U.S. Geol. Surv. Water-Supply Pap. 137, 140 pp., maps.

Development of underground waters in the Central Coastal Plain Region of Southern California. U.S. Geol. Surv. Water-Supply Pap. 138, 162 pp., maps.

Development of underground waters in the Western Coastal Plain Region of Southern California. U.S. Geol. Surv. Water-Supply Pap. 139, 105 pp., maps.

The hydrology of the San Bernardino Valley, California. U.S. Geol. Surv. Water-Supply Pap. 142, 124 pp., maps.

1908

Two mountain ranges of Southern California (San Bernardino and San Gabriel ranges). Geol. Soc. Am. Bull., 18:660–61.

Ground waters and irrigation enterprises in the Foothill Belt, Southern California. U.S. Geol. Surv. Water-Supply Pap. 219, 180 pp.

Preliminary report on the ground waters of San Joaquin Valley, California. U.S. Geol. Surv. Water-Supply Pap. 222, 52 pp.

1909

A phase of ground water problems in the West. Economic Geology, 4:35–45, map.

Some desert watering places in southeastern California and southwestern Nevada. U.S. Geol. Surv. Water-Supply Pap. 224, 98 pp.

Ground waters of the Indio Region, California, with a sketch of the Colorado Desert. U.S. Geol. Surv. Water-Supply Pap. 225, 56 pp.

Underground waters. U.S. Geol. Surv. Water-Supply Pap. 234, pp. 68–77. Also in: National Conservation Commission Report

(60th Congress 2d session, Senate Document No. 676), vol. 2, pp. 86–94.

The Colorado desert. Natl. Geogr. Mag., 20:681–701.

A coal prospect on Willow Creek, Morrow County, Oregon. U.S. Geol. Surv. Bull. no. 341, pp. 406–8.

1910

Notes on the geology of Carrizo Mountain and vicinity, San Diego County, California. Journal of Geology, 18:336–55.

1913

Development of the Survey's organization for land classification. In: The Classification of the Public Lands, by George Otis Smith, pp. 11–18. U.S. Geol. Surv. Bull. no. 537.

1916

With others. Ground water in San Joaquin Valley, California. U.S. Geol. Surv. Water-Supply Pap. 398, 310 pp., maps; Washington Academy of Science Journal, 6:502–3(A).

1920

Memorial of Grove Karl Gilbert. Geol. Soc. Am. Bull., 31(1):26–64.

1926

Trends in American geology (notice by T. C.). Nature, 117:489–91; Pan-American Geologist, 45(2):171(A).

Cooperative geologic surveys in Colorado. Mining and Metallurgy, 7(239):476–78.

1927

Oil possibilities of an area northeast of Petaluma, Sonoma County, California. American Association of Petroleum Geologists Bulletin, 11(4):425.

Volcano stations of the U.S. Geological Survey. National Research Council Bulletin no. 61, pp. 269–71.

1931

Geology and the state. Illinois State Geological Survey Bulletin 60, pp. 149–59.

Announcement concerning 16th International Geological Congress. Geol. Soc. Am. Bull., 42(1):177–79.

Annual Report of the Director of the U.S. Geological Survey to the Secretary of the Interior, 52nd, 1931, 95 pp., Washington (1931); 53rd, 94 pp., I plate (1932); 54th, U.S. Department of Interior, Annual Report, pp. 203–37 (1933); 55th, pp. 217–53 (1934); 56th, pp. 233–74 (1935); 57th, pp. 309–45 (1936); 58th, pp. 151–89 (1937); 59th, pp. 125–72, I plate (1938); 60th, pp. 139–90 (1939).

1932

Economies imposed on the U.S. Geological Survey. Science, 76: 77–78.

1933

The United States Geological Survey. Sci. Mon., 36:104–20.

The 16th International Geological Congress. Science, 78(2021): 247–54.

1935

David White (1862–1935). Science, 81(2097):244–46.

David White (1862–1935): an appreciation. Sci. Mon., 40(4):380–82.

1936

Establishment of Pennsylvania Survey, an outstanding event in development of sciences in U.S. Pennsylvania Department of Internal Affairs, Monthly Bulletin, 2(1):17–18.

1937

Development and present status of geology in North America. Geol. Soc. Am. Bull., 48(3):349–63.

Memorial of (Charles) David White (1862–1935). Geological Society of America Proceedings, 1936, pp. 271–80.

1940

(U.S.) Geological Survey. New International Yearbook, 1939, p. 305. New York, Funk and Wagnalls, Inc.

Occurrence of a deposit of Trona. Science, 91(2349):11–12.

Arthur Michael

ARTHUR MICHAEL

August 2, 1853–February 8, 1942

BY LOUIS F. FIESER

THE FOLLOWING MINUTES were placed upon the records of the Faculty of Arts and Sciences of Harvard University at the meeting of May 18, 1943.*

"Arthur Michael, Professor of Organic Chemistry, *Emeritus,* died on February 8, 1942, in Orlando, Florida, in the eighty-ninth year of his age. Michael was born in Buffalo, New York, on August 7, 1853, the son of John and Clara (Pinner) Michael. He attended the Briggs Classical School in Buffalo. No formal classes in chemistry were held there at that time but Michael had special instruction in this subject at school from one of his teachers, and he performed the experiments by himself with great enthusiasm in a laboratory which his father had fitted up for him at home.

"Thereafter, Michael had planned to go to Harvard College, but a serious illness intervened. As a result the Michael family, in the summer of 1871, went for a long sojourn in Europe. They arrived in Berlin just in time to see the German Army, fresh from the Siege of Paris, march triumphantly down *Unter den Linden.*

"After he had recovered from his illness and after an interval of preoccupation with art and literature, Michael suc-

* E. W. Forbes, L. F. Fieser, and A. B. Lamb, "Arthur Michael," *Harvard University Gazette* 38(1943):246.

331

ceeded, in spite of his meager chemical training, in gaining admission to the Chemical Laboratory of Professor Hofmann at the University of Berlin. A year later, Michael transferred to Heidelberg for two years of study under the renowned Bunsen, who ever remained his scientific paragon. He returned to Berlin in 1876 for two years of study, and it was then that he began the execution and publication of his remarkably long series of brilliant and important researches. Hofmann was the outstanding organic chemist of Germany and his laboratory at that time was the focal point of the world for research in organic chemistry, and there Michael became acquainted with many of the future leaders in that field, among them Ira Remsen and our own Charles Loring Jackson. Michael concluded his student years by spending another year at the *École de Médecine* in Paris under the great Wurtz.

"In 1880, Michael returned to America, and after a short period as Assistant in the Chemical Laboratory at Tufts College, was appointed Professor of Chemistry at that institution. He was able to devote practically all of his time to research and with the aid of private assistants and graduate students prosecuted his investigations with great energy and success. Among the graduate students who came to study with him at that time was Miss Helen Abbott of Philadelphia. She and Michael were married in 1889, and after an 18 months' tour around the world, Michael accepted a position as Head of the Department of Chemistry at the recently established Clark University. This position soon proved most uncongenial, and after a few months he resigned and established a residence and a private laboratory on the Isle of Wight, where he pursued his researches for four years. In 1894, he resumed his professorship at Tufts College and remained there until 1907 when he became Professor *Emeritus,* whereupon he established a private laboratory on his estate at Newton Center.

"In 1912, Michael was appointed Professor of Organic Chemistry at Harvard. He gave no lecture courses. At first his research students and his private assistants worked with him in his laboratory at Newton Center, but during his later years, they carried on their experimental work at the Converse Laboratory, reporting at frequent intervals to Professor Michael at his home. Michael became *Emeritus* here in 1936, nineteen years after he had taken a similar status at Tufts College.

"Next to chemistry, Michael's chief interest was in art, especially ancient and medieval art. He began collecting at an early date and his home in Newton was a repository of thousands of rare objects of art. Through his friendship with Professor Fenollosa, his attention had been directed particularly to oriental art, and objects from the Orient were numerous and conspicuous in his collections. He also had a fine collection of Early American silver. As might have been expected, Michael's erudition regarding the innumerable items of his collection was encyclopedic. At his death he bequeathed his American silver to the Smithsonian Institution and the remainder of his collection to the Albright Art Gallery in his native city of Buffalo.

"As a young man, Michael passed many of his vacations among the mountains; the Alps, the Canadian Rockies, and the Selkirks. Indeed, he became a real mountain climber. Thus, in 1897, he was in the party that made the first ascent of Mount Lefroy, and a few days later, with Professor Fay of Tufts College, he made the first ascent of Mt. Victoria. These are the two splendid ice-capped peaks which dominate the vista at Lake Louise.

"Michael was an eager, alert, but retiring personality, deeply immersed in his scientific and artistic pursuits. He had few intimates and he shunned publicity. Indeed, he declined to accept the award of a famous medal because of the publicity which this would entail. As a teacher, he was stimulating and inspiring and uncompromising in his insistence on thoroughness and accuracy. In his home, among his beautiful Chinese porcelains and bronzes, his Greek and Roman statuettes, his medieval works of art, with his extraordinary cosmopolitan background of experience and acquaintance, he was an incomparable host.

"Michael was always very fond of children, although he never had any of his own. It is not surprising, therefore, that in his will, after disposing of his art collection, his library, and his chemical apparatus, he bequeathed the residue of his considerable estate to three Buffalo institutions for the care of crippled, blind and needy children.

"Michael's research activities were prodigious and remarkably prolonged. The first of his 225 separate articles describing his researches was published when he was twenty-three years old; the last appeared a few months after his death sixty-six years later. It would be idle to attempt to recapitulate these many contributions; a few may be mentioned for which he will be particularly remembered.

"Michael was the first to synthesize a natural glucoside (hélicin, 1879), and the method that he introduced has become the standard synthetic route to this important class of compounds. Another landmark was his discovery, in 1887, of the addition of active-hydrogen reagents to α,β-unsaturated esters and carbonyl compounds; this, the Michael reaction, proved capable of wide elaboration and, in one or another of many modifications, constitutes an important tool of the modern builder of molecules. Another general synthetic method discovered by Michael, a modification of the Perkin Reaction, is extensively used for the condensation of aldehydes and malonic acid (1883). Finally may be mentioned his discovery of chlorine heptoxide, in 1900.

"This enumeration might seem to imply that Michael was concerned chiefly with the experimental rather than the theoretical aspects of chemistry. Actually the very opposite was the case. Michael was passionately interested in the theories of organic chemistry; that is, the fundamental laws and the mechanisms which might explain the marvelous variety and multiplicity of the compounds of carbon. All of his researches were undertaken to shed some light on these fundamental questions, and his numerous and far-ranging experimental investigations did, as a matter of fact, lead to the elaboration of a general theory of organic reactions. He developed special conceptions of the nature of valence, the condition of unsaturated systems, and the forces involved in chemical reactions, and he formulated a principle according to which 'every chemical system tends to so arrange itself that the maximum of chemical neutralization is attained.'

"While a few of Michael's collaborators learned to apply his method of reasoning, the Michaelian theories have had but little following, even though accorded the prominence of a special chapter in F. Henrich's treatise on the *Theories of Organic Chemistry*. Nevertheless, Michael himself, with his keen intuitive faculty, his wide experience in the laboratory, and his vast knowledge of the literature, could apply these concepts with extraordinary success both in the interpretation of known phenomena and in the prediction of unexplored happenings. Theories that can be thus applied certainly have a *prima facie* justification.

"The vigor of Michael's interest in theory and his extreme independence of thought were responsible for another important function which he performed throughout his long career to the great advantage of chemical science, namely, that of a sharp and penetrating critic of accepted views.

"When the van't Hoff theory of geometrical isomerism was gaining general acceptance through the able exploitation of Wislicenus and others, Michael flatly refused to accept what to him was an unproved hypothesis. Alert to any opportunity to attack current doctrine, he saw the weakness in Wislicenus' assumption that additions to unsaturated substances necessarily proceed in the *cis* direction and, in a series of carefully planned experiments, proved conclusively that *trans* addition does indeed occur. He thereby corrected an erroneous feature of this theory, but far from overthrowing the basic theory itself, his work extended and greatly strengthened a general concept that soon became a fully established tenet of the science. This example can be amplified by many others. Victor Meyer's view that the sulfone grouping is not comparable with the carbonyl and other acid-forming radicals was generally accepted until Michael (1889) succeeded in demonstrating the reactivity of the methylene groups in β-sulfonyl esters. Michael was the first to question the C-metal formulation of the metal derivatives of nitroparaffins (1888), and, in 1908, he challenged Claisen's views with regard to the relative stabilities of enolates. In 1920 he severely criticized Tiffeneau's interpretation of the pinacol and benzilic acid rearrangements, and, in 1935, he attacked the experimental basis for analogies accepted over a period of years as supporting the hypothetical addition—elimination mechanism of aromatic substitutions. His own astutely planned and faultlessly executed reinvestigations of the nitration and sulfonation of olefins proved the previously accepted analogies to be nonexistent, and indeed the hypothesis that he contested is now discarded.

"Summarizing, we can say that Michael was a powerful theorist, a keen critic and a consummate experimentalist. Or perhaps with equal appropriateness we can in conclusion quote the citation opposite his name in *American Men of Science* describing his field of activity, which reads, "Investigations in organic chemistry bearing on its fundamental laws and theory."

In a review of the Michael reaction published 112 years after the initial discovery, E. D. Bergmann, D. Ginsburg, and R. Pappo* cite 1045 references to its exploration and use. They note that in its original scope the condensation is a base-catalyzed addition of an addend or donor (A) containing an α-hydrogen atom in the system $O=C-CH$ to a carbon-carbon double bond that forms part of a conjugated system of the general formula-

* E. D. Bergmann, D. Ginsburg, and R. Pappo, "The Michael Reaction," *Organic Reactions* 10(1959):179.

tion C=C—C=O in an acceptor (B). Typical acceptors are
α,β-unsaturated aldehydes, ketones, and acid derivatives. All

$$
\begin{array}{cccc}
\text{R} \quad \text{R}^1 & \text{R}^3 \; \text{R}^5 \; \text{R}^6 & & \text{R} \quad \text{R}^1 \; \text{R}^3 \; \text{R}^5 \; \text{R}^6 \\
| \quad | & | \quad | \quad | & \text{Base} & | \quad | \quad | \quad | \quad | \\
\text{O=C—CH} + & \text{C=C—C=O} & \rightarrow & \text{O=C—C—C—C—C=O} \\
| \quad & | & & | \quad | \quad | \\
\text{R}^2 & \text{R}^4 & & \text{R}^2 \; \text{R}^4 \; \text{H} \\
\quad \text{A} & \text{B} & &
\end{array}
$$

structures containing O=C—CH— in which the hydrogen is
active by the Zerewitinoff test will serve as donors in the Michael
reaction. In addition, many compounds that do not meet this
test of hydrogen activity, such as acetophenone, are effective
Michael reactants. Typical acceptors are α,β-unsaturated aldehydes, ketones, and acid derivatives. By extension of the original scope, the Michael reaction has come to be understood to
include addends and acceptors activated by groups other than
carbonyl and carboalkoxyl. The wider scope includes as donors
nitriles, nitro compounds, sulfones, and certain hydrocarbons
such as cyclopentadiene, indene, and fluorene that contain sufficiently reactive hydrogen atoms. Another hydrocarbon acceptor is the conjugated tetraacetylenic compound (I), which
adds diethyl sodium malonate as follows:

$$
\text{CH}_3\text{C}\equiv\text{C—C}\equiv\text{C—C}\equiv\text{C—C}\equiv\text{CCH}_3 + \text{CH}_2(\text{CO}_2\text{C}_2\text{H}_5)_2 \xrightarrow{\text{Base}}
$$
$$
(\text{I})
$$

$$
\text{CH}_3\text{C}\equiv\text{C—C}\equiv\text{C—C}\equiv\text{C—CH=C(CH}_3)\text{CH(CO}_2\text{C}_2\text{H}_5)_2
$$

The review article cited discusses the mechanism of the
Michael reaction, the nature of the anion of the adduct, and
the reverse, or retrograde Michael reaction, used for example in
establishing the course of the biosynthesis of cholesterol, the
question of *para*-bridged intermediates, the stereochemistry of
the Michael condensation, and related topics. In presenting a

brief sketch of "an almost legendary figure, one of those giants of the days of the dawn of organic chemistry," W. T. Read * described Michael as "one of the most interesting figures that has ever appeared in the scientific world." In another review † Professor Albert B. Costa, historian of science of Duquesne University with research interests in nineteenth-century organic chemistry, described Michael's synthesis of natural glucosides and noted his preparation of pyrimidines by the reaction of ureas or thioureas with ethyl sodiomalonate. However, he states:

"Michael's primary concern was not these experimental contributions but organic theory. So concerned was he with fundamental principles that he elaborated a general interpretation of organic reactions and developed his own conceptions of the forces involved in chemical phenomena.‡ Energy conversions were for him the important controlling factors in all chemical changes, and he interpreted organic reactions in terms of energy in a long series of papers from 1888 on. His novel contribution to chemical theory was to introduce the thermodynamic conceptions of free energy and entropy into organic structural theory in order to overcome the pictorial and mechanical interpretation of chemical behavior.

"Michael's speculations included the genesis of the chemical elements in energetic terms (1910). The original corpuscles of matter were exclusively carriers of free chemical energy (convertible into less active chemical and physical energy), and all of the bound chemical energy (only partially reconvertible into free energy) appeared gradually in time from this original reservoir of free energy. Adopting the chemical evolutionary

---

* W. T. Read, "American Contemporaries; Arthur Michael," *Industrial and Engineering Chemistry* 22(1930):1137.

† A. B. Costa, "Arthur Michael (1853–1942). Meeting of Thermodynamics and Organic Chemistry," *Journal of Chemical Education* 48(1971):243.

‡ F. Henrich, *Theories of Organic Chemistry*, transl. T. B. Johnson and D. A. Hahn (New York: John Wiley & Sons, Inc., 1922).

ideas then in vogue, he argued that the elements appeared in sequential order. In the earlier stages of the formation of the atoms of the elements the free energy of the original corpuscles was converted largely into bound energy and heat; thus, the atoms of the less active elements were formed. As the temperature rose in the process of chemical evolution, such extensive conversions of free into bound energy did not occur and more reactive elements gradually emerged. With the genesis of the radioactive elements there appeared atoms with so much free energy that they were unstable.

"Having the chemical elements with their varying degrees of activity based on their free energy content, Michael set out to interpret chemical reactions. His starting point was Kekulé's idea that the first stage in every chemical reaction consisted in two molecules attracting each other through their chemical affinity to form a double molecule. Michael proposed that the free chemical energy in two unlike molecules was converted in part into bound energy and heat, the stability of the double molecule being determined by the extent of this conversion. He represented the reaction between sodium and chlorine in the following manner, using dotted lines to represent the free energy and solid lines the bound energy of atoms.

$$
\text{Na—Na} + \text{Cl—Cl} \rightarrow \quad
\begin{array}{c}
\vdots \quad \vdots \\
\text{Na—Na} \\
| \quad | \\
\text{Cl—Cl} \\
\vdots \quad \vdots
\end{array}
\tag{1}
$$

$$
\begin{array}{c}
\vdots \quad \vdots \\
\text{Na—Na} \\
| \quad | \\
\text{Cl—Cl} \\
\vdots \quad \vdots
\end{array}
\quad \rightarrow \quad
\begin{array}{c}
\text{Na—Na} \\
| \quad | \\
\text{Cl—Cl}
\end{array}
\tag{2}
$$

$$
\begin{array}{c}
\text{Na—Na} \\
| \quad | \\
\text{Cl—Cl}
\end{array}
\quad \rightarrow \quad 2\text{NaCl}
\tag{3}
$$

"In phase (1) the free energy in sodium and chlorine molecules resulted in the formation of a double molecule of the elements. Phase (2) represented the neutralization of the free energy as completely as possible. Finally, the bound energy between the two sodium atoms and two chlorine atoms was converted into bound energy between sodium and chlorine, the energy of the like atoms not being sufficient to hold these atoms together.

"In general, every spontaneous chemical change involved the conversion of free into bound energy. Every atom represented a definite quantity of potential chemical energy and had a tendency toward a condition of greater stability. Free energy and the affinity relationships of the atoms determined the chemical potential of a system.

"To Michael, the second law of thermodynamics was the most firmly established generalization in science. The increase in entropy that took place in every spontaneous chemical change must be the soundest basis for organic theory. For entropy, he substituted 'chemical neutralization,' meaning by this the neutralization of the free energy of the reacting atoms. The greater the conversion of free into bound energy that took place the more the neutralization of the chemical forces of the atoms. He then restated the second law in chemical terms: 'Every chemical system tends to arrange itself so that the maximum of chemical neutralization is attained.'

"Michael applied this general theory in detail to organic chemistry. Molecular rearrangements, addition and substitution reactions, tautomerism, and stereochemical phenomena were among the aspects of organic chemistry included within his theory. In the case of molecular rearrangements he proposed four factors which determined whether rearrangements might occur: (1) the extent of free energy among the interchanging atoms or groups; (2) their affinity for each other and for the atoms in the group to which they migrate; (3) the amount of energy required to separate migrating parts from the remaining part of the molecule; and (4) the heats of formation of the substances. He related these factors to the structures of the substances involved and explained a variety of rearrangement reactions, all of which entailed an increase in entropy, or in his terms, a neutralization of surplus free energy. A rearrangement might occur if a well neutralized substance was formed, provided that the increase in entropy due to the intramolecular neutralization was greater than the decrease in entropy due to factor (3).

"Michael's account of the tautomerism of nitromethane and nitrosomethane is an interesting example of the application of his ideas. Nitrosomethane (CH_3NO) is unstable and spontaneously forms the oxime ($CH_2:N \cdot OH$), whereas nitromethane (CH_3NO_2) is stable and its tautomer ($CH_2:NO \cdot OH$) is relatively unstable. He noted that the nitroso group has more free energy than the nitro group, the latter having the higher heat of formation. In nitrosomethane the oxygen has a strong affinity for the hydrogen of the methyl group. By changing into the oxime, much of the free energy in the nitroso group is converted into bound energy and heat; hence, there has been formed a well neutralized substance. However, the nitro group has less free energy, and its oxygen is less capable of overcoming the bound energy holding the hydrogen to carbon in the methyl group. Furthermore, nitromethane is poorer in free energy than the strongly acidic tautomer; hence, a rearrangement would result in a decrease in entropy and would not be favored.

"After the proof that tautomerism was the result of a mobile equilibrium between *keto* and *enol* forms, Michael investigated the conditions of stability of the forms and showed that the phenomena depended on the energy, affinity, and entropy relations of the tautomers and the solvent. He proposed an interaction between solvent and solute molecules: *Keto*-Solvent ⇌ *Enol*-Solvent. If the transformation was accomplished by an increase in entropy, tautomerization resulted with that particular solvent, the degree of tautomerization depending on the relative increase in entropy. With a large difference, only one form was stable; a small difference meant that both forms were stable.

"Michael concentrated much of his work on the theoretical aspects of addition to the double bond and the behavior of active methylene compounds. He claimed that addition reactions played a much more important role than chemists hitherto believed, and that many substitution reactions involved additions as a preliminary stage. A substitution was more often than not the end result of an addition followed by an elimination reaction. His interpretation of the mechanism of reactions according to an addition with the formation of an intermediate 'addition product' proved to be an important concept.

"The addition process meant that a substance was unsaturated, and unsaturated compounds have free energy potentially convertible into bound energy. His understanding of unsaturation in organic compounds was a consistent aspect of his general theory. By removal of a hydrogen atom from each carbon atom in ethane, the energy used to hold these hydrogen atoms was now employed in increasing the self-saturation of the carbon atoms. Hence, ethylene is a storehouse of potential chemical energy.

"Michael published many papers on the addition of unsymmetric addenda to unsymmetric unsaturated compounds. He proposed a 'positive–negative' rule as a way of determining the course of such addition reactions: the maximum neutralization is attained by the electronegative atom or group of the addendum combining with the more electropositive atom of the unsaturated molecule and the more electropositive atom or group to the more electronegative atom of the molecule. In propene ($CH_3CH:CH_2$), e.g., the positive methyl radical made the central carbon more positive than the end carbon atom. Hence, hydrogen iodide (H^+I^-) added to form mainly the secondary iodide (CH_3CHICH_3), although a small amount of primary iodide was also formed in agreement with Michael's distribution principle (see below). The addition of ICl and BrCl gave different results. ICl (I^+Cl^-) added to form mainly the primary iodide. Michael found experimentally that the isomeric addition products were present in a ratio of 3:1 of the primary to the secondary iodide. With BrCl the two atoms were more nearly equal in electronegativity and more nearly equal amounts of the primary and secondary bromide were formed. (He obtained them in a 7:5 ratio.) These relations were consistent with the energetic character of the compounds. In the addition of hydrogen iodide to propene the maximum entropy increase was realized in the formation of the secondary iodide; it has a greater heat of formation than the primary compound and thus a greater neutralization within the molecule.

"The positive–negative rule also clarified Michael's malonic and acetoacetic ester syntheses. These too were instances of heterogeneous addition. Both ethyl sodioacetoacetate and methyl iodide had pronounced positive–negative properties. Their reaction involved the separation of iodine from the methyl group, the attraction of sodium for iodine compared to the attraction of sodium for oxygen, and the attraction of methyl for one of the unsaturated atoms in the ester. The methyl would tend to combine with the most negative of the unsaturated atoms. The positive metal directed the course of reaction

$$
\begin{array}{c}
\overset{\displaystyle ONa}{\underset{}{|}} \\
CH_3 - \underset{+}{C} = \underset{-}{CH} \cdot COOC_2H_5 \ + \ \underset{+}{CH_3}\underset{-}{I} \ \rightarrow
\end{array}
$$

$$
\begin{array}{c}
\overset{\displaystyle ONa}{|} \qquad\qquad\qquad \overset{\displaystyle O}{\|} \\
CH_3 - C - CH \cdot COOC_2H_5 \ \rightarrow \ CH_3 \cdot C - CH \cdot COOC_2H_5 \ + \ NaI \\
\ \ | \ \ \ | \qquad\qquad\qquad\qquad\quad | \\
\ \ I \ \ CH_3 \qquad\qquad\qquad\qquad\quad CH_3
\end{array}
$$

"Michael found experimentally that if the metal was less positive and the addendum more negative, e.g., silver acetoacetate and acyl iodide, then the affinity relations were changed. The affinity to methyl was diminished more than that of metal to oxygen and the tendency of the reaction was toward substitution, not addition. Silver acetoacetate and methyl iodide still produced a methylated compound, but in decreased yield. If an acyl iodide was substituted for methyl iodide, substitution took place instead of addition, the acidic group attaching to oxygen. The positive and negative groups of both components distributed themselves to produce the maximum neutralization of affinities.

"Since all reactions do not produce one set of products, Michael introduced his 'distribution principle': 'If two unsaturated atoms A and B are present in a molecule which exhibits unequal affinity towards C and D of the addendum CD, and if A has greater affinity for C than has B, addition will occur if the affinity of AC–BD is greater than that of CD, and the more readily and completely the larger the difference. In this process of addition not only the affinity of A to C and of B to D comes into action, but also that of A to D and B to C, and therefore the further possibility is presented, not only of the combination of AC–BD, but of AD–BC, and the latter in increasing proportion the nearer the two combinations AC–BD is greater than AD–BC approach one another.' Thus, the more closely two atoms of a molecule resemble each other in chemical affinity for a third, the more nearly equal will be the relative number of molecules of the two compounds formed.

"Another important contribution, perhaps as important as his thermodynamic theory in its direct influence on organic chemists, was Michael's role as a critic. He responsibly throughout his long career was a sharp and penetrating critic of accepted views. When the theory of geometrical isomerism was gaining acceptance through the work of Wislicenus and others, he refused to accept what was to him the unjustified assumption that additions to unsaturated compounds always proceeded with the formation of cis products and that eliminations occurred more easily with cis than with trans isomers. In a series of carefully planned experiments Michael proved conclusively that trans additions did occur and that all of the then adopted configurations of geometric isomers were erroneous. He proved that fumaric acid derivatives were the direct products of the addition of halogens and hydrohalic acids to acetylenic acids and that the fumaric configurations of halo-succinic acids lost HX or halogen more readily than the isomeric compounds with the maleic acid configuration. He argued that both cis and trans additions and eliminations may occur in a given case to yield a mixture of isomers whose relative proportions depended on conditions incompatible with any mechanical conception of the process.

"Far from overthrowing the basic theory, Michael felt that his correction of it greatly strengthened stereochemistry and ensured that it would become a fully established part of organic chemistry. Where chemists such as Wislicenus had erred was in thinking that the stereochemical course of reactions could be represented by purely mechanical, geometric means; adequate understanding required the use of thermodynamic factors.

"Another example of his penetrating criticism was his reinterpretation of several types of rearrangements, as illustrated by his examination of the benzilic acid rearrangement

$$C_6H_5COCOC_6H_5 \xrightarrow{\text{KOH}} (C_6H_5)_2C(OH)COOK$$

He studied the explanations of the rearrangement of benzil into benzilic acid put forth by Nef and by Tiffeneau and found them to be chemically impossible. Tiffeneau, e.g., proposed the addition of an alkali molecule to each carbonyl group, followed by the elimination of water and isomerization to dipotassium benzilate. Michael pointed out that there was no experimental evidence that benzil could add two molecules of alkali or that benzilic acid formed a dibasic salt. His explanation was in terms of affinity and energy: the affinity of the carbon atoms of the two carbonyl groups in benzil was greatly decreased by the attached oxygen atoms, and the compound was easily ruptured at that point. But in the presence of alkali the following reaction took place

$$C_6H_5COCOC_6H_5 + KOH \rightarrow C_6H_5 \cdot \underset{\underset{OH}{|}}{\overset{\overset{OK}{|}}{C}}-COC_6H_5$$

The alkali greatly increased the amount of energy needed to rupture the carbon–carbon bond, while decreasing the amount of energy needed to break the bond between the phenyl group and the newly saturated carbon atom. Thus, a change in affinity relations had occurred, and the system, instead of rupturing a carbon–carbon bond, was converted by migration of the phenyl group and a hydrogen atom into a salt of benzilic acid with a large increase in entropy

$$C_6H_5-\underset{\underset{OH}{|}}{\overset{\overset{OK}{|}}{C}}-COC_6H_5 \rightarrow \underset{\underset{O}{||}}{\overset{\overset{OK}{|}}{C}}----\underset{\underset{C_6H_5}{|}}{\overset{\overset{OH}{|}}{C}}-C_6H_5$$

"Michael was a critic of all purely mechanical interpretations of organic reactions, such as Victor Meyer's steric hindrance concept and Baeyer's strain hypothesis. He experimentally showed that steric hindrance was very limited and was applicable to the esterification of substituted benzoic acids only when hydrochloric acid was used as a catalyst. He demonstrated that the formation of esters of such acids without this catalyst proceeded as smoothly as with other organic acids.

"Baeyer explained the ready formation and stability of five- and six-membered rings by postulating that the ease of formation of a ring depended on the amount a bond must deviate from the tetrahedral angle of 109°28′ in order to form the bond. Since the strain hypothesis did not consider the chemical affinity and energy relations nor the influence of side groups, it could not be for Michael a comprehensive explanation of ring formation. He proved experimentally that with certain side groups cyclobutyl derivatives were as easily formed as any derivatives of five- or six-membered rings. He prepared a four-membered ring compound by the addition of ethyl sodiomalonate to ethyl citraconate

$$CH_3-\underset{\underset{COOC_2H_5}{|}}{C}=CHCOOC_2H_5 \ + \ \underset{\underset{COOC_2H_5}{|}}{H}\underset{}{C}=\overset{\overset{ONa}{|}}{C}-OC_2H_5 \ \rightarrow$$

$$CH_3-\underset{\overset{|}{C}=\underset{\underset{COOC_2H_5}{|}}{C}}{\overset{\overset{COOC_2H_5}{|}}{C}}-CH_2COOC_2H_5 \quad \xrightarrow{-C_2H_5OH} \quad CH_3-\underset{\underset{COOC_2H_5}{|}}{\overset{\overset{COOC_2H_5}{|}}{C}}-CHCOOC_2H_5$$

To Michael, the strain hypothesis required significant modification before it could offer a satisfactory explanation of ring formation.

"Michael's speculations were an attempt to broaden and develop structural theory in organic chemistry. Structural theory was too mechanical and the attempts to remedy its defects were always along mechanical lines, such as conceptions of new kinds of valencies (partial, dissociated), oxonium and carbonium theories, steric hindrance, etc. All of these were inadequate to the challenge, for they all failed to consider energy–affinity relations. For Michael, all the forces in nature had the same end: the realization of the maximum increase in entropy, and a sound chemcial theory must have this fundamental law as a basis. He stressed the need for thermochemical and physico–chemical investigations in order to reveal the intimate connection between energy relations and chemical behavior and hoped that the union of thermodynamical principles with structural theory would lead to a more profound science of organic chemistry. His Harvard colleagues, in summarizing his contribution to chemistry, referred to him as 'a powerful theorist, a keen critic and a consummate experimentalist.' "

BIBLIOGRAPHY

KEY TO ABBREVIATIONS

Am. Chem. J. = American Chemical Journal
Ber. dtsch. chem. Ges. = Berichte der deutschen chemischen Gesellschaft
J. Am. Chem. Soc. = Journal of the American Chemical Society
J. Org. Chem. = Journal of Organic Chemistry
J. prakt. Chem. = Journal für praktische Chemie
Ann. Chem. = Justus Liebigs Annalen der Chemie

1876

Über die Einwirkung von Kaliumsulphhydrat auf Chloralhydrat. Ber. dtsch. chem. Ges., 9:1267.

With T. H. Norton. Über die Darstellung und Eigenschaften des Trijodresorcins. Ber. dtsch. chem. Ges., 9:1752.

1877

With S. Gabriel. Über die Einwirkung von wasserentziehenden Mitteln auf Säureanhydride. Ber. dtsch. chem. Ges., 10:391.

Zur Darstellung der Paramidobenzoësäure. Ber. dtsch. chem. Ges., 10:576.

With T. H. Norton. Über die Diamidosulphobenziddicarbonsäure. Ber. dtsch. chem. Ges., 10:580.

With A. Adair. Zur Kenntniss der aromatischen Sulphone. Ber. dtsch. chem. Ges., 10:583.

Über die Einwirkung des Broms auf Aethylphtalimid. Ber. dtsch. chem. Ges., 10:1644.

1878

With L. M. Norton. Über die Einwirkung des Chlorjodes auf aromatische Amine. Ber. dtsch. chem. Ges., 11:107.

With A. Adair. Zur Kenntniss der aromatischen Sulphone. Ber. dtsch. chem. Ges., 11:116.

1879

Über die Synthese des Phenolglykosides und des Orthoformylphenolglykosides oder Helicins. Comptes rendus hebdomadaires des séances de l'academie des sciences, 89:355; also in Ber. dtsch. chem. Ges., 12:2260; Am. Chem. J., 1:305.

With A. Kopp. Einwirkung verschidener Salzen auf Aldehyd Versuche angestellt. Ber. dtsch. chem. Ges., 12:2091.

On a new formation of stilbene and some of its derivatives. Am. Chem. J., 1:312; also in J. Am. Chem. Soc., 2:42 (1880).

Laboratory Notes. I. On mono-ethylphthalate. Am. Chem. J., 1:413; also in Ber. dtsch. chem. Ges., 13:1873 (1880); J. Am. Chem. Soc., 2:220 (1880).

Laboratory Notes. II. On a new formation of ethyl-mustard oil. Am. Chem. J., 1:416; also in J. Am. Chem. Soc., 2:221 (1880).

Laboratory Notes. III. On the preparation of methyl aldehyde. Am. Chem. J., 1:418; also in Ber. dtsch. chem. Ges., 13:1864 (1880); J. Am. Chem. Soc., 2:221 (1880).

Laboratory Notes. IV. On the "migration of atoms in the molecule" and Reimer's chloroform aldehyde reaction. Am. Chem. J., 1:420.

1880

Aethylsenfölbildung. Ber. dtsch. chem. Ges., 13:1866.

With L. M. Norton. On α- and β-monobromcrotonic acids. Am. Chem. J., 2:11.

With C. Gundelach. Preliminary note on the synthesis of methyl-conine and constitution of conine. Am. Chem. J., 2:171.

Darstellung von Methylaldehyd. J. Am. Chem. Soc., 2:221.

1881

With C. Gundelach. Vorläufige Notiz über die Synthese des Methyl-coniins und die Constitution des Coniins. Ber. dtsch. chem. Ges., 14:110.

Über die Einwirkung von aromatischen Oxysäuren auf Phenole. Ber. dtsch. chem. Ges., 14:656.

With L. M. Norton. Über α- und β-Monobromcrotonsäure. Ber. dtsch. chem. Ges., 14:1202.

Über die Synthese des Methylarbutins. Ber. dtsch. chem. Ges., 14:2097.

Zur Kenntniss des p-Coniins. Ber. dtsch. chem. Ges., 14:2105.

1882

Über die Synthese des Salicins und des Anhydrosalicylglucosids. Ber. dtsch. chem. Ges., 15:1922.

1883

On the action of aromatic oxy-acids on phenols. Am. Chem. J., 5:81; also in Ber. dtsch. chem. Ges., 16:2298.

With A. M. Comey. On some properties of phenylsulphonacetic ethers. Am. Chem. J., 5:116; also in Ber. dtsch. chem. Ges., 16:2300.

Synthetical researches in the glucoside group. Am. Chem. J., 5:171.

With A. Kopp. On the formation of crotonic and β-oxybutyric aldehydes from ethyl aldehyde. Am. Chem. J., 5:182; also in Ber. dtsch. chem. Ges., 16:2501.

Laboratory Notes. V. On the action of sodium ethyl oxide on bromethylidenebromide. Am. Chem. J., 5:192; also in Ber. dtsch. chem. Ges., 16:2499.

Laboratory Notes. VI. A new synthesis of allantoin and some suggestions on the constitution of uric acid. Am. Chem. J., 5:198; also in Ber. dtsch. chem. Ges., 16:2506.

Laboratory Notes. VII. On a convenient method for preparing bromacetic acid. Am. Chem. J., 5:202; also in Ber. dtsch. chem. Ges., 16:2502.

Laboratory Notes. VIII. On several cases of intermolecular rearrangement. Am. Chem. J., 5:203.

Laboratory Notes. IX. On a new synthesis of cinnamic acid. Am. Chem. J., 5:205.

With A. M. Comey. On the action of aldehydes on phenols. II. Am. Chem. J., 5:349.

Laboratory Notes. X. Some convenient quantitative lecture apparatus. Am. Chem J., 5:353.

Laboratory Notes. XI. Observations on the action of acetylchloride and acetic anhydride on corn and wheat starch. Am. Chem. J., 5:359.

On the constitution of resocyanin. Am. Chem. J., 5:434.

1884

With G. M. Palmer. On the action of sodium phenylsulphinate on methylene iodide. Am. Chem. J., 6:253.

With G. M. Palmer. On the conversion of organic isocyanates into mustard oils. Am. Chem. J., 6:257.

Synthetical researches in the glucoside group. III. Am. Chem. J., 6:336.

With J. F. Wing. On the action of methyl iodide on asparagine. Am. Chem. J., 6:419.

1885

With G. M. Palmer. On some properties of phenylsulphonacetic ethers. II. Am. Chem. J., 7:65.

With J. F. Wing. Note on the constitution of the addition-product of chlorhydric acid to ethylcyanide. Am. Chem. J., 7:71.

On the decomposition of cinchonine by sodium ethylate. Am. Chem. J., 7:182.

With G. M. Palmer. On simultaneous oxidation and reduction by means of hydrocyanic acid. Am. Chem. J., 7:189.

With J. F. Wing. On the action of alkyl iodides on amido acids. Am. Chem. J., 7:195.

With G. M. Palmer. On resacetophenone. Am. Chem. J., 7:275.

With J. F. Wing. On inactive aspartic acid. Am. Chem. J., 7:278.

1886

Über einen Zusammenhang zwischen Anilidbildung und der Constitution ungesättigter, mehrbasischer, organischer Säuren. Ber. dtsch. chem. Ges., 19:1372.

With G. M. Palmer. Über einen Zusammenhang zwischen Anilidbildung und der Constitution ungesättigter, Mehrbasischer, organischer Säuren. II. Ber. dtsch. chem. Ges., 19:1375.

Über die einwirkung des Anilins auf die Brommalein- und Chlorfumarsäure. Ber. dtsch. chem. Ges., 19:1377.

With G. M. Browne. Zue Isomerie in der Zimmtsäurereihe. Ber. dtsch. chem. Ges., 19:1378.

Zue isomerie in der Fettreihe. Ber. dtsch. chem. Ges., 19:1381.

Über die Nitrirung des Phenylhydrazins. Ber. dtsch. chem. Ges., 19:1386.

With J. P. Ryder. Zur Kenntniss der Einwirkung von Aldehyden auf Phenole. Ber. dtsch. chem. Ges., 19:1388.

Die Citraconsäure als Reagenz zur Erkennung und Scheidung der Aromatischen Amine. Ber. dtsch. chem. Ges., 19:1390.

With G. M. Browne. Überführung der α-Bromzimmtäther in Benzoylessigäther. Ber. dtsch. chem. Ges., 19:1392.

Einwirkung von Phosphorpentachlorid auf einige organische Verbindungen. Gesellschaft deutscher Naturforscher und Arzte. Tageblatt Naturforsch-Versammlung zu Berlin, 411.

1887

Über eine bequeme Darstellungsweise von bromirten Fettsäuren. J. prakt. Chem., 35:92.

Das Verhalten von Essigsäure und einigen Derivaten derselben gegen Fünffach-chlorphosphor. J. prakt. Chem., 35:95.

Über die Constitution der Trimethylentricarbonsäure. J. prakt. Chem., 35:132.

Über die Bildung des Indigblau aus Orthonitrophenylpropiolsäure mittelst Cyankalium. J. prakt. Chem., 35:254.

With G. M. Browne. Über alloisomerie in der Crotonsäurereihe. J. prakt. Chem., 35:257.

Über die Addition von Natriumacetessig- und Natriummalonsäureather zu den Äthern ungesättigter Säuren. J. prakt. Chem., 35:349; also in Am. Chem. J., 9:112.

Die Reduction von alpha- und alloalphabromzimmtsäuren zu Zimmtsäure. J. prakt. Chem., 35:357.

With G. M. Browne. Über aromatische Hydroxylamine. J. prakt. Chem., 35:358.

On some new reactions with sodium acetacetic and sodium malonic ethers. Am. Chem. J., 9:124; also in J. prakt. Chem., 35:449.

With J. P. Ryder. On the action of aldehydes on phenols. III. Am. Chem. J., 9:130.

Über das Verhalten von Oxalsäureäther zu Resorcin. J. prakt. Chem., 35:510.

Bemerkungen zu einer Abhandlung des Hrn. L. Claisen. Ber. dtsch. chem. Ges., 20:1572.

Researches on alloisomerism. I. A relation between the constitution of polybasic unsaturated organic acids and the formation of their anilides. Am. Chem. J., 9:180.

With G. M. Palmer. Researches on alloisomerism. II. Am. Chem. J., 9:197.

On the action of phosphorus pentachloride on the ethers of organic acids, and on some derivatives of acetic acid. Am. Chem. J., 9:205.

On the action of phosphorus pentachloride on acetanilide. Am. Chem. J., 9:217; also in J. prakt. Chem. 35:207.

Preliminary notes. Am. Chem. J., 9:219.

Antwort auf eine Bemerkung von L. Claisen. J. prakt. Chem., 36:113.

With G. M. Browne. Researches on alloisomerism. Am. Chem. J., 9:274.

With G. M. Browne. Zur isomerie in der Crotonsäurereihe. J. prakt. Chem., 36:174.

Remarks on the constitution of levulinic and maleic acids. Am. Chem. J., 9:364.

1888

Preliminary notes on the constitution of sodium acetacetic and malonic esters. Am. Chem. J., 10:158.

Über das verhalten von Natriummalonäther gegen Resorcinol. J. prakt. Chem., 37:469.

Zur constitution des Natriumacetessigäther. J. prakt. Chem., 37:473.

With H. Pendleton. Zur Alloisomerie in der Krotonsäurereihe. J. prakt. Chem., 38:1.

Zur kritik der Abhandlung von J. Wislicenus: "Über die räumliche Anordung der Atome in organischen Molekulen." J. prakt. Chem., 38:6.

1889

Bemerkung zu der Abhandlung von J. Wislicenus: "Zur geometrischen Constitution der Krotonsäuren und ihrer Halogensubstitutionsprodukte." J. prakt. Chem., 40:29.

With H. Pendleton. Zu Alloisomerie in der Zimmtsäurereihe. J. prakt. Chem., 40:63.

With P. Freer. Über die einwirkung von Jodwasserstoffsäure auf die Krotonsäuren. J. prakt. Chem., 40:95.

Über die Regelmässigkeiten bei der Anlagerung von Halogenverbindungen an ungesättigte Säuren. J. prakt. Chem., 40:171.

1890

Bemerkung zu der Abhandlung von Otto und Rossing über die Ersetzbarkeit des Natriums in Natriumphenylsulfonessigäther durch Alkyle. Ber. dtsch. chem. Ges., 23:669.

Bemerkungen zu der Abhandlung von Goldschmidt und Meissler über "Versuche zur Constitutionsbestimmung tautomerer Verbindungen." J. prakt. Chem., 42:19.

1891

With P. C. Freer. Über die Addition von Natriumacetessig- und Natriummalonsäther zu den Äthern ungesättigter Säuren. II. J. prakt. Chem., 43:390.

With O. Schulthess. Untersuchungen über Alloisomerie. I. Zur Kenntnis der Halogenentziehung bei organischen α-β-Halogensäureäthern. J. prakt. Chem., 43:587.

Zur Kenntnis der Lävulinsäure und des Acetondiessigsäuredilaktons. J. prakt. Chem., 44:113.

Bemerkung zu der Abhandlung von Ad. Claus: über die Umsetzung von Dibrombernsteinsäureester mit Zink. J. prakt. Chem., 44:399.

With G. Tissot. Zur Kenntnis der Homologen der Äpfelsäure. Ber. dtsch. chem. Ges., 24:2544.

1892

On the constitution of sodium acet-acetic ether. Am. Chem. J., 14:481.

With O. Schulthess. Über die Addition von Natriumacetessig- und Natriummalonsäureäther zu den Äthern ungesättigter Säuren. J. prakt. Chem., 45:55.

Zur Konstitution des Natriumacetessigäther. J. prakt. Chem., 45:580; 46:189.

Untersuchungen über Alloisomerie. II. Tul. I. Über die Addition von Brom zu Acetylendicarbonsäure und deren Äthyläther. J. prakt. Chem., 46:209.

With C. C. Maisch. Über die Einwirkung von Natriumäthylat auf Dibrombernsteinsäureäther. J. prakt. Chem., 46:233.

With O. Schulthess. Untersuchungen über Alloisomerie. II. III. Über die Crotonsäure und Derivate derselben. J. prakt. Chem., 46:236.

Untersuchungen über Alloisomerie. II. IV. Über die Bildung von fester Crotonsäure bei der Reduktion von allo-α-Brom- und -chlorcrotonsäure. J. prakt. Chem., 46:266.

With G. Tissot. Untersuchungen über Alloisomerie. II. VI. Beiträge zur Kenntniss einiger Homologen der Äpfelsäure. J. prakt. Chem., 46:285.

With G. Tissot. Untersuchungen über Alloisomerie. II. VII. Über die Addition von Chlor zu mehrbasischen ungesättigten Fettsäuren. J. prakt. Chem., 46:381.

Untersuchungen über Alloisomerie. II. VIII. Vergleich der Versuchsergebnisse mit den theoretischen Folgerungen aus den Hypothesen Le Bel-Van't Hoff und Wislicenus. J. prakt. Chem., 46:400.

Untersuchungen über Alloisomerie. II. IX. Die van't Hoff'sche Hypothese in ihrer Anwendung auf die Gegenseitegen Beziehungen gesättigter und ungesättigter Fettsäuren. J. prakt. Chem., 46:424.

1893

Untersuchungen über Alloisomerie. J. prakt. Chem., 47:197.

Über die Einwirkung von Diazobenzolimid auf Acetylendicarbonsäuremethylester. J. prakt. Chem., 48:94.

1894

Über die Addition von Natriumacetessig- und Natriummalonsäureäther zu den Äthern ungesättigter Säuren. J. prakt. Chem., 49:20.

Beiträge zur Kenntnis des Ringbildung bei organischen, stickstoffhaltigen Verbindungen. J. prakt. Chem., 49:26.

Über die Einwirkung von Natriummalonäthylester auf Benzalaceton. Ber. dtsch. chem. Ges., 27:2126.

With G. Tissot. Über die Brommesakonsäure. Ber. dtsch. chem. Ges., 27:2130.

1895

Zur Schmelzpunktbestimmung von hochschmelzenden und sogenannten unschmelzbaren organischen Verbindungen. Ber. dtsch. chem. Ges., 28:1629.

Über die Addition von Schwefel zu ungesättigten organischen Verbindungen. Ber. dtsch. chem. Ges., 28:1633.

With J. E. Bucher. Über die Einwirkung von Essigsäureanhydrid auf Säuren der Acetylenreihe. Ber. dtsch. chem. Ges., 28:2511.

Untersuchungen über Alloisomerie. III. J. prakt. Chem., 52:289.

With T. H. Clark. Relative Leichtigkeit der Kohlendioxydabspaltung aus den Silversalzen der β-Chlorcrotonsäuren. J. prakt. Chem., 52:326.

With G. Tissot. Dritter abschnitt. J. prakt. Chem., 52:331.

Vierter abschnitt: über die gesetze der Alloisomerie und Anwendung derselben zur Classificirung ungesättigter organischer Verbindungen. J. prakt. Chem., 52:344.

Bemerkungen zu Arbeiten von C. A. Bischoff, J. A. Wislicenus and J. H. van't Hoff. J. prakt. Chem., 52:365.

1896

Über die Einwirkung von Äthyljodid und Zinc auf $\Delta^{\alpha,\beta}$-Fettester. Ber. dtsch. chem. Ges., 29:1791.

With J. E. Bucher. Zur Constitution der Oxalessigsäure. Ber. dtsch. chem. Ges., 29:1792.

Zur Kenntniss der Additionsvorgänge bei den Natriumderivaten von Formyl- und Acetessigestern und Nitroäthanen. Ber. dtsch. chem. Ges., 29:1793.

Herrn. E. Erlenmeyer und C. Liebermann zur Erwiderung. J. prakt. Chem., 54:107.

1898

With J. E. Bucher. On the action of acetic anhydride on phenylpropiolic acid. Am. Chem. J., 20:89.

With F. Luehn and H. H. Higbee. On the formation of imido-1,2-diazol derivative from aromatic azimides and esters of acetylenecarboxylic acids. Am. Chem. J., 20:377.

Über das Verhalten von Benzaldehyd gegen Phenol. J. prakt. Chem., 57:334.

1899

Über die Ersetzung des Natriums in Natriumphenylsulfonessigester durch Alkyle. J. prakt. Chem., 60:96.

Über einige Gesetze und deren Anwendung in der organischen Chemie. I. J. prakt. Chem., 60:286.

With V. L. Leighton. Über einige Gesetze und deren Anwendung in der organischen Chemie. II. J. prakt. Chem., 60:409.

With W. T. Conn. On chlorine heptoxide. Am. Chem. J., 23:444.

1900

Zur Kenntniss der Natriumacetessigestersynthese und der Vierringbildung mittels Natriumäthylats. Ber. dtsch. chem. Ges., 33:3731.

1901

With W. T. Conn. On the behavior of iodine and bromine toward chlorine heptoxide and perchloric acid. Am. Chem. J., 25:89.

Zur Kenntniss der Perkin'schen Reaction. Ber. dtsch. chem. Ges., 34:918.

On methyl cyanide as a catalytic reagent and a criticism of J. U. Nef's views on the Frankland-Wurtz- and Conrad reactions. Am. Chem. J., 25:419.

With V. L. Leighton and F. D. Wilson. Über die isomeren Iso-butylenchlorhydrine und die Zersetzung der gemischten Äether durch Halogenwasserstoff. J. prakt. Chem., 64:102.

Zur Kenntniss der drei stereomeren Zimmtsäuren. Ber. dtsch. chem. Ges., 34:3640.

With W. W. Gerner and W. H. Graves. Zur Kenntniss der Sub-stitution-vorgänge in der Fettreihe. Ber. dtsch. chem. Ges., 34:4028.

Über einige Laboratoriumsapparate. Ber. dtsch. chem. Ges., 34:4058.

With T. H. Mighill. Zur Kenntniss des Additions-Abspaltungs-Gesetzes. Ber. dtsch. chem. Ges., 34:4215.

1903

Bemerkung zur der Mittheilung des Hrn. S. Svoboda "Über einen abnormalen Verlauf der Michael'schen Condensation." Ber. dtsch. chem. Ges., 36:763.

With W. W. Garner. Beiträge zur Frage der Isozmutsäure. Ber. dtsch. chem. Ges., 36:900.

Zur Geschichte der Isozimmtsäure. Ber. dtsch. chem. Ges., 36:2497.

On the condensation of oxalic ethylester with ethylene and tri-methylene cyanides. Am. Chem. J., 30:156.

Valenzhypothesen und der Verlauf chemischer Vorgänge. J. prakt. Chem., 68:487.

With V. L. Leighton. Über die Konstitution des Phenylcinna-menylakrylsäuredibromids. J. prakt. Chem., 68:521.

1905

Phenylisocyanat als Reagens zur Feststellung der constitution tauto-merer Verbindungen. Ber. dtsch. chem. Ges., 38:22.

With O. Eckstein. Über die Bildung von *o*-Acylderivaten aus Cyanessigester durch Anwendung von Pyridin und Chinolin. Ber. dtsch. chem. Ges., 38:50.

Zur Geschichte der Theorie über die Bildung und Constitution des Natracetessigesters. Ber. dtsch. chem. Ges., 38:1922.

Zur Kenntniss der Synthesen mit Natracetessigester. Ber. dtsch. chem. Ges., 38:2096.

Zur Frage über der Verlaug der Claisen'schen Zimmtsäurestersynthese. Ber. dtsch. chem. Ges., 38:2523.

Zur Kenntniss der Vorgänge bei der Synthesen mit Natrium Malonester und verwandten Verbindungen. Ber. dtsch. chem. Ges., 38:3217.

Herren Störmer und Kippe zur Erwiderung. Ber. dtsch. chem. Ges., 38:4137.

Über die Darstellung reiner Alkylmalonester. J. prakt. Chem., 72:537.

1906

On the isomerism and tautomerism question. Am. Chem. J., 35:201.

With H. D. Smith and A. Murphy, Jr. The question of isomerism and tautomerism. Ber. dtsch. chem. Ges., 39:203.

Zur constitution des Tribenzoylenbenzols. Ber. dtsch. chem. Ges., 39:1908.

With W. W. Garner. Cinnamylideneacetic acid and some of its transformation products. Am. Chem. J., 35:258.

With W. W. Garner. Magnesium permanganate as an oxidizing agent. Am. Chem. J., 35:267.

Zur constitution des "Kohlensuboxyds." Ber. dtsch. chem. Ges., 39:1915.

Über das Vertheilungsprincip. Ber. dtsch. chem. Ges., 39:2138.

Über den Verlauf der addition von Wasser an Hexin-2. Ber. dtsch. chem. Ges., 39:2143.

With R. N. Hartman. Zur Constitution des aus Mannit-Hexen dargestellten Hexylalkohols. Ber. dtsch. chem. Ges., 39:2149.

Über die Einwirkung von Chlor auf Hexan. Ber. dtsch. chem. Ges., 39:2153.

With V. L. Leighton. Über die Addition von Unterchloriger säure an Isobuten. Ber. dtsch. chem. Ges., 39:2157.

With F. D. Wilson. Über den Verlauf der Zersetzung von gemischten Fettäthern durch Jodwasserstoffsaure. Ber. dtsch. chem. Ges., 39:2569.

Über die Einwirkung von Salzsäure auf Propenoxyd und Propenalkohol. Ber. dtsch. chem. Ges., 39:2785.

With V. L. Leighton. Über die Einwirkung von Salzsäure auf Isobutenoxyd. Ber. dtsch. chem. Ges., 39:2789.

With A. B. Lamb. The isomerism of ethyl coumaric and ethyl coumarinic acids. Am. Chem. J., 36:552.

1907

With R. N. Hartman. Zur Konstitution des aus Mannit dargestellten Hexyljodids. Ber. dtsch. chem. Ges., 40:140.

With H. Hibbert. On the ammonia reaction as a means of distinguishing between enol and keto derivatives. I. Ber. dtsch. chem. Ges., 40:4380.

With H. Hibbert. The ammonia reaction as a means of distinguishing between enol and keto derivatives. II. Ber. dtsch. chem. Ges., 40:4916.

Die van't Hoff-Wislicenusache Konfigurationslehre. J. prakt. Chem., 75:105.

1908

Stereoisomerism and the law of entropy. Am. Chem. J., 39:1.

With H. D. Smith. The addition of halogens to cinnamic acid and some of its derivatives. Am. Chem. J., 39:16.

Über Desmotropie und Merotropie. I. Ann. Chem., 363:20.

With H. D. Smith. II. Die tertiären Amine als Reagentien zur Unterscheidung zwischen stabilen Enol- und Ketonderivaten. Ann. Chem., 363:36.

With P. H. Cobb. III. Phenylisocyanat als Reagens zur Festellung der Constitution Merotropen Vergindungen. Ann. Chem., 363:64.

With A. Murphy, Jr. IV. Acetylchlorid und Essigsäureanhydrid als Reagentien zur Unterscheidung zwischen Enol- und Ketonderivaten. Ann. Chem., 363:94.

With W. W. Garner. Magnesium permanganate as an oxidizing agent. Monatshefte fuer Chemie und Verwandte Teile Anderer Wissenschaften, 22:556.

With J. E. Bucher. Zur Frage über die Festellung der Konstitution der Phenylnaphthalindicarbonsäure; Hrn. Hans Stobbe zur Antwort. Ber. dtsch. chem. Ges., 41:70.

Über refraktometrischen Beweis der Konstitution des "Kohlensuboxyds." Ber. dtsch. chem. Ges., 41:925.

With H. Hibbert. Über die vermeintliche Beziehung zwischen Dielektrizitätskonstante und isomerisierender Kraft organischer Losungsmittel bei Enol-Keton-Desmotropen. Ber. dtsch. chem. Ges., 41:1080.

With O. D. E. Bunge. Über den stereochemischen verlauf der Addition von Chlor zu Crotonsäure. Ber. dtsch. chem. Ges., 41:2907.

1909

With H. Hibbert. V. Zur Constitution des Cyanwasserstoffs. Ann. Chem., 364:64.

With H. Hibbert. VI. Zur Constitution der Cyansäure. Ann. Chem., 364:129.

With R. F. Brunel. On the relative ease of addition in the alkene group. First paper on the laws of addition in organic chemistry. Am. Chem. J., 41:118.

Zur theorie der Esterfikation organischer Carbonsäuren. (Erste Mitteilung über die Natur der "sterischen Hinderung"). Ber. dtsch. chem. Ges., 42:310.

With K. J. Oechslin. Über den Einfluss der substituenten aromatischer Carbonsäuren auf ihre Esterifikation. II. Ber. dtsch. chem. Ges., 42:317.

Das chinon von Standpukt des Entropiegesetzes und der Partialvalenzhypothese. J. prakt. Chem., 79:418.

With K. Wolgast. Über die Beziehung zwischen Struktur des Fettalkohole und Geschwindigkeit der Esterifikation. III. Ber. dtsch. chem. Ges., 42:3157.

With K. Wolgast. Zur Darstellung reiner Ketone mittels Acetessigester. Ber. dtsch. chem. Ges., 42:3176.

1910

Über die Beziehung zwischen Structure der Fettalkohole und geschwindigkeit der Esterifikation. Ber. dtsch. chem. Ges., 43:464.

Über die "Additionstheorie," Hrn. S. J. Acree zur antwort. Ber. dtsch. chem. Ges., 43:621.

On the application of physical chemical methods to determine the mechanism of organic reactions. Am. Chem. J., 43:322.

Outline of a theory of organic chemistry founded on the law of entropy. J. Am. Chem. Soc., 32:990.

With A. Murphy, Jr. On the action of chlorine in solution in carbon tetrachloride and of carbon tetrachloride on metallic oxides. Am. Chem. J., 44:365.

With P. H. Cobb. Über die Reaktion zwischen Chinon und Salzsäure. J. prakt. Chem., 82:297.

Über den Mechanismus der Chinonreaktionen. Hrn. Theodor Posner zur erwiderung. J. prakt. Chem., 82:306.

1911

With H. Leupold. Zum verlauf der intramolekularen Umlagerungen bei den Alkylbromiden und zur Frage der Ursache des Gieichgewichtszustandes bei Unkehrbaren reaktionen. Ann. Chem., 379:263.

1912

With R. F. Brunel. Action of aqueous solutions of acids on alkenes. Am. Chem. J., 48:267.

With F. Zeidler. Chemistry of the amyl series. Ann. Chem., 385:227.

Number of isomers in merotropic and desmotropic compounds. I. Ann. Chem., 390:30.

Number of isomers in merotropic and desmotropic compounds. II. Isomeric keto forms of acetyldibenzoylmethane. Ann. Chem., 390:46.

With Harold Hibbert. Number of isomers in merotropic and desmotropic compounds. III. Isomeric keto forms of propionyldibenzoylmethane. Ann. Chem., 390:68.

Number of isomers in merotropic and desmotropic compounds. IV. Isomeric forms of formylphenylacetic ester. Ann. Chem., 391:235.

With G. P. Fuller. Number of isomers in merotropic and desmotropic compounds. Isomeric enol forms of formylphenylacetic ester. Ann. Chem., 391:275.

With F. Zeidler. Course of intramolecular rearrangements in alkyl bromides. Ann. Chem., 393:81.

Application of the "scale of combined influence" to explain the ionization constants of organic acids, and a reply to C. G. Derik. J. Am. Chem. Soc., 34:849.

1913

The Perkin reaction. Am. Chem. J., 50:411.

With E. Scharf. Über den Mechanisms der Einwirkung von Brom auf Fettsaurechloride. Ber. dtsch. chem. Ges., 46:135.

1914

With W. Schlenk, J. Appenrodt and A. Thal. Über Metalladitionen en mehrfache Bindungen. Ber. dtsch. chem. Ges., 47:473.

Number of isomers of merotropic and desmotropic compounds. VI. Isomeric forms of formylphenylacetic ester. Ann. Chem., 406:137.

1916

With E. Scharf and K. Voigt. Rearrangement of iso into tertiary butyl bromide. J. Am. Chem. Soc., 38:653.

1918

Configurations of organic compounds and their relation to chemical and physical properties. J. Am. Chem. Soc., 40:704.

Configurations of organic compounds and their relation to chemical and physical properties. II. The relations between the physical properties and the configurations of unsaturated acids. J. Am. Chem. Soc., 40:1674.

1919

Relations between the chemical structures of carbonyl derivatives and their reactivities towards salts of semicarbazide. J. Am. Chem. Soc., 41:393.

1920

The chemical mechanism of organic rearrangements. J. Am. Chem. Soc., 42:787.

The non-existence of valence and electronic isomerism in hydroxylammonium derivatives. J. Am. Chem. Soc., 42:1232.

1921

The structures and reactions of hydroxylamine and its derivatives. I. J. Am. Chem. Soc., 43:315.

1929

Castor-oil preparation. Australian patent 20,127.

1930

With J. Ross. Course of addition of sodium enol alkyl malonic esters to α,β-unsaturated esters. J. Am. Chem. Soc., 52:4598.

1931

With J. Ross. Course of addition of sodium enol alkylmalonic and sodium enol alkylcyanoacetic esters to unsaturated esters. J. Am. Chem. Soc., 53:1150.

With J. Ross. $\alpha\beta\gamma$-Trimethylglutaric acids. J. Am. Chem. Soc., 53:1175.

With J. Ross. Partition principles as applied to the structures of enolic sodium derivatives of 1,3-diketones and β-keto esters. J. Am. Chem. Soc., 53:2394.

1932

With J. Ross. Partition principles as applied to the structure of enolic sodium derivatives of 1,3-diketones and β-keto esters. II. J. Am. Chem. Soc., 54:387.

With J. Ross. Addition of sodium enol alkylmalonic ester to benzal-acetophenone. J. Am. Chem. Soc., 54:407.

1933

With J. Ross. Course of addition of the sodium enolates of malonic and methylmalonic esters to benzalacetophenone and to crotonic ester. J. Am. Chem. Soc., 55:1632.

With J. Ross. Carbon syntheses with malonic and related acids. I. J. Am. Chem. Soc., 55:3684.

1934

With N. Weiner. Formation of enolates from α-lactonic esters. J. Am. Chem. Soc., 56:2012.

1935

With G. H. Carlson. Mechanism of reactions of acetoacetic ester, the enolates and structurally related compounds. I. C- and O-Alkylation. J. Am. Chem. Soc., 57:159.

The mechanism of the reactions of metal enol acetoacetic ester and related compounds. II. Sodium enolates toward acyl chloride. J. Am. Chem. Soc., 57:165.

With G. H. Carlson. Mechanism of the nitration process. J. Am. Chem. Soc., 57:1268.

1936

With N. Weiner. Mechanism of the sulfonation process. J. Am. Chem. Soc., 58:294.

Mechanism of the reactions of metal enol acetoacetate ester and related compounds. III. Copper enolates. J. Am. Chem. Soc., 58:353.

With N. Weiner. Carbon syntheses with malonic acid and related compounds. II. Aromatic aldehydes. J. Am. Chem. Soc., 58:680.

With N. Weiner. Formation of enolates from lactonic esters. J. Am. Chem. Soc., 58:999.

1937

With N. Weiner. 1,2- and 1,4-Addition. I. The 1,4-addition of potassium isocyanate. J. Am. Chem. Soc., 59:744.

With G. H. Carlson. 1,2- and 1,4-Addition. II. Nitrogen tetroxide and trimethylethylene. J. Am. Chem. Soc., 59:843.

Course of the addition of malonic enolates to α,β-unsaturated esters. J. Org. Chem., 2:303.

1938

With N. Weiner. The partition principle as applied to the structures of enolic sodium derivatives of β-diketones and β-keto esters. III. J. Org. Chem., 3:372.

1939

With G. H. Shadinger. Influence of solvents on the stereochemical course of the addition of hydrogen bromide to monobasic acetylenic acids and the relation of solvent effect to chemical structure. J. Org. Chem., 4:128.

With G. H. Carlson. 1,2- and 1,4-Addition. III. Nitrogen trioxide and trimethylethylene. J. Org. Chem., 4:169.

The relations of "oxygen and peroxide effect," and of hypochlorous acid addition, to the structures of unsaturated organic compounds. J. Org. Chem., 4:519.

With N. Weiner. Solvent and peroxide effect in the addition of hydrogen bromide to trimethylethylene. J. Org. Chem., 4:531.

1940

With G. H. Carlson. 1,2- and 1,4-Addition. IV. Nitrogen tetroxide and isobutylene. J. Org. Chem., 5:1.

With G. H. Carlson. 1,2- and 1,4-Addition. V. Nitrogen tetroxide and tetramethylethylene. J. Org. Chem., 5:14.

With N. Weiner. Solvent and peroxide effect in the addition of hydrogen bromide to unsaturated compounds. IV. Isopropylethylene. J. Org. Chem., 5:389.

1943

With C. M. Saffer, Jr. The addition of triphenylmethylsodium and phenyllithium to cinnamic ester and benzalacetophenone. J. Org. Chem., 8:60.

With H. S. Mason. Normal addition of hydrogen bromide to 3-butenoic, 4-pentenoic and 5-hexenoic acids in hexane. J. Am. Chem. Soc., 65:683.

With H. S. Mason. Determination of the composition of mixtures of α-bromo-α-methyl, and α-bromo-β-methylsuccinic acids. J. Org. Chem., 9:393.

RICHARD JOEL RUSSELL

November 16, 1895–September 17, 1971

BY CHARLES A. ANDERSON

R ICHARD JOEL RUSSELL had an outstanding career in the earth sciences. He began with undergraduate work in forestry and vertebrate paleontology, followed by graduate studies in petrography and structural geology at the same time that he was teaching elementary geography. His subsequent professional activities ranged from work in climatology and geomorphology to the careful examination of the Mississippi River Delta and worldwide beach studies. He had the honor of serving as president of the Association of American Geographers (1948) and of the Geological Society of America (1957). He was a member of the faculty of Louisiana State University for forty-three years, dean of the Graduate School for thirteen years, and founder and director for seventeen years of the Coastal Studies Institute.

Richard was proud of his Scottish ancestry; it could be traced back to Robert Russell, one of the early settlers in New England and the first person to be buried in the old "South" cemetery at Andover, Massachusetts. Richard's grandfather, Joel Russell, sailed from Bangor, Maine, landing in San Francisco on January 4, 1850. After two years of gold mining in northern California, he obtained land on San Francisco Bay near Hayward and became a Superior Court judge in Alameda County. Richard's grandmother, Carrie Bartlett, came from Old Town,

369

Maine, by way of Panama to teach Latin in an elementary
school near Hayward. Richard's father, Frederick James, was
born on August 7, 1867.

Richard's maternal grandmother, Martha Brennan, a widow
with three daughters, sailed from New England in 1870 via
Panama to San Francisco to marry a childhood sweetheart
named Morril, and the family home was established in Alameda.
The youngest daughter, Nellie Potter Morril, was the mother of
Richard Joel Russell, who was born in Hayward, California,
November 16, 1895.

Richard's father had graduated from Hastings College of
Law but he always considered that his mother had forced him
into a disdainful career. Because Richard's mother had a strong
desire to move away from a domineering mother-in-law, the
family had an auction of personal effects in early 1899, and
arranged a passage to Honolulu on a three-masted schooner.
The father obtained a temporary job in the Customs House,
but was soon given a desk in a law office. Being an excellent
linguist, he quickly mastered Cantonese and acquired a large
share of the Chinese law practice in the Hawaiian Islands. On
the death of his mother in 1902, Frederick Russell returned to
the Hayward area in order to assume responsibility of handling
his share of the estate.

Richard's early education was not orthodox. Two years
were spent at Punahou kindergarten rather than in grammar
school because his mother admired the teachers. On the return
to California, Richard was enrolled in a private school in Oakland, California, where he was taught a little German. The
next experiment was enrollment in Dixon's Business College,
where at the age of nine, he learned to write Gregg shorthand
and mastered the touch system on a Smith Premier typewriter.
The next move was to Alameda because his mother knew the
second-grade teacher. He spent a few days in that grade and
within a month was active in the fifth grade. The next move

was back to Hayward where his mother knew the sixth grade teacher. From then through high school, his education became more regular.

By the time Richard had reached the eighth grade, the family moved to the "ranch," the original land acquired by his grandfather. Richard had the responsibility of breaking the ranch horses, both to saddle and harness, and he rode horseback to school as well as to many camp sites. Other farm chores involved milking cows, which were acquired in growing numbers and left little time for school until his father hired a Swiss milker. About this time, his father began to acquire automobiles; but Richard's first love was a rubber-tired buggy and Ruby, a Thoroughbred of Stanford stock. By the time Richard was fifteen years old, he had learned to drive an automobile and later won a county fair dirt track race, in which he averaged sixty miles per hour for twenty-five miles.

Hayward High School with an enrollment of about one hundred students and a staff of five teachers, offered a classical education. The athletic program was so small that Richard served as track captain for four years and won letters each year in football (rugby). In addition to ranch chores, athletic activities, and studies, Richard built up a business as a professional photographer, handling all of the commercial work for Hayward's three drug stores and taking pictures of houses for rent or sale by real estate agents. Income from this activity as well as from available temporary jobs permitted him to carry on experiments in color photography.

At the completion of high school in 1914, Russell had no desire to enroll in college. Instead, he spent about a year working in lumber yards where he designed small structures such as barns and chicken houses, made step ladders and baseball bats, and replaced window panes. While on a hunting trip in the Coast Ranges, a forest supervisor aroused Richard's interest for an outdoor career in forestry, which resulted in his enrollment in the College of Agriculture at the University of California (Berkeley) in 1915. In his sophomore year he took a required course in geology that stimulated him to take additional geology courses with the reluctant permission of his advisor in forestry.

Richard, one of the earliest students to be drafted for service in World War I, was discharged immediately for physical disability; he had a crooked left arm that had resulted from a compound fracture of the elbow that had been set incorrectly. After futile attempts to enlist in several military units, he was finally accepted in the naval reserve, where he was trained as a gunner's mate for assignment in the Merchant Marine. Although no openings were immediately available, he was finally accepted in the officer's class and commissioned ensign to teach seamanship and gunnery.

At the conclusion of World War I, Richard returned to the University of California, selected vertebrate paleontology as a major under John C. Merriam, and graduated with honors in 1920. In the summers of 1919 and 1920, he accompanied Chester Stock in collecting vertebrate fossils in Nevada and Oregon. After graduation, he had a choice of a graduate teaching fellowship in geography or in geology: He accepted the former because it involved only five quiz sections per week; the geology fellowship involved fifteen hours a week with the class in mineralogy. During the first year of Richard's teaching fellowship in geography, Professor Ruliff S. Holway became incapacitated and Richard had to take part of Holway's teaching assignments. He had taken almost no courses in geography and he had to learn as he taught. In 1923, Carl O. Sauer succeeded Professor Holway and Richard was advanced to the rank of Associate. He instructed large classes in elementary geography as well as a course in the geography of California and various courses in geomorphology. In 1920, John C. Merriam became president of the Carnegie Institution and Richard changed his major to petrography and structural geology under George D. Louderback. In 1926 he completed his Ph.D. thesis, "Basin Range Structure and Stratigraphy of the Warner Range, Northeastern California."

Richard Russell had definite convictions that new Ph.D.'s should not remain on the faculty of their alma mater; thus, in 1926, he accepted the position of Associate Professor of Geology at Texas Technological College at Lubbock. There he found that his personal library was larger than the school's geologic library and that his research activities were curtailed by a heavy teaching load. On the positive side, he found plant leaves and vertebrate teeth in nearby Permian and Triassic beds and he encouraged one of his able students to study paleobotany. He found the Carlsbad Caverns a fascinating place for geological observations, and trips to the Colorado Rockies sparked an interest in nivation and solifluction. Because his "Climates of California" (1926) had attracted considerable favorable comment, he used much of his spare time in Lubbock to compile the "Dry Climates of the United States" (1931), which emphasized frequency of median values as more significant than classification based on averages.

Henry V. Howe, an old friend during graduate school days at Berkeley, had started a department of geology at Louisiana State University in 1922 and he persuaded the LSU administration that Russell was needed to develop the field of geography. Richard was delighted at this opportunity, and in September 1928, he arrived in Baton Rouge where he spent the remainder of his professional career. Although he had many invitations to consider transfer to other institutions, he was supremely happy at LSU. He and Howe made a remarkable team and together built a major school of geology and geography. They were particularly proud of the modern university library that grew from two hundred thousand to well over one million volumes. Richard was gratified with the growth of the Department of

Geography, particularly in graduate studies and research. The establishment of the Louisiana Department of Conservation with its series of geology bulletins provided publication facilities for many of the studies of the Mississippi River Delta. Richard enjoyed the interdepartmental freedom at LSU; one could be a professor of geography yet teach structural geology and serve as a major professor for doctoral candidates in either geology or geography. Furthermore, research support was generous and the physical facilities excellent.

Russell's introduction to land forms was at Hayward High School where he had a course in physical geography based on a textbook written by William Morris Davis, and his first class in geography at Berkeley was strictly Davisian physiography. When Richard was a teaching assistant in geography in 1921, he selected the Donaldsonville, Louisiana, quadrangle as an example of "old age" topography, produced after the mountains and hills had worn away and the river wandered aimlessly on its floodplain. In 1925, Richard participated in a seminar given by Davis at Berkeley, and he became very critical of the Davisian methods of explanatory description of land forms based on superficial observations that were subjected to deductive methods. In Russell's fieldwork in the Warner Range, he used deductive methods during his first field trips but found that the fundamental structural features of the range history came as the result of good honest inductive study. This was not surprising as Russell was a protégé of George D. Louderback who counseled his students to keep open minds and to collect field data diligently before arriving at final conclusions. Carl O. Sauer had appreciable influence on Richard in emphasizing that points of view differing from those of Davis must be considered; in the summer of 1928 Russell participated with Albrecht Penck in field trips to many parts of California with particular emphasis on alpine land forms in the Sierra Nevada. That same summer, Richard met Davis again in Berkeley, and he later admitted that Davis did have a clear head and keen mind, but that the Davis methods of deduction were like chess— worthwhile, if one enjoys it.

After Russell moved to Louisiana, Davis asked him to "try and find out why the Mississippi River follows such a straight course below New Orleans." In later years, Richard reminisced that this request from an old friend was an important reason for starting serious studies on the floodplain and delta of the lower Mississippi River. The fact that Davis asked this specific question illustrated that even though he was old in years, he posed interesting and imaginative problems—and yearned for their solutions. It was some years later that the question was answered ["Aspects of Alluvial Morphology" (1957)] when subsurface data of the lower delta were available. The Mississippi River is comparatively straight below New Orleans because the channel is fixed in clay that was deposited ahead of an earlier delta some 4000 years ago; the present Mississippi River has been unable to scour its bed and therefore does not meander.

Russell's first paper described horizontal offsets along the Hayward fault, which was cited thirty years later in the U.S. Geological Survey's publication covering the Hayward quadrangle. (Richard was delighted to note that he could identify the house where he was born on the geologic map.) Many of his early papers dealt with climatology and, much to his surprise, these contributions were read widely. In 1931, while attending the International Geographical Congress in Paris, he discovered that he was considered a famous climatologist. Russell had written these papers more as a pleasant hobby involving little effort, but in five successive years he was offered a senior chair of climatology in the United States. He wanted to be a geomorphologist and did not believe he was prepared to accept a chair in his hobby field. In contrast, he was disappointed that little attention seemed to have been given to his early contributions to geomorphology; in 1937, however, he was given the first Wallace A. Atwood Award by the Association of American Geographers because of the publication of the "Physiography of the Lower Mississippi River Delta" (1936). This scholarly and comprehensive report clearly established Russell as one of the leading geomorphologists in America.

In 1928 serious geologic studies of the Mississippi River Delta were made possible by the availability of new topographic quadrangle maps and aerial photographs. At first the delta seemed flat and uninteresting to Richard after field studies in California and the Great Basin. In 1929, Fred Kniffen came to Louisiana State University from the University of California (Berkeley) with an excellent background in anthropology and geomorphology, and he and Russell started searching the swamps and coastal waters for Indian artifacts to establish dates. One memorable trip involved a visit to Larto Lake in central Louisiana, resulting in the proposal that this lake was a remnant channel of the Mississippi River miles from its present location.

"Physiography of the Lower Mississippi River Delta" was one of several contributions on delta studies published by the Louisiana Department of Conservation in which a combination of geomorphological, archeological and botanical reports were combined in a single bulletin. Russell's discussion in the 1936 publication emphasized the concept that the weight of the sedimentary deposits of successive deltas caused local downwarping of the earth's crust, thus developing a geosyncline. The physiography of the delta is characterized by dominant natural levees that form the high land; the gentle slopes of the natural levees lead away from the river to marshes, swamps, and open waters. Upstream, the floodplains have tributaries; downstream, the deltas have distributaries and abandoned channels that have been downtilted in the direction of the distal parts of old deltas. Meanders are present only on the floodplains where the channels encounter material deposited during the same cycle of alluviation and where the banks are lined by natural levees. He emphasized that the bottoms of large lakes are uniformly hard sand whereas those of small lakes are silty or oozy.

During the 1930s when petroleum resources of Louisiana required new appraisals of property values, remote and hardly used swamp and marshlands suddenly became valuable and questions arose about ownership. The state had title to navigable waterways as of the date of its admittance to the Union in 1812, and many titles hinged on the boundaries of water bodies at that time. Russell's noneconomic fieldwork in alluvial morphology focussed attention on him as having the best background to serve as an expert witness in the various land-title lawsuits. He and Henry Howe presented evidence that won state title to extensive waterbodies in southwestern Louisiana. One by-product of this activity was the addition of the term "chenier" (ridge of sand) to the terminology of geomorphology; it appeared in a geological bulletin (No. 6), published in 1935, on Cameron and Vermilion parishes. Another was a succession of other investigations for legal purposes, resulting in fees that in some years exceeded Russell's university salary.

Russell regarded the field experience in preparation for the witness stand as a rewarding research career. In order to establish precise locations for necessary boring, land surveyors and geologists had to cut trails through the swamps or walk miles on unstable floating marsh. In some cases, botanists, chemists, and other specialists were included in the field parties. No investigation was undertaken without a preliminary reconnaissance to determine if the litigant appeared to be scientifically correct, or, if there were refusals, to permit scientific publication of any data that were obtained. "Louisiana Stream Patterns" (1939) resulted from such a study.

The work of the Louisiana Geological Survey had the enthusiastic support of the petroleum industry, which sponsored a bill in the state legislature trebling their fee for drilling permits in order to expand the Survey's program. Henry Howe and Richard Russell felt compelled to refuse this expansion of their program because of the difficulty in training personnel to find and interpret geologic evidence in the essentially flat, deeply weathered, densely vegetated, and deep-soil region of the Gulf Coast. Harold N. Fisk, who appeared on the scene in 1935 after receiving his doctoral degree involving volcanic rocks in the Columbia River region, proved to be an exception. Within a few months, Fisk was making important discoveries in central Louisiana and promptly formulated an explanation of Quaternary deposits that received widespread acceptance. A close personal association soon developed between Fisk and Russell, involving work not only in Louisiana but on the Mississippi, Ohio, and Tennessee rivers and along the Atlantic Coastal Plain. Each published a number of papers, separately as a rule, emphasizing Gulf Coast Quaternary history. A number of their reports went into the files of the Mississippi River Commission that dealt with the problems of the levees along the river.

As Russell pursued his studies of the Quaternary terraces upstream along the Mississippi River, he became involved with exposures of loess—homogeneous, unstratified, slightly indurated and porous calcareous sedimentary rock composed of particles of silt size, yellowish or buff in color, that tend to crop out in vertical faces. Most American geologists favored the concept that, during the Ice Age, rivers transported to broad floodplains fine glacial debris, which was picked up by winds and deposited on or near adjacent bluffs; thus loess is an eolian deposit. Richard was convinced that along the central and southern Mississippi River, the field relations demonstrated that the parent materials were terrace deposits similar to the backswamp clays of the Recent Mississippi River; these weathered to brown loam that crept downslope and accumulated in valleys or as mantles on the bluffs. The abundant calcium carbonate found in them was contributed and moved about by groundwater and percolating waters. After an exhaustive literature search, he published "Lower Mississippi Valley Loess" (1944), pointing out similarities to the European loess exposures. He had the satisfaction that many European investigators subsequently accepted his interpretation but he admitted that his American colleagues, in general, were skeptical.

Russell loved to travel and as his university salary and consulting fees increased, he began a series of foreign trips, starting in 1931 with the International Geographical Congress in Paris. In 1937, he and Henry Howe attended the Geological Congress in Moscow where they presented papers on the Gulf Coast geosyncline and participated in field excursions across the Caucasus to Soviet Armenia and to Novaya Zemlya. After his return from this trip, Russell received the Atwood Award for his paper on the Mississippi River Delta, which enabled him to return to Europe in January 1938 to study the Rhone Delta ["Geomorphology of the Rhone Delta" (1942)] in which he noted that the chief contrasts between the Mississippi and Rhone deltas were quantitative; the ratio in area, as limited by marginal distributary streams, is about 20:1. Although there are striking rearrangements in channel patterns in each delta in modern geologic time and coarse sediment is more extensive in the Rhone Delta, channel patterns in both depend on previously existing channels. Both deltas face tideless seas and the modern drainage patterns indicate a decided increase in the Mississippi River Delta whereas the Rhone Delta has remained constant in area; also, the "bird's foot" delta of the Mississippi River is in contrast to the smooth shores and traditional deltoid shape of the Rhone.

After the completion of the field studies of the Rhone Delta, Russell attended the International Geographical Congress in Amsterdam and visited his old friend, Albrecht Penck in

Germany. In 1937 and again in 1938, he saw most of the coast of Norway and much of Finland in both summer and winter. Ten years later (1948) he attended the Geological Congress in Great Britain and made field trips to Wales. This was followed in 1952 by the Geological Congress in Algiers with field trips in the western Sahara and back through the Atlas Mountains. Russell was curious to find out if the Meander River in Anatolia actually meandered. In 1938 he had been unsuccessful in obtaining a visa; in 1952, however, he was appointed to the faculty at Istanbul and in exchange for a minimum requirement of delivering three lectures received the necessary documents permitting field investigations in Turkey. He was delighted to discover that the Great Meander is an excellent type locality for meanders.

The next Geological Congress was held in Mexico City in 1956 where Russell served as co-chairman of the Geomorphology Section. He was also a guest of the Brazilian Government in a memorable Amazon excursion. Two years later, he was active in a Congress of the Association of Sedimentologists in Geneva and Lausanne. In 1959, under the financial sponsorship of the National Science Foundation, Richard was sent to Indonesia to serve as an advisor to the Council for Sciences of Indonesia, and after visiting many centers of research in Java, Sumatra, and Celebes, he wrote *Report on Scientific Research in Indonesia* and many of his recommendations were effected in an amazingly short time. The International Geographical Congress in 1960 gave him the opportunity to join field symposia in Sweden on alluvial and coastal morphology. The following year, he organized a symposium, "Pacific Island Terraces: Eustatic?", for the Honolulu Pacific Science Congress, and he served as co-chairman of the Section of Geomorphology at the INQUA Congress in Warsaw. In 1962, Russell presided at the Geomorphology Section of the Kuala Lumpur meetings of the International Union and he participated in excursions that were made along the coast of Malaya.

Russell was a member of the Committee on Geophysics and Geography for the Department of Defense and a member of the Committee on Geography, Advisory to the Office of Naval Research. In 1949, he learned that progress in coastal research was lagging seriously in defense programs and he was urged by army and navy officers to give his attention to this problem. This offer came as he was named Dean of the Graduate School at LSU, but with the assistance of James P. Morgan, a proposal was presented to the Geography Branch of the Office of Naval Research for a study of trafficability of Louisiana coastal marshes. This study led to the establishment in 1954 of the Coastal Studies Institute with Russell as director. The program expanded rapidly, supported by the federal and state governments and by industrial groups. No classified research was accepted in the program, nor was there any appreciable deviation from basic research in shallow coastal waters and adjacent land areas.

Russell shifted his interest from floodplains and deltas to sea coasts in 1956. His first objective was the Lesser Antilles because that island arc possessed volcanic and organic debris beaches typical of oceanic islands as well as quartz–sand beaches characteristic of continental shores. But he soon became involved in cemented beach material that crops out at about mean sea level in areas of small tidal range. Commonly, several bands of this beach rock are separated by shallow strips of water with the oldest bands seaward and the youngest under the beach; the outer bands are tough and durable in contrast to the friable inner band. All beach rock localities occur where there is coastal recession and the groundwater is heavily charged with calcium carbonate, the cement of the beach rock. The initial studies of beach rock were on St. Lucia, but these led to additional studies in the Mediterranean, the coasts of northern and southern Africa, various Pacific and Indian Ocean islands, New Zealand, and both the east and west coasts of Australia. The work in western Australia revealed long bands of Pleistocene beach rock

20 feet above the present beach; strands of beach rock at the same elevation on islands in the Indian Ocean and West Indies strongly indicate crustal stability in these three areas extending back to the Pleistocene [*River Plains and Sea Coasts* (1967)].

Much of the early literature on sea coasts was concerned with their classification, but Russell firmly believed that taxonomy should follow the acquisition of precise and factual information. Much of his last years of field studies were spent obtaining background information to enable him to identify problems related to sea coasts. He emphasized that the glacio-eustatic changes of level between land and sea by the melting of continental ice sheets raised the level of oceans by 450 feet during the Recent rise of sea level. As a result, all sea coasts were drowned. Some are smooth with barrier islands fronting linear lagoons, but where the rocks are weak and poorly consolidated, other features considered proof of emergence are really demonstrations of the efficacy of wave attack and related shores processes that wear away headlands and fill embayments. In contrast, where resistant and durable rocks are exposed to wave attack, the forces of marine action are almost powerless to change the shorelines. Russell's reconnaissance investigations convinced him that the majority of beaches are diminishing in volume, probably resulting from the Recent still stand in sea level. When the seas were rising rapidly from their pre-Recent low level (eight to twelve inches per century), they encountered old coastal plains and new surfaces were flooded. These surfaces were the sources of the sand that was transported shoreward by wave action. But when still stand was reached, new sand supplies were no longer encountered [*River Plains and Sea Coasts* (1967)].

Writing for particular audiences was a challenge that Richard readily accepted and enjoyed. His "Climatic Change through the Ages" in the 1941 Yearbook of the Department of Agriculture was aimed at the level of the "intelligent farmer." Two books were issued by the Louisiana Department of Education, *The Mississippi River* for the fourth grade level and *Louisiana—Our Treasure Ground* for the eighth grade. Chapters in *The Pacific Ranges* and *The Sierra Nevada* were directed to the general public. His wide travels formed the basis of *Culture Worlds,* a widely used text for college geography; Fred B. Kniffen was joint author for three editions; Evelyn Pruitt of the Office of Naval Research participated in both the second and third editions.

Russell, elected to the National Academy of Sciences in 1959, was active in the affairs of the Division of Earth Sciences of the National Research Council, starting in 1936 when it was called the Division of Geology and Geography. He was one of the leaders in broadening the activities in 1953 and getting a more inclusive name for the expanding role of activities by geochemists, geophysicists, meteorologists, soil scientists, and oceanographers. He was chairman of the Division between 1954 and 1956, but he involved himself only with those committees that held a special interest for him.

One such committee was the Committee on Geography, Advisory to the Office of Naval Research, on which he served from 1949 to 1963. This committee did many useful things for the ONR but, as the navy budgets were tightened, the committee was dissolved. One of its major achievements was to assess the navy's need for research geographers, and it recommended that ONR support a program to enable young geographers to do research work outside the United States. The objective was to develop a group of people with first-hand knowledge and active contacts in some country where the navy was likely to maintain an interest. This led to the establishment of the Foreign Research Program, Screening Committee, that started in 1955 and continued until 1972. Richard served on every screening committee, except in 1959 when he was in Indonesia. He also served actively for ten years on the Committee on Waste Disposal, Advisory to the Atomic Energy Commission, starting in 1955. This committee had many ups and downs, but Richard took the work seriously and made one inspection trip alone to visit AEC installations to see what research was being done on methods of disposing of radioactive waste products. For some years, the annual meeting of the Division of Earth Sciences took a full day for committee reports, budget review, and rambling discussion. With Richard as prime mover, the annual meeting was converted to an hour of business followed by an extensive symposium on a timely research topic in the earth sciences.

Russell was the recipient of many honors during his long career as a geomorphologist and geographer. In 1943, he was Distinguished Lecturer ("Gulf Coast Geosyncline") for the American Association of Petroleum Geologists and in 1958 National Lecturer ("Instability of Sea Level") for Sigma Xi. He was a Special Fellow of the Belgian American Foundation and was honored by membership in the Academy of Natural Sciences of Göttingen, the Royal Danish Academy of Science, Royal Dutch Geographical Society, the Belgian Society of Geology, Paleontology and Hydrology, and the German Academy of Sciences. In 1961, Queen Louise of Sweden presented him the Vega Medal of the Royal Swedish Society of Anthropology and Geography, and in 1962 he received the Cullum Medal of the American Geographical Society. He was Hitchcock Lecturer at the University of California (Berkeley) in 1965; the subject of these lectures resulted in *River Plains and Sea Coasts,* published in 1967. The U.S. Navy Distinguished Service Award was given to Richard in 1967.

Russell had the reputation of being a superior but rigorous teacher. His conversation was ordinarily free and easy, but he could pour forth a tremendous sales pitch when he thought that the occasion warranted it. He was a good story teller, seasoned with his low keyed dry humor, who often saw the wry funny side of serious situations. He had a reputation for expertise in Chinese restaurants and could steer his friends into superb combinations of plates. He liked to adapt himself completely to the life in foreign countries and in some of the small places in Turkey, the natives thought that he was a Turk. When he was in Indonesia, he broke away from American ties as much as possible so that he could live like an Indonesian. He became a member of the Masonic Order while a student at Berkeley and was affiliated with Phi Kappa Sigma, Gamma Alpha, Phi Sigma, Sigma Xi, and Phi Kappa Phi. He was very active in Theta Tau, an engineering fraternity with a chapter at Berkeley limited to mining engineers and geologists, and he rose through the ranks to become Grand Regent between 1928 and 1932. He was a member of the Cosmos Club in Washington, D.C., where he usually stayed during his many trips to that city; in his spare moments, he could usually be found at the club playing billiards.

Richard Joel Russell married Mary Dorothy King of Covina, California, in 1924, and their son, Benjamin James, lives in Hermosa Beach, California. Dorothy died in Baton Rouge in 1936. Richard married Josephine Burke of Wabash, Indiana, in 1940, and had four sons, Robert Burke of Foley, Alabama, Charles Douglas of New Orleans, John Walter of Dayton, Ohio, and Thomas William of Montreal, Canada. Richard is survived by a sister, Helen (Mrs. George W. McCollum), of Oakland, California.

RICHARD JOEL RUSSELL left extensive biographical data that have been most helpful in the preparation of this biographical memoir. Correspondence from Russell, largely written from Lubbock, Texas, was loaned by A. O. Woodford, and William R. Thurston provided information on Russell's contribution to the National Research Council. The bibliography was assembled by Romaine L. Kupfer and the staff of the Coastal Studies Institute, Louisiana State University.

BIBLIOGRAPHY

KEY TO ABBREVIATIONS

Am. Assoc. Pet. Geol. Bull. = American Association of Petroleum Geologists Bulletin

Am. Meteorol. Soc. Bull. = American Meteorological Society Bulletin

Assoc. Am. Geogr. Ann. = Association of American Geographers Annals

C. R. Congr. Int. Géogr. = Comptes Rendus du Congrès International de Géographie

C. R. Congr. Int. Géol. = Comptes Rendus du Congrès International de Géologie

Coastal Stud. Bull. = Louisiana State University Coastal Studies Bulletin

Coastal Stud. Inst. Tech. Rep. = Louisiana State University Coastal Studies Institute Technical Report

Geogr. Rev. = Geographical Review

Geol. Soc. Am. Bull. = Geological Society of America Bulletin

J. Geogr. = Journal of Geography

K. Ned. Aardrijkskd. Genoot. Tijdschr. = K. Nederlandsch Aardrijkskundig Genootschap, Amsterdam, Tijdschrift

La. Conserv. Rev. = Louisiana Conservation Review

La. Dep. Conserv. Geol. Bull. = Louisiana Department of Conservation, Geology Bulletin

Proc. Conf. Coastal Eng. = Proceedings, Conference on Coastal Engineering

Univ. Calif. Publ. Geogr. = University of California Publications in Geography

Z. Geomorphol. = Zeitschrift für Geomorphologie

1926

Recent horizontal offsets along the Hayward fault. Journal of Geology, 34:507–11.

Climates of California. Univ. Calif. Publ. Geogr., 2:73–84.

1927

Landslide lakes on the northwestern Great Basin. Univ. Calif. Publ. Geogr., 2:231–54.

The land forms of Surprise Valley, northwestern Great Basin. Univ. Calif. Publ. Geogr., 2:323–58.

1928

Basin range structure and stratigraphy of the Warner Range, northeastern California. University of California Publications in Geological Sciences, 17:387–496.

1931

Dry climates of the United States. I. Climatic map. Univ. Calif. Publ. Geogr., 5:1–41.

Geomorphological evidence of a climatic boundary. Science, 74: 484–85.

1932

Dry climates of the United States. II. Frequency of dry and desert years 1901–20. Univ. Calif. Publ. Geogr., 5:245–74.

Significance of Baer's law. Science, 75:584–85.

Land forms of San Gorgonio Pass, southern California. Univ. Calif. Publ. Geogr., 6:23–121.

1933

Fixing the facts of climatic distribution. J. Geogr., 32:164–70.

Zachary, Louisiana, tornado of March 31, 1933. Am. Meteorol. Soc. Bull., 14:126–31.

Hailstorm of April 20, 1933, Baton Rouge, Louisiana. Am. Meteorol. Soc. Bull., 14:177–78.

Alpine land forms of western United States. Geol. Soc. Am. Bull., 44:927–50.

Larto Lake, an old Mississippi River channel. La. Conserv. Rev., 3:18–21, 46.

1934

Climatic years. Geogr. Rev., 24:92–103.

With R. D. Russell. Dust storm of April 12, 1934, Baton Rouge, La. Monthly Weather Review, 62:162–63.

1935

With H. V. Howe. Cheniers of southwestern Louisiana. Geogr. Rev., 25:449–61.

Earthquakes. Proceedings, Louisiana Academy of Sciences, 2:1–7.

With H. V. Howe and J. H. McGuirt. Physiography of coastal southwest Louisiana. In: Reports on the geology of Cameron and Vermilion parishes. La. Dep. Conserv. Geol. Bull., 6:1–72.

1936

The desert-rainfall factor in denudation. C. R. Congr. Int. Géol. (16th, Washington, D.C., 1933), 2:753–63.

Physiography of the lower Mississippi River Delta. In: Reports on the geology of Plaquemines and St. Bernard parishes. La. Dep. Conserv. Geol. Bull., 8:3–193.

With C. F. Dohm. Bibliography. In: Reports on the geology of Plaquemines and St. Bernard parishes. La. Dep. Conserv. Geol. Bull., 8:279–320.

Suggestions Concerning Desirable Lines of Research in Geology and Geography. Special Publication, National Research Council, pp. 49–50. Washington, D.C., National Academy of Sciences.

Climatology of Brown's hypothesis on origin of Gulf border salt deposits. Am. Assoc. Pet. Geol. Bull., 20:821–24.

1938

Physiography of Iberville and Ascension parishes. In: Reports on the geology of Iberville and Ascension parishes. La. Dep. Conserv. Geol. Bull., 13:3–86.

Quaternary surfaces in Louisiana. C. R. Congr. Int. Géogr. (15th, Amsterdam, 1938), 2(sec. F):406–12.

Suggestions on Geographic Classification of Surface Configuration. Annual Report for 1937–1938, National Research Council, Report of Division on Geology and Geography, Appendix N, pp. 3–4.

1939

Louisiana and the Ice Age. La. Conserv. Rev., 8:14–16, 18.

With R. D. Russell. Mississippi River Delta sedimentation. In: *Recent Marine Sediments,* ed. by P. D. Trask, pp. 153–77. Tulsa, American Association of Petroleum Geologists.

Morphologie des Mississippideltas. Geographische Zeitschrift, 45: 281–93.

Louisiana stream patterns. Am. Assoc. Pet. Geol. Bull., 23:1199–1227.

1940

Impressions of the Soviet Union. The Gear of Theta Tau, 29(2): 22–27.

Quaternary history of Louisiana.   Geol. Soc. Am. Bull., 51:1199–1234.

Gulf Coast geosyncline: America's great petroleum reserve.   C. R. Congr. Int. Géol. (17th, Moscow, 1937), 4:255–57; also in Russian, pp. 269–72.

1941

Modern channels of the Mississippi River.   Oil, 1:28–30, 44, 52.

Climatic change through the ages.   In: *Climate and Man,* pp. 67–97, 1941 Yearbook of Agriculture. Washington, D.C., U.S. Department of Agriculture.

1942

With Harold N. Fisk.   Isostatic effects of Mississippi River Delta sedimentation. International Union of Geodesy and Geophysics General Assembly (7th, Washington, 1939), Appendix III, pp. 56–59.

Geomorphology of the Rhone Delta.   Assoc. Am. Geogr. Ann., 32: 149–254; re-issued in Bobbs-Merrill Geography Reprint Series as G-199.

Flotant. Geogr. Rev., 32:74–98.

1943

Freeze-and-thaw frequencies in the United States.   American Geophysical Union Transactions, 24:125–33.

1944

Lower Mississippi Valley loess.   Geol. Soc. Am. Bull., 55:1–40.

Origin of loess—Reply.   American Journal of Science, 242:447–50.

The Mississippi River. Baton Rouge, State Department of Education. 120 pp.

1945

Climates of Texas.   Assoc. Am. Geogr. Ann., 35:37–52.

Post-war geography.   J. Geogr., 44:301–12.

1946

A Geografía de Após-Guerra.   Boletin Geográfico (Brazil), 4(37): 44–50.

Climatic transitions and contrasts.   In: *The Pacific Coast Ranges,* ed. by R. Peattie, pp. 357–79.   New York, Vanguard Press Inc.

1947

Sierra climate. In: *The Sierra Nevada,* ed. by R. Peattie, pp. 323–40. New York, Vanguard Press Inc.

1948

Coast of Louisiana. Société belge de Géologie, Paléontologie, et d'Hydrologie (Brussels) Bulletin, 57:380–94.

1949

Geographical geomorphology. (Presidential address) Assoc. Am. Geogr. Ann., 39:1–11.

1950

The Pliocene–Pleistocene boundary in Louisiana. C. R. Congr. Int. Géol. (18th, London, 1948), part 9, pp. 94–96.

Some problems in Pleistocene climate. In: Proceedings, 6th Plains Archeological Conference (1948), ed. by J. D. Jennings, pp. 39–42. Utah University Anthropological Papers, no. 11.

1951

Louisiana, Our Treasure Ground. Baton Rouge, State Department of Education. 149 pp.

With Fred B. Kniffen. *Culture Worlds.* New York, Macmillan Inc. 591 pp.

[Memorial to] Stanley Matthews McDonald. Am. Assoc. Pet. Geol. Bull., 35:1110–11.

1952

With J. P. Morgan. Photo-interpretation keys of selected coastal marshland features. Coastal Stud. Inst. Tech. Rep., 1:1–14.

Recent geology of coastal Louisiana. Proc. Conf. Coastal Eng. (2d, Houston, 1951), ed. by J. W. Johnson, pp. 101–10.

1953

Coastal advance and retreat in Louisiana. C. R. Congr. Int. Géol. (19th, Algiers, 1952), sec. 4, pp. 109–18.

Can higher education survive? Conference of Deans of Southern Graduate Schools. 12 pp. (booklet)

1954

Chairman. [1st] Coastal Geography Conference. Washington, D.C., Office of Naval Research. 71 pp.

Alluvial morphology of Anatolian rivers. Assoc. Am. Geogr. Ann., 44:363–91.

Alluvial morphology. Istanbul University Geography Institute Review (International Edition), no. 1, pp. 28–49.

1955

Editor. Guides to southeastern geology. Prepared for the 1955 annual meeting of the Geological Society of America and associated societies. New York, Geological Society of America. 592 pp.

Notes on loess in Mississippi and along U.S. 61 below Vicksburg. *Ibid.,* pp. 301–6.

1956

Environmental changes through forces independent of man. In: *Man's Role in Changing the Face of the Earth,* ed. by W. L. Thomas, Jr., pp. 453–70. Chicago, University of Chicago Press.

With H. O'R. Sternberg. Fracture patterns in the Amazon and Mississippi valleys. C. R. Congr. Int. Géogr. (17th, Washington, D.C., 1952), pp. 380–85.

1957

Instability of sea level. (Sigma Xi National Lecture, 1956–1957) American Scientist, 45:414–30.

Aspects of alluvial morphology. K. Ned. Aardrijkskd. Genoot. Tijdschr. (Leiden), 74:377–88.

Aspects of alluvial morphology. In: *The Earth, Its Crust, and Its Atmosphere—Geomorphological and Geophysical Studies,* pp. 163–74. (Presented to Professor Jacoba B. L. Hol on July 6, 1957) Leiden, Netherlands, E. J. Brill.

1958

Caribbean beach studies—preliminary notes on Caribbean beach rock. Coastal Stud. Inst. Tech. Rep. 11, part A. 15 pp.

Long, straight beaches. Ecologae Geological Helvetiae, 51:591–98.

Geological geomorphology. (Presidential address)   Geol. Soc. Am. Bull., 69:1–21.

1959

Chairman and editor. Second Coastal Geography Conference. (Coastal Studies Institute, Louisiana State University, 1959) Washington, D.C., Office of Naval Research. 472 pp.

With others. Field excursion itineraries (Louisiana) [Guidebook]. In: Second Coastal Geography Conference (1959), R. J. Russell, chairman, pp. 361–422.

Alluvial morphology of Louisiana salt marshes.   Salt Marsh Conference, Proceedings (1958).   University of Georgia Marine Institute (Sapelo Island), pp. 29–31.

Caribbean beach rock observation. Z. Geomorphol., 3(3):227–36.

1960

Report on scientific research in Indonesia.   Council for Sciences of Indonesia (M.I.P.I., Djakarta) Bull. 2. 74 pp.

Research needs and possibilities in the field of geology.   U.S. House of Representatives, 86th Congr., 2d Sess., H.R. No. 2226, Panel on Science and Technology, pp. 13–18.

Preliminary notes on Caribbean beach rock. Transactions of the 2d Caribbean Geological Conference (Mayaguez, Puerto Rico, 1959), pp. 43–49.

Instability of sea level.   In: *Science in Progress,* 11th ser., ed. by H. S. Taylor, pp. 39–59. New Haven, Yale University Press.

1961

Editor with others.   Louisiana coastal marsh ecology.   Coastal Stud. Inst. Tech. Rep. 14. 273 pp.

With Fred B. Kniffen and E. L. Pruitt.   *Culture Worlds—Brief Edition.*   New York, Macmillan Inc. 476 pp.

Editor. Pacific island terraces: eustatic? Z. Geomorphol. Suppl., 3:106 pp.

1962

Origin of beach rock. In: *1st National Coastal and Shallow Water Conference* (1961), pp. 454–56. Washington, D.C., National Science Foundation and Office of Naval Research.

Origin of beach rock. Z. Geomorphol., 6(1):1–16.

Coastal studies. Z. Geomorphol., 6:351–52.

Beach rock: geological observations. In: *Guidebook—Field Trip to Peninsula of Yucatan, 1962*, pp. 64–72. New Orleans, La., New Orleans Geological Society.

1963

Recent recession of tropical coasts. Science, 139:9–15.

Beach rock. Journal of Tropical Geography (Malaya), 17:24–27.

1964

Techniques of eustasy studies. Z. Geomorphol., 8(special issue):25–42.

Duration of the Quaternary and its subdivisions. Proceedings of the National Academy of Sciences, 52:790–96.

Mass-movement in contrasting latitudes. Sixth Congress of the International Association for Quaternary Research (Warsaw, 1961), vol. 4, pp. 143–51.

1965

With W. G. McIntire. Southern hemisphere beach rock. Geogr. Rev., 55:17–45.

With W. G. McIntire. Beach cusps. Geol. Soc. Am. Bull., 76:307–20.

With W. G. McIntire. *Australian Tidal Flats*. Coastal Studies Series no. 12. Baton Rouge, Louisiana State University Press. 48 pp.

Memorial to Harold N. Fisk. Geol. Soc. Am. Bull., 76:P53–P58.

1966

With W. G. McIntire. *Barbuda Reconnaissance*. Coastal Studies Series no. 16. Baton Rouge, Louisiana State University Press. 53 pp.

Coral cap of Barbados. K. Ned. Aardrijkskd. Genoot. Tijdschr. (Leiden), 83:298–302.

With C. J. Sonu. Topographic changes in the surf zone profile. Proc. Conf. Coastal Eng. (10th, Tokyo, 1966), 1:502–24.

River and Delta Morphology. Coastal Studies Series no. 20. Baton Rouge, Louisiana State University Press. 55 pp.

1967

River Plains and Sea Coasts. Berkeley, University of California Press. 173 pp.

Origins of estuaries. In: *Estuaries,* ed. by G. H. Lauff, pp. 93–99. Publ. no. 83. Washington, D.C., American Association for the Advancement of Science.

Aspects of coastal morphology. Geografiska Annaler Ser. A, 49:299–309.

1968

Algal flats of Port Hedland, western Australia. Louisiana State University, Coastal Studies Bulletin no. 2, pp. 45–55.

Glossary of Terms Used in Fluvial, Deltaic, and Coastal Morphology and Processes. Coastal Studies Series no. 23. Baton Rouge, Louisiana State University Press. 97 pp.

Where most grains of very coarse sand and fine gravel are deposited. Sedimentology, 11:31–38.

Foreword, Küstengeomorphologie. Z. Geomorphol. Suppl., 7:v–vii.

1969

South American marine energy. Coastal Stud. Inst. Tech. Rep. 73. 31 pp.

With F. B. Kniffen and E. L. Pruitt. *Culture Worlds—Brief Edition* (revised). London, Macmillan Inc. 557 pp.

1970

Oregon and northern California coastal reconnaissance. Coastal Stud. Inst. Tech. Rep. 86. 25 pp.

Florida beaches and cemented water-table rocks. Coastal Stud. Inst. Tech. Rep. 88. 53 pp.

1971

Beaches and ground water of Cape Sable, Florida, during extreme drought. Coastal Stud. Inst. Tech. Rep. 103. 18 pp.

The coast of Louisiana. In: *Applied Coastal Geomorphology,* ed. by J. A. Steers, pp. 84–97. London, Macmillan Inc.

Contributions to McGraw-Hill *Encyclopedia of Science and Technology,* vol. 5: Coastal landforms, pp. 257–58; Escarpment, pp. 75–76; Floodplains, pp. 331–32. New York, McGraw-Hill Book Co.

HENRY CLAPP SHERMAN

October 16, 1875–October 7, 1955

BY CHARLES GLEN KING

HENRY CLAPP SHERMAN was born on a farm in Ash Grove, Virginia, near Washington, D.C., and lived there during his early school years. His parents, Franklin and Caroline Clapp Alvord Sherman, were the offspring of immigrants from Britain who settled in America during the early history of New England. A former professor of mathematics at Columbia University, F. D. Sherman prepared a record of the family in "The Sherman Ancestry, 1420–1890." In Henry's immediate family there were five brothers and five sisters.

As was true of many other American leaders, Sherman's early education was in a one-room, one-teacher, gradeless school. His educational progress was rapid, however, as illustrated by his attainment of the Bachelor of Science degree from the Maryland Agricultural College (later the University of Maryland) in 1893. During the two years that followed, he continued at Maryland in graduate studies while serving as an assistant in chemistry. He received a fellowship in chemistry at Columbia University (1895–1897), where he received his Master of Science degree in 1896. In 1897, Sherman received the Doctor of Philosophy degree from Columbia—the youngest person to be awarded that degree from the university.

He continued as an assistant in analytical chemistry during 1897–1898 and, in the summer periods of 1898–1899, he served as an assistant with Dr. W. O. Atwater in the U.S. Department of Agriculture. Sherman was particularly interested in organic analysis and the measurement of energy values. Strong friendships and mutual interests with personnel in the department continued throughout his life.

From 1899 until his retirement he served as a faculty member in the Department of Chemistry at Columbia University, successively as lecturer, instructor, adjunct professor of analytical chemistry, professor of organic analysis, professor of food chemistry, Mitchell Professor of Chemistry, and Executive Officer of the Department of Chemistry (1919–1939). The university awarded him the honorary degree of Doctor of Science in 1929.

Leaves of absence during Dr. Sherman's service at Columbia University were extended to permit him to render important services during periods of national emergency. In 1917 with the rank of major he served with the American Red Cross Mission to Russia, and from April 1, 1943, to June 30, 1944, he was Chief of the Bureau of Human Nutrition and Home Economics in the Department of Agriculture.

He often recalled with pleasure an early experience in educating the public in scientific matters when, in 1913, he served during the summer with Dr. S. N. Babcock and H. E. Alvord at the World's Columbian Exposition in Chicago.

Dr. Sherman's early association with Dr. Atwater in the Department of Agriculture stimulated an interest in the accurate analysis of foods, feeds, and related products. Thirty-six of his first thirty-eight journal papers were on this general subject during the period from 1895 to 1910. The summer periods furnished background for his early papers and eventually led him to emphasize laboratory training in quantitative organic analysis for graduate students. Dr. Arthur Thomas accepted chief responsibility in this area for the department as demands on Professor Sherman's time increased. This

Thomas did very effectively in parallel with his own teaching and intensive research in colloid chemistry.

Dr. Sherman had a similar experience with another of his research projects. Beginning in 1910, when Edward C. Kendall was his graduate student, Dr. Sherman's interest in the chemistry of enzymes, particularly in relation to the starch-splitting amylases from plant and animal sources, developed rapidly. Twenty papers appeared within the first seven years of Sherman's research in this field. Then it was gradually accepted as a major field of emphasis by his former student and continuing faculty associate, Dr. Mary L. Caldwell. Their evidence that the enzyme was essentially a pure protein was one of the important contributions (in parallel with the evidence of James B. Sumner, John H. Northrop and others) that challenged the persistent views of Richard Willstätter and others in Europe that it was possible to prepare enzymes free from protein. Sherman pointed out two basic errors in Willstätter's interpretation: He and his associates had permitted hydrolysis of protein during long periods of dialysis, and then used tests for enzyme activity that were more sensitive than the tests used for protein.

As the evidence became increasingly clear that deficiencies of protein, iron, calcium and vitamins were major health problems, Sherman began to conduct short-term experiments on balances in relation to food intake. Then, he gradually turned to long-term quantitative studies of nutrition in relation to health. He also did much to encourage greater public and professional interest in these aspects of nutrition research. Two major types of life-span studies on food intake in relation to health in albino rats were emphasized: first, a comparison of experimental diets based on definite quantities of common foods through several generations and, second, observation of the improvement that resulted from adding known quantities of specific nutrients thought to be marginally deficient. One group of rats was fed a diet (No. 16) based *solely* on one-sixth part by weight of whole milk powder plus five-sixths parts by weight of ground whole wheat, 1.3 percent of table salt and distilled water. This diet supported fairly good growth, prevented any specific signs of malnutrition, and permitted reproduction through more than 40 generations. But the record of this group of rats for early maturity, longevity and surviving offspring clearly was not as good as the record of a group fed diet No. 13, which contained one-third whole milk powder and two-thirds whole wheat, plus salt and distilled water. Addition of calcium or vitamin A to diet No. 16 resulted in distinct improvement. But addition of good quality protein, which accelerated early growth, caused less favorable records—unless additional calcium was furnished to compensate for the early rapid growth and increased bone development. The meticulous care of experimental animals by H. Louise Campbell was of great assistance in these long-term studies that could not be readily conducted by graduate students.

Another example of improving diets of marginal value was shown in relation to vitamin A. In life-span tests about four times as much of the vitamin, supplied as fish liver oil, was required for best performance, compared to the quantity that prevented physical signs of vitamin A deficiency.

As there was no evidence of the exact nature of any of the vitamins at that time, and hence no certainty of chemical methods of measurement, Dr. Sherman recognized the need to develop reliable methods of biological assay, which would reflect a quantitative measure of the conjectured nutrient associated with such specific deficiency diseases as scurvy, beriberi, rickets, xerophthalmia and pellagra. For example, "one unit" of vitamin C could represent one-tenth of the quantity of vitamin C required per day to prevent scurvy in a standard guinea pig. Sherman's assay methods for vitamin A, vitamin B_1, vitamin B_2 (riboflavin), and vitamin C were widely adopted and made an important contribution to advancing nutrition on a quantitative basis. The thoroughness with which he sought to identify the approximate range of optimum intake of individual nutrients or specific types of food mixtures was remarkable—particularly in terms of numbers of animals used, length of time involved, number of surviving offspring, growth rate, longevity, tissue storage, and statistical evaluation of data as a basis for conclusions. His human balance experiments with calcium, phosphorus, iron and protein were regarded for many years as the best guides to health requirements for these minerals.

When queried or chided by his friends for devoting so much of his time, energy, and resources to biological research, his enthusiastic reply was, "These animals are my burettes and balances. They give quantitative answers in chemical terms to many of man's greatest problems!" Sherman was not interested in spectacular discoveries as such, but he was wholeheartedly devoted to research that he was confident would result in substantial advances in human health, greater efficiency in agriculture, improvements in food technology, or, in time, would accelerate chemical understanding of life processes.

Sherman was meticulous in his insistence on careful records from his graduate students in research (records were required in duplicate form, one for his files and one for the student), in the citation of others' publications, and in the exact wording of each manuscript. As reported by his associate, Dr. E. J. Quinn, when one of the students expressed a complaint at the requirement of so many successive drafts for journal papers, Dr. Sherman replied quietly, but with unmistakable firmness, "As many drafts may be required as there are paragraphs in the finished manuscript."

Sherman's immediate interest in possible applications of research to improvements in the full gamut of food practices, from agriculture to the consumer, was illustrated in 1927 when he was shown the assay data confirming a high concentration of vitamin C in green peppers. Knowing that this author had worked with peppers during earlier years on a farm, he asked a whole series of questions concerning how widely peppers could be grown in different areas, how well they met requirements for marketing, and the variety of ways they might be utilized in food practices. And, when he learned that samples of powdered milk from newly developed spray driers showed a distinctly higher content of vitamin C than was contained in the product from conventional drum driers, he smiled and said quickly, "I think the Borden Company will be glad to know that!"

Professor Sherman's keen interest in the relationship of food practices to health was evident in nearly all of his lectures and writing. Through many years, beginning in 1920, he joined with Professor C. E. A. Winslow and others in Reports on Nutrition Problems or reports on specific topics for the American Public Health Association and its journal. His textbooks on nutrition soon became the most widely used in their respective spheres, and his books of a more general nature or on specific topics had wide acceptance. Sherman's first text, *Methods of Organic Analysis* (1905) was published in a second edition in 1912; the second text, *Chemistry of Food and Nutrition* (1911; 7th ed., 1946) was the most widely used of all. The monograph entitled *The Vitamins*, with S. L. Smith as co-author, was a notable contribution sponsored by the American Chemical Society through two editions (1922 and 1931). Both as a public service and as a tribute to his outstanding contributions in nutrition education and research, Sherman's associates, with assistance from the Nutrition Foundation, prepared for the Macmillan Company a single volume, *Selected Works of Henry Clapp Sherman*, published in 1948.

His own evaluation of the science of nutrition is well expressed in the introduction to the book: "There is already a world-wide awakening of interest in the potentialities of the knowledge already gained, and of desire in almost every nation that the benefits of this newer knowledge of nutrition shall be brought within reach of all its people through more adequate and better-balanced food supplies. All over the earth there are now modern-minded men of affairs who, without necessarily having a scientific understanding of nutrition, have nevertheless grasped the fact of its significance for higher health and longer, more efficient life; and are working, both through education and governmental action to bring these benefits to their people. In the non-technical language of Lord Astor they see the importance to their people having, 'not only enough food, but further, enough of the right kinds of food.' Thinking nationally, each wants the higher efficiency of a better-nourished body of fellow-citizens. Thinking internationally, all are coming to want a more equitable distribution of the world's food among the world's people. Our increasingly scientific concept of better use of food and of resources for food production is keyed to the growing realization that all people live in one world."

The faculty at Teacher's College of Columbia University contributed extensively to Dr. Sherman's accomplishments in nutrition education and in the joint sponsoring of students for graduate degrees and research. Mary Schwartz Rose, Grace MacLeod, Clara Mae Taylor, and Orrea Pye were recognized nationally and internationally as among the most energetic and effective leaders in nutrition education. Professor Sherman served as chairman of a special committee in the Graduate School with responsibility for establishing requirements for Ph.D. students in nutrition and for guiding them in the selection of their course work. In chemistry and in other basic sciences, the students were required to meet the same standards in designated courses and examinations as other students in the respective disciplines. The large seminar originally chaired by Dr. Rose, but later by Dr. Sherman, in the chemistry department was interdepartmental and included faculty members and selected graduate students in other departments and in Teachers College.

In addition to postdoctoral scientists who participated in research with Professor Sherman, a large number studied with him as their major adviser for the Ph.D. degree. E. C. Kendall and A. O. Gettler were among his first students. Among others were A. W. Thomas, V. K. LaMer, and M. L. Caldwell, who remained on the department staff, and P. L. Day, J. H. Axtmayer, A. Spohn, R. T. Conner, M. Adams, M. D. Schlesinger, H. K. Stiebeling, E. L. Batchelder, E. N. Todhunter, M. L. Fincke, E. W. Toeper, F. L. MacLeod, and E. Woods.

The intensity and persistence with which Dr. Sherman normally worked made one hesitant to interrupt or ask for an appointment unless a serious issue were at stake. His sincere personal interest in his students and faculty associates and his remarkable sense of courtesy were so clear, however, that demands on his time were always heavy. Hence, it was delightful, and one of his great gifts, to see how quickly and naturally he would relax at luncheon, dinner, or other break periods and show a continuing sense of subtle humor that made his friendship doubly rewarding.

Sherman was by nature relatively quiet and shy, with a steadfast sense of courtesy, honesty, discipline, and kindliness. Both his home life and his spontaneous relationships with others were characterized by these qualities. As a teacher, Sherman was a continuing inspiration to his students.

His most famous student, Nobel Laureate Edward C. Kendall expressed his regard for Professor Sherman in terms that others would gladly endorse: "His scientific papers do not reflect his genial capacity for friendship, his deep understanding of human nature, his lack of malice and intrigue, his sense of humor, his modesty and in short, his kindly spirit which endeared him to his students and associates." And P. L. Day, an outstanding student, many years later wrote, "Although quick of wit he did not indulge in breezy repartee; neither did he ever raise his voice in argument or anger."

Beyond his direct services to Columbia University, Dr. Sherman accepted numerous professional appointments, including Research Associate with the Carnegie Institution, 1912–1929, 1933–1939; member of the Committee on Food and Nutrition, National Research Council, 1920–1928, 1940–1943, and chairman of the Committee on Human Nutrition, chairman of the Committee on Nutrition Problems, American Public Health Association, 1919–1933; Scientific Advisory Committee of the Nutrition Foundation, 1942–1952; President of the American Institute of Nutrition, 1931–1933; collaborator, U.S. Nutrition Laboratory 1940–1942; and Chief, U.S. Bureau of Human Nutrition, 1943–1944.

Special honors received by Dr. Sherman included medalist, American Chemical Society, 1934; Franklin Medal, Franklin Institute, 1946; Chandler Medal, Columbia University, 1949; Borden Award, American Institute of Nutrition, 1950; Vice-President, American Chemical Society, 1907–1908; President, American Society of Biological Chemists, 1926; member, National Academy of Sciences, 1933; honorary member, the Harvey Society.

There were four children in the Sherman family, Phoebe (deceased, 1929), Henry Alvord, William Bowen (deceased, 1971), and Caroline Clapp (Mrs. Oscar E. Lanford, Jr.). Henry, William, and Caroline all had outstanding careers, respectively, in chemical engineering, medicine, and biochemistry.

BIBLIOGRAPHY

KEY TO ABBREVIATIONS

Am. Food J. = The American Food Journal
Am. J. Physiol. = American Journal of Physiology
Am. J. Public Health = American Journal of Public Health
Am. Med. = American Medicine
Am. Public Health Assoc. Yearb. = American Public Health Association Yearbook
Ann. Rev. Biochem. = Annual Review of Biochemistry
Ann. Surv. Am. Chem. = Annual Survey of American Chemistry
Bull. N.Y. Acad. Med. = Bulletin of the New York Academy of Medicine
Carnegie Inst. Wash. Yearb. = Carnegie Institution of Washington Yearbook
Child Health Bull. = Child Health Bulletin
Columbia Univ. Q. = Columbia University Quarterly
J. Am. Chem. Soc. = Journal of the American Chemical Society
J. Am. Diet. Assoc. = Journal of the American Dietetic Association
J. Am. Med. Assoc. = Journal of the American Medical Association
J. Biol. Chem. = Journal of Biological Chemistry
J. Chem. Educ. = Journal of Chemical Education
J. Franklin Inst. = Journal of the Franklin Institute
J. Home Econ. = Journal of Home Economics
J. Ind. Eng. Chem. = Journal of Industrial and Engineering Chemistry
J. Nutr. = Journal of Nutrition
Proc. Natl. Acad. Sci. = Proceedings of the National Academy of Sciences
Proc. Soc. Exp. Biol. Med. = Proceedings of the Society for Experimental Biology and Medicine
Sch. Mines Q. = School of Mines Quarterly
Sci. Mon. = Science Monthly
U.S. Dep. Agric. Bull. = U.S. Department of Agriculture Bulletin

1895

The determination of nitrogen in fertilizers containing nitrates. J. Am. Chem. Soc., 17:567–78.

1896

A study of methods for the determination of starch. Sch. Mines Q., 17:356.

1897

The insoluble carbohydrates of wheat. J. Am. Chem. Soc., 19:291–324.

1900

With H. Hyde. On the determination of phosphoric acid as phosphomolybdic anhydride. J. Am. Chem. Soc., 22:652.

With P. B. Hawk. On the elimination of nitrogen, sulphates and phosphates after the ingestion of proteid food. Am. J. Physiol., 4:25–49.

1901

With J. F. Snell. On the heat of combustion as a factor in the analytical examinations of oils; and the heats of combustion of some commercial oils. J. Am. Chem. Soc., 23:164–72.

With W. O. Atwater. The effect of severe and prolonged muscular work on food consumption, digestion and metabolism. Office of Experiment Stations, U.S. Dep. Agric. Bull. no. 98. Washington, U.S. Government Printing Office. 67 pp.

With H. M. Burr. On the so-called gluten and diabetic foods of commerce. New York Medical Journal, 74:686.

1902

With J. L. Danziger and L. Kohnstamm. On the temperature reaction of oils with sulphuric acid-maumene's test. J. Am. Chem. Soc., 24:266–73.

With J. F. Snell. On the relation of the heat of combustion to the specific gravity in fatty oils. J. Am. Chem. Soc., 24:348–53.

The determination of sulphur and phosphorus in organic materials. J. Am. Chem. Soc., 24:1100–1109.

Experiments on the metabolism of nitrogen, sulphur and phosphorus in the human organism. Office of Experiment Stations, U.S. Dep. Agric. Bull. no. 121. Washington, U.S. Government Printing Office. 47 pp.

1903

On the composition of cow's milk. J. Am. Chem. Soc., 25:132–42.

With M. J. Falk. The influence of atmospheric oxidation upon the composition and analytical constants of fatty oils. J. Am. Chem. Soc., 25:711–16.

With H. Abraham. The viscosity of the soap solution as a factor in oil analysis. J. Am. Chem. Soc., 25:977–82.

On the influence of diet, muscular exertion and loss of sleep upon the formation of uric acid in man. J. Am. Chem. Soc., 25:1159–66.

1904

With C. B. McLaughlin and E. Osterberg. The determination of nitrogen in food materials and physiological products. J. Am. Chem. Soc., 26:367–71.

With M. J. Falk. The determination of nitrogen in organic compounds. J. Am. Chem. Soc., 26:1469–74.

1905

With W. N. Berg. The determination of ammonia in milk. J. Am. Chem. Soc., 27:124–36.

With M. J. Falk. The influence of atmospheric oxidation upon the analytical constants of fatty oils. J. Am. Chem. Soc., 27:605–8.

With A. W. Hahn and A. J. Mettler. Comparative experiments upon chemical preservatives in milk. J. Am. Chem. Soc., 27:1060–68.

With R. H. Williams. The detection, determination and rate of disappearance of formaldehyde in milk. J. Am. Chem. Soc., 27:1497–1503.

Methods of Organic Analysis. New York, Macmillan Inc. xvi + 407 pp.

1906

With W. G. Tice. Proteolysis in cow's milk preserved by means of formaldehyde. J. Am. Chem. Soc., 28:189–94.

With R. H. Williams. The osazone test for glucose and fructose as influenced by dilution and by the presence of other sugars. J. Am. Chem. Soc., 28:629–32.

Iron in food and its functions in nutrition. Office of Experiment Stations, U.S. Dep. Agric. Bull. no. 185. Washington, U.S. Government Printing Office. 80 pp.

With W. N. Berg, L. J. Cohen, and W. G. Whitman. Ammonia in milk and its development during proteolysis under the influence of strong antiseptics. J. Biol. Chem., 3:171–75.

Seasonal variations in the composition of cow's milk. J. Am. Chem. Soc., 28:1719–23.

With J. E. Sinclair. The balance of acid-forming and base-forming elements in foods. J. Biol. Chem., 3:307–9.

With F. C. Hinkel. Experiments on Barfoed's acid cupric acetate solution as a means of distinguishing glucose from maltose, lactose and sucrose. J. Am. Chem. Soc., 29:1744–47.

1908

With W. G. Whitman. The effect of pasteurization upon the development of ammonia in milk. J. Am. Chem. Soc., 30:1288–95.

With E. C. Kendall. The detection and identification of certain reducing sugars by condensation with para-brombenzylhydrazide. J. Am. Chem. Soc., 30:1451–55.

With H. Colwell. Chemical evidence of peptonization in raw and pasteurized milk. J. Biol. Chem., 5:247–51.

With A. H. Kropff. The calorific power. J. Am. Chem. Soc., 30:1626–31.

1909

With T. T. Gray and H. A. Hammerschlog. A comparison of the calculated and determined viscosity numbers (Engler) and flashing and burning points in oil mixtures. J. Ind. Eng. Chem., 1:13–23.

With D. A. Bartlett. A study of the effect of excess of reagent and time of reaction in the determination of iodine numbers of fatty oils. Sch. Mines Q., 31:55–63.

With W. H. Boynton. A comparison of the calculated and determined values for the specific temperature reactions of oil mixtures with sulphuric acid. Sch. Mines Q., 31:64.

1910

A source of error in the examination of foods for salicylic acid. J. Ind. Eng. Chem., 2:24–29.

With A. J. Mettler and J. E. Sinclair. Calcium, magnesium, and phosphorus in food and nutrition. Office of Experiment Stations, U.S. Dep. Agric. Bull. no. 227. Washington, U.S. Government Printing Office. 70 pp.

With E. C. Kendall and E. D. Clark. Studies on amylases. I. An examination of methods for the determination of diastatic power. J. Am. Chem. Soc., 32:1073–86.

With E. C. Kendall. Studies on amylases. II. A study of the action of pancreatic amylase. J. Am. Chem. Soc., 32:1087–1105.

1911

With M. D. Schlesinger. Studies on amylases. III. Experiments upon the preparation and properties of pancreatic amylase. J. Am. Chem. Soc., 33:1195–1204.

Quantitative aspects of nutrition. Teachers College Bulletin, 2d ser., no. 15. New York, Teachers College Press.

With A. Gross. The detection of salicylic acid. J. Ind. Eng. Chem., 3:492–96.

With C. G. Amend. The relation of chemical composition of calorific power in wood, peat and similar substances. Sch. Mines Q., 33:31–34.

Chemistry of Food and Nutrition. New York, Macmillan Inc. viii + 721 pp.

1912

Wtih A. O. Gettler. The balance of acid-forming and base-forming elements in foods and its relation to ammonia metabolism. J. Biol. Chem., 11:323–28.

Chemical investigation of amylases. (Annual report as research associate) Carnegie Inst. Wash. Yearb., 11:255.

With M. D. Schlesinger. Studies on amylases. IV. A further investigation of the properties of pancreatic amylase. J. Am. Chem. Soc., 34:1104–11.

1913

Continuation of the chemical investigation of the amylases. (Annual report as research associate) Carnegie Inst. Wash. Yearb., 12:288.

With M. D. Schlesinger. Studies on amylases. V. Experiments upon the purification of the amylase of malt. J. Am. Chem. Soc., 35:1617–23.

With M. D. Schlesinger. Studies on amylases. VI. A comparison of the amyloclastic and saccharogenic powers. J. Am. Chem. Soc., 35:1784–90.

With A. O. Gettler. Studies on amylases. VII. The forms of nitrogen in amylase preparations from the pancreas and from malt, as shown by the Van Slyke method. J. Am. Chem. Soc., 35: 1790–94.

1914

Food and sanitary chemistry in the schools of science. Columbia Univ. Q., 16:256.

Continuation of the chemical investigation of the amylases. (Annual report as research associate) Carnegie Inst. Wash. Yearb., 13:353.

Food Products. New York, Macmillan Inc. ix + 594 pp.

1915

With A. W. Thomas. Studies on amylases. VIII. The influence of certain acids and salts upon the activity of malt amylase. J. Am. Chem. Soc., 37:623–43.

With M. D. Schlesinger. Studies on amylases. IX. Further experiments upon the purification of malt amylase. J. Am. Chem. Soc., 37:643–48.

With M. D. Schlesinger. Studies on amylases. X. Comparison of certain properties of pancreatic and malt amylase preparations. J. Am. Chem. Soc., 37:1305–19.

Continuation of the chemical investigation of the amylases. (Annual report as research associate) Carnegie Inst. Wash. Yearb., 14:366.

1916

With A. P. Tanberg. Experiments upon the amylase of *Aspergillus oryze.* J. Am. Chem. Soc., 38:1638–45.

With P. W. Punnett. On the products of the action of certain amylases upon soluble starch, with special reference to the formation of glucose. J. Am. Chem. Soc., 38:1877–85.

With J. C. Baker. Experiments upon starch as substrate for enzyme action. J. Am. Chem. Soc., 38:1885–1904.

With D. E. Neun. An examination of certain methods for the study of proteolytic action. J. Am. Chem. Soc., 38:2199–2216.

Continuation of the chemical investigation of the amylases. (Annual report as research associate) Carnegie Inst. Wash. Yearb., 15: 356.

1917

With J. A. Walker. Influence of certain electrolytes upon the course of the hydrolysis of starch by malt amylase. J. Am. Chem. Soc., 39:1476–93.

With L. H. Gillett. The adequacy and economy of some city dietaries. New York Association for Improving the Condition of the Poor, no. 121.

Continuation of the chemical investigation of the amylases. (Annual report as research associate) Carnegie Inst. Wash. Yearb., 16:302.

1918

A glimpse of Russia in the year of her revolution. Columbia Univ. Q., 20:11.

The food supply of Russia. Political Science Quarterly, 33:210–29.

Food chemistry in the service of human nutrition. (Harvey Lecture) J. Ind. Eng. Chem., 10:383–90.

With L. H. Gillett and H. M. Pope. Monthly metabolism of nitrogen, phosphorus and calcium in healthy women. J. Biol. Chem., 34:373–81.

With L. Wheeler and A. B. Yates. Experiments on the nutritive value of maize protein and on the phosphorus and calcium requirements of healthy women. J. Biol. Chem., 34:383–93.

Use of corn (maize) as human food. J. Am. Med. Assoc., 70:1580–81.

With I. D. Garard. A study of the glucosazone reaction. J. Am. Chem. Soc., 40:955–69.

Place of milk and vegetables in the diet. Am. Med., 24:361.

With D. E. Neun. Action of pancreatic enzymes upon casein. J. Am. Chem. Soc., 40:1138–45.

With J. C. Winters. Efficiency of maize protein in adult human nutrition. J. Biol. Chem., 35:301–11.

Fundamental requirements of human nutrition. Proceedings of the Institute of Medicine of Chicago, 2:33.

Food and conservation from the standpoint of the chemistry of nutrition. Proceedings of the American Philosophical Society, 57:491.

Continuation of the chemical investigation of the amylases. (Annual report as research associate) Carnegie Inst. Wash. Yearb., 17:284.

1919

With A. W. Thomas and M. E. Baldwin. Influence of hydrogen ion concentration upon the enzymic activity of three typical amylases. J. Am. Chem. Soc., 41:231–35.

Permanent gains from the food conservation movement. Columbia Univ. Q., 21:1–14.

With F. Walker and M. L. Caldwell. Action of enzymes upon starches of different origin. J. Am. Chem. Soc., 41:1123–29.

With J. C. Winters and V. Phillips. Efficiency of oat protein in adult human nutrition. J. Biol. Chem., 39:53–62.

Proteolytic activity of pancreatic amylase preparations. J. Am. Chem. Soc., 41:1855–62.

With F. Walker. Influence of aspartic acid and asparagin upon the enzymic hydrolysis of starch. J. Am. Chem. Soc., 41:1866–73.

With M. E. Rouse, B. Allen, and E. Woods. Growth and reproduction upon simplified food supply. Proc. Soc. Exp. Biol. Med., 17:9.

Continuation of the chemical investigation of the amylases. (Annual report as research associate) Carnegie Inst. Wash. Yearb., 18:328.

1920

With C. E. A. Winslow, H. S. Grindley, A. G. Woodman, and E. L. Fisk. Second report of Committee on Nutritional Problems, American Public Health Association. Am. J. Public Health, 10:86.

Protein requirement of maintenance in man and the nutritive efficiency of bread protein. J. Biol. Chem., 41:97–109.

The protein requirement of maintenance in man. Proc. Natl. Acad. Sci., 6:38–40.

Phosphorus requirement of maintenance in man. J. Biol. Chem., 41:173–79.

With I. D. Garard and V. K. LaMer. A further study of the process of purifying pancreatic amylase. J. Am. Chem. Soc., 42:1900–1907.

Calcium requirement of maintenance in man. J. Biol. Chem., 44:21–27.

With F. L. MacLeod and M. M. Kramer. Preliminary experiments with the fat soluble vitamin (vitamin A). Proc. Soc. Exp. Biol. Med., 18:41.

Chemical investigation of amylases and related enzymes. (Annual report as research associate) Carnegie Inst. Wash. Yearb., 19:338.

1921

With V. K. LaMer and H. L. Campbell. The effect of temperature and of hydrogen ion concentration upon the rate of destruction of antiscorbutic vitamin. Proc. Soc. Exp. Biol. Med., 18:122.

With C. E. A. Winslow, E. L. Fisk, and I. Greenwald. Third annual report, Committee on Nutritional Problems, American Public Health Association. Am. J. Public Health, 11:166.

With A. M. Pappenheimer. A dietetic production of rickets in rats and its prevention by an inorganic salt. Proc. Soc. Exp. Biol. Med., 18:193.

With M. E. Rouse, B. Allen, and E. Woods. Growth and reproduction upon simplified food supply. I. J. Biol. Chem., 46:503–19.

With A. M. Pappenheimer. Experimental rickets in rats. J. Exp. Med., 34:189–98.

The vitamins. Physiological Reviews, 1:598–630.

With V. K. LaMer and H. L. Campbell. The effect of temperature and of the concentration of hydrogen ions upon the rate of destruction of antiscorbutic vitamin (vitamin C). Proc. Natl. Acad. Sci., 7:279–81.

With M. Wayman. Effect of certain antiseptics upon the activity of amylases. J. Am. Chem. Soc., 43:2454–61.

With M. L. Caldwell. A study of the influence of arginine, histidine, tryptophane, and cystine upon the hydrolysis of starch by purified pancreatic amylase. J. Am. Chem. Soc., 43:3469–76.

With F. Walker. The study of the influence of certain amino acids upon the enzymic hydrolysis of starch. J. Am. Chem. Soc., 43:2461–69.

Chemical investigation of amylases and related enzymes. (Annual report as research associate) Carnegie Inst. Wash. Yearb., 20:386.

1922

With C. E. A. Winslow, E. L. Fisk, and I. Greenwald. Dried milks. Report of the Committee on Nutritional Problems, American Public Health Association. Am. J. Public Health, 12:113–16.

With V. K. LaMer and H. L. Campbell. The quantitative determination of the antiscorbutic vitamin (vitamin C). J. Am. Chem. Soc., 44:165–72.

With V. K. LaMer and H. L. Campbell. The effect of temperature and the concentration of hydrogen ions upon the rate of destruction of antiscorbutic vitamin (vitamin C). J. Am. Chem. Soc., 44:172–81.

With M. Muhlfeld. Growth and reproduction upon simplified food supply. II. Influence of food upon mother and young during the lactation period. J. Biol. Chem., 53:41–47.

With E. Hawley. Calcium and phosphorus metabolism in childhood. J. Biol. Chem., 53:375–99.

With E. Hawley. Calcium requirements of children. J. Home Econ., 14:413.

Food and health. The Nation's Health, 4:513.

With C. E. A. Winslow, E. L. Fisk, I. Greenwald, and T. P. B. Jones. Present status of our knowledge of the vitamins and its application to the dietary. Report of the Committee on Nutritional Problems, American Public Health Association. Am. J. Public Health, 12:908–15.

The place of the laboratory man in the world of food economics. Am. Food J., 17:9–10.

With M. L. Caldwell. Influence of amino acid in protecting amylase from inactivation by mercury. J. Am. Chem. Soc., 44:2923–26.

With M. L. Caldwell. Influence of lysine upon the hydrolysis of starch by purified pancreatic amylase. J. Am. Chem. Soc., 44:2926–30.

With N. M. Naylor. Influence of some organic compounds upon the hydrolysis of starch by salivary and pancreatic amylase. J. Am. Chem. Soc., 44:2957–66.

Chemical investigation of amylases and related enzymes. (Annual report as research associate) Carnegie Inst. Wash. Yearb., 21:334.

With S. L. Smith. *The Vitamins.* New York, Chemical Catalogue Company. 575 pp.

1923

An investigation of the chemical nature of two typical enzymes: pancreatic and malt amylase. Proc. Natl. Acad. Sci., 9:81–86.

Vitamins in the food supply. The Survey, 49:782.

With F. Walker. Effect of amino acids in retarding the hydrolytic decomposition of an enzyme (pancreatic amylase). J. Am. Chem. Soc., 45:1960–64.

With H. Edgeworth. Experiments with two methods for the study of vitamin B. J. Am. Chem. Soc., 45:2712–18.

With A. Spohn. A critical investigation and an application of the rat growth method for the study of vitamin B. J. Am. Chem. Soc., 45:2719–28.

With M. R. Grose. A quantitative study of the destruction of vitamin B by heat. J. Am. Chem. Soc., 45:2728–38.

The fat-soluble vitamin in relation to health. The Nation's Health, 5:682.

Vitamins as factors in food values. Industrial Engineering and Chemistry News Edition 1, 22:3, 5.

Nutrition and vigor. American Physical Education Review, 28: 462.

Chemical investigation of amylases and related enzymes. (Annual report as research associate) Carnegie Inst. Wash. Yearb., 22:296.

1924

With H. L. Campbell. Growth and reproduction upon simplified food supply. IV. Improvement in nutrition resulting from an increased proportion of milk in the diet. J. Biol. Chem., 60: 5–15.

With M. M. Kramer. Experiments upon vitamin A. J. Am. Chem. Soc., 46:1055–63.

A message to the food manufacturer. Am. Food J., 19:105.

With C. E. A. Winslow, E. L. Fisk, I. Greenwald, and T. P. B. Jones. Mineral elements in nutrition with special reference to calcium and phosphorus. Report of the Committee on Nutritional Problems, American Public Health Association. Am. J. Public Health, 14:513.

With A. W. Thomas and M. L. Caldwell. The iso-electric point of malt amylase. J. Am. Chem. Soc., 46:1711–17.

The optimum amount of milk for children. Proceedings of the World's Dairy Congress, 1:455.

Iodine in nutrition: goiter as a nutritional problem. Am. J. Public Health, 14:1038.

With F. L. MacLeod. Relation of vitamin A to growth, reproduction and longevity. Proc. Soc. Exp. Biol. Med., 22:75.

Chemical investigation of amylases and related enzymes. (Annual report as research associate) Carnegie Inst. Wash. Yearb., 23:243.

1925

With A. T. Merrill. Cystine in the nutrition of the growing rat. J. Biol. Chem., 63:331–37.

With H. E. Munsell. The quantitative determination of vitamin A. J. Am. Chem. Soc., 47:1639–46.

With L. C. Boynton. Quantitative experiments upon the occurrence and distribution of vitamin A in the body, and the influence of the food. J. Am. Chem. Soc., 47:1646–53.

With L. B. Storms. The bodily store of vitamin A as influenced by age and other conditions. J. Am. Chem. Soc., 47:1653–57.

With F. L. MacLeod. The relation of vitamin A to growth, reproduction and longevity. J. Am. Chem. Soc., 47:1658–62.

With M. L. Caldwell and N. M. Naylor. Influence of tryptophan and enzymic activity of pancreatic amylase. J. Am. Chem. Soc., 47:1702–9.

With F. L. MacLeod. The calcium content of the body in relation to age, growth, and food. J. Biol. Chem., 64:429–59.

The prevention of rickets. Child Health Bull., 1:57.

With E. Woods. The determination of cystine by means of feeding experiments. J. Biol. Chem., 66:29–36.

Chemical investigation of amylases and related enzymes. (Annual report as research associate) Carnegie Inst. Wash. Yearb., 24:306.

1926

With E. L. Fisk, I. Greenwald, T. P. B. Jones, and C. E. A. Winslow. The prevention of rickets. Am. J. Public Health, 16:139.

With M. L. Caldwell and M. Adams. Further experiments upon

the purification of pancreatic amylase. Proc. Soc. Exp. Biol. Med., 23:413.

With E. J. Quinn. The phosphorus content of the body in relation to age, growth, and food. J. Biol. Chem., 67:667–77.

With M. L. Cammack. A quantitative study of the storage of vitamin A. J. Biol. Chem., 68:69–74.

With M. L. Caldwell and M. Adams. Enzyme purification by adsorption: an investigation of pancreatic amylase. J. Am. Chem. Soc., 48:2947–56.

With G. W. Burton. Effect of hydrogen ion concentration upon the rate of destruction of vitamin B upon heating. J. Biol. Chem., 70:639–45.

Nutrition and health. J. Ind. Eng. Chem., 18:1261–63.

With C. E. A. Winslow, E. L. Fisk, I. Greenwald, and T. P. B. Jones. The relation of dairy products to health through nutrition. Am. J. Public Health, 16:1205.

1927

The vitamins, I-VI. J. Chem. Educ., 3:1240–47.

Chemical investigation of amylases and related enzymes. (Annual report as research associate) Carnegie Inst. Wash. Yearb., 26:302–4.

With M. C. Hessler. Quantitative differentiation of vitamins A and D. J. Biol. Chem., 73:113–20.

With E. H. MacArthur. A quantitative study of the determination of vitamin B. J. Biol. Chem., 74:107–15.

With O. H. M. Gloy. Vitamin B determination and requirement with special reference to protein intake. J. Biol. Chem., 74:117–22.

With M. L. Caldwell and M. Adams. Establishment of the optimal hydrogen-ion activities for the enzymic hydrolysis of starch by pancreatic and malt amylases under varied conditions of time and temperature. J. Am. Chem. Soc., 49:2000–2005.

With J. H. Axtmayer. A quantitative study of the problem of the multiple nature of vitamin B. J. Biol. Chem., 75:207–12.

With M. L. Caldwell and J. E. Dale. A quantitative study of the influence of sodium acetate, sodium borate, sodium citrate, and sodium phosphate upon the activity of pancreatic amylase. J. Am. Chem. Soc., 49:2596–98.

1928

With C. E. A. Winslow, E. L. Fisk, I. Greenwald, T. P. B. Jones, and D. B. Jones. The vitamins as factors in health and in food values. Am. J. Public Health, 18:331–37.

With M. P. Burtis. Vitamin A in relation to growth and to subsequent susceptibility to infection. Proc. Soc. Exp. Biol. Med., 25:649–50.

With E. J. Quinn, P. L. Day, and E. H. Miller. The relative stability of vitamin A from plant sources. J. Biol. Chem., 78: 293–98.

With M. P. Burtis. Factors affecting the accuracy of the quantitative determination of vitamin A. J. Biol. Chem., 78:671–80.

With M. L. Caldwell and M. Adams. The influence of concentration of neutral salt on the activation of pancreatic amylase. J. Am. Chem. Soc., 50:2535–37.

With M. L. Caldwell and M. Adams. A quantitative comparison of the influence of neutral salts on the activity of pancreatic amylase. J. Am. Chem. Soc., 50:2538–43.

The chemical nature of certain amylases. In: *A Comprehensive Survey of Starch Chemistry*, 2d ed., ed. by Robert P. Walton, pp. 77–86. New York, Chemical Catalog Company, Inc.

Feeding the municipal family. The American City, 39:101.

Supplementary relations among nutritive values of foods. Am. Med., 34:767.

Revision of "Food," by Edward K. Dunham. In: *Public Health and Hygiene in Contributions by Eminent Authorities*, 2d ed., ed. by William H. Park, pp. 334–46. Philadelphia and New York, Lea & Febiger.

Food laws and standards: the preservation and adulteration of food. In: *Public Health and Hygiene in Contributions by Eminent Authorities*, 2d ed., ed. by William H. Park, pp. 353–70. Philadelphia and New York, Lea & Febiger.

Nutritional significance of our present knowledge of the multiple nature of vitamin B. J. Nutr., 1:191–99.

With H. L. Campbell. The influence of food upon longevity. Proc. Natl. Acad. Sci., 14:852–55.

The meaning of vitamin A. Science, 68:619–20.

Chemical investigation of amylases and related enzymes. (Annual report as research associate) Carnegie Inst. Wash. Yearb., 27:359.

1929

Food Products. New York, Macmillan Inc. 687 pp.

With M. R. Sandels. Experiments with reference to the more heat-stable factor of the vitamin B group (factor P-P, vitamin B_2 or G). Proc. Soc. Exp. Biol. Med., 26:536–40.

With D. B. Jones, T. P. B. Jones, E. L. Fisk, and C. E. A. Winslow. Vitamins as factors in health and in food values. II. Am. J. Public Health, 19:482.

The problem of sweets for children. Child Health Bull., 5:65.

With H. K. Stiebeling. Quantitative studies of responses to different intakes of vitamin D. J. Biol. Chem., 83:497–504.

Food and Health. (De Lamar Lectures, 1928–1929) Baltimore, Williams & Wilkins Co.

Chemical investigation of amylases and related enzymes. (Annual report as research associate) Carnegie Inst. Wash. Yearb., 28:351.

1930

With H. K. Stiebeling. The relation of vitamin D to deposition of calcium in bone. Proc. Soc. Exp. Biol. Med., 27:663–65.

With H. I. Campbell. Further experiments on the influence of food upon longevity. J. Nutr., 2:415–17.

The vitamins as factors in nutrition. Illinois Department of Public Health, Educational Health Circular, 5:3.

With M. L. Caldwell and H. H. Boynton. A quantitative study of the influence of acetate and of phosphate on the activity of malt amylase. J. Am. Chem. Soc., 52:1669–72.

With M. L. Caldwell and M. Cleaveland. The influence of certain neutral salts upon the activity of malt amylase. J. Am. Chem. Soc., 52:2436–40.

A glimpse of the social economics of Porto Rico, 1930. J. Home Econ., 22:537–45.

Some aspects of the chemistry of nutrition in relation to health. Porto Rico Journal of Public Health and Tropical Medicine, 5:407.

With M. L. Caldwell and M. Adams. Enzyme purification: further experiments with pancreatic amylase. J. Biol. Chem., 88:295–304.

With H. K. Stiebeling. Quantitative differentiation of vitamins A and D. II. J. Biol. Chem., 88:683–93.

Chemical investigation of the amylases and related enzymes. (Annual report as research associate) Carnegie Inst. Wash. Yearb., 29:370.

The vitamins. In: *Annual Survey of American Chemistry*, vol. IV, pp. 312–21. New York, Chemical Catalog Company.

1931

Nutritional problems: new light on the significance of the protective foods. Am. Public Health Assoc. Yearb., 1930–1931, p. 213.

With M. L. Whitsitt. A study of the effect of nitrous acid upon components of the vitamin B complex. J. Biol. Chem., 90:153–60.

With M. R. Sandels. Further experimental differentiation of vitamins B and G. J. Nutr., 3:395–409.

Chemistry. In: *A Quarter Century of Learning*, p. 275. New York, Columbia University Press.

Enzymes and vitamins in present-day chemistry. J. Chem. Educ., 8:652.

With E. L. Batchelder. Further investigation of quantitative measurement of vitamin A values. J. Biol. Chem., 91:505–11.

With M. L. Caldwell and L. E. Booher. Crystalline amylase. Science, 74:37.

With L. E. Booher. The calcium content of the body in relation to that of the food. J. Biol. Chem., 93:93–103.

With A. Bourgquin. Quantitative determination of vitamin G (B$_2$). J. Am. Chem. Soc., 53:3501–5.

With E. F. Chase. A quantitative study of the determination of the antineuritic vitamin B. J. Am. Chem. Soc., 53:3506–10.

Some recent advances in the chemistry of nutrition. J. Am. Med. Assoc., 97:1425–30.

Emergency nutrition. Child Health Bull., 7:185–88.

The vitamins. In: *Annual Survey of American Chemistry*, vol. V, pp. 333–42. New York, Chemical Catalog Company.

1932

With E. L. Fisk, C. E. A. Winslow, and E. M. Nelson. The practical significance of the vitamins to health. Am. Public Health Assoc. Yearb., 1931–1932, p. 126.

The vitamins from the view-point of the official chemist. (Wiley Memorial Lecture) Journal of the Association of the Official Agricultural Chemists, 15:103–12.

Some recent advances in the chemistry of nutrition. The significance of protective foods. (Forsyth Lecture for 1930) Boston, Forsyth Dental Infirmary for Children.

Calcium, phosphorus and vitamins as they promote the development and health of the teeth. Dental Survey, 8:29–30.

With I. A. Derbigny. Studies on vitamin G (B_2) with special reference to protein intake. J. Biol. Chem., 99:165–71.

1933

The trend of recent advances in the chemistry of food and nutrition. J. Am. Diet. Assoc., 9:373.

With N. Halliday. Adsorption experiments with vitamins B (B_1) and G (B_2). J. Am. Chem. Soc., 55:332–35.

Food and health. Am. J. Public Health, 23:335–38.

Guard against the hidden hunger. Child Health Bull., 9:135.

Thomas Bruce Freas. Columbia Univ. Q., 25:230.

Natural and induced variations in the vitamin values of milk. Am. J. Public Health, 23:1031–34.

A century of progress in the chemistry of nutrition. Sci. Mon., 37:442.

Relation of food to length of life. Carnegie Inst. Wash. Yearb., 32:317.

1934

With L. N. Ellis. Necessary versus optimal intake of vitamin G (B_2). J. Biol. Chem., 104:91–97.

With M. L. Caldwell and W. E. Doebbeling. Further studies upon the purification and properties of malt amylase. J. Biol. Chem., 104:501–9.

Chemistry of the vitamins with special reference to quantitative aspects. (Nichols Medal Award Address) J. Ind. Eng. Chem., 26:583.

With H. L. Campbell. Observations upon growth from the viewpoint of statistical interpretation. Proc. Natl. Acad. Sci., 20:413–16.

The twentieth century science of nutrition. Proceedings of the West Virginia Academy of Science, 7:17–20.

General review of our present knowledge of the vitamins. Bull. N.Y. Acad. Med., 10:457.

With E. N. Todhunter. The determination of vitamin A values by a method of single feedings. J. Nutr., 8:347–56.

Foods for health protection. J. Home Econ., 26:493–96.

Relation of food to length of life. Carnegie Inst. Wash. Yearb., 33:295.

Food and Health. New York, Macmillan Inc. 290 pp.

Food chemistry, 1933 and 1934. Ann. Surv. Am. Chem., 9:206.

1935

Food as a far-reaching factor in health. Child Health Bull., 11:1–4.

With H. L. Campbell. Rate of growth and length of life. Proc. Natl. Acad. Sci., 21:235–39.

With M. L. Fincke. The availability of calcium from some typical foods. J. Biol. Chem., 110:421–28.

With H. L. Campbell. Relation of food to regularity of nutritional response. Proc. Natl. Acad. Sci., 21:434–36.

With H. L. Campbell and O. A. Bessey. Adult rats of low calcium content. J. Biol. Chem., 110:703–6.

With O. A. Bessey, C. G. King, and E. J. Quinn. The normal distribution of calcium between the skeleton and soft tissues. J. Biol. Chem., 111:115–18.

Food supply and human progress. J. Ind. Eng. Chem., 27:995–96.

With H. L. Campbell. Effects of increasing the calcium content of a diet in which calcium is one of the limiting factors. J. Nutr., 10:363–71.

With B. Bisbey. Experiments upon the extraction and stabilities of Vitamin B (B_1) and of lactoflavin. J. Biol. Chem., 112:415–20.

Relation of food to length of life. Carnegie Inst. Wash. Yearb., 34:306.

1936

Calcium as a factor in the nutritional improvement of health. Proc. Natl. Acad. Sci., 22:24–26.

Lafayette Benedict Mendel. Science, 88:45–47.

With M. Speirs. Calcium and phosphorus retention in growth in relation to the form of carbohydrate in the food. J. Nutr., 11:211–18.

Nutritional improvement in health and longevity. Sci. Mon., 43: 97–107.

With H. L. Campbell. A further study of regularity of nutritional response to chemical intake. Proc. Natl. Acad. Sci., 22: 478–81.

With L. B. Whitcher and L. E. Booher. Further studies on the calcium content of the body in relation to calcium and phosphorus content of the food. J. Biol. Chem., 115:679–84.

With E. W. Toepfer. The effect of liberal intakes of calcium or calcium and phosphorus on growth and body calcium. J. Biol. Chem., 115:685–94.

With R. T. Conner. Some aspects of protein intake in relation to growth and rate of calcification. J. Biol. Chem., 115:695–706.

Relation of food to length of life. Carnegie Inst. Wash. Yearb., 35:314.

1937

The bearing of the results of recent studies on nutrition on health and length of life. (Biggs Memorial Lecture) Bull. N.Y. Acad. Med., 13:311.

With F. G. Benedict, H. L. Campbell, and A. Zmachinsky. Basal metabolism of rats in relation to old age and exercise during old age. J. Nutr., 14:179–98.

With H. L. Campbell and P. B. Rice. Nutritional well-being and length of life as influenced by different enrichments of an already adequate diet. J. Nutr., 14:609–20.

With C. C. Sherman. The vitamins. Ann. Rev. Biochem., 6: 335–74.

Relation of food to length of life. Carnegie Inst. Wash. Yearb., 36:323.

1938

With E. V. Carlson. Riboflavin and a further growth essential in the tissues. J. Nutr., 15:57–65.

With H. C. Kao and R. T. Conner. The availability of calcium from Chinese cabbage. J. Biol. Chem., 123:221–28.

Human nutrition. In: *Seventh International Management Congress Proceedings and Papers,* vol. 3: *Agriculture Papers,* p. 117. Sponsored by the National Management Council of the U.S.A. Baltimore, Waverly Press, Inc.

With C. S. Lanford. Further studies of the calcium content of the body as influenced by that of the food. J. Biol. Chem., 126: 381–87.

With H. L. Campbell. Nutritional effects of the addition of meat and green vegetables to a wheat and milk diet. J. Nutr., 16: 603–12.

The influence of nutrition upon the chemical composition of the normal body. In: Cooperation in research, papers prepared in honor of John Campbell Merriam by staff members and research associates, pp. 415–23. Carnegie Institution of Washington Publication 501. Washington, Carnegie Institution of Washington.

Relation of nutrition to optimal health. Journal of Health and Physical Education, 9:406–7.

Influence of nutrition upon the chemical composition of the normal body. Carnegie Inst. Wash. Yearb., 37:331.

1939

With H. L. Campbell and C. S. Lanford. Experiments on the relation of nutrition to the composition of the body and the length of life. Proc. Natl. Acad. Sci., 25:16–20.

With L. N. Ellis. Responses to different levels of nutritional intake of riboflavin (formerly called vitamin G). Proc. Natl. Acad. Sci., 25:420–22.

Research on influence of nutrition upon the chemical composition of the normal body. Carnegie Inst. Wash. Yearb., 38:297.

Calcium and phosphorus requirements of human nutrition. In: *United States Department of Agriculture Yearbook for 1939,* p. 187. Washington, U.S. Government Printing Office.

1940

With H. C. Kao. Influence of nutritional intake upon concentration of vitamin A in body tissues. Proc. Soc. Exp. Biol. Med., 45:589–91.

Research on influence of nutrition upon the chemical composition of the normal body. Carnegie Inst. Wash. Yearb., 39:257.

With C. S. Lanford. *Essentials of Nutrition.* New York, Macmillan Inc. 504 pp.

1941

Significance of different levels of vitamin intake. J. Am. Diet. Assoc., 17:1.

With K. E. Briwa. The calcium content of the normal growing body at a given age. J. Nutr., 21:155–62.

With C. S. Lanford and B. Finkelstein. Riboflavin contents of some typical fruits. J. Nutr., 21:175–77.

With C. S. Lanford and H. L. Campbell. Influence of different nutritional conditions upon the level of attainment in the normal increase of calcium in the growing body. J. Biol. Chem., 137:627–34

With F. O. Van Duyne, C. S. Lanford, and E. W. Toepfer. Lifetime experiments upon the problem of optimal calcium intake. J. Nutr., 21:221–24.

Some aspects of the present significance of nutrition. J. Franklin Inst., 231:305.

With R. T. Conner and H. C. Kao. Further studies on the relationship of the plane of protein intake to the rate of normal calcification during growth. J. Biol. Chem., 139:835–41.

With F. O. Van Duyne. Riboflavin contents of tissues as stabilized in the adult at liberal levels of intake. Proc. Natl. Acad. Sci., 27:289–91.

With H. C. Kao and R. T. Conner. Influence of protein intake upon growth, reproduction and longevity. J. Nutr., 22:327–31.

Progress in the chemistry of food and nutrition. The American Scholar, 10:369.

Mary Swartz Rose. J. Biol. Chem., 140:687–88.

Some relations of food chemistry to the time of aging and the length of life. News Edition, American Chemical Society, 19:1081–82.

Research on influence of nutrition upon the chemical composition of the normal body. Carnegie Inst. Wash. Yearb., 40:287.

1942

With M. S. Ragan. Quantitative distribution of phosphorus and calcium in certain fruits and vegetables. J. Nutr., 23:283–92.

With N. Jolliffe and J. S. McLester. The prevalence of malnutrition. J. Am. Med. Assoc., 118:944–50.

Adequate nutrition and human welfare. Proceedings of the National Nutrition Conference for Defence, May 1941, p. 30. Washington, U.S. Government Printing Office.

Research on influence of nutrition upon the chemical composition of the normal body. Carnegie Inst. Wash. Yearb., 41:245.

With C. S. Pearson. *Modern Bread from the Viewpoint of Nutrition.* New York, Macmillan Inc. vi + 118 pp.

The training of analytical chemists from an industrial point of view. J. Chem. Educ., 19:589–97.

Training and opportunities for women in chemistry. In: *The Chemist at Work,* by R. I. Grady, J. W. Chittum, and others, pp. 368–72. Easton, Pennsylvania, Journal of Chemical Education.

1943

The Science of Nutrition. New York, Columbia University Press. 253 pp.

With L. N. Ellis and A. Zmachinsky. Experiments upon the significance of liberal levels of intake of riboflavin. J. Nutr., 25:153–60.

With R. W. Little and A. W. Thomas. Spectrophotometric studies of the storage of vitamin A in the body. J. Biol. Chem., 148:441–43.

Foods of animal origin. J. Am. Med. Assoc. Handbook of Nutrition, 122:228–31.

With A. B. Rohrer. The bodily store of vitamin A as influenced by age and by food. J. Nutr., 25:605–9.

With C. S. Lanford. Nutrition, 1941 and 1942. Ann. Rev. Biochem., 12:397–424.

With H. L. Campbell and C. S. Pearson. Effect of increasing calcium content of diet upon rate of growth and length of life of unmated females. J. Nutr., 26:323–25.

With C. S. Lanford. *An Introduction to Foods and Nutrition.* New York, Macmillan Inc.

1944

Principles of nutrition and nutritive value of food. United States Department of Agriculture, Miscellaneous Publication no. 546. Washington, U.S. Government Printing Office. 40 pp.

Nutritional engineering, I-IV. J. Franklin Inst., 238:37–38, 97–105, 273–89, 319–24.

Nutritional principles in wartime food problems. Chemical and Engineering News, 22:2011–12.

Research on influence of nutrition upon the chemical composition of the normal body. Carnegie Inst. Wash. Yearb., 43:165.

1945

With H. L. Campbell, M. Udiljak, and H. Yarmolinsky. Vitamin A in relation to aging and to length of life. Proc. Natl. Acad. Sci., 31:107–9.

With H. L. Campbell. Stabilizing influence of liberal intake of vitamin A. Proc. Natl. Acad. Sci., 31:164–66.

Food and nutrition—today and tomorrow. (Isabel Bevier Memorial Lecture) Urbana, University of Illinois.

With H. L. Campbell. Influence of the calcium intake level upon the complete life cycle of the albino rat. Am. J. Physiol., 144: 717–19.

With H. L. Campbell, M. Udiljak, and H. Yarmolinsky. Bodily storage of vitamin A in relation to diet and age, studied by the assay method of single feedings. J. Nutr., 30:343–48.

With A. B. Caldwell and G. MacLeod. Bodily storage of vitamin A in relation to diet and age, studied by means of the antimony trichloride reaction using a photoelectric colorimeter. J. Nutr., 30:349–53.

Research on influence of nutrition upon the chemical composition of the normal body. Carnegie Inst. Wash. Yearb., 44:160.

1946

With M. S. Ragan. Further studies of the influence of nutrition upon the chemical composition of the body. Proc. Natl. Acad. Sci., 33:266–68.

With A. E. H. Houk and A. W. Thomas. Some interrelationships of dietary iron, copper and cobalt in metabolism. J. Nutr., 31:609–20.

With A. Z. Murray and W. C. Zmachinsky. Riboflavin as a factor in the adequacy of the American food supply. Sci. Mon., 63: 151–53.

Research for better nutrition. J. Franklin Inst., 242:1.

The expanding opportunity of the science of nutrition. Nutrition Reviews, 4:225–27.

The nutritional improvement of life. J. Am. Diet. Assoc., 22:577–81.

With A. Z. Murray and L. M. Greenstein. Fluorometric studies of the riboflavin contents of muscle and liver. J. Biol. Chem., 165:91–94.

Increasing the useful life span. In: *The Science of Nutrition; Papers Presented at Meetings of the Nutrition Foundation,* Nov. 13–14, 1946, pp. 31–35. New York, Nutrition Foundation, Inc.

Nutrition policy. In: *Nutrition for Young and Old,* pp. 53–59. Albany, New York State Joint Legislative Committee on Nutrition.

Foods: Their Value and Management. New York, Columbia University Press. viii + 221 pp.

1947

With M. S. Ragan and M. E. Bal. Effect of increasing food protein upon the calcium content of the body. Proc. Natl. Acad. Sci., 33:356–58; Nutrition Abstracts and Reviews, 18:128.

Calcium and Phosphorus in Foods and Nutrition. New York, Columbia University Press. 117 pp.

1949

With H. Y. Trupp. Long term experiments at or near optimal level of intake of vitamin A. J. Nutr., 37:467–74.

With H. C. Campbell and M. S. Ragan. Analytical and experimental study of the effects of increased protein with liberal calcium and riboflavin intakes: complete life cycles. J. Nutr., 37:317–27.

1950

The Nutritional Improvement of Life. New York, Columbia University Press. 270 pp.

With C. S. Pearson and M. E. Bal. Quantitative effects of protein enrichment of diet upon growth and early adult life. Proc. Natl. Acad. Sci., 36:106–9.

GEORGE ELBERT KIMBALL MEMOIR

Volume 43

BY PHILIP M. MORSE

.

BIBLIOGRAPHY*

KEY TO ABBREVIATIONS

J. Chem. Phys. = Journal of Chemical Physics
J. Colloid Sci. = Journal of Colloid Science
Phys. Rev. = Physical Review

1931

With J. R. Bates. The band structure of arsenic monohydride. Nature, 128:969. (L)

1934

With G. H. Shortley. Numerical solution of eigenvalue problems in any number of dimensions. Phys. Rev., 45:560. (A)

1935

The electronic structure of diamond. J. Chem. Phys., 3:560.

1937

With I. Roberts. The halogenation of ethylenes. Journal of the American Chemical Society, 59:947.

---

* Subsequent to the publication of the memoir of George Elbert Kimball in Volume 43 of the National Academy of Sciences' series, additional bibliographical material has come to light. This additional information, prepared by W. H. Stockmayer, is shown on the following pages.

1941

With S. Glasstone and A. Glassner.   Overvoltage and the structure of the electrical double layer at a hydrogen electrode.   J. Chem. Phys., 9:91.

1944

With G. R. Hennig.   The kinetics of the electroreduction of acetone.   J. Chem. Phys., 12:415.

1945

With A. J. De Béthune.   Hydrogen overvoltage in concentrated sulfuric and phosphoric acid solutions.   J. Chem. Phys., 13:53.

1946

Thermodynamics of relaxation processes.   Phys. Rev., 69:688.   (A)

1948

With M. Metlay.   Ionization processes on tungsten filaments.   I. The electron affinity of the oxygen atom.   J. Chem. Phys., 16:774.

With M. Metlay.   Ionization processes on tungsten filaments.   II. The adsorption of fluorine on tungsten.   J. Chem. Phys., 16:779.

With G. E. Cogin.   The vapor pressures of some alkali halides.   J. Chem. Phys., 16:1035.

1949

With F. C. Collins.   Diffusion-controlled reaction rates.   J. Colloid Sci., 4:425.

With M. B. Oakley.   Punched card calculation of resonance energies.   J. Chem. Phys., 17:706.

With F. C. Collins.   Diffusion-controlled reactions in liquid solutions.   Industrial and Engineering Chemistry, 41:2551.

1950

With H. Markovitz.   The effect of salts on the viscosity of solutions of polyacrylic acid.   J. Colloid Sci., 5:115.

With E. Blade.   The determination of energy levels from thermodynamic data.   I. The effect of experimental error.   J. Chem. Phys., 18:626.

With E. Blade. The determination of energy levels from thermodynamic data. II. The heights of potential energy barriers restricting intramolecular rotation. J. Chem. Phys., 18:630.

1951

With V. A. Lewinson. Application of a modified quantum-mechanical cellular method to the hydrogen molecule. J. Chem. Phys., 19:690.

Quantum theory. Annual Review of Physical Chemistry, 2:177.

With M. Cutler. Effect of adsorption on measurements of viscosities of very dilute polymer solutions. Journal of Polymer Science, 7:445.

With S. Grand and F. C. Collins. Quenching of fluorescence in liquid solution. Phys. Rev., 82:338.

The liquid state. In: *States of Matter,* pp. 353–419, vol. 2 of *A Treatise on Physical Chemistry,* 3d ed., ed. by H. S. Taylor and S. Glasstone. New York, D. Van Nostrand Co.

1952

With M. Cutler and H. Samelson. Theory of polyelectrolytes. Journal of Physical Chemistry, 56:57.

1953

Philosophy of operations research. Operations Research, 1:145.

1957

With G. F. Neumark. Use of Gaussian wave functions in molecular calculations. J. Chem. Phys., 26:1285.

1958

With J. G. Trulio. Quantum mechanics of the H_3 complex. J. Chem. Phys., 28:493.

IRVING WIDMER BAILEY MEMOIR

Volume 45

BY RALPH H. WETMORE

Change of wording in last paragraph, page 43, from:

To Mrs. Howard Mumford Jones and Mrs. Lyle Boyd, authors of *History and Work of the Harvard Observatory* (McGraw-Hill Book Co., New York, 1971), the author would like to indicate how much of the boyhood life of Irving Bailey he obtained from their vivid portrayal of Irving's father's two expeditions to Peru. . . .

to:

To Mrs. Howard Mumford Jones and Mrs. Lyle Boyd, authors of *The Harvard College Observatory—The First Four Director-ships, 1839–1919* (The Belknap Press of the Harvard University Press, Cambridge, Massachusetts, 1971), the author would like to indicate how much of the boyhood life of Irving Bailey he obtained from their vivid and discriminating portrayal of Irving's father's two expeditions to Peru. . . .

ACKNOWLEDGMENTS FOR THE PHOTOGRAPHS

Photograph of Clarence Henry Graham
by R. Shlaer

Photograph of William King Gregory
from a portrait by Charles Chapman

Photograph of Donald Forsha Jones
from a portrait by Deane Keller

Photograph of Arthur Remington Kellogg
Smithsonian Institution

Photograph of Charles Christian Lauritsen
California Institute of Technology

Photograph of Walter Curran Mendenhall
U.S. Department of the Interior
Geological Survey

Photograph of Henry Clapp Sherman
by Warman
Columbia University